OUR "REGULAR" READERS RAVE!

"Thank you. Thank you. Thank you!!!
"I have been a bathroom reader since I was a little kid, starting with *MAD* magazine when I was 10....You have given the frowned-upon habit a new respectability. We have every *Bathroom Reader* ever published, and love all of them. In fact, we are known in our circle of friends as the "household with the best bathroom reading material." Keep up the great work; we are crossing our legs waiting for the next volume!"

—*Brenda B., Illinois*

"The BRI is a fine upstanding (er...downsitting) organization...that takes the facts and runs with them, no matter how large the load. I, like other readers, salute you as you go about your business, logging all this information and getting a handle on the facts. Bravo!"

—*Todd G., Prince Edward Island*

"Thanks to the BRI, I won a BBQ for 25 people on a radio show for knowing who invented the parking meter."

—*Linda L., Arizona*

"I'm thinking of changing my religion!!!"

—*Joel A., Saskatchewan*

"Mothers introduce you to the world. Mine is better than most because she also introduced me to the wonderful world of the Bathroom Readers Institute when she bought me the *Ultimate Bathroom Reader* for my 16th birthday. At first, I was a little skeptical...but then I opened up the first page and was captivated. Thank you, BRI! Without you I don't know where I'd be!"

—*Andrew G., Wisconsin*

"Well what can I say? Because of you guys, my wife never sees me, I miss work, and basically have no social life anymore. I have become an Uncle John junkie. I can't help [but] listen to other people's conversations and interrupt them if they say or do something that I found in your wonderful books. Well, it's *that* time again. I have to go. Thank you."

—*"The Wilsonator," Florida*

"This past year my grandson went off to college, where he wouldn't have access to his family's *Bathroom Reader*. So I got him his own to take back to school, accompanied by a letter pointing out that over the course of one's life there were various rites of passage: the first haircut, wearing long pants, sitting at the adult table for holiday meals, etc. It was my honor to acknowledge another rite of passage by providing him with his own personal copy of the *Bathroom Reader*."

—*Thomas O'H., Tennessee*

"Until the BR came into my life, my visits to the WC were oh so stressful, as many a time I was forced to resort to reading the items in my wallet. Now, thanks to the *Bathroom Reader*, I will never have that problem again!"

—*John R., California*

"Every year for the past 11 years, my husband has given me your latest edition of the *Bathroom Reader* for Christmas. Why? Because he really likes to read them! If you ever stop printing these books, I may get some alternative presents…such as jewelry or lingerie."

—*Janice C., Oregon*

"Me and my sister, Liz, bought a *Bathroom Reader* for my grandpa for his birthday, but we liked it so much we kept it. Now each of our four bathrooms has a different volume. I just quote random stuff from your books at school and know I am the Dalai Lama of my high school. Thanks and keep writing."

—*Mary D., Michigan*

Uncle John's

ABSOLUTELY ABSORBING

BATHROOM READER®

The Bathroom Readers'
Institute

Bathroom Readers' Press
Ashland, Oregon

THANK YOU!

The Bathroom Readers' Institute sincerely thank the people whose advice and assistance made this book possible.

John Javna
John Dollison
Jeff Altemus
Gordon Javna
Jennifer & Sage
Erin Keenan
Jay Newman
Jack Mingo
Erin Barrett
John Darling
Jeff Cheek
Antares Multimedia
Michael Brunsfeld
Sharilyn Hovind
Claudia Bauer
Paul Stanley
Lonnie Kirk
Julie Roeming
Bennie Slomski
Barb Porshe
Dale Vidmar
Jay Ingram
Bill Crawford

Lisa Cooper
Debra Gates
Dee Smith
Mike Schuster
Douglass Keeslar
Peter Workman
Janet Harris
Paula Leith
Tessa Vanderkop
Uncle Edgester
Douglas Sigler
Lorien Sekora
Rich Stim
Mustard Press
Thomas Crapper
Faye Courtenay
Jim McCluskey
Kathy Dratch
Hi Pastor Bob
Marley & Catie Pratt
Bloomsbury Books
Jesse & Sophie, *B.R.I.T.*
Hi to Emily and Molly!

*   *   *

Random Fact: In the 1800s, drinking "tea" made from boiled old shoes was thought to cure disease.

CONTENTS

NOTE
Because the B.R.I. understands your reading needs, we've
divided the contents by length as well as subject.
Short—a quick read
Medium—1 to 3 pages
Long—for those longer visits, when something
a little more involved is required.
* Extended—for a leg-numbing experience.

☆　☆　☆

BATHROOM NEWS
Medium
Long

THE NAME GAME
Short
Medium

LAW & ORDER
Short
Medium

THAT'S LIFE!
Short
Medium

*   *   *

Random Fact: Ulysses S. Grant's favorite breakfast:
"a cucumber drenched in vinegar."

INTRODUCTION

Well, we did it again.

Every year at this time—the last minute—we flip through the book to see what's missing...and realize we still haven't written the introduction.

It's almost a tradition. Jennifer says nervously, "John, the book has to go to the printer tomorrow. Will you *please* write the intro?" And Uncle John pays no attention at all, because he still has, oh, six hours before complete panic sets in.

A few hours later, we get an ultimatum from Sharilyn: If it's not here by three o'clock, she won't have time to copyedit it. It's do-or-die. Now or never. Truth or consequences.

In the end, it always gets done—barely—just like the rest of the *Bathroom Reader*. And all is forgiven, because our readers seem to enjoy these books so much.

Actually, we really like this edition. In fact, a lot of the BRI thinks it's the best *Bathroom Reader* we've ever done (although it's hard to tell when you've been working on something for so long). Good sign: Our proofreader says she had a hard time proofing the manuscript—she got involved in the stories and started reading them instead of correcting them. But we'll wait to see what you have to say before we take any bows.

Let us know via *www.bathroomreader.com*. We'll be waiting.

A few notes:

• There are more three-page and two-part articles in this *Bathroom Reader* than in the previous few—we had more topics we wanted to cover in depth. To make up for it, we didn't feature one story running through the whole book, as we did in previous *Readers* with the *Tonight Show*, Miss America, etc. (We did, however, include the final installment of the *Tonight Show* story this time.) Which do you prefer?

• A call to our many Canadian readers: Help us include more Canadian-oriented material—send us articles or appropriate book titles, so we find the best resources. We promise, next edition, to include the best of what we receive (and if we use your submission, you get a free *Reader*!).

• Our next edition is our 13th! That gives us a whole range of possible subjects to cover. Got any good info on superstitions? We're all ears.

Let's see, what else? Oh, yes—our Web site. Last year we introduced the Throne Room; this year, we're introducing the Salon (a chat room). Now you can actually talk to us...and each other. Plus, we've decided to start putting original material online that you can't get in our books—starting with the History of the Bra, which we promised to include in the *Great Big Bathroom Reader*. Well, better late than never...and at least it's free. Print it out and leave it in the "reading room." Or use your laptop—a whole new concept in bathroom reading!

Thanks so much for your support. We are perpetually delighted—and astonished—by your enthusiasm for our work. As we've said before, that's what keeps us going through the long months of research and writing. We know that someone out there—you—is waiting for it.

And, as always, remember:

Go with the flow!

Bathroom Readers' Institute,
October 4, 1999

YOU'RE MY INSPIRATION

It's always fascinating to find out who, or what, inspired cultural milestones like these.

OSCAR THE GROUCH. "At a restaurant called Oscar's Tavern in Manhattan, Jim Henson and Sesame Street director Jon Stone were waited on by a man so rude and grouchy that…going to Oscar's became a sort of masochistic form of lunchtime entertainment for them. They immortalized him as the world's most famous grouch." (*Sesame Street Unpaved*)

FREDDY KRUEGER. Writer/director Wes Craven reportedly named the evil character of his *Nightmare on Elm Street* film after a kid at high school who harassed and bullied him.

MEN ARE FROM MARS… In the early 1980s, "John Gray was looking for a playful way to talk [to an audience] about the differences between men and women." He borrowed the interplanetary theme from Steven Spielberg. "Men, he said, were like the alien E.T.—and from Mars to boot, the planet of the warriors. The audience loved it, [so he added that] women…were from Venus, the planet of love and affection." (*USA Today*)

BMW SYMBOL. The Bavarian Motor Works once manufactured airplanes. Their logo represents a plane's propeller.

LAVERNE & SHIRLEY. In 1959 Gary Marshall was eating at a Brooklyn restaurant with his date when "another woman approached the table and began arguing with Marshall's companion. Before he knew what was happening, his quiet, demure date was shucking her coat and wrestling in the aisle." The incident made such an impression on Marshall that in 1975 he wrote it into an episode of his TV show, "Happy Days." He named the two brawling women Laverne and Shirley. Audiences loved the pair, and the following year they had their own sitcom. (*New York Daily News*)

What food are you most likely to be allergic to? Nuts.

COURT TRANSQUIPS

We're back, with one of our regular features. Do court transcripts make good bathroom reading? Check out these quotes. They're things people actually said in court, recorded word for word.

Q: "James shot Tommy Lee?"
A: "Yes."
Q: "Then Tommy Lee pulled out his gun and shot James in the fracas?"
A: "No sir, just above it."

Q: "Doctor, did you say he was shot in the woods?"
A: "No, I said he was shot in the lumbar region."

Q: "Have you lived in this town all your life?"
A: "Not yet."

Q: "The hospital is to the right?"
A: "It was on this side."
Q: "When you say this side, can you say right or left?"
A: "Sure. Right or left."

Judge (to jury): "If that be your verdict, so say you all."
Two Jurors: "You all."

Q: "Doctor, will you take a look at those X-rays and tell us something about the injury?"
A: "Let's see, which side am I testifying for?"

Q: "How would you expect somebody to react, being stabbed six times in this fashion?"
A: "Well, it might slow him down a little."

Q: "How was your first marriage terminated?"
A: "By death."
Q: "And by whose death was it terminated?"

Q: "And what did he do then?"
A: "He came home, and next morning he was dead."
Q: "So when he woke up the next morning he was dead?"

Q: "Can you describe the individual?"
A: "He was about medium height and had a beard."
Q: "Was this a male or a female?"

The Court: "You've been charged with armed robbery. Do you want the court to appoint a lawyer to represent you?"
Defendant: "You don't have to appoint a very good lawyer, I'm going to plead guilty."

Q: "What happened then?"
A: "He says, 'I have to kill you because you can identify me.'"
Q: "Did he kill you?"
A: "No."

Judge: "Well, gentlemen of the jury, are you unanimous?
Foreman: "Yes, your Honor, we're all alike—temporarily insane."

Leaf-cutter ants can build anthills 16 feet deep and an acre square.

MADE IN THE USA

*You've heard of inventors Thomas Edison and Alexander
Graham Bell. But what about Chester Greenwood
and Frank Rose? Let's give them their due, too.*

THE EAR-MUFF. When he was 15 years old, Chester Greenwood went ice skating on a pond near his home in Farming-
ton, Maine. He nearly froze his ears off. The next day he covered his ears with a thick woolen scarf...but it was too heavy and
itchy. So the next day, he bent some wire into ear-shaped loops and
asked his grandmother to sew fur around them. That worked perfectly. So many neighbors asked Chester for a pair of "muffs for ears"
that he patented his design and founded the Greenwood Ear Protector Factory in 1877. He became extremely wealthy supplying them
to U.S. soldiers during World War I.

THE OUTBOARD MOTOR. According to company lore, Ole
Evinrude, a Norwegian immigrant, got the idea for an outboard
motor while on a picnic with his sweetheart Bessie. They were on
a small island in Lake Michigan, when Bessie decided she wanted
some ice cream. Ole obligingly rowed to shore to get some, but by
the time he made it back the ice cream had melted. So Ole built a
motor that could be attached to his rowboat, and founded the Evinrude company in 1909.

THE FLY SWATTER. Dr. Samuel J. Crumbine of the Kansas
State Board of Health was watching a baseball game in Topeka in
1905. It was the bottom of the eighth inning, the score was tied, and
Topeka had a man on third. Fans were screaming "Sacrifice fly! Sacrifice fly!" to the batter, or "Swat the ball! Swat the ball!" Crumbine, who'd spent much of the game mulling over how to reduce the
spread of typhoid fever by flies during hot Kansas summers, suddenly
got his inspiration: "Swat the fly!" Crumbine didn't actually invent
the fly swatter; he just popularized the idea in a front-page article titled "Swat the Fly," in the next issue of *Fly Bulletin*. A schoolteacher
named Frank Rose read the article and made the first fly swatter out
of a yardstick and some wire screen.

More babies are born in the month of September than in any other month.

FOREIGN FUNDS

*Ever wonder why different kinds of money are called what they are?
Why is a franc called a franc, for example? We did. So, we put together
a list of various currencies and how they got their names.*

POUND. (*English*) Named for its weight in *Sterlings*—the unit of currency in Medieval England. The first *pound* coin was issued in 1642.

LIRA. (*Italy*). From the Latin word *libra*, or "pound."

DRACHMA. (*Greece*) Means "handful."

RUPEE. (*India*) Comes from the Sanskrit *rupa*, which means "beauty" or "shape."

KORUNA. (*Czechoslovakia*) Means "crown."

GUILDER. (*Netherlands*) From the same root as "gilded," the guilder was originally a gold coin. It was first introduced from Florence in the 13th century.

ROUBLE. (*Russia*) Means "cut-off," a term that dates back to the days when portions of silver bars were literally "cut off" from the bars and used as coins. The rouble was first issued as a silver piece in 1704.

PESO. (*Mexico*) Means "weight." It was introduced by Spain in 1497, then adopted by Mexico and other Latin American countries in the late 19th century.

PESETA. (*Spain*) Means "little peso," and was created in the 18th century as a "companion" coin to the Spanish peso (no longer in circulation.)

FRANC. (*France*) First issued in 1360, as a gold coin. Gets its name from its original Latin inscription, *Francorum Rex*, which means "King of the Franks," the title given to kings of France in the 1300s.

RIYAL. (*Saudi Arabia*) Borrows its name from the Spanish *real*, meaning "royal."

ESCUDO. (*Portugal*) Means "shield," referring to the coat of arms on the original coin.

YEN. (*Japan*) Borrowed from the Chinese *yuan*, which means "round," and describes the coin. First issued in 1870.

Take a guess: How many muscles are there in your ear? Nine.

OOPS!

Everyone's amused by tales of outrageous blunders—probably because it's comforting to know that someone's screwing up even worse than we are. So go ahead and feel superior for a few minutes.

HAPPY BIRTHDAY!

"Matt Brooks of Cheshire, England, a furnaceman, thought he was 63 years old in 1981. When he applied for early retirement, he learned that he was really 79 and should have retired 14 years earlier."

—*Encyclopedia Brown's Book of Facts*

BLIND JUSTICE

"Judge Claudia Jordan caused panic in her court in Denver when she passed a note to her clerk that read: 'Blind on the right side. May be falling. Please call someone.' The clerk rang for help. Informed that paramedics were on the way, the judge pointed to the sagging Venetian blinds on the right side of the room. 'I wanted someone from maintenance,' she said."

—*The Fortean Times*

HIGH WIRE ACT

"During a parade through Ventura, California, a drum major twirled his baton and threw it high into the air.

"It hit a power cable and melted. It also blacked out ten blocks, put a radio station off the air and started a grass fire."

—*The World's Greatest Mistakes*

AMEN

"Warren Austin, U.S. ambassador to the United Nations in 1948, expressed the wish that Arabs and Jews would settle their differences 'like good Christians.' "

—*Not A Good Word About Anybody*

FLOUR POWER

"After great expense and preparation, British climber Alan Hinkes attempted to scale the 26,000-foot-high Nanga Parbot mountain in

First TV show to win an Emmy for Outstanding Drama: "Pulitzer Prize Playhouse," in 1950.

Pakistan. He got about halfway up and was eating a Pakistani bread called *chapati*, which is topped with flour, when the wind blew the flour in his face, causing him to sneeze. It resulted in a pulled back muscle that made further climbing impossible."

—*News of the Weird*, Nov. 28, 1998

THAT'S B-U-R-T, RIGHT?

"Scrawling his way into immortality in the concrete in front of Mann's (formerly Grauman's) Chinese Theater in Hollywood, Burt Reynolds misspelled his own name."

—*Hollywood Confidential*

LETTER BOMB

NORWALK, Conn.—"The Caldor department store chain apologized this week after 11 million copies of an advertising circular showed two smiling boys playing Scrabble around a board with the word 'rape' spelled out. Caldor said it does not know who did it or how it got past the proofreaders. 'Obviously, it's a mistake,' said Caldor spokeswoman Jennifer Belodeau."

—*The Progressive*, February 1999

FORGET ABOUT THAT RAISE

LONDON—"A trader cost his employers an estimated $16 million when he pressed the wrong key on his computer during training, launching the largest single trade in German futures.

"The *Daily Telegraph* did not name the trader of the firm, but described him as a junior trader working out of London for a German finance house.

"Apparently, while training on what he thought was software *simulating* financial transactions, he posted an offering of 130,000 German bond futures contracts, worth $19 billion. But he had pressed the wrong button, entering the system for actual dealing."

—*Medford Mail Tribune*, Nov. 20, 1998

AND EYES LIKE BONZO?

"During a high-level meeting with Arab leaders, Reagan offhandedly remarked to the Lebanese foreign minister, 'You know, your nose looks just like Danny Thomas's.'"

—*Hollywood Confidential*

Surprising poll result: 53% of Americans think they're paid "the right amount."

LET ME WRITE SIGN— I GOOD SPEAK ENGLISH

When signs in a foreign country are in English, any combination of words is possible. Here are some real-life examples.

At a Tokyo bar: "Special cocktails for the ladies with nuts."

At a Budapest zoo: "Please do not feed the animals. If you have any suitable food, give it to the guard on duty."

At a Budapest hotel: "All rooms not denounced by twelve o'clock will be paid for twicely."

In a Hong Kong supermarket: "For your convenience, we recommend courteous, efficient self-service."

At a Norwegian cocktail lounge: "Ladies are requested not to have children in the bar."

In a tailor shop in Rhodes: "Order your summer suit. Because is big rush we will execute customers in strict order."

A laundry in Rome: "Ladies, leave your clothes here and spend the afternoon having a good time."

In a Czech tourist agency: "Take one of our horse-driven city tours—we guarantee no miscarriages."

On a Viennese restaurant menu: "Fried milk, children sandwiches, roast cattle and boiled sheep."

In a Swiss mountain inn: "Special today—no ice cream."

A doctor's office in Rome: "Specialist in women and other diseases."

In a Moscow hotel room: "If this is your first visit to the USSR, you are welcome to it."

At a Vienna hotel: "In case of fire, do your utmost to alarm the hotel porter."

At a Hong Kong dentist: "Teeth extracted by the latest Methodists."

At a Swedish furrier: "Fur coats made for ladies from their own skin."

Vitamin rule of thumb: The darker green a vegetable is, the more vitamin C it contains.

FAMILIAR PHRASES

Here are the origins to some common phrases.

STUMP SOMEONE
Meaning: Ask someone a question they can't answer
Origin: Actually refers to tree stumps. "Pioneers built their houses and barns out of logs...and they frequently swapped work with one another in clearing new ground. Some frontiersmen would brag about their ability to pull up big stumps, but it wasn't unusual for the boaster to suffer defeat with a stubborn stump." (From *I've Got Goose Pimples*, by Marvin Vanoni)

PAINT THE TOWN RED
Meaning: Spend a wild night out, usually involving drinking
Origin: "This colorful term...probably originated on the frontier. In the nineteenth century the section of town where brothels and saloons were located was known as the 'red light district.' So a group of lusty cowhands out for a night on the town might very well take it into their heads to make the whole town red." (From *Dictionary of Word and Phrase Origins Vol. 3*, by William and Mary Morris)

STAVE OFF
Meaning: Keep something away, albeit temporarily
Origin: "A *stave* is a stick of wood, from the plural of staff, *staves*. In the early seventeenth century *staves* were used in the 'sport' of bull-baiting, where dogs were set against bulls. [If] the dogs got a bull down, the bull's owner often tried to save him for another fight by driving the dogs off with a *stave*." (From *Animal Crackers*, by Robert Hendrickson)

WING IT
Meaning: Do something with little or no preparation
Origin: "Originally comes from the theater. The *Oxford English Dictionary* suggests that it refers to the hurried study of the role in the wings of the theater." (From *The Whole Ball of Wax*, by Laurence Urdang)

First announcer to say, "He shoots, he scores!" during a hockey game: Foster Hewitt, in 1933.

CEREAL STORIES

We didn't realize how familiar cereal and its ads have become until we read Cerealizing America, *by Scott Bruce and Bill Crawford. Some anecdotes from the book, to prove the point:*

RAISIN' CONSCIOUSNESS

In the late 1960s, a thirty-something adman named Danny Nichols was sweating it out to come up with a new ad campaign for Kellogg's Raisin Bran. He had done all his research and had spent many long hours analyzing the product, trying to come up with a new commercial angle.

Following the advice of a colleague, Danny took the box of Raisin Bran home. He stared at it. He smelled it. He ate it. He fiddled with it. Finally, he dumped the entire box out on his kitchen table and began to play with it. He picked up a little scoop he had for coffee and filled it with raisins. He emptied the scoop and filled it again. The next day he rushed in to his office and announced excitedly, "I've got a great idea! There are two scoops of raisins in every box of Raisin Bran!"

PINK-ENSTEIN

In 1971, inspired by the TV shows "The Addams Family" and "The Munsters," General Mills created Franken Berry and Count Chocula cereals. They immediately ran into a public relations problem with Franken Berry. "Within weeks they had to recall it; they pulled all of it off the shelves," laughs the artist who designed the scary breakfast characters, "because when kids went to the bathroom, their stools were pink from the food coloring." This probably happened with both characters, "But with Count Chocula being brown, who would know?"

YABBA-DABBA-DOUGH

In 1969, Hanna-Barbera's long association with Kellogg ended. The animation studio—creators of Yogi Bear, Scooby Doo, the Flintstones, and other cartoons—sent out a mailing to other companies announcing that their characters were now available for licensing.

When mating, a hummingbird's wings beat 200 times per second.

As it happened, Post was in the process of phasing out its line of sugar-coated rice krispies, Rice Krinkles…but still had a fruit-flavored version they wanted to market. With Krinkles defunct, they had no name or character to put on the box. That's when the Hanna-Barbera flyer arrived.

Post needed something quickly. Figuring the fruit cereal looked enough like little rocks to make it compatible with the Flintstones, they made a deal to use Fred and Pebbles. Post execs hoped they'd get a few years out of Pebbles cereal. Thirty years later, they're still making it. "That's probably the longest license in existence," says Bill Hanna.

LUCKY CHOICE

In 1960, Post began experimenting with multicolored marshmallow candy bits—"marbits" in industry jargon—in a cereal called Huckle Flakes. The cereal combined cornflakes with "little marshmallow balls dyed dark blue like huckleberries," recalls a package designer. "They came up with the concept of an Italian moustachioed organ grinder character for it…I never figured out the association between huckleberries and Italians, but we did the package." Huckle Flakes died in test markets. But the concept of an "ethnic cereal" with marbits survived.

"Somebody came up with the idea of [an] Irish cereal," says a former Post adman. They added marbits in the shapes of shamrocks, stars, half moons, and diamonds—and had Lucky Charms.

DOIN' THE FLAKE

The breakfast table's first real rock hit was "Doin' the Flake," a 1965 Kellogg's Corn Flakes promotion recorded by Gary Lewis and the Playboys. A surfer-type song co-written by Leon Russell (who also provided the deep-throated "flake-flake-flake" background vocals), "Doin' the Flake" was a bargain for only thirty-five cents and a box top. The flip side of the record featured the Playboys' hits "This Diamond Ring" and "Little Miss Go-Go."

Crazy new dance, it's the talk of the town, it's the Flake

"'Doin' the Flake'…was within this promotional thing of, 'Hey, your career needs this,'" Gary Lewis explained nearly thirty years later. "But all it got me was about 43,000 cases of Corn Flakes."

FAMOUS FOR 15 MINUTES

Here it is again—our feature based on Andy Warhol's prophetic remark that "in the future, everyone will be famous for 15 minutes." Here's how a few folks have used up their allotted quarter-hour.

T HE STAR: Jeff Maier, a kid from Old Tappan, New Jersey
THE HEADLINE: *Most Valuable Player? 12-year-old Cinches Playoff Game for Yankees*

WHAT HAPPENED: On October 9, 1996, Jeff Maier was sitting in the front row of Yankee Stadium's right-field stands, watching a critical playoff game between the Yankees and the Baltimore Orioles. In the eighth inning New York's Derek Jeter hit a long fly to right field. The Orioles' outfielder probably would have caught it, but Maier stuck out his hand…and deflected it into the stands for a game-tying home run. The Yankees went on to win, 5-4, in 11 innings.

THE AFTERMATH: The home run was replayed on TV so many times that by the end of the game Maier was famous. The next day he made appearances on *Good Morning America, Live with Regis and Kathie Lee* and *Hard Copy*. But he turned down a chance to appear on the *Late Show With David Letterman, The Larry King Show* and *Geraldo* so that he could take a limo (provided by the *New York Daily News*) to see the next playoff game from front-row seats behind the Yankee dugout.

THE STAR: John Albert Krohn, an ex-newspaperman
THE HEADLINE: *Circular Logic: Man Pushes Wheelbarrow Around the Country—Literally*

WHAT HAPPENED: In 1908 Krohn decided to become the first person to push a wheelbarrow around the perimeter of the United States. He did it for the money—Krohn figured he could sell aluminum souvenir medals along the way, and then sell the rights to his story when he made it home. "Sure, money is the root of all evil," he admitted, but "most of us need the 'root.' "

Ketchup was once sold as a medicine.

Krohn left Portland, Maine, on June 1, 1908, and wheelbarrowed his way west to Washington State, then south to the Mexican border, then east to the Atlantic and north back to Maine. He covered 9,024 miles in 357 days, wearing out 11 pairs of shoes, 121 pairs of socks, and 3 rubber tires. TV and radio didn't exist, but he received plenty of news coverage and an enthusiastic response nearly everywhere he went; in some communities he was even "arrested" and sentenced to a meal and a bed at the best hotel in town.

THE AFTERMATH: Krohn did write a book—no word on how well it sold—and then spent the rest of his life working in his garden.

THE STAR: Fawn Hall, a 27-year-old, $20,000-a-year government secretary assigned to the U.S. National Security Council in 1987. Her boss: Lt. Col. Oliver North.

THE HEADLINE: *Fawn Stood by Her Man...And He Fed 'er Into the Shredder*

WHAT HAPPENED: Oliver North was the mastermind behind the Iran-Contra scandal, a plan to sell arms to Iran in exchange for the release of U.S. hostages, then divert the profits to the Contras in Nicaragua—a direct violation of U.S. law.

As word of the scheme began leaking to the press in mid-1986, North, assisted by loyal secretary Fawn Hall, began altering and destroying incriminating documents. After North was fired from his post, Hall continued the shredding on her own. When she testified about her role in the coverup before a nationally televised congressional hearing, she became a celebrity overnight.

THE AFTERMATH: Hall kept a low profile, turning down several lucrative endorsement offers (including one from Revlon to become part of the "America's Most Unforgettable Women" campaign). "I was so out of my league," she says. "One day you're a normal girl walking down the street; the next, they want to put you in movies."

Hall worshipped North as "a hero," and at the end of her congressional testimony let his friends know she "wanted to hear from him"...but North never spoke to her again, not even to thank her for the risks she'd taken on his behalf.

Two dogs were hanged for witchcraft in Salem, Massachusetts, during the Salem witch trials.

Hall later transferred to a job at the Pentagon, but she attracted so much attention that she eventually had to quit. "People would come in and stare at me," she says.

She moved to Los Angeles to write a book and married Danny Sugerman, former manager of the rock group The Doors, and an ex-heroin addict. He introduced his new wife to crack cocaine. "I took one hit on the crack pipe, and I was addicted, instantly," she told *Redbook* magazine.

Hall surfaced again in mid-1994, when the *National Enquirer* revealed she was being treated for crack addiction at a Florida half-way house. By late 1995, both Hall and Sugerman had kicked their habits. Still no word from North, not even a postcard or a phone call. "Ollie used me," she says. "I was like a piece of Kleenex to him."

THE STAR: Lenny Skutnick, 28, a clerk in the Congressional Office Building in Washington, D.C., in 1982

THE HEADLINE: *Just Plane Brave: Man Saves Woman from Icy Grave*

WHAT HAPPENED: Skutnick was driving home from work one winter day in 1982 when Air Florida's Flight 90 crashed into the Potomac River. Skutnick parked his car and went down to the river, where a crowd was gathering.

A rescue helicopter managed to pluck four passengers from the icy water, but by the time it got to 23-year-old Priscilla Tirado, she was too cold to grab the dangling life ring, and the helicopter propeller wash kept pushing it out of reach. "Won't somebody please come out here and save me?" she screamed.

Skutnick jumped into the Potomac, swam to Tirado, and dragged her back to shore. "She was going to drown if no one moved," he explained later. Meanwhile, a television crew recorded the entire rescue and broadcast it live to 50 million viewers.

THE AFTERMATH: One of the people watching was President Reagan. He was so impressed that he invited Skutnick to the White House and publicly thanked him during the State of the Union Address.

The navel divides the body of a newborn baby into two equal parts.

"IT'S NOT A WORD...
IT'S A SENTENCE"

A page by people who know the true meaning of "wedded bliss."

"Bigamy is having one husband too many. Monogamy is the same."

—**Erica Jong**

"Marriage is the triumph of imagination over intelligence. Second marriage is the triumph of hope over experience."

—**Anonymous**

"Marriage is really tough because you have to deal with feelings and lawyers."

—**Richard Pryor**

"Marriage is a three-ring circus: engagement ring, wedding ring, and suffer-ring."

—**Anonymous**

"A man in love is incomplete until he has married. Then he's finished."

—**Zsa Zsa Gabor**

"Love is blind, but marriage restores the sight."

—**Georg Lichtenberg**

"Politics doesn't make strange bedfellows—marriage does."

—**Groucho Marx**

"Before marriage, a man yearns for the woman he loves. After marriage, the 'Y' becomes silent."

—**Anonymous**

"The poor wish to be rich, the rich wish to be happy, the single wish to be married, and the married wish to be dead."

—**Ann Landers**

"Marriage teaches you loyalty, forbearance, self-restraint, meekness, and a great many other things you wouldn't need if you had stayed single."

—**Jimmy Townsend**

"Love is an ideal thing, marriage a real thing; a confusion of the real with the ideal never goes unpunished."

—**Johann von Goethe**

"It's a bit dangerous out there, and I guess men have to choose between marriage and death. I guess they figure that with marriage at least they get meals. But then they get married and find out we don't cook anymore."

—**Rita Rudner**

The only tree from which we eat the flower is the fig.

HOW TO TELL IF YOUR HEAD'S ABOUT TO BLOW UP

Some people call the Weekly World News *a low-brow tabloid. Uncle John, however, considers it one of America's great satire magazines (along with the* Onion, *from Madison, Wisconsin). This article, reprinted from the May 24,1994 edition, supplies important information about the dreaded affliction HCE.*

S URPRISE!
MOSCOW—Doctors blame a rare electrical imbalance in the brain for the bizarre death of a chess player whose head literally exploded in the middle of a championship game!

No one else was hurt in the fatal explosion but four players and three officials at the Moscow Candidate Masters' Chess Championships were sprayed with blood and brain matter when Nikolai Titov's head suddenly blew apart. Experts say he suffered from a condition called Hyper-Cerebral Electrosis, or HCE.

"He was deep in concentration with his eyes focused on the board," says Titov's opponent, Vladimir Dobrynin. "All of a sudden his hands flew to his temples and he screamed in pain. Everyone looked up from their games, startled by the noise. Then, as if someone had put a bomb in his cranium, his head popped like a firecracker."

AN EXPLOSIVE SITUATION

Incredibly, Titov's is not the first case in which a person's head has spontaneously exploded. Five people are known to have died of HCE in the last 25 years. The most recent death occurred... in 1991, when European psychic Barbara Nicole's skull burst. Miss Nicole's story was reported by newspapers worldwide, including *WWN*. "HCE is an extremely rare physical imbalance," said Dr. Anatoly Martinenko, famed neurologist and expert on the human brain who did the autopsy on the brilliant chess expert. "It is a condition in which the circuits of the brain become overloaded

---

If the average male never shaved, his beard would be 13 feet long on the day he died.

by the body's own electricity. The explosions happen during periods of intense mental activity when lots of current is surging through the brain. Victims are highly intelligent people with great powers of concentration. Both Miss Nicole and Mr. Titov were intense people who tended to keep those cerebral circuits overloaded. In a way it could be said they were literally too smart for their own good."

Although Dr. Martinenko says there are probably many undiagnosed cases, he hastens to add that very few people will die from HCE. "Most people who have it will never know. At this point, medical science still doesn't know much about HCE. And since fatalities are so rare it will probably be years before research money becomes available."

In the meantime, the doctor urges people to take it easy and not think too hard for long periods of time. "Take frequent relaxation breaks when you're doing things that take lots of mental focus," he recommends.

THE WARNING SIGNS

Although HCE is very rare, it can kill. Dr. Martinenko says knowing you have the condition can greatly improve your odds of surviving it. A "yes" answer to any three of the following seven questions could mean that you have HCE:

1. Does your head sometimes ache when you think too hard? (Head pain can indicate overloaded brain circuits.)

2. Do you ever hear a faint ringing or humming sound in your ears? (It could be the sound of electricity in the skull cavity.)

3. Do you sometimes find yourself unable to get a thought out of your head? (This is a possible sign of too much electrical activity in the cerebral cortex.)

4. Do you spend more than five hours a day reading, balancing your checkbook, or other thoughtful activity? (A common symptom of HCE is a tendency to over-use the brain.)

5. When you get angry or frustrated do you feel pressure in your temples? (Friends of people who died of HCE say the victims often complained of head pressure in times of strong emotion.)

6. Do you ever overeat on ice cream, doughnuts and other sweets? (A craving for sugar is typical of people with too much electrical pressure in the cranium.)

7. Do you tend to analyze yourself too much? (HCE sufferers are often introspective, "over-thinking" their lives.)

THE WORLD'S WEIRDEST PLANTS

Here is a list of 10 of the most peculiar plants and trees in the world from The Best Book of Lists Ever *compiled by Geoff Tibballs.*

1. The **Sausage Tree** of Africa (*Kigelia Africana*) gets its name from the long, thick fruits which hang from the tree like sausages. The fruits have a different connotation to the Ashanti people of Ghana, who call it the "hanging breast tree," comparing it to old tribeswomen whose life of unremitting breastfeeding results in very long breasts.

2. The **Starfish Flower** (*Stapelia variegata*) from Africa looks like a brown and yellow starfish nestling in the sand. It also smells like a dead animal, as a result of which flies, thinking it's a lump of rotten meat, decide it is the perfect place to raise a family. As they lay their eggs on the surface, they inadvertently pollinate the flower at the same time.

3. *Welwitschia mirabilis*, from the deserts of Namibia, can live for over 2,000 years, yet its central trunk never grows more than 3 feet in height. Instead the energy is transmitted into its two huge leaves which nev-er fall and continue growing throughout the plant's life. The leaves can be as long as 20 feet.

4. The **Banyan Tree** (*Ficus benghalensis*) of India has more than one trunk. When the tree attains a certain size, it sends down ropelike roots, which, on reaching the soil, take root and then thicken to form additional trunks. So the tree can spread outwards almost indefinitely. A 200-year-old specimen in the Calcutta Botanic Gardens had over 1,700 trunks, whilst during Alexander the Great's Indian campaign, 20,000 soldiers are said to have sheltered under a single banyan tree.

5. The merest touch causes the **Sensitive Plant** (*Mimosa pudica*) to collapse in one-tenth of a second. The wilting pose deters grazing animals from eating it. Ten minutes later, when the danger has passed, the plant reverts to its upright position.

6. *Puya Raimondii* of Bolivia can take up to 150 years to bloom. And once it has flowered, it promptly dies. Although it is an herbaceous plant, it is built like a tree with a stem strong enough to support an human adult.

7. The **Grapple Tree** (*Harpagophytum procumbens*) of South Africa produces a fearsome fruit called the "Devil's Claw" which has been known to kill a lion. The fruit is covered in fierce hooks, which latch on to passing animals. In trying to shake the fruit off, the animal disperses the seeds but at the same time, the hooks sink deeper into the creature's flesh. If the animal touches the fruit with its mouth, the fruit will attach itself to the animal's jaw, inflicting great pain and preventing it from eating. Antelopes are the usual victims.

8. The **Sugarbush** (*Protea repens*), the national flower of South Africa, depends on forest fires for survival. When its seeds have been fertilized, they are encased inside tough fireproof bracts which don't reopen until they have been scorched by fire. When the fire has passed, the seeds emerge undamaged.

9. As it reaches upwards, the trunk of California's **Boojum Tree** (*Idris columnaris*) gradually reduces to long, tentacle-like protuberances. Sometimes these droop down to the ground and root so that the tree forms a complete arch. The tree has no branches but is instead covered with thorny stems.

10. When the fruit of the South American **Sandbox Tree** (*Hura crepitans*) is ripe, it explodes with such force that the seeds can be scattered up to 15 feet from the main trunk. The explosion is so loud that it can scare the life out of unsuspecting passers-by.

* * *

POKER ODDS

- Odds of getting one pair in a hand of poker: 1 in every 1.37 hands.
- Three of a kind: 1 in every 46 hands.
- A straight: 1 in every 508 hands
- A full house: 1 in every 693 hands.
- A straight flush: 1 in every 72,192 hands.
- A royal flush: 1 in every 649,739 hands.

If you lined up all the Slinkys ever made in a row, they could wrap around the Earth 126 times.

RESCUED FROM THE TRASH

In the last few BRs, we've included a section called "Lucky Finds"
(see page 322), about the amazing things people have picked up at
flea markets and garage sales. Here's a variation on the theme:
the unexpected treasures is this section were literally rescued
from the trash, as they were about to be lost forever.

CARRIE, *Stephen King's first novel*
Trash: King, 24, was making $9,500 a year teaching high-school English and living in a trailer—a rented trailer—with his wife and two kids when he began work on *Carrie*. At the time, he was selling short stories to magazines just to make ends meet. "Carrie" started out as a short story, but the author couldn't finish it because it was "too realistic" and too focused on the "world of girls," which he didn't understand. "After six or eight pages," he says,

> I found myself in a high-school locker room with a bunch of screaming girls who were all throwing sanitary napkins and screaming "Plug it up!" at a poor, lost girl named Carrie White who had never heard of menstruation and thought she was bleeding to death.

Appalled by what he'd written, he threw the pages away.

Rescue: That night, as King's wife was emptying the wastebasket, she noticed the crumpled papers. "[She] got curious about what I'd been writing, I guess," he says. She thought it was great, and insisted that he finish it.

> I told her it was too long for the markets I'd been selling to, that it might turn out to be a short novel, even. She said, "Then write it." I protested that I knew almost nothing about girls. She said, "I do. I'll help you." She did, and for the last 28 years, she has.

Doubleday paid a meager $2,500 advance for the book, thinking it might be a sleeper. It wasn't—it was a blockbuster. *Carrie* became a nationwide best-seller, and was later made into a hit film. "The book's reception floored everyone, I think," King says, "except my wife."

Cost, in parts and labor, for an Academy Award Oscar statuette: about $300.

EMILY DICKINSON'S POEMS

Trash: Dickinson was a homebody and virtual recluse. She hid her writings from everyone, including family, and was so private that she asked her sister Lavinia to burn her letters, unopened packages, and manuscripts after she died. So when Emily passed away in 1886 at age 56, Lavinia respected her wishes.

After destroying hundreds of manuscripts and letters without reading them, Lavinia opened a bureau drawer and found more than 600 poems in one box, and hundreds more "totally unordered and in various stages of completion." Surprised by the discovery, she stopped to read some before burning them...and was astonished by the quality of the writing.

Rescue: Years later editor Mabel Loomis Todd recounted what happened next:

> Soon after Emily's death, Lavinia came to me, in late evening, actually trembling with excitement. She told me she had discovered a veritable treasure—quantities of Emily's poems which she had no instructions to destroy. She had already burned without examination hundreds of of manuscripts, and letters...carrying out her sister's expressed wishes but without intelligent discrimination. Later she bitterly regretted such inordinate haste. But these poems, she told me, must be printed at once.

Todd spent the next four years sorting and editing Dickinson's surviving letters and poems. The first volume of poems was published in November 1890, and sold out six printings in the first five months. Today, she is considered one of America's greatest poets.

JACKSON BROWNE'S CAREER

Trash: Browne was still an unknown singer in the late 1960s, when David Crosby, of Crosby, Stills, and Nash, urged him to send a demo tape to manager David Geffen. Browne did...and as Fred Goodman writes in *Mansion on the Hill*, "Geffen did exactly what most people in the entertainment industry do with unsolicited material from unknown performers—he threw it away without a listen."

Rescue: "As luck would have it, Geffen's secretary happened to notice the 8 x 10 glossy" that Browne had sent and thought he was attractive. Curious about how he sounded, she fished the recording out of the trash. Goodman writes:

> "You know that record and that picture you threw out?" she asked Geffen the next day.
> "You go through my garbage?" asked her boss.
> "Well, he was so cute that I took it home. And he's very good. Listen to the record."

Geffen did...and took Browne on as a client. When he couldn't get anyone to sign Browne to a record contract, he started his own label, Asylum—and Browne became its first star. Browne then helped fill out the label's roster, turning it into a monster success by bringing Geffen acts like the Eagles and Linda Ronstadt. The "rescue" made Geffen a billionaire.

YOU BET YOUR LIFE, *a quiz show starring Groucho Marx*
Trash: "You Bet Your Life"—featuring hours of Groucho's comedy—was one of America's top 10 shows in the 1950s. But by 1973, it was off the air and long forgotten. In August of that year, the program's producer/creator, John Guedel, got a call from NBC:

> They asked me, "Would you like to have a set of films for your garage as mementos of the show?" I said, "What do you mean?" They said, "We're destroying them to make room in our warehouse in New Jersey." I said, "You're kidding. How many have you destroyed so far?" They said 15 of the 250 negatives. I said, "Stop! Right now! Let me talk to New York."

Rescue: Guedel immediately called NBC's top brass and made a deal to syndicate "You Bet Your Life" rather than destroy it. He approached several TV stations...but no one bought it. Finally he went to KTLA, Channel 5 in Los Angeles, and asked them to run the show as a favor to Groucho—so he wouldn't have to drag out his projector every time he wanted to watch it. They agreed and, to everyone's surprise, it was a hit. In fact, it was so popular that other stations signed up, sparking a Groucho fad. "The boom in Groucho-related merchandise exceeds the Davy Crockett craze of twenty years ago," a surprised Groucho told a reporter in the 1970s, "So now, they tell me, I'm a cult." Groucho remained a pop icon until his death in 1977.

> *"Hollywood is the place where they shoot too many pictures and not enough actors."* —Walter Winchell

FLUBBED HEADLINES

These are 100% honest-to-goodness headlines.
Can you figure out what they were trying to say?

British Left Waffles on
Falkland Islands

*Shot Off Woman's Leg Helps
Nicklaus to 66*

Plane Too Close to Ground,
Crash Probe Told

**Juvenile Court To Try
Shooting Defendant**

Stolen Painting Found by Tree

BOMB HIT BY LIBRARY

After Detour to California
Shuttle Returns to Earth

**Boy Declared Dead, Revives
as Family Protests**

*Dead Coyote Found in Bronx
Launches Search for Its Mate*

CHILDBIRTH IS BIG STEP
TO PARENTHOOD

42 Percent of All Murdered
Women Are Killed by the
Same Man

**National Hunting Group
Targeting Women**

*Fire Officials Grilled Over
Kerosene Heaters*

POLICE CAN'T STOP
GAMBLING

**Ability to Swim May Save
Children from Drowning**

LOW WAGES SAID KEY
TO POVERTY

Youth Hit by Car Riding
Bicycle

**Hostage-Taker Kills Self;
Police Shoot Each Other**

TESTICLE CARGO SEIZED

Check With Doctors Before
Getting Sick

*Police Kill Youth in Effort to Stop
His Suicide Attempt*

INTERN GETS TASTE OF
GOVERNMENT

Convicted S&L Chief Donated
to University

**Study: Dead Patients Usually
Not Saved**

PARKING LOT FLOODS
WHEN MAN BURSTS

U.S. Ships Head to Somalia

**U.S. Advice: Keep Drinking
Water from Sewage**

SUICIDES ASKED TO
RECONSIDER

Cold Wave Linked to
Temperatures

**Gators to Face Seminoles
With Peters Out**

New Autos to Hit 5 Million

What do rabbits and horses have in common? They can't vomit.

"I SPY"...AT THE MOVIES

You probably know the kids' game "I spy, with my little eye..." that was turned into a popular series of books called I Spy. Well, moviemakers have been playing that game with each other (and their actors) for years. Here are some in-jokes and gags you can look for the next time you watch these films (from Reel Gags, *by Bill Givens and* Television In-Jokes, *by Bill van Heerden).*

S CREAM (1996)
I Spy...Wes Craven, the film's director
Where to Find Him: He's the school janitor, wearing a Freddy Krueger sweater from his *Nightmare on Elm Street* movie.

E.T.—THE EXTRA-TERRESTRIAL (1982)
I Spy... Harrison Ford
Where to Find Him: He's the biology teacher who explains that "the frogs won't feel a thing." Screenwriter Melissa Mathison wrote this bit part for her husband. You won't see his face, because his back is to the camera.

CLOSE ENCOUNTERS OF THE THIRD KIND (1977)
I Spy... The Grateful Dead's Jerry Garcia
Where to Find Him: Among the masses in the Indian crowd scene.

BEETLEJUICE (1988)
I Spy... Elwood (Dan Aykroyd) and Jake (John Belushi) Blues from the *Blues Brothers*
Where to Find Them: The scene in which Barbara (Geena Davis) and Adam (Alec Baldwin) go to their caseworker's office. Elwood and Jake are peeking through the blinds.

THE ADDAMS FAMILY (1991)
I Spy... Barry Sonnenfeld, the film's director
Where to Find Him: The scene in which Gomez (Raul Julia) is

Bestselling posthumous hit of all-time: *(Just Like) Starting Over,* by John Lennon.

playing with his train set. When he looks into the window of a train car, a tiny commuter looks back up at him. That's Sonnenfeld.

THE LOST WORLD: JURASSIC PARK (1997)

I Spy...Ads for some improbable new movies: *King Lear*, starring Arnold Schwarzenegger; *Jach and the Behnstacks*, starring Robin Williams; and *Tsunami Surprise*, with Tom Hanks's head attached to a surfer's body

Where to Find Them: In the window of a video store.

THE ROCKY HORROR PICTURE SHOW (1975)

I Spy...Easter eggs

Where to Find Them: Various places during the movie. For example, one is under Frank's throne, one is in a light fixture in the main room, and you can see one when the group goes into an elevator to the lab. What are they doing there? The film crew had an Easter egg hunt on the set, but didn't find all the eggs...so they show up in the film.

TRUE ROMANCE (1993), PULP FICTION (1994), FOUR ROOMS (1995), FROM DUSK TILL DAWN (1996)

I Spy...Big Kahuna burgers and Red Apple cigarettes

Where to Find Them: They're writer/director Quentin Tarantino's special signature on his work. They first showed up in *True Romance*. "In *Pulp Fiction*," says Bill Givens in his book, *Reel Gags*, "Samuel L. Jackson recommends Big Kahuna burgers and both Bruce Willis and Uma Thurman smoke Red Apple cigarettes. In *From Dusk Till Dawn*, George Clooney carries a Big Kahuna burger bag, and you can spot a pack of Red Apples in his car. In *Four Rooms*, Red Apple smokes are near the switchboard."

HALLOWEEN (1978)

I Spy...William Shatner

Where to Find Him: On the psycho's face. The film's budget was so small, they couldn't afford a custom-made mask. So they bought a William Shatner mask, painted it white, and teased out the hair.

Politics aside: The heel of a sock is called the "gore."

CLASSIC (B)AD CAMPAIGNS

Companies are always trying to come up with new ways to make their products look attractive. These efforts are notable for achieving the opposite result.

CASHING IN YOUR CHIPS
Brilliant Marketing Idea: In 1998 the Bangkok subsidiary of the American ad agency Leo Burnett came up with a novel way to sell Thailand's "X" brand potato chips: show that they're so much fun, even "the sourest man in history" can't help turning into a fun guy.

Oops: The historical figure they used was Adolf Hitler. In the commercial, Hitler eats some chips, then strips off his Nazi uniform and dances merrily as a Nazi swastika morphs into the brand's "X" logo. The ad generated so many complaints— especially from the Israeli Embassy in Bangkok—that they had to pull it and issue apologies. "The campaign was never intended to cause ill feelings," an agency spokesperson told reporters.

MYSTERY OF THE EAST
Brilliant Marketing Idea: In England, Smirnoff Vodka's ad agency created a campaign using the slogan "I thought the Kama Sutra was an Indian restaurant...until I discovered Smirnoff."

Oops: They were forced to cancel it, a company spokesperson admitted, "when we conducted a survey and discovered that 60% of people *did* think it was an Indian restaurant."

HIGH FLYER
Brilliant Marketing Idea: In 1967 Pacific Airlines, a commuter airline on the West Coast, hired award-winning adman/comedian Stan Freberg to design an unorthodox new campaign. As Bruce Nash and Allan Zullo write in *The Misfortune 500*, Freberg "suggested PAL poke fun at the one thing airlines never mention— fear of flying."

The tomato comes in over 4,000 varieties.

Oops: Pacific Airlines, at Freberg's direction, placed full-paged ads in newspapers that read:

> Hey there! You with the sweat in your palms. It's about time an airline faced up to something: Most people are scared witless of flying. Deep down inside, every time that big plane lifts off that runway, you wonder if this is it, right? You want to know something, fella? So does the pilot deep down inside.

Freberg also arranged for flight attendants to hand out survival kits containing rabbits' feet and the book *The Power of Positive Thinking*, and instructed that when the plane touched down on the runway, flight attendants were supposed to exclaim, "We made it! How about that!" The airline went under two months after the campaign started.

AH-NOLD GO BOOM!

Brilliant Marketing Idea: In 1993, Arnold Schwarzenegger was America's #1 box-office attraction. Columbia Pictures decided to promote his latest movie, *The Last Action Hero*, with a 75-foot-tall balloon of Schwarzenegger's character in New York's Times Square. Instead of holding a gun, like he does in the movie, Ahnold had a fistful of dynamite in his hand. "We thought a gun was too violent an image," a Columbia spokesperson explained.

Oops: After months of planning, Columbia Pictures finally launched the balloon. Unfortunately, it was just days after the terrorist bombing of the World Trade Center. The studio tried replacing the dynamite with a police badge, but ended up just taking the balloon down. *The Last Action Hero* was one of the biggest flops of the decade.

LOVELY RING, MRS....UH...

Brilliant Marketing Idea: Executives in the jewelry department of Neiman-Marcus, an upscale department store, thought it would be good business to send a personal note of thanks to each of their biggest customers.

Oops: According to *The Business Disaster Book of Days*: "Most of the notes were addressed to the men, the people who had paid for the expensive baubles. But most of the envelopes were opened by women. Unfortunately for Neiman-Marcus, many of these women—wives of the purchasers, mostly—had not been the recipients of the costly purchases."

THE RIGHT STUFF

Thoughts from a conservative with a sense of humor—P. J. O'Rourke.

"Remember the battle between the generations twenty-some years ago? Remember all the screaming at the dinner table about haircuts and getting jobs and the American dream? Well, our parents won. They're out there living the American dream on some damned golf course, and we're stuck with the jobs and haircuts."

"Seriousness is stupidity sent to college."

"Every government is a parliament of whores. The trouble is, in a democracy the whores are us."

"A number of...remarkable things show up in holiday dinners, such as...pies made out of something called 'mince,' although if anyone has ever seen a mince in its natural state he did not live to tell about it."

"There's one...terrifying fact about old people: I'm going to be one soon."

"Everybody knows how to raise children, except the people who have them."

"You can't shame or humiliate modern celebrities. What used to be called shame and humiliation is now called publicity."

"A fruit is a vegetable with looks and money. Plus, if you let fruit rot, it turns into wine, something Brussels sprouts never do."

"Feminism is the result of a few ignorant and literal-minded women letting the cat out of the bag about which is the superior sex."

"The sport of skiing consists of wearing three thousand dollars' worth of clothes and equipment and driving two hundred miles in the snow in order to stand around at a bar and get drunk."

"Politicians *are* interested in people. Not that this is always a virtue. Dogs are interested in fleas."

"I like to do my principal research in bars, where people are more likely to tell the truth or, at least, lie less convincingly than they do in briefings and books."

About 8,000 Americans are injured by musical instruments each year.

"SHE'LL ALWAYS BE DAD TO ME!"

What would you do if your gender prevented you from pursuing the career of your choice? Many women faced this problem in the past. For a rare few the solution was, "If you can't beat 'em, join 'em." They literally lived their lives as men.

D R. JAMES BARRY, *British army surgeon and pioneer of sanitary reforms in medicine in the 19th century*
Background: Barry entered Edinburgh University's medical school in 1808 when he was just 15 (only men were admitted to medical school then). He rose to become one of the most skilled doctors in England. As Carl Posey writes in *Hoaxes and Deceptions*, the "tiny, beardless doctor" was no shrinking violet:

> Far from keeping a low profile, the medic courted attention, picked quarrels, fought a duel, flirted outrageously with the ladies, and once horsewhipped a colonel in public. Adored by patients, but despised by colleagues, Barry was finally forced into early retirement in 1859.

Surprise! Shortly after Barry died in 1865, at the age of 73, acquaintances discovered why, despite his having spent 57 years in the army, no one had ever see him naked: he was a woman.

Note: Apparently, not everyone had been fooled. "Many people seem to have known her secret all along," Posey writes, "and simply—perhaps because of Barry's powerful patrons—declined to mention it."

CHARLIE PARKHURST, *"one of the toughest stagecoach drivers of the Old West"*
Background: Parkhurst worked for the California Stage Company at the height of the Gold Rush in the 1850s. He was 5'7" tall, had broad shoulders, gambled, and chewed tobacco. "Once," Carl Sifakis writes in *Hoaxes and Scams*, "this legendary master of the whip raced a team across an unstable bridge, reaching the other site just before it collapsed. Another time, stopped by highwaymen, Charlie shot the leader and escaped with passengers and goods intact."

Chance that public road in the U.S. is unpaved: 1%. In Canada: 75%.

Parkhurst, who claimed to be an orphan, never grew any facial hair, something that friends attributed to a "fetish" for shaving every day. Unlike his rowdy friends, he also avoided prostitutes, and preferred to sleep apart from other men. Other than that, for all appearances he was one of the guys.

Surprise! In the late 1860s, an illness forced Parkhurst into retirement, and on December 31, 1879, he died alone in his cabin near Watsonville, California. A doctor called in to investigate the death found not only that he had died of cancer, but also that he was a woman who had given birth at some point in her life. Who was this mystery woman? Nobody knows—that was one secret she did manage to take to the grave.

BILLY TIPTON, *jazz musician and leader of the Tipton Trio*
Background: Tipton was a popular jazz musician in Washington from the 1930s to the late 1980s. He married three times and his last marriage, to Kitty Oakes, lasted 19 years. He had three children, all adopted, a fact he attributed to an "injury" that he claimed made "normal" sexual relations impossible. Early in his jazz career his baby face and high-pitched voice caused some listeners to joke that he was too feminine to be a man. But that was about as close as anyone came to suspecting the truth.

Surprise! After years of refusing to see a doctor despite his failing health, Tipton died in 1989 of a bleeding ulcer at his mobile home in Spokane, Washington. He was 74. The paramedics who responded to the call quickly discovered that Tipton was a female, something that apparently only Kitty Oakes had known.

It turns out that at the age of 18, Tipton had borrowed her brother's name and began dressing as a man so she could work as a jazz musician. In those days, most women in jazz were "girl singers," whose careers were short and of limited range.

Tipton's children were shocked. "I'm just lost," her son Jon Clark told reporters after learning his father was a woman. "The guy at the funeral home showed me a little yellow piece of paper where it was marked 'female' under sex. I said, 'What?' and he said it was true. Even so, she'll always be Dad to me."

VEGETABLE TRIVIA

*Did you eat your vegetables today? BRI member Jeff Cheek,
a former CIA man (no kidding) loves to write about food.
He sent us this potpourri of vegetable facts.*

CORN. The most versatile of all food plants, it can be eaten at every stage of development. You can find it in more than 3,000 grocery items. In fact, according to *The Great Food Almanac,* "the average American eats the equivalent of three pounds of corn each day in the form of meat, poultry, and dairy products."

GARLIC. One of the first foods ever cultivated. First written reference: 5,000 years ago, in Sanskrit. At banquets, ancient Greeks served each guest a bowl of parsley, believing it would mask "garlic breath." A vestige of this custom survives. Many restaurants still drop a sprig of parsley on every plate.

LETTUCE. The name comes from the Latin *lactuca* (milk) because of the white liquid that oozes from broken stalks. The Romans prized it so highly that any slave caught eating lettuce was given 30 lashes.

EGGPLANT. Originated in China, where it was grown as a decoration. The Chinese called eggplants "mad apples," believing they caused insanity. It was accepted as a food only after it was brought to the Mediterranean.

LEEKS. These members of the onion family originated in Egypt, then spread to Rome. (Emperor Nero drank a quart of leek soup every day, thinking it improved his singing voice.) The Romans introduced the leek to Wales and it became the Welsh national symbol in 640, when Saxons invaded from England. With no uniforms, it was hard to tell friend from foe in the battle, so each Welsh soldier pinned a leek on his cap to identify himself. They won, and every March 1, St. David's Day, the Welsh pin a leek to their hats or lapels to commemorate the victory.

RADISHES. Since they're ready to harvest after only 42 days, the Greeks named them *Raphanos,* meaning "easy to grow." The Romans changed this to *Radix,* meaning "root."

In medieval Japan, dentists extracted teeth with their hands.

IT ISN'T 2000
FOR EVERYONE

*Does the new millennium mean the end of the world?...the
beginning of the New Age?...We've all got an opinion, but
for much of the world the question is irrelevant—because,
according to their calendars, it's not a new millennium....*

...It's 5760
Who Says? The Hebrew (Jewish) calendar. Their year 2000 occurred in 1760 B.C.
Origin: It's a lunar calendar that dates to 3760 B.C.—according to Jewish tradition, the date the world began.

...It's 4698
Who says? The Chinese calendar. Their year 2000 occurred in 698 B.C.
Origin: A lunar calendar dating from 2600 B.C., when the Emperor Huang Ti introduced the first cycle of the zodiac. It begins at the second new moon after the winter solstice.

...It's 1921
Who Says? The Reformed Indian Calendar. Their year 2000 will arrive in 2079 A.D.
Origin: India gained independence from England in 1947. In 1957, it officially adopted this calendar, based on the beginning of the Saka Era (a Hindu time cycle).

...It's 1421
Who Says? The Muslim Calendar. Their 2000 will arrive in 2579 A.D.
Origin: A lunar calendar that dates back to 622 A.D., the year Muhammad and his followers migrated from Mecca to Medina to escape persecution.

...It's 1378
Who Says? The Persian calendar. Their year 2000 arrives in 2622 A.D.
Origin: This solar calendar was created by the poet and mathematician Omar Khayyám. Iranians and many Central Asians celebrate their new year every spring equinox.

...It's 2543
Who Says? The Thereveda Buddhist calendar. Their year 2000 occurred in 1457 A.D.
Origin: Dates from 544 B.C., the commonly accepted date of Buddha's death (he was 80). Thereveda Buddhists celebrate the new year in mid-April.

Do you alphabetize your spice rack? Only one in twelve Americans does.

THE ORIGIN OF BASKETBALL, PART I

Unlike baseball and football, which trace their roots to games that have been played for centuries, basketball was invented by one man— a Canadian named James Naismith—in a couple of days in 1891. It is the only major sport considered native to the USA. Here's its history.

SOMETHING NEW

Today the YMCA is synonymous with sports, but that hasn't always been the case. In the mid-1880s, it was primarily a missionary group. "In fact," Ted Vincent writes in *The Rise and Fall of American Sport*, "the Young Men's Christian Association condemned almost all sports, along with dancing, card playing, and vaudeville shows, on the grounds that these activities were 'distinctly worldly in their associations, and unspiritual in their influence,' and therefore 'utterly inconsistent with our professions as disciples of Christ.'"

Good Sport

Then, at the YMCA's national convention in 1889, 24-year-old Dr. Luther Gulick started a revolution when he suggested that "good bodies and good morals" might actually go together. He insisted that keeping physically fit could make someone a better person, rather than inevitably leading them down the path of sin….And he proposed that the YMCA use organized athletics to reach out to youngsters who might otherwise not be interested in the Y's traditional emphasis on religion.

His proposal met with heavy opposition from conservatives, who argued that a "Christian gymnasium teacher" was a contradiction in terms. But when Gulick's idea was put to a vote, he won. Gulick was put in charge of a brand-new athletics teaching program at the YMCA School for Christian Workers in Springfield, Massachusetts.

CHANGING TIMES

Gulick's ideas were actually part of a larger social movement. For decades, America had been making the transition from a largely rural, farm-based society to an industrialized economy, in which

In 1797 James Hetherington invented the top hat and

much of the population lived and worked in cities. Americans who had once labored in fields from sunup to sundown were now spending much of their working lives cooped up inside a factory, or behind a desk or sales counter.

"Middle-class Americans in particular reacted to the growing bureaucracy and confinement of their work lives, and to the remarkable crowding of their cities, by rushing to the outdoors, on foot and on bicycles," Elliot Gorn writes in *A Brief History of American Sports*. "Hiking, bird-watching, camping, rock-climbing, or simply walking in the new national parks—participation in all of these activities soared in the years around the turn of the century."

MASS APPEAL

Middle-class Americans who embraced physical activity as the answer to their own yearnings also began to see it as an answer to some of society's ills. The repeal of child labor laws and high levels of immigration meant that the tenement districts in America's major cities were full of immigrant youths who had little or nothing to do. Leaders of the "recreation movement," like Dr. Gulick, felt that building public playgrounds and bringing organized play programs into the slums would help the kids stay out of trouble and make it easier for them to assimilate into American life.

"Reformers thought of themselves as being on an exciting new mission, Americanizing children by helping them to have fun," Gorn says. "Playground reformers sought to clean up American streets, confine play to designated recreational spaces, and use their professional expertise to teach 'respectable' athletics." In an era in which public playgrounds were virtually unheard of, the facilities and athletic programs that organizations like the YMCA were beginning to offer often provided the only positive outlet for urban kids' energies.

BACK TO SCHOOL

As Gulick set up his program to train YMCA physical education instructors, he also decided to require men training to be "general secretaries" (the official title for men who ran local YMCA chapters) to take phys ed classes.

These students were older and more conservative than other

students. They hadn't been sold on Gulick's newfangled sports ideas and, left to their own devices, would avoid physical education classes entirely. Gulick feared that if he didn't bring these future YMCA leaders around to his point of view while they were in Springfield, they wouldn't implement his programs when they got back home…and his efforts would be fruitless.

Cold Shoulder

Working with the general secretaries was a snap at first: in the early fall they just went outside and played football or soccer. But when the weather turned cold and they were forced indoors, things got difficult. The best recreation Gulick could come up with was a schedule of military drills…followed by German, French, and Swedish gymnastics. Day after day, the routine was the same, and the students became thoroughly bored.

THE INCORRIGIBLES

Within weeks, the class was in open rebellion, and two successive physical education instructors resigned rather than put up with their abuse. They told Gulick that he might as well give up on "The Incorrigibles," as the class had become known.

Gulick wasn't ready to quit yet. For weeks, an instructor named James Naismith had been arguing that The Incorrigibles weren't to blame for the situation. "The trouble is not with the men," he said, "but with the system we are using. The kind of work for this class should be of a recreative nature, something that would appeal to their play instincts." At one faculty meeting, he even proposed inventing a new indoor game. So when Gulick put Naismith in charge of the class, he commented pointedly: "Now would be a good time for you to work on that new game that you said could be invented."

For Part II, turn to page 181.

*   *   *

"I cannot imagine any condition which could cause this ship to founder. I cannot conceive of any vital disaster happening to the vessel. Modern shipbuilding has gone beyond that."
—E.I. Smith, captain of the Titanic

Attention Pentagon! The United States has never lost a war in which mules were used.

THE UNFINISHED MASTERPIECE

Even if you're not an art lover, you've probably seen the best and most famous picture of the first U.S. president, George Washington, painted by Gilbert Stuart—it's the one on the dollar bill. But did you know that it was never finished? Here's the story.

PRESIDENTIAL PORTRAITURE

Before photography, sitting for a portrait was a long, tedious process. George Washington never liked it, and by the time he retired from the presidency, he'd vowed never to do it again. He routinely refused requests from artists who wanted to capture his likeness one more time for posterity. But in 1796, he got a request he couldn't refuse: his wife Martha wanted them both to pose for portraits to be hung together in a central place in their home.

The painter Martha had in mind was Gilbert Stuart—a celebrated artist in both Britain and America and the portraitist of choice for hundreds of politicians and dignitaries. George agreed with her decision; he'd already posed for two other paintings with Stuart and found him relatively easy to sit for.

STUART'S STORY

Stuart didn't feel the same way about Washington. He thought the ex-president was too stiff, and complained to friends about his stony countenance, his foul teeth, and the dead look in his eyes.

But Stuart still took Mrs. Washington's assignment gladly. Alcoholism and exorbitant spending had put him in debt, and he needed cash. Besides, he'd made quite a bit of money from his first two Washington portraits:

• He sold the first one to a wealthy merchant for a tidy sum…but before delivering it, quickly painted and sold at least 15 copies. (One was later used for the image on U.S. quarters.)

• The second painting—a full-length portrait this time—was so well received that Stuart was able to sell dozens of copies before delivering it to the banker who originally commissioned it.

During the 1980s, the average speed of traffic in New York City was less than 10 mph.

Aware of Stuart's past duplicities and not wanting to spend months waiting while the artist copied her paintings, Martha Washington made a careful deal: she insisted that Stuart agree to deliver the portraits the moment they were finished.

WORKING WITH GEORGE

The sitting with Washington began much like the previous efforts. Stuart was relieved to see that the president was wearing a new set of false teeth that made his face look more natural. But he was exasperated when, once again, Washington's face turned to stoniness the minute he sat down.

Stuart told jokes and anecdotes trying to capture an engaging, interested look. It didn't work...but in the middle of the sitting, Washington's face momentarily lit up with a pleasant expression. Stuart began drilling him to find out what had happened...and discovered that Washington had seen a horse go by outside.

Stuart began talking horses—anything and everything he could think of. Then he talked about farming, and anything to do with rural life. Washington's entire demeanor changed: he became more natural, more lighthearted; his face became brighter.

CREEP OR GENIUS?

The result was the best portrait of the first president ever painted. In fact, Stuart was so pleased that he immediately began trying to figure out a way to keep it. If he could just get out of his deal with Mrs. Washington, he could make more than just a dozen hurried copies—he could do *hundreds* at his leisure and finally get out of debt. But how could he pull it off?

Then he hit on a plan. He stopped a few brushstrokes short of completing the painting, leaving a little canvas peeking through where Washington's collar should have been. Then he told messenger after messenger from the impatient ex-First Lady, "Sorry, it's not finished yet."

SECOND-RATE ART

Even a visit from the former president couldn't shake the painting loose. Instead Stuart sent along one of his copies of the original. Mrs. Washington hung it up, but told her friends: "It is not a good likeness at all."

In fact, not many of the copies *were*. Stuart was interested in speed, not quality. According to one of his daughters, on a "good day" he could pump out a copy every two hours. Many had little or no resemblance to Washington at all. An acquaintance of Stuart's wrote, "Mr. Stuart told me one day when we were before this original portrait that he could never make a copy of it to satisfy himself, and that at last, having made so many, he worked mechanically and with little interest."

Regardless, the portrait became a wildly popular commodity and Stuart dashed off more than 200 copies, calling them his "hundred dollar bills." But he still couldn't completely rid himself of debt. Ironically, in the end there were so many inferior copies of the Unfinished Portrait (by other artists as well) that they actually did significant damage to Stuart's reputation. When he died in 1828, he still owed considerable money, and his youngest daughter, Jane—also a portrait painter—had become the breadwinner for the family.

BY THE WAY

The original paintings, still technically "unfinished," never were delivered to the Washington family. The Boston Athenaeum wound up owning them, and today they're shared part of the year with the Boston Museum of Fine Arts and the National Portrait Gallery in Washington.

* * *

LAST LAUGH

"On Nixon's death in 1994 President Clinton declared an official day of mourning and closed the federal government for a day, as had been done upon the deaths of former Presidents Truman, Eisenhower, and Johnson. The cost of closing the federal government for one day in 1994? More than $400 million. Of that total, $23 million was extra premium pay for 'essential' workers who had to go to work anyway to keep the government functioning. They received time and a half for that day."

—*Stupid Government Tricks,* by John Kohut

IT'S A WEIRD, WEIRD WORLD

Proof that truth really is stranger than fiction.

A STRANGE BE-LEAF

"A Swiss woman has left over a half-million dollars to a houseplant. The millionairess, from Geneva, once described her newly rich jade plant as her 'best and only friend.' She is believed to have conversed with the plant for the last five years."

—The *Edge,* April 19, 1999

LOOK AT THOSE MELONS!

"Britain's biggest supermarket chain has asked growers to supply smaller melons after research showed women shoppers subconsciously compared them to the size of their breasts.

"The *Daily Telegraph* said buyers working for Tesco were told by researchers that a current preference for smaller busts was the reason why traditional big, fleshy melons were remaining unsold.

"'We were surprised,' said a Tesco spokesman. 'But it's certainly produced results. Since we introduced smaller melons two months ago we have sold more than a million.'"

—Reuters, May 3, 1999

A SILLY SUPERSTITION?

"Gerald Steindam, 24, of Miami, Florida, vowed never to fly Eastern Airlines' flight 401 (New York–Miami) after luckily missing a flight 401 in 1972 that went down in the Everglades.

"In 1980 he overcame his superstitious fear and took the flight. The plane was hijacked to Cuba."

—*Encyclopedia Brown's Book of Strange Facts*

A REAL CONDOM-NATION

"Police in Sri Lanka recently arrested a man after finding a condom in his wallet. 'Why would anyone want to carry a condom in his wallet, unless of course he was up to some mischief,' a police officer was quoted as saying. The man was released after questioning."

—*San Francisco Chronicle,* 1993

There are an estimated 171 billion U.S. pennies in circulation.

Q & A:
ASK THE EXPERTS

Everyone's got a question or two they'd like answered—basic stuff, like "Why is the sky blue?" Here are a few of those questions, with answers from books by some of the nation's top trivia experts.

KNUCKLE UNDER
Q: *Why do our knuckles crack?*

A: "The bones in our fingers are separated by small pads of cartilage, and in between are small pockets of a thick liquid. When you bend your fingers, the bones pull away from the pads of cartilage and a vacuum forms. As the bending continues...the vacuum bubble bursts, making the cracking sound you hear. The process is very similar to what happens when you pull a rubber suction cup off a smooth surface." (From *Ever Wonder Why?*, by Douglas B. Smith)

SEEING THINGS
Q: *What are those little squiggles you see floating on your eyes when you look at the sky?*

A: "They're called 'floaters.' To some people they look like spots; to others, like tiny threads. They're not on your eyes, though; they're *in* your eyes. That's why blinking doesn't make them go away. Floaters are all that's left of the hyaloid artery. The hyaloid artery carried blood to your eye and helped it grow...when you were still inside your mother's womb.

"When your eyes were finished growing, the hyaloid artery withered and broke into pieces. But since these pieces were sealed up inside your eye, they had no place to go. You'll see them floating around the rest of your life." (From *Know It All!*, by Ed Zotti)

STOP, POP AND ROLL
Q: *How does quicksand work?*

A: "Not by pulling you down. Quicksand is nearly always found above a spring, which creates a supersaturated condition that makes the sand frictionless and unable to support weight. In

---

Bird rule of thumb: If they could sweat, they wouldn't be able to fly.

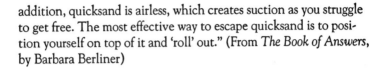

addition, quicksand is airless, which creates suction as you struggle to get free. The most effective way to escape quicksand is to position yourself on top of it and 'roll' out." (From *The Book of Answers*, by Barbara Berliner)

LONG-DISTANCE RUNAROUND

Q: *Why does the alphabet on a phone start on the #2 button rather than on the #1?*

A: Back when dial phones were used, a pulse or clicking sound was made whenever you dialed. The pulses corresponded to the number dialed, so "when you dialed the number 1, it sent out one click...2, sent two clicks, and so on. Sometimes a random clicking caused equipment to think someone was dialing a number beginning with 1, when they actually weren't. Thus a rule was made: No phone number can start with 1. This rule is still observed, though solely for the sake of tradition." (From *Why Things Are, Volume II: The Big Picture*, by Joel Achenbach)

I CAN SEE CLEARLY NOW

Q: *How does an X-ray photograph your bones but not your flesh?*

A: "An X-ray camera fires electrons at a plate covered with silver halide crystals, which are sensitive to light. Your leg is put in the way of the penetrating stream of particles. When an electron reaches the plate unimpeded, it turns a halide crystal black. The crystals that receive no electrons fall away when the plate is developed and leave that area white under the light. X-ray particles are so highly energized that most of them pass right through flesh. Bones, on the other hand, are very densely packed and contain large amounts of calcium. They stop the X-rays by absorbing them—the crack in your tibia shows up black on the plate because that's where bone isn't." (From *How Do They Do That?*, by Caroline Sutton)

*   *   *   *

Slippery when wet

Ice isn't slippery. What makes people and things slip on ice is water. A thin layer of ice melts when pressure is applied to it and it is this wet layer on top of the ice that is slippery.

Queen termites can lay an egg every second, or 86,000 eggs a day.

POLITICALLY INCORRECT

Observations from Bill Maher, host of TV's late-night political talk show.

"I believe Dr. Kevorkian is onto something. I think he's great. Because suicide is our way of saying to God, 'You can't fire me. I quit.'"

"The economy is incredibly good. It's too good. It's happy, excited. The GNP is up, the Dow Jones is up. Inflation is at its lowest level since 1963. I went to the ATM today, and I inserted my card—it moaned."

"We survived the 1980s. Back then, the economic program was called 'trickle down.' That actually meant they were pissing on you. How the whole theory goes was this: 'We have all the money. If we drop some, it's yours. Go for it.'"

"My mother is Jewish, my father Catholic. When I went to confession, I'd pray, 'Bless me, father, for I have sinned. And I think you know my lawyer, Mr. Cohen.'"

"Kids, they're not easy, but there has to be some penalty for sex."

"I saw a product in the market, Mr. Salty pretzels. Isn't that nerve? Everything nowadays is low salt or salt-free. Here's a guy who says, 'The hell with you, I'm Mr. Salty pretzels.' Like Mr. Tar and Nicotine cigarettes, or Mr. Gristle and Hard Artery beefsteak."

"This country loves guns; we even have salad shooters. This country thinks that salad is too peaceable, you have to find some way to shoot it."

"Remember, kids, guns aren't for fun. Guns are for killing things like songbirds, and deer, and intruders, and Spice Girls, and busybodies who just won't leave your cult alone, and women who don't understand you're the best man for them. That may sound crazy, but when you're holding a gun, you decide who's crazy."

"They added up all the people in this country who consider themselves a minority and it added up to more than the population of the country."

Food for thought: Peanut butter sandwiches weren't popular until the 1920s.

TWINKIE
FAILURE TESTING

*Everyone seems to think that Twinkies, the eternally maligned snack
cake, can last forever and withstand any kind of abuse. The folks
at Spy magazine put that common belief to a test. Here are
the results, reprinted from their July 1989 issue.*

IN AN EFFORT to clarify questions about the purported durability and unusual physical characteristics of Twinkies, we subjected the Hostess snack logs to the following scientific experiments:

EXPOSURE: A Twinkie was left on a window ledge for four days, during which time an inch and a half of rain fell. Many flies were observed crawling across the Twinkie's surface, but contrary to hypothesis, birds—even pigeons—avoided this potential source of sustenance. Despite the rain and prolonged exposure to the sun, the Twinkie retained its original color and form. When removed, the Twinkie was found to be substantially dehydrated. Cracked open, it was observed to have taken on the consistency of industrial foam insulation; the filling, however, retained its advertised "creaminess."

RADIATION: A Twinkie was placed in a conventional microwave oven, which was set for precisely 4 minutes—the approximate cooking time of bacon. After 20 seconds, the oven began to emit the Twinkie's rich, characteristic aroma of artificial butter. After 1 minute, this aroma began to resemble the acrid smell of burning rubber. The experiment was aborted after 2 minutes, 10 seconds, when thick, foul smoke began billowing from the top of the oven. A second Twinkie was subjected to the same experiment. This Twinkie leaked molten white filling. When cooled, this now epoxy-like filling bonded the Twinkie to its plate, defying gravity; it was removed only upon application of a butter knife.

EXTREME FORCE: A Twinkie was dropped from a ninth-floor window, a fall of approximately 120 feet. It landed right side up, then bounced onto its back. The expected "splatter" effect was not observed. Indeed, the only discernible damage to the Twinkie was a narrow fissure on its underside. Otherwise, the Twinkie remained structurally intact.

Estimated cost of maintaining a chimpanzee in captivity for 60 years: $300,000.

EXTREME COLD: A Twinkie was placed in a conventional freezer for 24 hours. Upon removal, the Twinkie was not found to be frozen solid, but its physical properties had noticeably "slowed": the filling was found to be the approximate consistency of acrylic paint, while exhibiting the mercury-like property of not adhering to practically any surface. It was noticed that the Twinkie had generously absorbed freezer odors.

EXTREME HEAT: A Twinkie was exposed to a gas flame for 2 minutes. While the Twinkie smoked and blackened and the filling in one of its "cream holes" boiled, the Twinkie did not catch fire. It did, however, produce the same "burning rubber" aroma noticed during the irradiation experiment.

IMMERSION: A Twinkie was dropped into a large beaker filled with tap water. The Twinkie floated momentarily, began to list and sink, and yellow tendrils ran off its lower half, possibly consisting of a water-soluble artificial coloring. After 2 hours, the Twinkie had bloated substantially. Its coloring was now a very pale tan—in contrast to the yellow water that surrounded it. The Twinkie bobbed when touched, and had a gelatinous texture. After 72 hours, the Twinkie was found to have bloated to roughly 200 percent of its original size, the water had turned opaque, and a small, fan-shaped spray of filling had leaked from one of the "cream holes."

Unfortunately, efforts to remove the Twinkie for further analysis were abandoned when, under light pressure, the Twinkie disintegrated into an amorphous cloud of debris. A distinctly sour odor was noted.

SUMMARY OF RESULTS: The Twinkie's survival of a 120-foot drop, along with some of the unusual phenomena associated with the "creamy filling" and artificial coloring, should give pause to those observers who would unequivocally categorize the Twinkie as "food." Further clinical inquiry is required before any definite conclusions can be drawn.

*　　*　　*

"A wife lasts only for the length of a marriage, but an ex-wife is there for the rest of your life."
　　　　　　　　　　　　　　　　—Woody Allen

THE DONALD

What can you say about Donald Trump? Nothing he hasn't already said about himself, in one way or another.

"In the second grade...I punched my music teacher because I didn't think he knew much about music....I'm not proud of that, but it's clear... that...early on I had a tendency to stand up."

"You know, it really doesn't matter what [the media] write as long as you've got a young and beautiful piece of ass."

"I'll tell you, it's Big Business. If there is one word to describe Atlantic City, it's Big Business. Or two words—Big Business."

"There's no one my age who has accomplished more. Everyone can't be the best."

"I love creating stars. To some extent I have done that with Ivana. To a certain extent I have done that with Marla. I have really given a lot of women great opportunity. Unfortunately, after they are a star, the fun is over for me."

"It's a lot better to side with a winner than a loser."

"How about the guys that stand there grabbing the urinal for balance? I watch in amazement. Then they come up and say, 'I'm a big fan, can I shake your hand?' And I'm a bad guy for saying, 'Excuse me!' They were just holding the big wonger, and they want to shake your hand!"

"The worst thing a man can do is go bald. Never let yourself go bald."

"I allow Ivana to stay there because it gives her something to do." —*on why his ex-wife was still president of the Plaza Hotel*

"Germ phobia is a problem. You have to be selective. It's pretty dangerous out there. It's like Vietnam! Dating is my personal Vietnam!"

"I like thinking big. If you're going to be thinking anything, you might as well think big."

"There has never been anything like this built in four hundred years."
—*on the Trump Tower*

The first movie shown in a drive-in theater was *Wife Beware*, in 1933.

WEIRD THEME RESTAURANTS

For a while, it looked as though restaurants modeled after the Hard Rock Cafe were going to sweep the world. Guess which of the following is Uncle John's personal favorite.

THE ROADKILL CAFE, Greenville, Maine

Theme: Animals squashed on the highway

Details: The menu features only "critters that don't move fast enough" to get out of traffic. Sample items: "The Chicken That Didn't Make It Across the Road," and "Bye Bye Bambi Burgers." It's actually just a little black humor, but the staff gets into the act: "A cook named Freddy is fond of yelling 'down boy, down boy' as he pounds on chicken breasts before grilling them. When he's done, he might throw handfuls of feathers out the door."

THE OUTHOUSE, Winnipeg, Manitoba

Theme: Bathrooms

Details: The entire restaurant was decorated to look like a public restroom—"toilet bowls alternate with tables in the main dining room. And their logo, a toilet seat, was on all the menus." Shortly after the Grand Opening in the mid-1970s, health officials shut it down. The reason: "Not enough working bathrooms."

ALACATRAZ BC, Tokyo

Theme: Maximum-security prison

Details: "Diners are handcuffed, eat in cells, and must beg permission from the guards to be allowed out to visit the restroom."

CRASH CAFE, Baltimore

Theme: Disasters and human carnage (just what we like to contemplate over dinner)

Details: The smoking fuselage of what appears to be a crashed DC3 juts from the exterior of the flagship restaurant. "The roof is askew, windows are cracked and the outer wall is shattered in spots. In the drive, a car looks as if it has just smashed into a fire hydrant, which

---

President Grover Cleveland's nickname was "Uncle Jumbo."

is spewing water." Inside, diners are "entertained" by film clips of train wrecks and collapsing bridges and buildings. "Some may say that it teeters on the verge of unacceptable," says founder Patrick Turner, "but that is precisely its strength. Crash Cafe seduces us to look closer, to indulge our undeniable fascination with the destructive, erotic nature of crashing."

DIVE!, Los Angeles and Las Vegas

Theme: Submarines

Details: "A submarine-shaped restaurant that specialized in gourmet submarine sandwiches." Partners included Hollywood moguls Steven Spielberg and Jeffrey Katzenberg. It had "millions of dollars in special effects," including "computer-controlled flashing light, steam blasts, deep-sea scenes on video screens, and a surging water wall to recreate the experience of 'an actual submarine dive.'" Singer Thomas Dolby provided interactive sound effects that were just a little too real: "Apparently, the virtual aquatic experience was so convincing that it prompted an upsurge in customers visiting the toilet. The L.A. restaurant closed in 1999.

HOUSE OF MAO, Singapore

Theme: Chairman Mao Tse-tung—who ruled China from 1950 until his death in 1976—as a pop icon

Details: "Scores of Mao pictures, poems and sculptures peer down from the walls. The staff wear uniforms similar to those of China's People's Liberation Army (though waitresses are miniskirted)."

"Chairman Mao was one of the most feared individuals in the world," the founder says, "but when you come to the restaurant, you see the human side of him, swimming, playing poker." On the menu: Mao burgers, Mao pizza, Mao fajitas, and Mao pasta. "Mao would probably turn in his grave," one Singapore journalist wrote following the restaurant's grand opening.

* * *

Truth or Urban Legend?

On an American one-dollar bill, there's supposedly an owl in the upper left-hand corner of the "1" encased in the "shield" and a spider hidden in the front upper right-hand corner.

STRANGE LAWSUITS

These days, it seems that people will sue each other over practically anything. Here are a few real-life examples of unusual legal battles.

THE PLAINTIFF: A Chinese restaurant in Stansted, England

THE DEFENDANT: Kevin Clifford, a customer

THE LAWSUIT: In 1996 Clifford walked into the restaurant and ordered a large meal. While he was waiting for it, he explained later, the smells from the kitchen made him so hungry that he lost control. He began ripping the leaves off potted plants, eating them. "By the time his order was ready," according to one report, "he had eaten the leaves off every plant in the place." The restaurant owner sued him for the cost of the plants.

THE VERDICT: Guilty. Clifford's unusal salad cost him $700.

THE PLAINTIFF: Donald Drusky

THE DEFENDANT: "God, the sovereign ruler of the universe"

THE LAWSUIT: In 1999 the 63-year-old Drusky filed suit against God for "taking no corrective action" against an ex-employer who'd fired him 30 years before. His demands: God must grant him guitar-playing skills and resurrect either his pet pigeon or his mother.

THE VERDICT: Drusky claimed that since God didn't show up in court, he won by default. The judge declared the suit "frivolous."

THE PLAINTIFF: Nellie Mitchell, a 98-year-old Arkansas woman

THE DEFENDANT: Globe International, publishers of the supermarket tabloid the *Sun*

THE LAWSUIT: In 1990 the *Sun* ran a "report" about a 101-year-old newspaper carrier in Australia "who'd quit her route because she'd become pregnant by a millionaire customer." They picked a photo of Mitchell to illustrate it. Why? They assumed she was dead. She wasn't, and sued for invasion of privacy.

THE VERDICT: The jury awarded her $1.5 million (later

Proper English: Technically speaking, a female "dude" is known as a "dudine."

reduced to $850,000). A judge compared her experience to being "dragged slowly through a pile of untreated sewage."

THE PLAINTIFF: Dave Feuerstein
THE DEFENDANT: Tesco supermarkets, an English chain
THE LAWSUIT: Enthusiastic about Tesco's low prices during a special promotion, Feuerstein kept going back to buy more. In three days, he redeemed over 300 coupons...then claimed he'd hurt his back carrying all the cheap merchandise, and sued. "Offers like this are too good to refuse," he told a reporter. "Tesco should have been more considerate and made it impossible to do what I did. If Tesco hadn't had this offer, I wouldn't have hurt my back."
THE VERDICT: Unknown.

THE PLAINTIFF: Kenneth Bruckner of Gering, Nebraska
THE DEFENDANT: Presbyterian/St. Luke's Medical Center in Denver
THE LAWSUIT: In the spring of 1993, Bruckner sued the hospital, claiming the "highly toxic" cleanser they used to disinfect toilet seats had caused him "permanent burns, neurological injuries, and urologic and sexual dysfunction." Said Bruckner's attorney: "What's the world coming to if it's not safe to sit on the toilet and read the paper?"
THE VERDICT: Unknown...but you know how *we'd* rule.

THE PLAINTIFFS: Two college students
THE DEFENDANT: Pace University, Long Island, New York
THE LAWSUIT: The students took an introductory computer-programming course at Pace. One day the teacher required them, as homework, to calculate the cost of an aluminum atom. The answer is $6.22054463335 x 10^{-26}—less than a *trillionth* of a penny. Outraged that such a high level of work was required in an introductory course, the pair sued.
THE VERDICT: Believe it or not, the judge found their instructor guilty of "educational malpractice."

NO GOOD DEED GOES UNPUNISHED

Some Good Samaritans, like Lenny Skutnick (see p. 25),
wind up honored by the president of the United States.
Others get their cars stolen. Life isn't fair.

LATE FEE

"In 1994, New York City's Metropolitan Transit Authority docked Michael Durant, a 31-year-old bus driver, a day's pay for being twelve minutes late for work. His excuse: He had stopped to pull a man out of a burning car on the highway."

—Esquire, **January 1995**

THANKS, YOU ##*!#@!

"New York Jets quarterback Boomer Esiason...was driving home after a 28-24 loss to the Miami Dolphins when he had to stop his car because of an accident....He got out and asked a woman in the car in front of him whether she was all right. Her window was broken and she was crying. Esiason recalls: 'She looked at me and said, 'Boomer?' I said, 'Yes.' She said, 'You guys really (stink). How'd you lose that game today?'"

—San Francisco Chronicle, **December 7, 1995**

ALL WET

"In 1981 Peter Stankiewicz of Rockville, Maryland stopped his car and dove into the Potomac River to rescue a driver whose lumber truck had crashed through a bridge railing and plunged 60 feet into the icy water. After hauling the driver to shore, Stankiewicz was informed that his car had been towed to the pound because it was blocking traffic."

—Encyclopedia Brown's Book of Strange Facts

THAT'S WHAT YOU GET

"When Lorne Murdock saw a delivery truck collide with a car in L.A., he pulled over his own car and rushed out to calm the bleeding motorist until help arrived. For his trouble, somebody stole

the word *agnostic* in 1869? He got tired of being called an atheist.

Murdock's 1980 AMC Spirit.

"'It's incredible, you try and save someone's life, do the right thing, help somebody out, and this happens,' said the 29-year-old Murdock.

"'That's what you get for being a Good Samaritan,' said officer Kirk Hunter."
—*Santa Rosa Press-Democrat*, May 2, 1993

METER-FEEDING GRANNY

"Sylvia Slayton was just trying to spare a stranger a ticket in Cincinnati, when she plunked a dime and a nickel into two expired parking meters. Instead she got handcuffed and arrested, and Thursday was convicted of a misdemeanor for interfering with an officer trying to ticket overdue cars.

"'I tried to do what I thought was the right thing,' the 63-year-old grandmother of 10 said. She faces as many as 90 days in jail and a $750 fine when she is sentenced later this month."
—Burlington, Vermont, *Free Press*, February 7, 1997

REWARD FOR VALOR

"In 1982 Timothy George, a part-time busboy at a family restaurant in Vallejo, California, chased and captured a mugger who had robbed a customer in the men's room. Timothy was promptly fired for 'leaving work' and 'fighting'."
—*Encyclopedia Brown's Book of Strange Facts*

GULL OF MY DREAMS

"In June 1994, Don Weston found a young seagull squawking on the ground in his driveway in Gloucester, England, and put the bird on top of his garage to keep it safe from cats. A few hours later it flew off. Mr. Weston thought he'd done a good deed, but every June and July for the last three years he has been pursued by a vengeful seagull—the very one, he believes, whose life he saved.

"'Its evil squawking is so distinctive,' he said. 'It sounds like a banshee wailing. I've had nightmares about it.' The bird pecks his head, bombs him with droppings...and stalks him through the city by air. 'At the sight of me, it goes crazy,' said Weston."
—*The Fortean Times*

If you visit, bring sunblock: Neptune's summer is 40 years long.

WHO'S ON FIRST?

*America's national pastime is more than just a game—it's
a tradition. The component parts are traditions, too.
We got curious about where the they come from.*

BASEBALL GLOVES
Introduced by: Charles Waite, first-baseman for the Boston
team of the National Association (forerunner of the National
League), in 1875

History: Until Waite started wearing a thin, unpadded, flesh-color
glove, everyone played barehanded. In fact, when he showed up on
the field with it, rivals jeered that he was a softy. One contemporary
wrote: "Waite confessed that he was a bit ashamed to wear it, but
had to save his hand. He also admitted he'd chosen a color as incon-
spicuous as possible, because he didn't want to attract attention."

Note: Though a few players copied Waite, it took a superstar to
popularize the use of gloves. In 1883 the shortstop for the Provi-
dence, Rhode Island, team broke a finger on his left hand. To protect it, he wore an oversized, padded buckskin glove. One of baseball's biggest heroes, John Montgomery Ward, decided to wear one
too…which inspired manufacturers to begin mass-producing them.
(From *The Baseball Catalog*, by Dan Schlossberg)

SHIN GUARDS
Introduced by: "One of two black second-basemen, Binghamton
[New York]'s Bud Fowler or Buffalo's Frank Grant, who played mi-
nor league ball in the 1880s in the International League." (From
Only the Ball Was White, by Robert Peterson)

History: In the 1880s, white ballplayers openly tried to injure black
players. Grant and Fowler "knew that about every player that came
down to second base on a steal…would, if possible, throw their
spikes into them." So one of them came up with the idea of wrap-
ping wooden slats around their shins.

Note: It only worked for a while…and then the bigots got more vicious. As one player recalled in 1891: "[When] Grant put wooden
armor on his legs for protection, the opposition just proceeded to

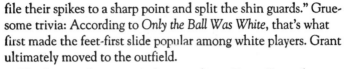

file their spikes to a sharp point and split the shin guards." Gruesome trivia: According to *Only the Ball Was White*, that's what first made the feet-first slide popular among white players. Grant ultimately moved to the outfield.

The first catcher to wear shin guards was Roger Bresnahan in 1907. He fashioned them after the leg guards used in the English game of cricket.

SEVENTH-INNING STRETCH

Introduced by: No one's sure

History: According to legend, the stretch began in 1910 when President William Howard Taft got up to leave during the seventh inning of a game between Washington and Philadelphia. "His entourage followed," the story goes, "and fans, seeing a crowd of people standing, stood up also."

That may have happened, but according to *Baseball's Book of Firsts*, the seventh-inning stretch was already part of baseball tradition: "In reality, fans had been standing and stretching at about the seventh inning since the early 1870s." The book says it started in Boston, where the local team tended to score most of its runs near the end of the game. Around the seventh inning, fans would stand and "cheer on the hometown boys."

Note: There's one other claimant—Manhattan College. According to one sports historian: "In 1882 during a baseball game at New York's Manhattan College, the athletic director, a man named Brother Jasper, called a time out during the seventh inning so that the fidgeting students in the stands would have a moment to stretch." True? Who knows?

UNIFORM NUMBERS

Introduced by: The New York Yankees

History: Around 1915, teams experimented with small numbers on uniform sleeves, but they made no difference to fans. In 1929, however, the Yankees—realizing they were attracting lots of new fans who didn't know the players by sight—put big numbers on the backs of uniforms. The original numbers followed the batting order. For example: Babe Ruth, who batted third, got number 3; Lou Gehrig, who batted fourth, was number 4. Later, numbers

In 1947 Marilyn Monroe was crowned the first Queen of Artichokes.

were assigned at random. It took another 31 years before teams started putting names on the uniforms. Why so long? Apparently, clubs were afraid they'd lose the profits they made from selling scorecards.

CATCHER'S MASKS

Introduced by: Fred Thayer, coach of Harvard University, in 1875 or 1877, depending on the source

History: Catchers originally wore no protection—they stood off to one side of the plate so they wouldn't get hit. In 1877, Thayer decided his catcher would have an advantage if he stood right behind the plate. But the student, James Tyng, refused. Thayer explained: "He had been hit by foul tips and had become timid....I [had] to find a way to bring back his confidence."

Thayer's solution: armor. He took a fencer's mask to a tinsmith, who cut eyeholes in the wire mesh. "Tyng placed the contraption over his head for a game against the Lynn Live Oaks Baseball Club," writes Lloyd Johnson in *Baseball's Book of Firsts*.

Note: Thayer later changed the mesh to wide-spaced iron bars, and added forehead and chin rests. He patented the mask in 1878, and it immediately became popular. Chest protectors were added in 1885.

BATTING HELMETS

Introduced by: Willie Wells, in 1939

History: In 1905 a "pneumatic batting helmet" that looked like a leather football helmet was introduced, but it was too cumbersome and no one used it. Even after Ray Chapman died when he was hit in the head by a pitch in 1920, there was no interest in helmets.

Once again, one player trying to protect himself changed baseball tradition. Wells, a good-hitting shortstop in the Negro Leagues, hung his head over the plate when he batted—which made him especially vulnerable. He finally got sick of being hit in the head, and showed up at a game wearing a miner's helmet. (No word on whether it had the light in front.) In 1942 he switched to a construction hardhat...which eventually led to helmets made especially for the Major Leagues in 1952.

UNCLE JOHN'S "STALL OF FAME"

You'd be amazed at the number of newspaper articles BRI members send in about the creative ways people get involved with bathrooms, toilets, toilet paper, etc. So we're creating Uncle John's "Stall of Fame."

Honoree: Will Simmons, a freshman at Duke University
Notable Achievement: Turning toilet paper into a political issue
True Story: In his first year at Duke, Simmons discovered that the toilets in his dorm were outfitted with single-ply toilet paper. Outraged, he decided to run for a seat in the student government. His single campaign platform: a promise that students would get two-ply paper in dorm bathrooms.

Simmons won, of course—students know what's important. After the election, university housing officials pledged to cooperate.

Honoree: Donna Summer, pop singer
Notable Achievement: Writing a Top 10 song in the bathroom
True Story: At a posh hotel, Summer was washing her hands in the ladies' room. She mused to herself that the washroom attendant there had to work awfully hard for her money. It suddenly hit Summer that she had a song title. So she rushed into a stall and wrote lyrics for it. "She Works Hard for the Money" was an international hit that went to #3 on the *Billboard* charts.

Honoree: Jacob Feinzilberg, a San Jose, California, inventor
Notable Achievement: Inventing the ultimate port-a-potty
True Story: In 1993 Feinzilberg came up with the Inflate-a-Potty, a toilet so portable it can actually fit in a purse. It can be inflated in seconds and is used with an ordinary eight-gallon kitchen bag as a disposable liner. He came up with the idea for it at a picnic when his young daughter suddenly "heard nature's call and found no place to answer it."

In the old days, freckles were called "moth-patches" and were considered an affliction.

Honorees: Philip Middleton and Richard Wooton of Chantilly, Virginia
Notable Achievement: Creating a "commode for dogs"
True Story: According to a 1993 news report, it's called the Walk-Me-Not. The dog walks up stairs at the side of the bathroom toilet, steps onto a platform over the toilet bowl, and squats down to use.

Honorees: Chiu Chiu-kuei and Lee Wong-tsong, a Taiwanese couple
Notable Achievement: Creating a public bathroom nice enough for a wedding...and then getting married in it
True Story: In the mid-1990s, Chiu Chiu-kuei designed, and her fiancé Lee Wong-tsong built, a bathroom for a public park in the city of Taichung. According to news reports: "The couple said the lavatory, complete with elaborate decoration, had cost about $1 million to build." Chiu explained: "Since the bathroom is the creation of me and my husband it is very meaningful to us and therefore we decided to have our ceremony in here." Not explained: Why seven other couples joined them, making it the largest group wedding ever performed in a lavatory.

Honoree: Bryan J. Patrie, a Stanford graduate student
Notable Achievement: Inventing the *Watercolor Intelligent Nightlight*, which informs bleary-eyed midnight bathroom-goers whether the toilet seat up is or down...without turning on a blinding light.
True Story: Patrie introduced the device in the early 1990s. He explained: "When you get within five feet of the dark commode, it will sense your motion. It looks to see if the room is dark. Then it looks upward by sending out an infrared beam. If it gets a reflection, it knows the seat is up. If it is, the red light comes on."

*   *   *

...And some vital "Stall-of-Fame" info: According to the *Philadelphia Inquirer* Toilet Paper Report, women's #1 bathroom complaint is men leaving the toilet seat up. Men's #1 complaint is having to wait to get into the bathroom.

Before he became an explorer, Amerigo Vespucci (for whom America is named) was a pickle merchant.

MR. TOAD'S WILD RIDE

*The Wind in the Willows is one of the best-loved books in the
English language, and a milestone in children's literature. But
it took some very unusual circumstances to get it written and
published. And then it took the intervention of the president of
the United States to make it a success. Here's the story.*

BACKGROUND

By the 1890s, Kenneth Grahame was already a celebrated
author. His two books, *The Golden Age* and *Dream Days*—
tales of childhood written for adults—had established him as an authority on children's literature. Editors were constantly asking him
to review new books and to edit collections of poems and stories.

But Grahame didn't want to write for a living. He was solidly
middle-class, and the English middle-class ideal at the time was to
be a "gentleman author"—someone who wrote part-time, for love,
not money. In his professional life, Grahame was a successful banker—in 1898 he landed the prestigious job of Secretary of the Bank
of England.

Wedded Miss

In 1899 Grahame married Elspeth Thompson. It was an unmiti-
gated disaster. Elspeth wound up writing despondent letters and
poems to her friends; Grahame developed a severe case of writer's
block. He became so distracted that, less than a decade later, he
was asked to retire from the bank.

The only good thing to come from the marriage was their son,
Alastair. But he had problems, too—he was born "blind in one eye
and squinting out of the other." His parents called him Mouse.

MAN OF LETTERS

Writing was difficult for Grahame, but he could still tell stories.
Every evening he invented one for Mouse, letting the little boy
choose the subject.

Actor with the most leading roles ever in Hollywood films: John Wayne, at 141.

One night, Mouse asked his father to make up something about a rat, a mole, and a giraffe. (The giraffe was soon replaced with Toad—a loose caricature of Alastair). The trio's ongoing experiences became such a favorite that in 1907, when Mouse was supposed to leave on a vacation with his governess, he refused to go— he didn't want to miss his father's bedtime stories.

Grahame promised to write down a new adventure every day and send it to his son...luckily, he kept his word. According to Elspeth, the child's governess was so impressed by the unusual stories that she saved the 15 letters and brought them back to her. These later became the basis for *The Wind in the Willows*.

A SAMPLE LETTER

[Ed. note: Toad was sent to prison for stealing a newfangled motorcar (it was 1907, remember) but escaped dressed as a washerwoman. Now, as he nears home, he looks up and sees the same car he stole headed toward him, and assumes it's pursuing him.]

16 Durham Villas
Campden Hill, W.
7th August, 1907

Dear Mouse:

When the Toad saw that his enemies were close upon him...he sank down in a shabby miserable heap in the road, murmuring to himself ..."It's all over now! Prison again! Dry bread and water again!...O what a fool I have been! What did I want to go strutting around the country for, singing conceited songs?...O unhappy toad! O miserable animal! And his head sank down in the dust.

The terrible motor-car drew nearer and nearer...Then it stopped. Some gentlemen got out. They walked round the trembling heap of misery lying in the road, & one of them said—"O dear! Here is a poor washerwoman who has fainted in the road...Let us lift her into the motor-car and take her to the nearest village.

...When the Toad heard them talk that way, & knew he was not recognized, his courage began to revive, & he opened one of his eyes. Then one of the gentlemen said: "See, she is feeling better already! The fresh air is doing her good! How do you feel now, washerwoman?"

The toad answered in a feeble voice, "Thank you kindly, Sir, I'm feeling rather better. I think if I might sit on the front seat, beside the chauffeur, where I could get more air, I should soon be quite right again."

"That's a very sensible woman," said the gentleman. So they helped ~~her~~ him into the front seat....The Toad began to sit up & look about & presently he said to the chauffeur, "Please Mr. Chauffeur, I wish you would let me try to drive the car for a little; it looks so easy; I'm sure I could do it quite well!"

The chauffeur laughed, heartily. But one of the gentlemen said, "Bravo, washerwoman! I like your spirit! Let her try. She won't do any harm."

So the chauffeur gave up his seat to the toad, & he took the steering wheel in his hands, and set the car going, & off they went, very slowly and carefully at first, for the toad was prudent. The gentlemen clapped their hands & cried, "Bravo, washerwoman! How well she does it! Fancy a washerwoman driving a motor-car! Bravo!"

Then the Toad went a little faster. The gentlemen applauded....The Toad began to lose his head. He went faster and faster still. The gentlemen called out warningly, "Be careful, washerwoman!" Then the Toad lost his head entirely. He stood up in his seat and shouted "Ho, ho! Who are you calling washerwoman! I am the Toad! The famous Mr. Toad! The motor-car driver, the toad who always escapes, who baffles his enemies, who dodges policemen, who breaks our of prison, the always victorious, the triumphant Toad!...

Grahame had already written much of the story, but he had no intention of turning it into a commercial work. Nothing could have been further from his mind.

For Part II of Mr. Toad's Wild Ride, turn to page 391.

*   *   *

"All women become like their mothers. That is their tragedy. No man does. That's his." —Oscar Wilde

THEY WENT THATAWAY

*Malcolm Forbes wrote a fascinating book, about the deaths of
famous people. Here are a few of the stories he found.*

POCAHONTAS

Claim to Fame: Daughter of Native American chief Powhatan and friend of the Jamestown, Virginia, settlers in the early 17th century

How She Died: "Old World" fever

Postmortem: In 1616 Pocahontas, her husband John Rolfe, their infant son Thomas, and 12 Native Americans sailed to England. Their purpose: to expose Pocahontas and her entourage to the charms of the Old World. Instead, they were exposed to Old World diseases...for which they had no natural immunity. By the time they set sail for Virginia in March 1617, Pocahontas was suffering from tuberculosis and possibly pneumonia. The party made it only about 20 miles downriver from London when Pocahontas fell so ill that they had to pull into port and take her ashore. Pocahontas, 22, died there three weeks later.

CLARK GABLE

Claim to Fame: One of the biggest film stars in Hollywood history

How He Died: Heart attack, probably caused by the strain of working with Marilyn Monroe

Postmortem: In 1960 Gable was offered the lead role in *The Misfits*, which co-starred Marilyn Monroe. His salary: $750,000 plus a percentage of the film's profits—the largest film deal ever (at the time). Friends warned Gable not to make a film with Monroe, who had a reputation for being extremely difficult to work with. But he liked the script and couldn't resist the money, so he took the deal. Filming began on location in the desert outside of Reno, Nevada, in the summer of 1960.

Working with Marilyn turned out to be even worse than Gable's friends had warned. Her marriage to playwright Arthur Miller was disintegrating and she was in the early stages of the mental breakdown that would eventually lead to her suicide. She threw tan-

---

Cool fact: The average American eats 5 gallons of frozen desserts a year.

trums, arrived for scenes hours late—when she showed up at all—and rarely knew her lines. Gable was so frustrated and bored that he dismissed his stuntmen and began doing his own stunts, hoping that it would help him blow off some steam. At 59, he wasn't in the best shape, and the stunts—including lassoing horses and being dragged by ropes behind a truck across the desert—left him battered, bruised, and sometimes even bloodied. "Christ I'm glad this picture's finished," he told a friend when filming ended, "Marilyn damn near gave me a heart attack."

Two days later, Gable was changing the tire on his Jeep when he felt chest pains. He didn't think much of it, but that night he complained of a headache and "indigestion." By the next morning he was doubled over in pain. His wife took him to the hospital, where doctors diagnosed a mild heart attack. He seemed to be making a quick recovery, but 10 days later suffered a second, massive heart attack and died.

NERO

Claim to Fame: Ruthless Roman emperor who killed his mother, wife, half-brother, and countless others. Was emperor during the fire that destroyed half of Rome in 64 A.D.

How He Died: Committed suicide to avoid an even worse fate

Postmortem: Contrary to popular belief, he never "fiddled while Rome burned." In fact, as one historian says, "Nero didn't even own a fiddle—he owned a lyre—and he was 50 miles away when the fire began." And he responded to the emergency admirably, "opening shelters for the homeless, reducing the price of corn, and bringing in food from the provinces."

Nevertheless, the fire sealed his fate. In its aftermath, he imposed heavy taxes to rebuild Rome. The huge construction project was never finished—he spent much of the money on himself while ordinary Romans starved and the military went unpaid. Finally, Rome revolted against his tyranny. Nero tried to flee to Egypt, but never made it out of the city: when the Senate learned he was hiding in his mansion, they sent a messenger to tell him he'd been declared a public enemy and would be punished in the "ancient style"—"stripped naked and, with his head thrust into a wooden fork, flogged to death with rods." Just as the cavalry arrived to take him away, Nero cheated fate by stabbing himself in the throat.

The tiniest snowflake ever recorded: 1/500th of an inch in diameter. Largest snowflakes:

AMERICAN TRADITIONS

There are some things Americans do because...well it's just what we do. How many of you know how these three traditions started?

THE PLEDGE OF ALLEGIANCE

Tradition: At the beginning of events or meetings, Americans face the U.S. flag with hand on heart and recite:

I pledge allegiance to the flag of the United State of America.
And to the Republic for which it stands, one nation under
God, with liberty and justice for all.

Is it an old patriotic verse dating back to the American Revolution? Was it written by the Founding Fathers? Nope. It was created as a promotional gimmick by a magazine in 1892.

Origin: As the 400th anniversary of Columbus's voyage to the New World approached in 1892, the U.S. made plans to celebrate the event with a huge World's Fair in Chicago (the Columbian Exposition). Editors at *The Youth's Companion*—the *Reader's Digest* of its day—jumped on the bandwagon and became sponsors of the National Public School Celebration for Columbus Day, 1892. Their goal: To get every public school in the U.S. to honor the occasion by raising a U.S. flag and reciting a flag salute. This meant, of course, that they needed an official flag salute.

The man assigned to write it was an editor named Francis Bellamy, a former Baptist minister who had been forced out of his Boston church for delivering socialist sermons. The pledge he wrote—which was recited by an estimated 10 million schoolchildren on that day in 1892—is slightly different than the one we know now. It was:

I pledge allegiance to my Flag and the Republic for which it stands,
one nation, indivisible, with liberty and justice for all.

According to scholar John W. Baer, Bellamy "considered placing the word 'equality' in his Pledge, but knew that the state superintendents of education...were against equality for women and African-Americans." The pledge Bellamy wrote quickly became part of

---

15 inches in diameter and eight inches thick. They fell in Montana in 1887.

America's culture. But people couldn't leave it alone. Baer adds:

> In 1923 and 1924 the National Flag Conference, under the "leadership of the American Legion and the Daughters of the American Revolution, changed the Pledge's words, "my Flag," to "the Flag of the United States of America." Bellamy disliked this change, but his protest was ignored.
>
> In 1954 Congress, after a campaign by the Knights of Columbus, added the words, "under God," to the Pledge. The Pledge was now both a patriotic oath and a public prayer.
>
> Bellamy's granddaughter said he also would have resented this second change....In his retirement in Florida, he [had] stopped attending church.

HAIL TO THE CHIEF

Tradition: When a U.S. president enters a room on a formal occasion, the song "Hail to the Chief" is played.

Origin: The 11th president, James K. Polk (1845–49), was so "physically undistinguished" that visitors to the White House often didn't notice when he'd entered a room. To make sure they knew Polk was there, his wife Sarah arranged for the Marine band to play this old Scottish anthem whenever he walked through the door. It was immediately adopted as a tradition, and all presidents have honored it since.

THE PURPLE HEART MEDAL

Tradition: U.S. soldiers who are wounded in combat are awarded the Purple Heart.

Origin: At the time of the American Revolution, European military tradition dictated that only officers could receive medals; it was unheard of to honor a common soldier for bravery. George Washington changed this practice. On August 7, 1782, he ordered the creation of the Badge of Military Merit, in the "figure of a heart in purple cloth or silk." (Purple was traditionally the color reserved for royalty.) The medal was awarded for "any singularly meritorious action," not necessarily for being wounded in action.

The medal fell into disuse for more than 150 years, but in 1932, to commemorate the 200th anniversary of Washington's birth, Gen. Douglas MacArthur revived it and gave it its current meaning.

Less is more: 95% of the creatures on Earth are smaller than a chicken egg.

THE NOSE KNOWS

*Smell is an amazing and complex function carried out in a tiny
chamber, half the size of an egg, situated just behind our nose.
With it, we are able to smell thousands of different odors.*

T**HE SCIENCE OF SMELL**
How do we smell things? The mystery is still unfolding, but
it starts with "odor molecules." Scientists tell us the air is
filled with them. They enter your nasal cavity every time you
breathe, 23,000 times a day.

• Just behind your nose, these molecules are absorbed by mucous-
covered tissue.

• This tissue is covered with "receptor" cells. (Some scientists say
you have millions of them.) Each one is mounted on a microscopic
hair.

• The receptor cells stick out and wave in the air currents we
inhale. Forty of them must detect odor molecules before a smell is
registered.

• When a new smell is detected, the tiny olfactory bulb, located
just above the nasal cavity, flashes data directly to the most ancient
and mysterious part of your brain—the limbic system—which
"handles feelings, lust, instincts, and invention." The limbic system
reacts immediately, without intervention of reason or language,
and may provoke powerful emotions, images, or nostalgia.

THE DARK AGES OF SMELLING
A keen sense of smell is now accepted as part of the good life—
coffees, wines, cheeses, and gourmet foods would all be lost on us if
we lacked our immense range of smell. However, this faculty wasn't
always appreciated.

• The ancient philosopher Plato looked down on smell as a lowly
instinct that might lead to gluttony and lust, while vision and hearing opened one to geometry and music and were therefore "closer to
the soul."

• During the 18th and 19th centuries, it was commonly believed
that many diseases were caused by smells. Odors from corpses, feces,
urine, swamps, and Earth fissures were called "miasmas" and were

---

The first open-heart surgery was performed in 1893.

thought to have the power to kill you. To ward off these smells, people carried and inhaled "antimephitics," such as garlic, amber, sulphur, and incense. When exposed to miasmic odors, people did not swallow their saliva, but spit it out. The Viennese physician Semmelweis was ostracized by colleagues when he declared that washing one's hands, not breathing antimephitics, would stop most disease from spreading.

• According to some sources, the stethoscope was invented not to hear the heartbeat better, but to give doctors some distance from a patient's bodily odors.

TASTE AND SMELL

• We taste only four things: sweet, sour, salt and bitter. It's the smells that make things really taste. For example, wine's smell, not its taste, is what makes it delicious. With a head cold, drinking wine is an entirely different experience.

• Scientists have categorized smells into seven groups: minty like peppermint, floral like roses, ethereal like pears, musky like—well—musk, resinous like camphor, foul like rotten eggs, and acrid like vinegar.

• Talking with your mouth full expels taste molecules and diminishes the taste of food.

SMELL FACTS

• Women have a keener sense of smell than men.

• By simply smelling a piece of clothing, most people can tell if it was worn by a woman or man.

• Each of us has an odor that is, like our fingerprints, unique. One result, researchers say: Much of the thrill of kissing comes from smelling the unique odors of another's face.

• Smells stimulate learning. Students given olfactory stimulation along with a word list retain much more information and remember it longer.

• Many smells are heavier than air and can be smelled only at ground level.

• We smell best if we take several short sniffs, rather than one long one.

THE WILD, WILD WEST

The Wild, Wild West, starring Will Smith, was one Hollywood's biggest hits of 1999. Thirty-four years earlier, however—before Smith was born—it was a hit TV show starring Robert Conrad. Here's a bit of TV nostalgia from Cult TV, by John Javna.

BACKGROUND
In 1960 the Western was king of TV: there were 22 of them in prime time. But by 1964, there were only 5. The new fad was spy shows—James Bond–type secret agents, equipped with ultramodern gadgets to fight assorted lunatics bent on world domination.

The two genres seemed utterly incompatible—but TV still managed to combine them. In a masterstroke of exploitation, producer Michael Garrison introduced *The Wild, Wild West* in 1965. It was TV's first "sci-fi/spy/cowboy" series and it was just like any other secret-agent show, with two important differences: James T. West lived in the 1870s, and his boss was Ulysses S. Grant.

In this program, the real bad guys of the Old West weren't Jesse James and Billy the Kid. They were evil scientists like Miguelito Loveless, who routinely invented things like laser weapons, atomic bombs, plastic, and instant photography. America hadn't seen so much out-of-place technology since *The Flintstones*. But that was the beauty of *WWW*; it took the ideas that fueled the spy craze and carried them to their silliest extremes.

Garrison happily acknowledged that he was just cashing in on a fad. "Apologize for it? I'm in this for the money," he said. "I see nothing wrong with TV following the Bond or any other trend. It's necessary. TV reflects what people are thinking." Garrison lived to see his show succeed, but died from a fall a year after its premiere.

ORIGIN
Strangely James West really did have a legitimate connection to 007. In 1955 Garrison and his partner, Gregory Ratoff, had discovered a novel by a little-known author named Ian Fleming. It was called *Casino Royale* and introduced a character named James Bond. "What a great movie this could be," they thought—so they bought the rights and tried to convince 20th Century-Fox to finance a film.

Poll results: 57% of women would rather go on a shopping spree than have sex.

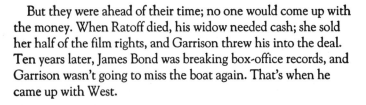

But they were ahead of their time; no one would come up with the money. When Ratoff died, his widow needed cash; she sold her half of the film rights, and Garrison threw his into the deal. Ten years later, James Bond was breaking box-office records, and Garrison wasn't going to miss the boat again. That's when he came up with West.

WEST...JAMES WEST

The Star. The first actor picked to play Jim West was old-time cowboy star Rory Calhoun. Then, at the last minute, he was dumped for a younger man who could do his own stunts—Robert Conrad (real name: Robert Conrad Falk).

The Fall Guy. Conrad did all his own fight choreography and stunts, until he almost killed himself in an episode called "The Night of the Fugitives." He was supposed to sail off a balcony and land on a bad guy below...but his timing was off, and he landed on his neck and head instead. After that, all the falls were taken by stunt men.

Short Story. Conrad was supposedly 5'10", but wore 3" heels as West. The CBS casting office had orders not to hire any women over 5'6" for the show. There was no similar limitation on men, but you'll never see James West surrounded by a group of tall actors—the producers didn't permit it.

GORDON...ARTIE GORDON

The Costar. West's sidekick, Artemus Gordon, was played by veteran actor Ross Martin (real name: Martin Rosenblatt).

The Human Chameleon. Gordon was supposed to be a master of disguises, and Ross Martin, who played the character, really was. "Ross came up with all his makeup himself," Conrad says. "I used to watch him sit down and put all the goop on his face; it was just fantastic. We counted once, and figured that he'd done over 100 different characters during the four years (104 episodes) we were on the air."

Man of 1,000 Faces. Martin had a unique approach to each new *WWW* role. First he read the script. Then he did a pen-and-ink drawing of the character he was going to play, down to the last detail: glasses, mustache, clothes, posture, shoes, etc. Then he brought the sketch to the show's makeup man, and together they

---

Food for thought: Twinkie inventor Jimmy Dewar ate 40,177 Twinkies in his lifetime.

molded his face until it looked like the drawing. "As the face emerges," Martin said, "I begin to really feel the character. By the time we're through, I'm beginning to behave like the character."

LOVELESS...MIGUELITO LOVELESS

The Evil Dwarf. In the film, Miguelito Loveless is played by Shakespearean actor Kenneth Branagh. But on TV, he was played by 3'6" Michael Dunn (real name: Gary Neil Miller). The name was a joke. In Spanish, Miguelito means "little Michael."

Big Impact. Dunn, considered by some critics "the ultimate TV villain of all time"—despite the fact that he was only in 10 episodes—was an accomplished actor who'd been nominated for both a Tony Award (*Ballad of a Sad Cafe*, 1963) and an Oscar (*Ship of Fools*, 1965). But he was frustrated that producers thought of him only as a "midget actor." "I don't want to play Charlton Heston parts," he complained, "but there are a lot of roles I can do."

Sad Ending. While filming on location in England in 1973, he died, an apparent suicide. He was 39 years old.

POW! THWAP! BAM!

Every episode of *WWW* featured at least one meticulously choreographed brawl. Conrad explained: "We always put in a lot more (fighting) than we really wanted to see. [Then the censors] would say: 'We're going to take out two punches...two of this...three of that.' So when they finished, we were still left with what we really wanted anyway."

Unfortunately, the show's reputation for its fights got it cancelled. In 1969 there was an outcry against violence on TV, and CBS offered up *WWW* as a sacrificial lamb. "The president of the network was kind enough to call me," recalls Conrad. "He said, 'We're cancelling the show. There's just too much pressure from Washington.'"

SILVER SCREEN

In 1994 Conrad found out there was going to be a film version of the show. Reporters asked him who he thought should play James West. "Dana Carvey," he answered. "He's hilarious....I'd like to play a small part as Dana's father and he'd be my illegitimate son." Conrad didn't appear in the movie.

According to *Guinness*, the longest recorded bout of hiccups lasted for 65 years.

THE SAGA OF RANGER JOE

Among the weird stuff in Uncle John's office is a box of Zucaritas—frosted flakes from Mexico. The other day one of our researchers picked up the box and wondered who invented sugar-coated cereal...which led to our discovery of the book Cerealizing America, *by Scott Bruce and Bill Crawford. Here's the story they tell.*

THE HEALTHY ALTERNATIVE

In 1939 a heating-equipment salesman named Jim Rex sat at the breakfast table in disgust and watched his children bury their puffed-wheat cereal in spoonful after spoonful of sugar. It was sickening. Wasn't there some way to get them to eat cereal without plunging into the sugar bowl? The solution came to him in a flash of inspiration: Why not create a cereal that already *had* sugar on it!

Putting his heating-equipment expertise to use, Rex devised a process that enabled him to dip puffed cereal into a diluted mixture of honey and corn syrup. Then he flash-baked it at a high temperature to give the coating a hard, varnishlike seal.

When he found that his kids liked the concoction, he hit up his friends for cash, scraped together a few thousand dollars, and—inspired by the radio success of the Lone Ranger—launched his own cereal company under the name Ranger Joe.

M-M-M—SUGAR BRICKS!

First, Rex hired an artist to draw the company logo: a portrait of Ranger Joe wearing a white cowboy hat and standing next to his white horse. Then he began packaging his cereal in little cellophane bags (not boxes). Soon, Ranger Joe Popped Wheat Honnies began appearing in Philadelphia-area stores.

"The Original Coated Popped Wheat Honnies" ran into serious trouble right away, however. Poor air conditioning at the plant and leaky cellophane bags caused the product to solidify into sticky bricks which were impossible to eat, and impossible to sell. Rex couldn't raise the money to buy new equipment. Within nine

---

Gezundheit! The longest recorded sneezing fit was 978 consecutive days.

months, the fledgling Ranger Joe Company "just flopped."

Rex sold it to a 45-year-old Philadelphia stockbroker named Moses Berger who was intrigued by the Ranger Joe ethos. "The name caught his imagination," his wife recalled. "He decided it was something he could promote."

RANGER JOE RIDES INTO THE SUNSET
Berger expanded the plant, improved the manufacturing process, and created an edible product. Then he drove around to super- markets in the Northeast, setting up Ranger Joe displays, handing out Ranger Joe cereal bowls and "ranch" mugs, and serving up free samples in cold milk for shoppers. The factory dropped toy airplanes and sheriff badges into packages. Orders poured in.

For over a decade, Ranger Joe, the original sugar-coated cereal, thrived. But the company was still a regional phenomenon; Ber- ger didn't have the resources to compete nationally. And when his product started attracting serious attention from big cereal companies, he realized it was time to get out. He sold his plant to Nabisco, which began marketing the product as Nabisco Wheat Honeys and Nabisco Rice Honeys. They replaced Ranger Joe with an animated cowboy insect named Buffalo Bee.

Ranger Joe may have been gone, but his offspring were round- ing up millions of kiddies at breakfast tables every day.

That's how sugar-coated cereal was born. But we haven't gotten to Frosted Flakes yet. If you want to know more, turn to page 289.

* * * *

CEREALIZING AMERICA
In 1957 General Mills was trying to develop a successful sugar- coated cereal. Al Clausi, head of product development, didn't know much about cereal, but he knew pasta. "The thought crossed my mind," he says, "to take pasta—which comes in all kinds of shapes—and puff it up." He tried it with a bunch of al- phabet pasta and General Mills execs loved it. They bought macaroni manufacturing equipment, and put out the cereal as Alpha-Bits.

Roll over, Rover: 63% of pet owners sleep with their pets.

NEVER SAY NEVER

A few pearls of wisdom from 599 Things You Should Never Do, edited by Ed Morrow.

"Never lend your car to anyone to whom you have given birth."
—Erma Bombeck

"Never test the depth of a river with both feet."
—African adage

"Never stand between a dog and the hydrant."
—John Peers

"Never raise your hand to your children—it leaves your midsection unprotected."
—Robert Orben

"Never teach your children to be cunning, you'll be one of their very first victims."
—Josh Billings

"Never say 'oops' in the operating room."
—Dr. Leo Troy

"Never try to pick up a woman who's wearing a Super Bowl ring."
—Garry Shandling

"Never interrupt an enemy while he's making a mistake."
—Napoleon Bonaparte

"Never ask what goes into a hot dog."
—American adage

"Never call a man a fool; borrow from him."
—Addison Mizner

"Never be afraid of the deafeningly obvious. It is always news to somebody."
—P. J. Kavanagh

"Never marry for money. You can borrow it a lot cheaper."
—Ann Landers

"Never feel remorse for what you have thought about your wife; she has thought much worse things about you."
—Jean Rostand

"Never tell a woman she doesn't look good in some article of clothing she has just purchased."
—Lewis Grizzard

"Never start a project until you've picked someone to blame."
—Johnny Hart and Brent Parker

Belgians once tried to deliver mail using cats. (It didn't work.)

JUST PLANE WEIRD

If you bought this book in an airport, you might want to skip reading this chapter until your flight is over and you're safely back on the ground.

NOTHING TO SNOOZE AT
In May 1995, a the pilot of Delta Airlines Flight 198, approaching Palm Beach International Airport, was unable to make contact with the control tower. The pilot landed the plane without any assistance, then alerted the Federal Aviation Administration. According to news reports, "Palm Beach sheriffs deputies entered the control tower and found the lone air traffic controller shoeless and apparently just waking up." The deputies also found a pistol, ammunition, and a gun-cleaning kit nearby (it's against federal law to have a gun in a control tower), and speculate he was cleaning the gun and fell asleep. FAA officials launched an investigation. "Meanwhile," the Associated Press reported, he "remains on the job."

UNLUCKY BREAK

In June 1999, a plane approaching Benbecula Airport in Western Scotland was forced to circle for half an hour while the air traffic controller stopped working to eat lunch. According to wire service reports, "Officials at the airport said there was just one controller at Benbecula, and she had to take a break at the time she did because national air traffic rules forbid any controller from working more than two hours without one....There was an uproar in the terminal building as families watched the plane from Glasgow linger in a holding pattern, 'tantalizingly within view.'"

UNLUCKIER BREAK

In 1999 the air traffic controller in Bournemouth Airport in southern England stepped away from his post for a few minutes to get some coffee...but was gone a lot longer than he'd planned. Greg Fanos, 39, fell down a flight of stairs and broke his ankle. "Crawling back to the tower was only two or three yards," Fanos says, "but it took forever." By the time he made it back to his desk and called an ambulance, several planes, unable to reach the tower on the radio, had gone into a holding pattern over the airport. Two other planes landed safely without assistance.

CLOSE ENCOUNTER

In April 1998, an air traffic supervisor at New York's LaGuardia Airport spilled some coffee in the control tower. One of the controllers turned from his position to help clean it up, and the momentary distraction caused what may be the closest near-miss in U.S. aviation history. A landing U.S. Airways plane came within 20 feet of colliding with an Air Canada plane that was taking off from an intersecting runway. According to news reports, "experts were unable to immediately cite another incident in which two airborne passenger jets came so close without colliding." When the National Transportation Safety Board investigated the incident and began taking statements from people in the control tower, "neither the supervisor nor the controller mentioned the spilled coffee in their statements."

RATS!

In August 1999, a woman on an Air New Zealand flight from Los Angeles to Auckland felt something on her leg. She lifted her blanket and saw a rat sitting on her knee. The rat had been spotted earlier, but according to an airline spokesperson, "attempts by the crew to catch it failed." According to wire service reports, "Quarantine officials met the plane when it landed in Auckland and conducted a search of the plane including passengers' hand baggage. The rat wasn't found, so the plane was quarantined and fumigated."

SUFFICIENT GROUNDS

In 1999 guards manning security checkpoint at more than 300 U.S. airports began ordering travelers carrying cups of coffee to sip their coffee to prove it really *was* coffee. "That's policy," says security spokesman Jeff Sledge. "It's so we'd be able to make sure that what's supposed to be in the cup is in the cup—not a weapon of some sort." The policy was reportedly put into place following an FAA test in which an FAA employee made it past security with a "simulated device in a coffee cup." But the FAA denies that it's behind the "clearing of liquids," or "sip test." "It's not an FAA requirement at all," a spokesperson told the *Wall Street Journal*. If the airlines are doing it, she said, "they're doing it on their own."

The average American receives their first romantic kiss at age 13.

HIS NAME IS MY NAME, TOO!

Remember the tune that goes, "John Jacob Jingleheimer Smith, his name is my name too…"? If you do, you probably won't be able to get it out of your head for the rest of the day. Sorry. Anyway, we've come across some stories about people with the same names as other folks (and one Supreme Being). Here they are.

NOT THE DICTTATTOR

"Adolf Hittler is alive and well. But probably not the guy you're thinking about. Unlike the Nazi leader, this gentleman spells his last name with two Ts, disdains fascism, and never aspired to take over the world. He's a 61-year-old retired school bus driver from Landeck, Austria, and he doesn't like to be teased. 'My whole life this has been a problem,' he says. 'Just try checking into a hotel with my name.…But it is in part my choice. I decided not to change my name. I thought it would be an insult to my parents.'

"Hittler's problem is rare. Only about 2% of German men before World War II were named Adolf, and during his reign, Hitler forbade Germans to name children after him."

—*The Wolf Files*, October 1, 1998

GOD AMONG MEN

"A man who legally changed his name to Ubiquitous Perpetuity God began serving a nine-month sentence for indecent exposure in Marin County, California on Wednesday. God, 68, has been convicted 18 times for similar offenses since 1968. His latest arrest came in October, when he exposed himself to a woman waiting in line at a coffee shop. He did it so that women 'could have some type of awareness of God,' according to police reports.…God will be released to a residential mental health facility, if one agrees to admit him."

—Ashland, Oregon, *Daily Tidings*, 1996

FRANK STATEMENT

"Say hello to Frank J. Manibusan and his brother, Frank, both of Alameda, California. And their brother, Frank. And their other brother, Frank. And his brother, Frank, and one other brother: Frank. Then, of course, there are children: Frank, Frank, Frank, Frank, Frank, and Frank. Frankly speaking, there are 12 Franks in all, at the moment—13 if you count the patriarch, 58-year-old Francisco. …The sons and grandsons all have middle initials: J., J., J., J., J., J., J., J., J., J., J., and J.

"Of course, the advantages definitely outweigh the detriments, they explain. Can't do jury duty? Not to worry. Which Frank are the authorities going to chastise? And if one brother is out of cash, who cares? He need only tear out a check from the wallet of one of his siblings. 'We don't leave no checks lying around,' explained Frank Joe, No. 2 son, while his brothers and father nodded in agreement."

—*San Jose Mercury News*

A FAN AMONG FANS

"A fanatical British pop fan has changed his name to include the titles of his favorite group's records. And for good measure, Anthony Hicks, 23, added the names of the original line-up of the group, Level 42.

"Hicks this week signed legal papers changing his name to: 'Ant Level Forty Two The Pursuit Of Accidents The Early Tapes Standing In The Light True Colors A Physical Presence World Machine Running In The Family Platinum Edition Staring At The Sun Level Best Guaranteed The Remixes Forever Now Influences Changes Mark King Mike Landup Phil Gould Boon Gould Wally Badarou Lindup-Badarou'.

"'If they release any album or single, I will alter my name to have the new title incorporated into it,' Hicks told reporters."

—Reuters, July 30, 1994

SPLIT DECISION

"When Denise Mason of Glasgow, Scotland, gave birth to a son six weeks ago, picking a name created a stir. Clark Kearny, the child's father and a big fan of the Glasgow Rangers soccer team, wanted to name the boy after his favorite Ranger but couldn't make a decision. So, he didn't. The lad is named Cairo Lionel Sergio Lorenzo Colin Giovanni Barry Ian Jorge Gabriel Stephane Rod Mason Kearney—after 11 Rangers."

—*USA Today*, February 3, 1999

Crocodiles can't move their tongues.

FAMILIAR PHRASES

Here are some more origins to everyday phrases.

P UT ON YOUR THINKING CAP
Meaning: Carefully and thoughtfully consider something
Origin: In previous centuries, it was customary for judges to put a cap on before sentencing criminals. Because judges were respected thinkers, it was referred to as a "thinking cap." (From *Gordon's Book of Familiar Phrases*)

PLAY FAST AND LOOSE
Meaning: Stretch the truth or meaning of words or rules, deceive or trifle with someone
Origin: This term dates from the 16th century. It comes from a game called "fast and loose," which was played at fairs. Operators rolled up a strap and left a loop hanging over the edge of a table. To win, a player had to catch the loop with a stick before the strap was unrolled. But they never won. Cheating operators rolled it up in such a way that the feat was impossible. (From *Have a Nice Day— No Problem!*, by Christine Ammer)

BOTCH A JOB
Meaning: Repair badly
Origin: "In old England, bodgers were peasant chairmakers....They produced, by traditional handicraft methods, simple and serviceable objects. When chairmaking was transformed into high art, the bodger was correspondingly downgraded to 'bodge' or '*botch*,'" which came to mean an item or service of poor quality. (From *To Coin a Phrase*, by Edwin Radford and Alan Smith)

IN HOCK
Meaning: Broke; have all of your belongings in a pawn shop
Origin: Comes from the Old West. In a common gambling card game called "faro," "the last card [to be played] was called the *hocketty card*. It was said to be *in hocketty* or *in hock*. When a player bet on a card that ended up *in hock* he was himself *in hock*, at risk of losing his bets." (From *The Whole Ball of Wax*, by Laurence Urdang)

The annual odds of dying by falling from your bed: 2 in 1 million.

TAKE ANOTHER TACK

Meaning: Try a different strategy

Origin: "Sailing ships could not move directly into the wind but had to tack—zigzag back and forth with the wind first on one side, then on the other. If a skipper approaching harbor found that his vessel couldn't make the harbor mouth on the starboard tack, he was obviously on the *wrong tack*, and would have to take the other (port) tack." (From *Loose Cannons and Red Herrings*, by Robert Claiborne)

GET OFF (OR GO) "SCOT-FREE"

Meaning: Escape punishment.

Origin: "In the thirteenth century, *scot* was the word for money you would pay at a tavern for food and drink, or when they passed the hat to pay the entertainer. Later, it came to mean a local tax that paid the sheriff's expenses. *To go scot-free* literally meant to be exempted from paying this tax." (From *How Does Olive Oil Lose Its Virginity?*, by Bruce Tindall and Mark Watson)

SLUSH FUND

Meaning: A hidden cache of money used for illegal or corrupt political purposes

Origin: "Derived from Scandinavian words meaning 'slops,' this phrase is derived from the nineteenth-century shipboard practice of boiling up large pots of pork and other fatty meats. The fat that rose to the top of the kettles was stored in vats and then sold to soap and candle makers. The money received from the sale of the 'slush' was used for the crew's comfort and entertainment." (From *Eatioms*, by John D. Jacobson)

TAKE SOMEONE DOWN A PEG

Meaning: Humble someone who is self-important and conceited

Origin: "The expression probably originally referred to a ship's flags. These were raised or lowered by pegs—the higher the position of the flags, the greater the honor. So to take someone down a peg came to mean to lower the esteem in which that person is held." (From *Get to the Roots*, by Martin Manser)

COURT TRANSQUIPS

Here's more 100% real-life courtroom dialogue.

Q: "Could you see him from where you were standing?"
A: "I could see his head."
Q: "And where was his head?"
A: "Just above his shoulders."

Q: "Do you drink when you're on duty?"
A: "I don't drink when I'm on duty…unless I come on duty drunk."

Q: "When he went, had you gone and had she, if she wanted to and were able, for the time being excluding all the restraints on her not to go, gone also, would he have brought you, meaning you and she, with him to the station?"
D. A.: "Objection. That question should be taken out and shot."

Q: "What is your relationship with the plaintiff?"
A: "She is my daughter."
Q: "Was she your daughter on February 13, 1979?"

Q: "How did you happen to go to Dr. Cherney?"
A: "Well, a gal down the road had had several of her children by Dr. Cherney, and said he was really good."

Q: "Was that the same nose you broke as a child?"
A: "I have only one, you know."

Q: "What can you tell us about the truthfulness and veracity of this defendant?"
A: "Oh, she will tell the truth. She said she'd kill that son of a bitch—and she did!"

Q: "Were you alone or by yourself?"

Q: I understand you're Dean Roberts' mother.
A: Yes.
Q: How long have you known him?

Q (to opposing attorney): "Why don't you let her ask a question?"
Witness: "I thought you did."
Opposing Attorney: "I thought I did, too."
Q: "Well, I don't know what it is."
Opposing Attorney: "Well, the witness does, and I do."
Witness: "What's your question? "

Q: "What is the meaning of sperm being present? "
A: "It indicates intercourse."
Q: "Male sperm?"
A: "That is the only kind I know."

Q: "You say you're innocent, yet five people swore they saw you steal a watch."
A: "Your Honor, I can produce 500 people who didn't see me steal it."

Q: "How long have you been a French Canadian?"

POLI-TALKS

*Politicians aren't getting much respect these days—but
then, it sounds like they don't deserve much, either.*

"I have the most reliable friend
you can have in American politics and that is ready money."
—**Sen. Phil Gramm**

"Do you come here often?"
—**Ted Kennedy,
to a patron of a
Brooklyn soup kitchen**

"There's nothing wrong with
this country that we couldn't
cure by turning it over to the
police for a couple of weeks."
—**George Wallace,
in 1967**

"We've never had a president
named Bob. And I think it's
time."
—**Bob Dole**

"There's no ethical problem
there. I used to teach ethics—
trust me."
—**William Bennett,
Bush's antidrug czar,
championing the idea of
decapitating drug dealers**

"Too bad ninety percent of the
politicians give the other ten
percent a bad reputation."
—**Henry Kissinger**

"I've got a lot to learn about
Washington. Why, yesterday I
accidentally spent some of my
own money."
—**Sen. Fred Thompson**

"Liberals feel unworthy of their
possessions. Conservatives feel
they deserve everything they've
stolen."
—**Mort Sahl**

"I never use the words 'Democrats' and 'Republicans.' It's
'liberals' and 'Americans.'"
—**James Watt, interior
secretary in the Reagan
administration**

"Washington is a city of southern efficiency and northern
charm."
—**John F. Kennedy**

"You can lead a man to Congress, but you can't make him
think."
—**Milton Berle**

"You might be interested to
know that the Scriptures are on
our side on this."
—**Ronald Reagan,
defending his arms-
buildup program**

Goldfish have a memory span of three seconds.

THE SHAPE OF THE EARTH

What shape is Earth? You'd say round, right? But scientists would hem and haw about it...and then answer "oblate spheroid." Read on...

YOU ARE HERE
In the age of space travel, we all know the world is "round." But ancient civilizations had no way to measure the size or shape of the Earth. So they came up with their own imaginative explanations. For example:

• In the Cherokee nation, people believed that mud rose from under the waters and formed an island with four corners—the Earth. The sun went underneath the island at night, and rose again the next day.

• Ancient Babylonians thought the Earth was inside a hollow mountain, floating on a sea. Everything—the sun, moon, sky, stars, water—was inside this mountain.

• Ancient Egyptians believed the whole Earth was part of their god, Keb. The stars were the jewels of a goddess in the sky and their god of air held her aloft.

• Ancient Hindus thought the Earth was in an upside-down bowl, being carried by elephants. The elephants stood on the back of a turtle that was standing on top of a snake. What the snake stood on, they hadn't quite worked out.

• Polynesian creation stories set the Earth in a basket with a lid. A hole cut in the top by a god lets in light. The woven grass at night lets light peek through in the form of stars.

THE GREEKS KNEW
Many people believe that Columbus was the first to realize that the world is round. Actually, the round-earth concept has been with us since ancient Greece.

The very early Greeks thought Earth was a flat disc floating on water. But in about 540 B.C., the renowned mathematician

---

Siberia contains more than 25% of the world's forests.

Pythagoras proposed the theory that the world was a sphere. The concept had many supporters, including Aristotle.

All's Well...

In about 250 B.C., Eratosthenes, librarian at the Library of Alexandria, even came up with a calculation of the Earth's spherical size.

He'd heard that in midsummer in the town of Syene, Egypt, the noonday sun shone directly into a deep well. He measured and discovered that in Alexandria, 787 kilometers north, the angle of the sun was about 7.2 degrees on the same date. With these measurements, he computed the circumference of the Earth.

Amazingly enough, considering how he came up with the numbers and how little he had to prove them, Eratosthenes's estimates were very close.

Another scholar, Posidonius (135–51 B.C.) did something similar over a century later, using the bright star Canopus. He measured the angles of the star from the horizon in two locations to get a fairly accurate estimate of the Earth's circumference.

IN FOURTEEN HUNDRED AND NINETY-TWO...

Fifteen hundred years later, Christopher Columbus came along, trying to make his now-famous voyage to Asia by going west. The decision of whether to fund his trip came down to analyzing the accumulation of estimates that had been gathered over the centuries.

Based on Eratosthenes' numbers, King Ferdinand believed that Columbus's fleet could never make it all the way to Asia: it was simply too far. He didn't see any reason to supply ships and crews only to have them die halfway from their goal.

Columbus used a ploy common in modern-day politics, marketing, and engineering: If the numbers don't support your conclusion, find some numbers that do. He found another estimate by Ptolemy dating from about 150 A.D. It was completely erroneous, but estimated that the Earth was about half its true size...so Queen Isabella agreed to support the voyage.

Luckily for Columbus, America got in his way, or he never would've reached India or anywhere else. Crossing both the Atlantic and the Pacific combined would've been an impossible feat with the ships and supplies he had.

No wonder they're gone: In ancient Egypt, pillows were made of stones.

FLAT AND FAT

It wasn't until 1958 that the Vanguard I satellite took the first photographs of earth from space and scientists were able to determine the planet's exact shape. The photographs proved the world is round...right?

Well, not exactly. Scientists reported that the Earth is an *oblate spheroid*—i.e., it's not *quite* round.

Since the Earth spins, it gets a slight bulge near the equator. Near yes, but not (as you might suspect) exactly *on* the equator.

Because of this bulge, the Earth is flattened very slightly on either end. Its circumference at the equator is 24,902 miles, and the circumference around the poles is 27 miles less than that: 24,875 miles. Not a big deal, really—if the world were the size of a basketball, it would be more perfectly round than a real basketball is. But still, after guessing for so long, scientists can't resist the opportunity to get it exactly right.

* * * *

THE WORLD IS PEAR-SHAPED

Ironically, toward the end of his life, Columbus came to believe the Earth was shaped like a pear. He developed this theory during his third voyage to the New World: When he was sailing west near the equator, he noticed that the North Star made a wider circle around the Pole than it did when he was sailing in more temperate latitudes.

From this he deduced that he had been sailing gradually uphill and therefore closer to the sun, which explained why the weather was getting warmer. "I have come to the conclusion," he wrote in a letter to Queen Isabella, "...that the Earth is not round, but of the form of a pear....Where the stalk grows being the highest and nearest the sky."

Columbus believed that if he sailed far enough, he would eventually reach the Garden of Eden, which was located in the pear's stalk. (*Ripley's Believe It or Not*)

Oldest form of surgery on Earth: *trepanning*—drilling holes into the skull.

THE EARTH IS FLAT!

For centuries, scientists have been able to prove that the Earth is round, but that hasn't stopped people from developing their own unique—and entertaining—theories about its shape.

THE EARTH IS FLAT

Who Says So: The International Flat Earth Research Society

What They Believe: The world is a big flat disc, with the North Pole at the center. What is mistakenly believed to be the South Pole is actually a 150-foot-high mass of ice that forms a big square around the Earth-disc (the way an album cover makes a square around a record). People who *think* they're sailing around the world are actually sailing in a circle on the surface of the disc.

Flat-Earthers believe the Bible must be interpreted literally. Passages like Revelation 7:1 and 20:8, which refer to "the four corners of the earth," are all the proof they need.

History: In 1849 an English "itinerant lecturer" named Samuel Birley Rowbotham resurrected the flat-Earth theory (which had been widely discredited by the eighth century). The flat-Earth movement grew sporadically over the next 70 years, finally peaking in the 1920s when Wilbur Glen Voliva organized a flat-Earth religious community with several thousand followers in Zion, Illinois. Voliva owned one of the country's first 100,000-watt radio stations, and used it to preach the flat-Earth gospel to folks in the American Midwest.

Today the movement lives on in Charles Johnson's Flat Earth Society, which published *Flat Earth News*...until Johnson's house burned down in 1995, incinerating the 3,500-person mailing list. No word on what he's doing now.

THE EARTH IS HOLLOW

Who Said So: Captain John Cleves Symmes, a hero of the War of 1812.

What He Believed: The Earth has four layers, like a big onion. Each is a "warm and rich land, stocked with vegetables and animals, if not men...." What we perceive as the surface of the Earth is actually the fifth and outer layer. And the North and South poles aren't

---

A spider's blood is transparent.

just poles, they're also *holes* leading to the four interior worlds.
History: In 1823 Symmes managed to get a bill introduced in the
U.S. Congress to finance a steamship voyage to the "North Hole"
and to the inner worlds beyond. When the bill received only 25
votes, Johnson talked President Adams's secretaries of the Navy
and the Treasury into outfitting three ships for a voyage to the middle of the earth. But before it got underway, Andrew Jackson became president and scuttled the trip. Symmes died in 1829, unful-
filled, but his theory remained popular with unconventional
thinkers until 1909, when Robert Peary set foot on the North Pole
(or at least came close)...and found no hole.

Even after 1909, the hollow-Earth theory had its admirers—
including Adolf Hitler. Today, a few diehard hollow-Earthers
believe that Hitler survived World War II, escaped to an interior
world under the South Pole, and may still be hiding there, min-
gling with "a race of advanced hollow-Earth beings who are responsible for the UFO sightings throughout history."

THE EARTH IS SHAPED LIKE THE INSIDE OF AN EGG
Who Said So: Cyrus Reed Teed, in the late 1860s.
What He Believed: Instead of living on the outside of a solid
round ball, we're on the inside surface of a hollow one. The rest
of the universe—sun, stars, etc.—is where the yolk would be.
Background: For years, Teed grappled with the notion of an infi-
nite universe...but just couldn't accept it. Then one night in 1869,
he had a dream in which a beautiful woman explained everything:

> The entire cosmos...is like an egg. We live on the inner surface of
> the shell, and inside the hollow are the sun, moon, stars, planets,
> and comets. What is outside? Absolutely nothing! The inside is all
> there is. You can't see across it because the atmosphere is too
> dense. The shell is 100 miles thick....

The woman in Teed's dream also said he would be the new Mes-
siah, and he took it to heart. In the 1890s, he bought land outside
Fort Meyers, Florida, and founded a community called The New
Jerusalem that he preached would one day be the capital of the
world. He expected 8 million residents, but only got 200. In 1908
Teed died from injuries suffered during a run-in with the local mar-
shal; his dwindling community held on until the late 1940s, when
the last of his followers disbanded following a property dispute.

Mmm-mmm good: In the Middle Ages, chicken soup was considered an aphrodisiac.

THE WHO?

Ever wonder how rock bands get their names? So did we.
After some digging around, we found these "origin" stories.

THE GIN BLOSSOMS. A gin blossom is slang for the capillaries in your nose and face that burst because of excessive drinking.

PROCUL HARUM. Named after a friend's cat. It's Latin for "Beyond All Things."

THE BOOMTOWN RATS. Named after a gang in Woody Guthrie's autobiography, *Bound for Glory*.

GENERATION X. Named after a book that singer Billy Idol found in his mother's bookcase. It was a mid-1960s sociological essay by Charles Hamblett and Jane Deverson that featured interviews with U.K. teenagers in competing gangs called the Mods and Rockers.

10,000 MANIACS. Came from the cult horror film *2,000 Maniacs*. One of the band members misunderstood the film's name.

FOO FIGHTERS. World War II fighter pilot slang for UFOs.

RAGE AGAINST THE MACHINE. Name refers to a (hoped-for) reaction of ordinary people against corporations, governments and other invasive institutions that control our society.

HOT TUNA. Originally Hot S**t. The band's record label made them change the second word to Tuna.

DIRE STRAITS. Suggested by a friend who was concerned about the state of the band's finances.

MOTHERS OF INVENTION. Frank Zappa's group was originally just The Mothers. But their record company was concerned it would be interpreted as an Oedipal reference and insisted they change it. The band chose the name from the old saying "necessity is the mother of invention."

PEARL JAM. Singer Eddie Vedder suggested the name in honor of his Aunt Pearl's homemade jam, supposedly a natural aphrodisiac containing peyote. "Pearl Jam" is also slang for semen.

BEASTIE BOYS. Beastie supposedly stands for Boys Entering Anarchistic States Towards Inner Excellence.

SQUIRREL NUT ZIPPERS. From a brand of old-time peanut-flavored candy containing caramel and nuts.

BLIND MELON. According to bassist Brad Smith, the name was slang for unemployed hippies in his Mississippi town. Also sounds supiciously like an anagram of blues singer Blind Lemon.

BLUE ÖYSTER CULT. An anagram of "Cully Stout Beer." It was chosen by a band member one night as he was mindlessly doodling while at a bar with the band's manager.

DEVO. An abbreviation of *de-evolution*, something that the members of the group believe is happening to the human race.

REM. An acronym for rapid eye movement. REM sleep is the state of sleep in which dreams occur.

MATCHBOX 20. Took its name from the combination of a softball jersey bearing the number 20 and a patch that read "matchbox." The name is meaningless. "The two parts aren't even related," singer Rob Thomas has said.

311. The police code for indecent exposure in California.

ZZ TOP. Said to be have been inspired by a poster of Texas bluesman Z. Z. Hill, and rolling-paper brands "Zig Zag" and "Top."

COUNTING CROWS. A reference to an old British poem that said life is as meaningless as counting crows.

L7. Fifties slang for someone who is "square," or uncool.

THE WHO. According to legend, the group, first called The High Numbers, was looking for a new name. Every time someone came up with an idea, they jokingly asked, "The *who?*" Finally, a friend said "Why not just call yourselves 'The Who'?"

THE LAST LAUGH: EPITAPHS

Some unusual epitaphs and tombstone rhymes from the U.S. and Europe, sent in by our crew of wandering BRI tombstone-ologists.

In New York:
Harry Edsel Smith
Born 1903–Died 1942
Looked up the
  elevator shaft
To see
If the car was on the
  way down.
It was.

In Massachusetts:
Matthew Mudd
Here lies Matthew
  Mudd,
Death did him no
  hurt;
When alive he was
  only Mudd,
But now he's only
  dirt.

In England:
Sir John Strange
Here lies an honest
  lawyer,
And that is Strange.

In Scotland:
Stranger, tread
This ground with
  gravity:
Dentist Brown is
  filling
His last cavity.

In England:
My wife is dead
And here she lies:
Nobody laughs
And nobody cries:
Where she is gone to
And how she fares
Nobody knows
And nobody cares.

In New York:
He angled in the
  babbling brook
With all his angler's
  skill.
He lied about the fish
  he took
And here he's lying
  still.

In Ireland:
Tears cannot
Restore her:
Therefore I weep.

In England:
Beneath this stone
Lie Humphrey and
  Joan,
Who rest together in
  peace,
Living indeed,
They disagreed,
But now all quarrels
  cease.

In Belgrave:
John Racket
Here lies John Racket
In his wooden jacket:
Kept neither horses
  nor mules
Lived a hog
Died a dog
And left all his money
  to fools.

In Massachusetts:
Here lies Ann Mann.
She lived an old
  maid
But died an old
  Mann.

In England:
Mrs Nott
Nott born, Nott dead
…Here lies a woman
  Who was,
And who was Nott.

In England:
Dr. I. Lettsom
When people's ill,
  they comes to I,
I physics, bleeds, and
  sweats 'em;
Sometimes they live,
sometimes they die;
What's that to I?
  I. Lettsom.

Half of all forest fires are started by lightning.

BIRTH OF A GIANT

Ever wonder why Uncle John drives an old Buick? Part of the reason is because he likes old Buicks…and part is because David Buick was more than a car manufacturer—he was a bathroom hero. Here's the story of Mr. Buick…and the giant auto company that grew out of his work.

A BATHROOM HERO

In 1882 the Alex Manufacturing Company of Detroit, a maker of iron toilet bowls and wooden water-closet tanks, went bankrupt. The company's plant foreman, David Dunbar Buick, and a partner, William Sherwood, took over the company, renamed it Buick and Sherwood, and nursed it back to health.

Buick was an ingenious man; he received 13 patents on various plumbing fixtures between 1881 and 1889, including valves, flushing devices, and even a lawn sprinkler. But his most signficant patent was for an improved method of fixing white porcelain onto an iron surface, such as a bathtub.

In other words, Buick is the father of the modern bathtub.

QUIT WHEN YOU'RE A HEAD

If there was ever a time to be in the plumbing business, the early 1890s was it. "With the rapid growth of urban areas and the great increase in the adoption of indoor plumbing facilities, David Buick's fortune would seem to have been assured," George S. May writes in *A Most Unique Machine.* "Instead, he threw this away in favor of another interest—gasoline engines and automobiles."

In 1899 Buick and Sherwood sold their company for $100,000. Buick used his share of the money to found the Buick Auto-Vim and Power Company, which manufactured gasoline motors for use in industry, in farming, and on riverboats. In 1902 Buick changed the name to the Buick Manufacturing Company and began making automobiles. Buick's automobile engine was one of the most advanced of its day, but Buick himself was apparently a terrible businessman.

Down the Drain

By the fall of 1903, Buick had used up all the money he'd made sell-

---

Side by side, 2,000 cells of the human body would cover about one square inch.

ing his plumbing business...and still owed so much money to Briscoe Brothers (his sheet metal supplier) that he signed over ownership of nearly the entire company to Benjamin and Frank Briscoe—on the condition that he'd get it back when he repaid them. But Buick never did repay them, so in September 1903, the Briscoes sold their stake in the company to Flint Wagon Works, a carriage maker in Flint, Michigan.

Buick, still in debt, stayed on to manage the company for the new owners.

ENTER WILLIAM DURANT

The owners of the Flint Wagon Works quickly came to realize that running an automobile company was going to cost a lot more than they were willing to spend. Furthermore, for all his talent as an inventor, David Buick was a terrible manager; the auto company would probably never make any money as long as he was in charge. So in 1904, Flint Wagon Works shoved David Buick aside and turned the reins of the company over to William "Billy" Crapo Durant, owner of a competing carriage company in Flint. Their plan: Flint Wagon Works would continue to own a stake in Buick, but Durant would run it and would raise new money by selling stock to outside investors.

If anyone could turn Buick around, Billy Durant could. In 1884 Durant, then a young insurance salesman, had seen a horse-drawn road cart while on a selling trip in Michigan. He was so impressed with the design that he abandoned insurance, bought the patent rights to the cart, and, together with a hardware clerk named Dallas Dort, formed a company to manufacture and sell the cart.

Tycoon

By the time Durant joined Buick in November 1904, he'd built Durant-Dort into the largest carriage company in the nation, with 14 factories across the U.S. and Canada and a nationwide network of dealerships that sold more than 75,000 carriages a year. It was an awesome achievement, and the owners of the Flint Wagon Works hoped that Durant would be able to work the same magic at Buick.

Americans consume an average 736 million pounds of peanut butter each year.

BOO-ICK

As for David Buick: He retained the title of company secretary and still had a seat on the board of directors, but his days of running the firm that bore his name were over. In fact, the Flint Wagon Works considered changing the name to the Durant Motor Company to capitalize on Durant's business fame.

Durant, however, insisted that the car retain the name of its inventor, even though he was worried that the public might mispronounce it "Boo-ick."

For Part II, turn to page 370.

*   *   *   *

CONSUMER REPORTS

BRI member Diana Wynn sent us this list, which originated in England, along with the comment: "In case you needed further proof that the human race is doomed through stupidity, here are some actual label instructions on consumer goods."

On a Sears hairdryer: *Do not use while sleeping.*

On a bag of Fritos: *You could be a winner! No purchase necessary. Details inside.*

On a bar of Dial soap: *Directions: Use like regular soap.*

On some Swanson frozen dinners: *Serving suggestion: Defrost.*

On packaging for a Rowenta iron: *Do not iron clothes on body.*

On Boot's Children's Cough Medicine: *Do not drive car or operate machinery.*

On Tesco's Tiramisu dessert (printed on bottom of box)**:** *Do not turn upside down.*

On Marks & Spencer Bread Pudding: *Product will be hot after heating.*

On Nytol sleep aid: *Warning: may cause drowsiness.*

On a Korean kitchen knife: *Warning keep out of children.*

On a string of Chinese-made Christmas lights: *For indoor or outdoor use only.*

On Sainsbury's peanuts: *Warning: contains nuts.*

The earliest form of electric shock treatment involved the use of electric eels.

SILENCE IS GOLDEN

The old adage may be true, but would you buy a "recording" with absolutely nothing on it? Apparently, some people would. Here are a few examples of silent "music"…proof that you can sell anything.

UN-CAGED. "The highly eccentric American composer, John Cage, is responsible for composing the sheet music for his extremely quiet opus '4 minutes 33 seconds,' which is exactly that much silence. The sheet music is blank and just tells you how long *not* to play."
—*The Worst Entertainment*

YOURS AND MIME. "In the 1970s, a record company in Los Angeles issued a record entitled, 'The Best of Marcel Marceau.' It contained forty minutes of silence followed by a burst of applause. Strangely enough, it sold very well. The company also issued a recording especially for children—it was exactly the same pressing, but had a redesigned cover."
—*The Mammoth Book of Oddities*

STOP THE MUSIC! In 1953 jukeboxes were so popular that there was no way to get a moment of quiet in some places…until Columbia Records issued a disc called "Three Minutes of Silence." According to jukebox operators, it was a big hit.
—*The Worst Entertainment*

SILENCE THERAPY. "In the 1960s, a Staten Island, New York speech pathologist named Jerry Cammarata did a brisk business with a 52-minute LP designed to 'conjure up previously learned musical experiences, and provide a welcome relief from noise pollution….' It had no sound on it."
—*Oops*

SOUND FREE EUROPE. "The Netherlands' Foundation of the Museum of Silence opened an exhibition featuring 75 years of great silences from Dutch radio and television. The silent moments, on loan from the Museum of Broadcasting in Hiversum, are played to visitors over loudspeakers in the museum. Curator Bob Vrakking said he started the foundation in 1990 to promote silence "because it is so scarce."
—*Dumb, Dumber, Dumbest*

The single most ordered item in American restaurants: French fries.

TRICK SHOTS: FAMOUS FAKED PHOTOS

If there's a lesson to be learned from these historic phonies, it's that people believe what they want to believe. In the face of overwhelming logic—or even solid contrary evidence—people have clung to the notion that the real truth was revealed in these photographs.

FAIRY TALE

Famous Photo: English fairies

Trick Shot: In 1917 Sir Arthur Conan Doyle, "an ardent believer in the occult," announced that, just as he'd always believed, sprites, gnomes, and other types of fairies really did exist. His proof: photographs of fairies taken by 16-year-old Elsie Wright and her 10-year-old cousin Frances Griffiths. "The pictures showed the girls by a wooded stream, with winged sprites and gnomes who danced and pranced and tooted on pipes," Michael Farquhar writes in the *Washington Post*. "Several of the photography experts who examined the pictures declared them free of superimposition or retouching," and the photos, backed by Conan Doyle's testament to their authenticity, launched a national fairy craze.

The Real Picture: "In 1983, the girls, by then old women, admitted that they had posed with paper cutouts supported by hatpins."

SECOND TIME AROUND

Famous Photo: American troops raising the flag on Iwo Jima

Trick Shot: The bloody battle of Iwo Jima (an island 650 miles from Tokyo) took place on February 23, 1945. The Japanese were nearly wiped out, and the Americans lost over one-third of their troops. When the U.S. Marines finally took Iwo Jima's highest point, Mt. Suribachi, they raised an American flag at the summit. AP photographer Joe Rosenthal was on hand to catch it on film; his dramatic picture is one of the most famous images of the 20th century. It won the Pulitzer Prize, was commemorated with a postage stamp, and was the inspiration for the Marines Memorial in Arlington National Cemetery.

The Real Picture: Rosenthal's photograph was so good that *Life*

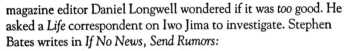

magazine editor Daniel Longwell wondered if it was *too* good. He asked a *Life* correspondent on Iwo Jima to investigate. Stephen Bates writes in *If No News, Send Rumors:*

> The correspondent reported, that as Longwell suspected, the photo had been staged. The marines had raised a small flag for a photographer from *Leatherneck*, the Marine Corps magazine. Rosenthal had arrived four hours later. At his request, the marines had reenacted the event with a larger flag.

Longwell refused to use a staged photograph in *Life*, but other publications did run it, and it caught on with the public. "The country believed in that picture," Longwell recounted later, "and I just had to pipe down."

UN-LOCH-ING THE TRUTH

Famous Photo: Loch Ness monster

Trick Shot: On April 19, 1934, Robert Wilson and a companion were walking along the shore of Loch Ness when the friend suddenly shouted, "My God, it's the monster!" Wilson grabbed his camera and snapped a quick photograph of what appears to be "a sea beast with a humpback and a long neck"—the legendary Loch Ness monster, an elusive creature with sightings dating as far back as 565 A.D. The *Daily Mail* ran the photograph, and news of the find spread round the world. Based largely on the strength of Wilson's photograph, it remains one of the most widely believed monster legends to this day. Nearly one million tourists visit Loch Ness each year, hoping to spot "Nessie" and pumping $37 million into the local economy while they're there.

The Real Picture: In 1995 a friend of Wilson's named Christian Spurling made a deathbed confession that the photograph was a hoax and the "monster" was actually "a toy submarine fitted with a fake sea-serpent head" that Spurling had made himself. "Wilson," the Associated Press reported in 1995, "was part of a hoax hatched by his friend Marmaduke Wetherell, a film maker and self-styled big game hunter hired by London's *Daily Mail* newspaper in 1933 to look for Nessie."

Note: Hard-core believers are unimpressed by the revelation. "Eyewitness accounts still suggest that there is something powerful in the loch," says Adrian Shine, founder of a group called The Loch Ness Project.

In Antarctica, sunsets can be green.

WEIRD TOYS

Looking for a gift for a special young friend or relative? Want to surprise them with something out of the ordinary? Well, if you don't mind being thrown out of the house, you might want to pick up one of these 100% real (we guarantee it) playthings.

The Tamahonam. Sold in Hong Kong, the Tamahonam is a Tamagotchi toy with Mob connections. Instead of feeding Tamahonam like you would other virtual pets, you "care" for Tamahonam by plying him with cigarettes and booze; instead of playing him, you give him a knife "to let him wage turf battles."

Feral Cheryl. "A doll that has unshaved legs, dreadlocks, tattoos, pubic hair, and pierced nipples." Made in Australia.

The Grossinator. Made by SRM, the company that brought you the Insultinator. "A minicomputer with a sound chip and programmable buttons with phrases you can mix and match." This one says things like, "I'm going to make a horrible, gross fart" and "How about a foul, smelly barf?"

Brian Jones Pool Toy. "An inflatable, life-size pool toy of Brian Jones, deceased member of the Rolling Stones, that floats facedown in the water, simulating the guitarist's death by drowning in his pool."

Gooey Looey. Exciting action! "Children use their fingers to relieve Louie's congested proboscis before the top of his head flies off."

Savage Mondo Blitzers. "A line of 48 characters named Bad Fart, Snot Shot, Projectile Vomit, Puke Shooters, Loaded Diaper, Eye Pus, and the like."

Letter Bomb. The manufacturer urges kids to "have fun and become a terrorist." Looks like an airmail envelope—"kids write the target's name on it, clap on it heavily, and then give it to the victim within seven seconds so it 'explodes' in his hand." Sold in the Philippines.

Nothing's new: Ancient Rome had rent-a-chariot businesses.

OLDER & WISER

Here are some observations about aging from folks who should know. They're from the book Older & Wiser, *by Gretchen B. Dianda and Betty J. Hofmayer.*

"I will never be an old man. To me, old age is always 15 years older than I am."
—**Bernard Baruch, at age 85**

"I don't deserve this award, but I have arthritis and I don't deserve that either."
—**Jack Benny**

"You know you're getting old when you stoop to tie your shoes and wonder what else you can do when you're down there."
—**George Burns**

"If you continue to work and to absorb the beauty in the world around you, you will find that age does not necessarily mean getting old."
—**Pablo Casals, at age 93**

"Old age isn't so bad when you consider the alternative."
—**Maurice Chevalier, at age 64**

"We don't grow older, we grow riper."
—**Pablo Picasso**

"An archaeologist is the best husband any woman can have; the older she gets, the more interested he is in her."
—**Agatha Christie, at age 64**

"We are happier in many ways when we are old than when we were young. The young sow wild oats. The old grow sage."
—**Winston Churchill**

"To be 70 years young is sometimes far more cheerful and hopeful than to be 40 years old."
—**Oliver Wendell Holmes, Sr., at age 80**

"Since I came to the White House I got two hearing aids, a colon operation, skin cancer, a prostate operation, and I was shot. The damn thing is, I've never felt better in my life."
—**Ronald Reagan, at age 69**

"What a wonderful life I've had! I only wish I'd realized it sooner."
—**Colette**

FOUNDING FATHERS

You already know the names. Here's who they belonged to.

William Colgate. In the early 1800s, making soap at home was a matter of pride with American housewives: 75% of U.S. soap was made at home (although it smelled terrible). In 1806 Colgate opened a soap business and succeeded by offering home delivery, and by adding perfume to his soap.

Gerhard Mennen. While recovering from malaria in the 1870s, he learned so much about the pharmaceutical trade that he opened his own drug store. He made his own remedies, including Mennen's Borated Talcum Infant Powder—America's first talcum powder.

Dr. William Erastus Upjohn. Until he invented a process for manufacturing soft pills, prescription pills were literally hard as a rock—you couldn't smash them with a hammer, and they often passed through a person's system without being absorbed by the body. Upjohn's invention changed all that.

John Michael Kohler. A Wisconsin foundry owner in the 1880s. One of his big sellers was an enameled iron water trough for farm animals. In 1883, convinced that demand for household plumbing fixtures was growing, he made four cast-iron feet, welded them to the animal trough, and began selling it as a bathtub.

William Boeing. When he wasn't working for his father, a timber and iron baron, Boeing and a friend named Conrad Westervelt built seaplanes as a hobby. In 1916 the pair founded Pacific Aero Products. When the U.S. entered World War I in 1917, the Navy bought 50 of his planes. He never worked for his father again.

William Rand and Andrew McNally. Rand and McNally printed railroad tickets and timetables. In 1872 they added maps to their line. Other companies using wood or metal engravings for their maps; Rand McNally used wax engravings, allowing them to update and correct maps at a fraction of the cost. By the early 1900s Rand McNally was one of the largest mapmakers in the country.

Lubberwort is another word for junk food.

ROCK GOSSIP

*Honorary BRI member and Texas author Bill Crawford
submitted these outrageous tales of rock heroes. For more of the
same, check out Margaret Moser and Bill Crawford's book*
Rock Stars Do the Dumbest Things.

BATTLE OF THE STARS
• Neil Diamond collaborated for many years with guitarist
Robbie Robertson of The Band. In 1976 Robertson invited
Diamond and Bob Dylan to perform at The Last Waltz, The Band's
final concert, which was documented by Martin Scorsese. Diamond
sang first, went backstage, and smugly said to Dylan, "You'll have to
be pretty good to follow me." Dylan snapped back, "What do I have
to do, go onstage and fall asleep?"

• Though many musicians put them down, former Beatle George
Harrison appreciates the true talent of the Spice Girls. "The good
thing about them," Harrison said, "is that you can look at them with
the sound turned down."

BEATLEMANIAC
In 1967 John Lennon decided that a TV repairman named John
Alexis Mardas was his guru. Lennon called him Magic Alex and
gave him a bunch of money to build a flying saucer, an artificial sun,
and "loudpaper"—wallpaper which was really a speaker system.
None of the inventions worked.

HELL ON EARTH
Kurt Cobain, of Nirvana, was not a housekeeper. There was old garbage and rotting food all over his Seattle digs. When the Cobains
tried to hire some help, the maid walked into their house, then ran
out screaming, "Satan lives here!"

WHAT CHILD IS THIS?
For a while, Mick Jagger introduced Bebe Buell as "the mother of
one of my illegitimate children." Jagger got a bit jealous, though,
when Buell informed him that Steven Tyler of Aerosmith was actually the father of her daughter, who grew up to be actress Liv Tyler.

Snow skiing rule of thumb: Most men fall on their faces, most women on their behinds.

GROUPIE PROBLEMS

When Linda McCartney died, Paul revealed that he and his wife had spent almost every day together since marrying. That wasn't always how he felt. When she came to visit him in London in 1968, Paul complained to a friend that "an American groupie" was "flying in. I've thrown her out once," explained Paul, "had to throw her suitcase over the wall, but it's no good, she keeps coming back."

VIOLENT OUTBURSTS

In 1988 after allegedly shooting at the walls of his bedroom, the Godfather of Soul, James Brown, pulled out a shotgun at an insurance seminar in Augusta, Georgia, and threatened people because someone had used the bathroom in his trailer. Brown then jumped into his truck and led police on a high-speed chase through two states. Brown finally stopped when police blasted the tires out from under his bullet-riddled vehicle. He was arrested and served two years in a penitentiary.

DOG DAYS

Madonna's pet chihuahua Ciquita was reportedly depressed over the attention lavished on Madonna's new baby, Lourdes. So Madonna sent the pooch to a canine shrink.

PETER PAN

Michael Jackson spent a lot of time with one young friend, trying to fly. Jackson and the boy would close their eyes, hold hands, stand in the middle of his room and concentrate on floating to the ceiling. "I'd get bored after half an hour or so," recalled the youngster years later, "but Jackson just kept standing there with his eyes closed, wishing he could fly. Once he asked Tinkerbell to sprinkle him with pixie dust. No, I'm sure he wasn't kidding."

POOR TABLE MANNERS

In 1971, brothers Ray and Dave Davies of the Kinks were dining in Manhattan. Dave tried to steal one of Ray's french fries. Ray responded by stabbing his brother in the chest with a fork.

Ropesville, Lariat, and Loop are all towns in Texas.

HOW WE GOT THE DOLLAR, PART I

Ever wondered why we call our money the "dollar"? At the BRI,
we've been trying to find a good explanation for years. Finally,
courtesy of BRI member Erin Keenan, we've got the answer.

BACKGROUND
In 1519 Stephan Schlick, a Czech nobleman, discovered a
rich vein of silver on his estate in the Joachimsthal Valley.
He began minting his own coins, which were accepted as *groschen*,
the official currency of the Holy Roman Empire, in 1520.

Schlick's coins were first referred to as *Joachimsthalergroschen*,
after the valley in which they originated. But that was too hard to
pronounce; people began shortening it. The coins became known
as *thalergroschen*...and eventually *talers* or *thalers*.

What Goes Around...
Schlick and his neighbors produced millions of thalers. By 1600
there were 12 million of the coins (an enormous amount for the
time) circulating around Europe. One result was that the thaler—
which started out as the equivalent of three German marks—lost its
specific value. It was considered local currency wherever it was used,
and its value changed from region to region.

After a while, the term *thaler* didn't even refer to Schlick's money
anymore. It became generic—synonymous with "any large silver
coin." Eventually, many cultures came up with their own version of
the word. In Italy, for example, a large silver coin became known as
a "*tallero*"; in Holland, it was a "*daalder*"; Denmark and Sweden had
"*dalers*"; in Hawaii, silver coins were "*dalas*"; Ethiopians exchanged
"*talari*", and in English-speaking countries, a silver coin was called a
"*dollar*."

COMING TO AMERICA
The term *dollar* was particularly popular in Scotland. As Jack
Weatherford writes in *The History of Money*:

> The Scots used the name dollar to distinguish their currency, and

---

There are twice as many billionaires in the U.S. today as there were 10 years ago.

thereby their country and themselves, more clearly from their domineering English neighbors to the south [who used *pounds, shillings, pence*, etc]. Thus from very early usage, the word 'dollar' carried with it a certain anti-English or antiauthoritarian bias that many Scottish settlers took with them to their new homes in the Americas and other British colonies. The emigration of Scots accounts for much of the subsequent popularity of the word "dollar" in British colonies around the world.

THE AMERICAN WAY

That explains how the term dollar got here...but not why it became the official currency of the U.S. After all, American colonists were still mostly loyal British subjects, and would have preferred to trade in pounds, shillings, and other English currency.

The problem was that the colonists suffered from a constant shortage of all coins—especially English ones. Starting in 1695, laws aimed at keeping gold and silver inside Britain's borders were passed by Parliament. "Britain forbade exporting gold and silver to anywhere in the world," Weatherford writes, "including its own colonies."

For a while, colonies minted their own money. But in the mid-1700s, Parliament prohibited that, too. As a result, the only coins available to the American colonists in adequate supplies were Spanish silver *reales* (pronounced ray-ahl-ehs; "royals" in Spanish), which were minted in Mexico, Bolivia, and Peru. The colonists didn't call them *reales*; they preferred the already familiar term *dollar*.

By the time the colonists declared independence in 1776, the "Spanish dollar" was the *de facto* currency of the United States.

WHAT NOW?

In 1782 Thomas Jefferson began to address the issue of a new national currency. It was logical to call it a dollar, as he wrote in his *Notes of a Money Unit for the U.S.*, "The unit or dollar is a known coin and the most familiar of all to the mind of the people. It is already adopted from south to north."

So on July 6, 1785, Congress declared that "the money unit of the United States of America be the dollar." Interesting note:

Big shoes to fill: George Washington's feet were size 13.

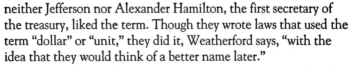

neither Jefferson nor Alexander Hamilton, the first secretary of the treasury, liked the term. Though they wrote laws that used the term "dollar" or "unit," they did it, Weatherford says, "with the idea that they would think of a better name later."

The U.S. allowed the Spanish dollar to continue as unofficial U.S. currency until the Mint was finally constructed nine years later. The Mint was the first public building, and the dollars it turned out were silver coins—not paper. It wasn't until many years later that the dollar bill came into existence. (We'll tell you about that in our next edition.)

* * *

WHERE DID PENNIES, DIMES, AND QUARTERS COME FROM?

• In the 1700s, the relationship of values between coins was arbitrary and confusing. In England, for example, 4 farthings were worth 1 pence, 12 pence were worth 1 shilling, and 20 shillings were worth 1 pound. Plus, the guinea—a slightly larger coin than the pound—was worth 1 pound and 1 shilling. Prices had to be written out explicitly for each coin (12 pounds, 13 shillings, and 4 pence, abbreviated to £12 s.13 p.4). Making change or converting prices from one coin to another was complex and time-consuming.

• In 1535 the Russians realized it would be easier to use a decimal system, and experimented by splitting the ruble into 100 coins, called *denga* (later *kopeks*). But as Jack Weatherford writes, "No matter how rational the new Russian system might have appeared to be, no other monarch wanted to copy Russia, which they regarded as a backward country."

• After the American Revolution, the U.S. was "eager to break with all things royal." In 1782 the "U.S. superintendent of finance sent a report to Congress recommending that the U.S. adopt a decimal system of currency." The goal: To divide the dollar into 100 equal parts. "Jefferson suggested that the smallest part, $1/_{100}$ of a dollar, be called a *cent*, from the latin word for 'hundred,' and that a tenth of a dollar be a *dime*, from the latin for 'tenth.'...In 1792, America became the first country with a completely decimalized money system." *Note*: England didn't adopt a decimal system of currency until 1971.

The average cat has 24 whiskers—12 on each side of its nose.

UNCLE JOHN'S TOP 12 "CURES" FOR BALDNESS

Now we've got Rogaine and other assorted chemicals to grow hair. But in the past, desperate baldies (like Uncle John) had to resort to everything from shock treatment to "hair-popping." These are 100% real, from the book Baldness: A Social History, *by Kerry Seagrave.*

12. BEAR GREASE. In the Old Testament, the second book of *Kings*, Chapter 2, the prophet Elisha tried to cure baldness by applying bear grease to his head. Bad news for bears: It was a popular remedy until the 16th century.

11. SNAKE "SOUP." A popular remedy prescribed by first-century physicians: "boil snakes and rub the broth into the bald areas."

10. ESTROGEN. In the 1980s, doctors found that the female hormone estrogen rubbed on a man's scalp could restore hair. Downside: It could also turn a man's voice from bass to soprano, reduce his libido, enlarge his breasts, and produce other female secondary-sex characteristics.

9. DOG PEE. From a pharmaceutical text in 17th-century Scotland came this recipe: "Wash the Head with a Dog's urine, and you shall not be bald."

8. HAIR IN A CAN. Invented in the early 1990s. GLH Formula #9, an aerosol-based dye with some polymers to frizz up the hair and thicken it. With the scalp dyed the same color as the hair, it gave the appearance of making balding men hair-bearing...at least on television. (By the way—it was created by Veg-o-Matic's Ron Popeil...and GLH stood for Great-Looking Hair.)

7. THE "ZOO" TECHNIQUE. The *Ebers Papyrus*, the first known medical record, was written around 1500 B.C. and recommended applying a mixture containing "the fat of a lion, a hippopotamus, a crocodile, a cat, and a serpent to the bald area." Alternate suggestion: apply the "burned prickles of a hedgehog, fingernail scrapings, and a mixture of honey, alabaster, and red ocher."

6. FILING IT. A "remedy" used in the 1980s, "head-filing" was a treatment that involved slitting open the scalp and filing the tissue between the skull and hair follicles to thin membranes over the skull. This was supposed to "wake up the follicles."

5. "LOVE" POTION. In the 1880s and '90s, French physician M. Vidal used *cantharides* (crushed insects better known as the so-called aphrodisiac Spanish fly) applied to the scalp....His formula combined the crushed bugs with acetic acid in a solution of 90% alcohol.

4. RUBBING IT RAW. A popular baldness treatment during the late 19th century was blistering (*vesication*) of the scalp. Irritating the area in this manner was thought to produce pooling of blood in the scalp (*hyperemia*), which provided more nourishment for the hair follicles there.

3. POP CURE. Cosmetologist Rita Hartinger was the foremost practitioner of the "hair popping" technique of hair preservation and regrowth in the 1980s. "When you lift up the scalp from the bone structure by popping," she says, "it stimulates circulation and nourishes the tissue." A journalist described the sound: "as if a kernel of popcorn had exploded on [the] head."

2. SHOCK THERAPY. In the 1890s, a German doctor named Seeger recommended the application of frictional electricity to the scalp by means of a special plate. This was rubbed over a dry cloth or piece of soft leather and then over the bald areas several times a day.

And the top baldness cure of all time...

1. THE COW LICK. In 1983 John Coombs of Wiltshire, England, was feeding his cow, Primrose, when dust from the feed settled on his bald head. As he bent to fill the trough, Primrose licked his scalp. Eight weeks later, Coombs's wife noticed his hair returning. Coombs went public with his story, and people were soon lining up to get their heads licked by cows.

Average surface temperature of Venus: 864°F, the hottest of any planet in the solar system.

UNCLE JOHN'S PAGE OF LISTS

For years, the BRI has had a file full of lists. We've never been sure what to do with them...until now.

TITLES OF 4 HOLLYWOOD FILMS RE-DUBBED IN HONG KONG:

1. **Fargo:** "Mysterious Murder in Snowy Cream."
2. **The English Patient:** "Don't Ask Me Who I Am."
3. **Boogie Nights:** "His Powerful Device Makes Him Famous."
4. **Nixon:** "The Big Liar."

4 NAMES FOR THINGS YOU DIDN'T KNOW HAD NAMES

1. **Aglet:** "The covering on the end of a shoelace."
2. **Phosphenes:** "The lights you see when you close your eyes hard."
3. **Kick or Punt:** "The indentation at the bottom of wine bottles."
4. **Harp:** "The metal hoop that supports a lampshade."

2 PRESIDENTIAL SUPERSTITIONS

1. Franklin Roosevelt (1933-1945) refused to sit at a table set for thirteen guests.
2. Woodrow Wilson (1913-1921) Believed 13 was his lucky number. He once ordered a ship to slow down so he would arrive in Europe on the 13th instead of the 12th.

9 BEANS THAT CAUSE THE MOST GAS

1. Soybeans
2. Pink beans
3. Black beans
4. Pinto beans
5. California small white beans
6. Great northern beans
7. Lima beans
8. Garbanzos
9. Blackeyes
—*U.S. Department of Agriculture*

3 MOST INFLUENTIAL PETS OF THE MILLENNIUM

1. Lassie
2. Snoopy
3. Arnold the Pig (from TV's *Green Acres*)
—*The American Pet Product Manufacturers Association*

5 THINGS YOU SHOULDN'T SAY WHEN A COP PULLS YOU OVER

1. "Aren't you the guy from the Village People?"
2. "That's great. The last guy only gave me a warning also."
3. "You're not gonna check the trunk, are you?"
4. "Hey, you must've been doing 100 just to keep up with me."
5. "I thought you had to be in good physical condition to be a cop."

Two most dangerous jobs in the U.S.: commercial fishing and logging.

JUST THE FAX, PLEASE

*Here are a few things to think about the next time
you find yourself standing at a fax machine.*

ONE WORLD

Fax machines are so common today that it's easy to forget how rare they once were. In 1977 fax machines cost more than $20,000 each...and transmitted one blurry, hard-to-read page every six minutes.

By 1989, fax machines began changing not just the way the world did business, but perhaps even the course of history. For example:

• When Lithuania seceded from the USSR, the secessionist government bypassed Soviet censors and communicated directly with the outside world using fax machines.

• Pro-democracy demonstrators on China's Tiananmen Square used fax machines to communicate with supporters within the country and around the world.

• When Nelson Mandela, still a political prisoner in South Africa, began negotiating the terms of his release from prison, the end of apartheid, and South Africa's transition to a full democracy, he did it using a fax machine.

The fax machine revolution "makes totalitarianism impossible," says Max Kampelman, the head of Freedom House, a human rights organization. "Totalitarianism requires the total control of information. That isn't possible anymore."

FAX HISTORY

The fax machine isn't a new idea. Believe it or not, the first one—called a *pantelegraph* because it was supposed to transmit messages over telegraph lines—was patented in 1843, 33 years before Alexander Graham Bell patented the telephone. It was created by Alexander Bain, a Scottish clockmaker who envisioned using pendulums at each end of the telegraph to transmit messages, (we won't get into exactly how it worked—it's too confusing). Unfortunately, Bain never figured out how to synchronize the pendulums, and he eventually gave up.

However, in 1864 a Catholic priest named Giovanni Caselli and his partner, Gustav Froment, finally got all the bugs out of Bain's invention. Their version not only worked, it sent messages written on ordinary paper, and could send several of them simultaneously over a single wire.

The duo demonstrated their machine to Emperor Napoleon III of France...and he loved it. Under his direction, the French legislature passed a law establishing the world's first fax service between Paris and Lyons—a distance of more than 200 miles. It was inaugurated on May 16, 1865, and by 1868 it was capable of sending more than 110 telegrams an hour. But it never really had a chance to catch on with the public. The system was disrupted by war and the siege of Paris in 1870, and was never resumed.

PHOTO AGE

Over the next four or five decades, scientists worked at perfecting the technique of sending not only messages, but pictures. In 1902 a German physicist named Arthur Korn figured out how to send photo-quality images using special wires. And in 1913 Edouard Belin invented what he called a "Belinograph" (Belino for short), a portable machine, smaller than a typewriter, that could transmit photographic images over standard telephone lines.

This invention revolutionized news reporting. For the first time in history, a newspaper could send someone to any corner of the globe (or at least any corner that had telephones) and, with the portable Belino machine, get photographic images in a matter of minutes—not weeks or months as had been the case before. Invented just in time for the outbreak of World War I, the Belino had an immediate impact on wartime news coverage. By the early 1920s, it was even possible to send "wirephotos" using radio waves, eliminating the need for telephones.

MODERN FAXES

For the next 50 years, these early machines were used almost exclusively to send news pictures around the world and to transmit weather maps by radio to ships at sea. The system was too expen-

A whale's heart beats about once every 6½ seconds.

sive and too slow to be of much interest to other types of businesses. Besides, AT&T had a monopoly on telephone service in the United States—and because they didn't manufacture fax machines, they fought to prevent customers from using telephone lines for anything other than voice. However, by the late 1960s, the FCC and the courts abolished most AT&T restrictions, opening the way for big companies like Xerox, IBM and others to create the technology that resulted in the modern fax.

MADE IN JAPAN

• Still, fax machines might never have come into widespread use were it not for the fact that the Japanese language uses thousands of characters (too many to fit on a typewriter keyboard). Typing and telexing is thus much more difficult in Japanese than it is in English.

• Japanese businessmen needed a way to send handwritten communications quickly and accurately over the telephone, so companies like Matsushita, Ricoh, Canon, and NEC spent tens of millions of dollars figuring out how to make fax machines cheaper, faster, and easier to use. They succeeded.

• Sales of fax machines boomed in Japan in the early 1980s, and by the late 1980s the fever had spread to the rest of the world. The steady decline of the price of the machines fueled the boom: by 1983 fax machines that had cost $21,000 in 1977 were selling for $2,600; by 1988 the price slipped under $1,000 for the first time, enabling millions of small business to afford them. By the mid-1990s, the price as low as $130 and most companies—even small ones—couldn't afford *not* to have a fax machine. Of course, *now* everyone needs computers and e-mail…but, that's another story.

*   *   *   *

FAX LINGO

Fax Potato: Someone who faxes materials from one floor of a building to another, because they're too lazy to use the elevator.

There are more telephones than people in Washington, D.C.

ZORRO

"Out of the night, when the full moon is bright, comes a horseman known as Zorro." Here's the story of how the masked man known as Zorro was created.

PULP FICTION

In 1919 a hack fiction writer name Johnston McCulley published a story called "The Curse of Capistrano" in *All-Story Weekly*, the country's premier serial fiction magazine.

The story was set in Los Angeles during the Spanish Mission period of the late 18th and early 19th centuries. The hero was Don Diego de la Vega, son of a wealthy hacienda owner—a foppish dilettante who detested violence as much as he loved poetry, intellectual pursuits, and finely tailored clothing. By night, however, Don Diego was El Zorro—"the Fox"—a sword-fighting, masked man in black who protected the helpless peasants from the territory's corrupt and greedy land barons.

THE END...AND A NEW BEGINNING

"The Curse of Capistrano" ran for five installments. In the end, Zorro defeats his enemy and reveals his true identity to the assembled crowd, saying, "It was difficult to fool you all...and now Señor Zorro shall ride no more."

The story was over...or so McCulley thought.

Using pen names, McCulley had written hundreds of stories, featuring such characters as Captain Fly-By-Night, Señor Vulture, Señor Devil-May-Care, and Don Peon. None of these survive today, and the same fate might have befallen El Zorro if actor Douglas Fairbanks hadn't picked up a copy of *All-Story Weekly* while he was on his honeymoon in March 1920.

Fairbanks, the "King of Hollywood," was famous for his action-comedy films. They were hits at the box office, but appealed mostly to men...and in the early 1920s, afternoon matinee audiences were made up mostly of females, who preferred romances. Theater owners complained that although Fairbanks's films packed the house in the evening, they played to empty theaters during the day.

When he read "The Curse of the Capistrano," Fairbanks knew he'd found the role that would allow him to combine the athletics for which he was famous with romantic subplots that would bring women into the theater. He was right.

OPENING NIGHT

The Mark of Zorro, which opened in the Capital Theater in New York—then the world's largest movie theater—made more money on opening day than any previous film had. The theater was so full that the police had to be called after the 9:00 show to disperse the crowds.

The film propelled Fairbanks's career to even greater heights: by the end of 1920, he ranked higher in film popularity polls than his wife, Mary Pickford, and higher even than Charlie Chaplin. But it also made Zorro a star. Over the next 80 years, the masked avenger would make hundreds of appearances on film and TV, becoming one of the best-known and most influential icons of pop culture.

For the "Return of Zorro," turn to page 325.

For the "Return of Zorro," turn to page 325.

* * *

THE TRUTH ABOUT TAROT CARDS?

Apparently, Tarot cards weren't always used to tell peoples' fortunes—they originally made up a game called *tarocchi* that was popular with the Italian nobility in the 15th century. Tarocchi was played much like bridge or whist, except that there was a fifth suit of cards which trumped all the other suits. The earliest recorded use of tarot cards in fortune telling is in Venice, Italy in 1527, but the fad didn't take off until 1781, when a French scholar proposed that cards in the deck contained the knowledge of the Egyptian hieroglyphic *Book of Thoth*, which he claimed had been saved from the ruins of sacked and burned Egyptian temples centuries earlier.

MADONNA: TEST-MOUSE OR HUSSY-WOMAN?

Many thanks to BRI member Pete McCracken for sending this article to us. It was found in the Edge section of the Portland Oregonian.

GROUND RULES

According to the Edge, when Madonna was in Hungary filming *Evita*, she granted an interview to *BLIKK*, a Budapest magazine.

First, the magazine would ask a question in Hungarian. The question was then translated into English for Madonna. Then, Madonna's answer was translated into Hungarian for the magazine. Finally, Madonna's words were translated again into English at *USA Today's* behest. The resulting chat was, like most events on Planet Madonna, freakishly entertaining. A sampling:

BLIKK: "Madonna, Budapest says hello with arms that are spead-eagled. Did you have a visit here that was agreeable?"

MADONNA: "Thank you for saying these compliments. [Holds up hands.] Please stop with taking sensationalist photographs until I have removed my garments for all to see [laughs]. This is a joke I have made."

BLIKK: "Madonna, let's cut toward the hunt: Are you a bold hussy-woman that feasts on men who are tops?"

MADONNA: "Yes, yes, this is certainly something that brings to the surface my longings. In America, it is not considered to be mentally ill when a woman advances on her prey in a discotheque setting with hardy cocktails present."

BLIKK: "Is this how you met Carlos, your love-servant who is reputed? Were you dating many other people in your bed at the same time?"

MADONNA: "No, he was the only one I was dating in my bed then, so it is a scientific fact that the baby was made in my womb

On average, 25% of the fish you eat are raised on fish farms.

using him. But as regards these questions, enough! I am a woman and not a test-mouse!"

BLIKK: "OK, here's a question from left space: What was your book *Slut* about?"

MADONNA: "It was called *Sex*, my book."

BLIKK: "Not in Hungary. Here it was called *Slut*."

> *Note: We called Uncle Edgester, and he says this may be an urban legend. Oh well, it's still great.*

*   *   *

"I'M HERE FOR THE PAYCHECK. ISN'T EVERYBODY?"

OfficeTeam, a temporary employment agency in Menlo Park, California, asked clients to describe the strangest things they've seen in job interviews. Here are some of the answers they received:

• A candidate waiting in the lobby opened a large bag of cheese curls and began eating them. When the interviewer greeted him, the applicant extended a hand covered with orange dust.

• An interviewer walked into the lobby to meet a nervous candidate, whose mouth displayed a ring of antacid from the bottle he was holding.

• When asked why she wanted the job, a recent graduate replied, "I'm here for a paycheck—isn't everybody?"

• When asked where she saw herself in five years, the candidate replied, "How am I supposed to know—isn't that your job?"

• A candidate who was chewing gum noticed the interviewer staring at her mouth. The candidate said: "Oh, I'm sorry. Did you want a piece?"

• A candidate with long fingernails, when asked to take a typing test, reached over the interviewer's desk, grabbed his scissors and snipped off the nails, one by one. She then said, "That just doubled my number of words per minute."

Virus means "poison" in Latin.

ZAP! MODERN DEBT COLLECTION

At the beginning of the 20th century, people regarded electricity as a miracle of modern science. Many imagined that by the year 2000, electricity would be used to solve every social problem. Does that seem absurd now? It's food for thought—we may be doing the same thing with contemporary scientific marvels, like computers. Here's an example of what they were thinking at the turn of the last century excerpted from Looking Forward, *a 1903 science-fiction novel by Arthur Bird.*

In 1899, the relations between creditor and debtor were not as cordial as they should be. [But that gradually changed.]

Beginning in 1930, creditors and debtors kept in closer electrical touch with one another. If the sum due was $50 or over and of long standing, the law allowed the creditor to connect his debtor with an electrical battery....If the debt was over three months due, the creditor was allowed to occasionally "touch up" his debtor without having to hunt him up. The creditor always had him "on the string" so to speak.

It was further specified by law that creditors must employ only as many volts as there were dollars due on account in shocking a debtor. These electrical shocks were merely reminders, intended to refresh the memory of the debtor. A man owing $200 was liable to receive two hundred volts until the debt was satisfied.

This plan for the collection of bad debts worked very successfully. In 1999 no debtor could tell when his creditor might touch him up. The shock reminding him of his old debt might come during the night and disturb his pleasant sleep. Perhaps while seated at the family table, or perhaps even while engaged in family worship, an electric shock might come that would raise him three feet off the floor.

Such little occurrences were rather embarrassing, especially if the debtor was talking at the time to some lady friend. A man owing $500 was in danger of his life. His creditor

Sleeping around: Louis XIV owned 413 beds.

was liable to dun him by giving him a shock of five hundred volts. Such sensations, certainly, are not as pleasant as watching a yacht race, with your boat an easy winner.

A curious illustration of the operation of this new condition between creditors and bad debtors came to light in a parish church on the banks of the St. Lawrence. The members of the choir were in their places, while the village school teacher stood near the communion-rail, facing the choir, with his back turned towards the empty pews. He was speaking, when suddenly his red hair stood on end, his whiskers straightened out at right angles, while his eyes looked big as door knobs. He then gave a leap in the air, turned a somersault backwards and cleared ten pews before landing again on his feet. It appears that he owed his landlord an old board bill of $120 and the latter had just given him an electrical dun. The choir was astounded at the professor's performance. The latter excused himself and merely said it was a slight attack of the "grippe."

* * * *

PLANNING TO WATCH
TV TONIGHT?

The TV remote control has become a vital instrument in modern homes. According to a 1994 survey by Magnavox:

• One third of Americans say that TV "wouldn't be as pleasurable" without it.

• 18 percent of women and nine percent of men would rather give up sex for a week than their remote control.

• Some 55 percent lose their remote five times a week and 63 percent spend at least five minutes a day looking for it. (Most frequent places the remote is left: under furniture, 38 percent, kitchen or bathroom, 20 percent and in the fridge, 6 percent.)

• Twice as many men lose the remote as women. And twice as many men as women get to hold the remote.

What's a *melcryptovestimentaphiliac*? Someone who compulsively steals ladies underwear.

RANDOM ORIGINS

Once again, the BRI asks—and answers—the
question: where did this stuff come from?

G OLD RECORDS
In 1941 RCA Victor released Glenn Miller's "Chattanooga
Choo Choo" after he performed it in the movie *Sun Valley
Serenade*. It was a huge hit: 1.2 million records were sold in less
than three months. So RCA came up with a great publicity
gimmick to promote it: They sprayed one of the "master records"
with gold paint and on February 10, 1942, presented it to Miller
during a radio broadcast in honor of his selling a million copies.
Eventually the Record Industry Association of America (RIAA)
copied the idea and started honoring million-selling records with
an official Gold Record Award.

Nobody knows for sure what the first million-selling record was.
One likely candidate: "Ragging the Baby to Sleep," recorded by
Al Jolson on April 17, 1912. (*Yankee Ingenuity*)

CIRCUS TIGHTS
"Tights are believed to have been introduced in 1828 by Nelson
Hower, a bareback rider in the Buckley and Wicks Show, as
the result of a mishap. The performers wore short jackets, knee
breeches, and stockings, but Hower's costume failed to arrive and
he appeared for the show in his long knit underwear." (*The People's
Almanac*)

KITTY LITTER
In January 1948, in Cassopolis, Michigan, a woman named Kay
Draper ran into trouble: the sandpile she used to fill her cat's litter
box was frozen solid. She tried ashes, but wound up with paw prints
all over the house. Sawdust didn't work, either.

As it happened, her neighbors, the Lowes, sold a product called
Fuller's Earth, a kiln-dried clay that was used to soak up oil and
grease spills in factories. Ed Lowe, their 27-year-old son, had been
looking for a new market for the stuff—he'd tried unsuccessfully to
sell it to local farmers as nesting material for chickens. On the spur

In India, playing cards are round.

of the moment, he convinced Draper that this stuff would make great cat litter. He really had no idea if it would…but it did! He sensed the sales potential, put some Fuller's Earth in paper bags and labeled it "Kitty Litter" with a grease pen. Then he drove around, trying to sell it. (Actually, he gave it away at first to get people to try it.) Once people tried it, they invariably came back for more.

"The success of kitty litter enabled pet owners to keep cats inside their homes with little muss or fuss (let's not discuss smell). As a result, an entire industry consisting of cat foods, toys, grooming products, and the like was launched." (*Useless Information* Web site)

RUGBY
William Webb Ellis was playing soccer at the Rugby School in Warwickshire, England, in 1823. His team was losing so badly that he grabbed the ball (a foul—in soccer, you're not allowed to touch the ball with your hands) and started running for the opposing goal. When he got close he drop-kicked the ball into the goal. The score didn't count, of course, and the captain of Ellis's team was so embarrassed that after apologizing to the officials, he suspended Ellis from the team.

The tale of "that play at Rugby" circulated for years afterward, and in 1839 Arthur Pell, the star forward of the Cambridge soccer team, drew up some rules for a new game—named after the Rugby School—that legalized holding, throwing, and running with the ball. The new sport was also the direct forerunner of American football. (*Fenton & Fowler's Best, Worst and Most Unusual*)

AEROSOL CANS
In 1943 the U.S. Agriculture Department came up with an aerosol bug bomb. It used liquid gas inside steel cans to help WWII soldiers fight malaria-causing insects (malaria was taking a heavy toll on the troops). By 1947, civilians could buy bug bombs, too, but they were heavy "grenadelike" things. Two years later, Robert H. Abplanalp developed a special "seven-part leak-proof" valve that allowed him to use lightweight aluminum instead of heavy steel, creating the modern spray can.

In the U.S., what sporting good outsells baseballs, basketballs, and footballs *combined*? Frisbees.

IT FITS YOU TO A "T"

A brief history of the most popular shirt in the world.

YOU BE THE JUDGE
T-shirts have been around so long that nobody knows for
sure where they originated or how they got their name. One
theory: They were first worn by longshoremen who unloaded tea
from merchant ships in Annapolis Maryland during the 17th century. They became known as "tea shirts" and eventually "T-shirts."

Another theory: They were invented by the British Royal Family
for use by sailors in the Royal Navy. According to that version,
"the monarchy ordered sailors to sew sleeves on their undershirts to
spare royalty the unseemly experience of witnessing an armada of
armpits. Ergo, the shirt shaped like the letter T."

UNDERSHIRTS ARE SUNK

T-shirts were part of American life as early as 1913, when the U.S.
Navy added crew-necked cotton undershirts to its uniform. But
they were generally limited to military use. To most American
men, the only *real* undershirt was the sleeveless variety, "with over-
the-shoulder straps, a deep neck and totally exposed armpits."

These, however, were dealt a serious blow in 1934 by actor Clark
Gable. In the Oscar-winning film *It Happened One Night*, Gable
took off his shirt...and wasn't wearing anything underneath.

"Hardly a young man from coast to coast would be caught wearing one after that." Jim Murray writes in the *Los Angeles Times*. "It
almost wrecked an industry, put people out of work."

By then, the T-shirt's transition from underwear to outerwear
was already underway, and in the early 1930s, some sports shops began selling shirts with university insignias on them. But they were
still primarily considered undershirts. In 1938 Sears, Roebuck &
Co. added the "gob-style" short-sleeved undershirts (U.S. Navy
sailors were known as "gobs") to its catalog. Price: 24¢ apiece. They
sold poorly—it was still too soon after the Gable fiasco.

If you tried to count off a billion seconds, it would take you 31.7 years.

T-SHIRT FASHION

It wasn't until World War II that T-shirts really began to take hold in American culture. Each branch of the military issued millions of "skivvies" in its own color, and in the Pacific islands it was so hot that they were virtually the only shirts that most soldiers wore. When the fighting boys returned home from the war, they brought their taste for T-shirts with them.

"For a while," says J. D. Reed in *Smithsonian* magazine, the T-shirt suggested the kind of crew-cut cleanliness and neatness indigenous to the new, postwar suburbs." Then in 1951, the movies struck again: Marlon Brando electrified audiences by wearing a skin-tight T-shirt in Tennessee Williams's *A Street Car Named Desire*. The actor's rippling muscles "gave the garment a sexual *je ne sais quoi* from which America has never recovered," writes one critic. "Elvis Presley cheered it on, sneering in a T-shirt and leather jacket. And James Dean perpetuated the Attitude-with-a-T look in *Rebel Without a Cause* in 1955."

By the end of the 1950s, the T-shirt was no longer just a piece of underwear—it was a fashion statement. Today the American T-shirt industry sells over a billion T-shirts a year. The average American owns 25 of them.

* * *

NEXT TIME YOU USE DUCT TAPE...

...Think about this: "Duct tape was invented in 1930 by Johnson & Johnson—the Band-Aid people—as a white waterproof cloth tape for use in hospitals. They called it Drybak. It didn't acquire its modern name and distinctive gray color until after World War II, when air-conditioning took off and sealing air-conditioning ducts became an occupation....

"Americans use 250 million square yards of duct tape a year. How much is that? Well, if it takes a foot or so to reattach a floppy shoe sole, you could fix 13.5 billion shoes a year, a pair for everyone on the planet, and still have enough left over to repair a La-Z-Boy recliner."

—Vince Staten, *Did Monkeys Invent the Monkey Wrench?*

The Statue of Liberty is patented.

STRANGE CELEBRITY LAWSUITS

Uncle John noticed that a number of the cases in our "Strange Lawsuits" file involve celebrities of one sort or another. Here's a sampling.

THE PLAINTIFF: Mark Twain

THE DEFENDANT: Estes and Lauriat Publishing Co.

THE LAWSUIT: In 1876 the Canadian publishers pirated the text of Twain's book *Tom Sawyer* and put out a low-priced edition. It cut into legitimate U.S. sales and deprived Twain of royalties. When he wrote *The Adventures of Huckleberry Finn* in 1884, he was determined to prevent a recurrence. He decided to publish *Huck Finn* himself...but hold off printing it until he had orders for 40,000 copies. That way, the book pirates wouldn't have a chance to undercut him.

Yet somehow, Estes and Lauriat got hold of a manuscript and started selling a pirated edition two months *before* Twain's authorized edition was available. Livid, Twain sued them.

THE VERDICT: Believe it or not, Twain lost the case. He issued this statement: "[The judge has allowed the publisher] to sell property which does not belong to him but me—property which he has not bought and I have not sold. Under this same ruling, I am now advertising the judge's homestead for sale; and if I make as good a sum out of it as I expect, I shall go on and sell the rest of his property."

THE PLAINTIFFS: Ten people named Jeff Stone, including the mayor of Temecula, California, a guy who works for NASA; and Paul Peterson—who isn't actually a Jeff Stone, but played a character with that name on TV's "Donna Reed Show" from 1958 to 1966

THE DEFENDANT: Jeff Gillooly, Tonya Harding's infamous ex-husband, who had served seven months in jail for plotting the 1994 attack on her skating rival, Nancy Kerrigan

---

The Oval Office in the White House is only 22 feet long.

THE LAWSUIT: In 1995 Gillooly filed to change his name to Jeff Stone (so he could have some anonymity.) Other Jeff Stones announced that they were outraged. Mayor Stone said his "hard-earned good name would be sullied"; Peterson insisted Gillooly was mocking his sitcom; NASA's Stone spread the word that he simply didn't want to share his name with Gillooly. And then they sued to prevent it.

THE VERDICT: In a ten-minute hearing, the judge ruled there was no basis for stopping Gillooly from becoming a Jeff Stone.

THE PLAINTIFF: Saddam Hussein

THE DEFENDANT: *Le Nouvel Observateur,* a French magazine

THE LAWSUIT: In an article about Hussein, the magazine described him as a "monster," an "executioner," "a complete cretin," and a "noodle." Saddam sued for libel.

THE VERDICT: Case dismissed.

THE PLAINTIFF: A dentist

THE DEFENDANTS: Johnny Carson and NBC

THE LAWSUIT: In the early 1980s, during a broadcast of the "Tonight Show," Carson mentioned he'd seen a report saying that dentists were closing their offices due to lack of business. "News like this," he quipped, "hasn't made me so happy since I heard the Gestapo disbanded." An angry dentist immediately sued Carson and the station for $1 million for libel.

THE VERDICT: Case dismissed.

THE PLAINTIFF: Dustin Hoffman

THE DEFENDANT: *Los Angeles* magazine

THE LAWSUIT: In its March 1997 issue, the magazine superimposed a picture of Hoffman's face—from the film *Tootsie,* in which he dressed as a woman—on a the body of a model "wearing a smashing gown and smart high heels." The caption: "Dustin Hoffman isn't a drag in a butter-colored silk gown by Richard Tyler and Ralph Lauren heels." Hoffman sued for $5 million, saying they had turned him into "an unpaid fashion model."

THE VERDICT: Calling Hoffman "one of our greatest living treasures," the judge ordered the magazine to pay the actor $3 million.

HOW TO MAKE A MONSTER, PART I

Godzilla is one of the most popular movie monsters in film history.
We told you the story of King Kong in the Giant 10th Anniversary
Bathroom Reader. *Now here's the story behind Japan's largest export.*

NUCLEAR AGE

On March 1, 1954, at the Bikini atoll in the South Pacific, the United States tested the world's first hydrogen bomb. It was 1,000 times more powerful than the A-bombs that had been dropped on Hiroshima nine years earlier.

American ships were warned to stay out of the test area...but because the project was top-secret, the U.S. government provided little advance warning to other countries. U.S. officials were certain that the resulting nuclear fallout would land in an empty expanse of the Pacific Ocean and no one would be in jeopardy.

Unfortunately, they were wrong. The fallout didn't travel in the direction they expected, and a small Japanese fishing boat named the *Daigo Fukuryo Maru* ("Lucky Dragon") was in the area where the nuclear cloud came to earth. Within hours of the blast, the boat's entire crew became violently ill from radiation poisoning. On September 23, 1954, after more than six months of agony, a radioman named Aikichi Huboyama died.

The fate of the crew of the *Daigo Fukuryo Maru* made international news. In Japan, headlines like "The Second Atomic Bombing of Mankind" compared the incident to the bombing of Hiroshima and Nagasaki in 1945.

ART IMITATES LIFE

While all of this was going on, Japanese movie producer Tomoyuki Tanaka arrived in Indonesia to oversee a film called *Beyond the Glory*. It was scheduled to be the main release for Japan's Toho Studios the following year but it never got off the ground; the Indonesian government refused to issue work visas to the film's two stars.

Suddenly, Tanaka found himself with time, money, and actors— but no film to make. In addition, Toho Studios had a big hole in their release schedule. The producer had to come up with a new movie concept...*fast.*

On his flight back to Tokyo, Tanaka stared out the window at the ocean below, desperately trying to think of something. His mind wandered to the H-Bomb tests in the South Pacific and the crew of the *Daigo Fukuryo Maru*...and then it hit him: He would combine an American-style monster movie with a serious message about the threat of radiation and nuclear weapons tests.

PROJECT G

Commercially, it made sense. For obvious reasons, the Japanese public was very concerned about nuclear testing. And in theaters, monster movies were hot. The 1933 classic, *King Kong*, had been re-released in 1952 and made more than $3 million in international ticket sales—four times what it had earned the first time around. *Time* magazine even named the giant ape "Monster of the Year." Its huge success inspired a "monster-on-the-loose" film craze.

One of the first to cash in on the fad was *The Beast from 20,000 Fathoms*, which featured a dinosaur attacking New York City after nuclear tests awakened it from a million-year sleep. The film cost $400,000 to make and was a critical flop—but with $5 million in box office receipts, it was one of the top-grossing movies of the year.

Tanaka got approval from his studio to do a Japanese version. He hired a prominent Japanese science fiction writer to write a knock-off screenplay tentatively titled *Big Monster from 200,000 Miles Beneath the Sea*, but he still wasn't sure what kind of monster to use, or what to call it. So to start out, the film was referred to simply as "Project G" (for Giant).

A PAIR OF EXPERTS

Meanwhile, he began assembling a crew. For director, Tanaka picked Ishiro Honda, a documentary filmmaker who had been Akira Kurosawa's assistant on *The Seven Samurai* (considered the best Japanese film ever made by most critics). Like many of the Toho Studios crew, Honda was a veteran of the Imperial Army. He had visited Hiroshima several months after the atomic bomb was dropped. "When I returned from the war and passed through Hiroshima," he told an interviewer years later, "there was a heavy atmosphere—a fear that the Earth was already coming to an end. That became my basis. Believe it or not, we naively hoped that Godzilla's death in the film was going to coincide with the end of nuclear testing."

Special effects were handled by Eiji Tsuburaya. During the war, he had made unusual propaganda films for the Imperial Army—he recreated battles in miniature, so Japanese movie audiences could follow the progress of the war. His work was so skillful that when the American occupation forces got hold of his reenactment of the bombing of Pearl Harbor, they were convinced they were watching actual combat footage. Since childhood, Eiji had dreamed of making monster movies with his miniature sets. Now he would have his opportunity.

FAT CHANCE

As it turned out, finding a name for the monster was easy. "At the time there was a big—I mean huge—fellow working in Toho's publicity department," director Ishiro Honda recalled. "Employees would argue, 'that guy is as big as a gorilla.' 'No, he's almost as big as a *kujira* (whale).' Over time, the two mixed and he was nicknamed 'Gojira' (pronounced GO-dzee-la). So when we were stuck for a name, Tanaka said, 'Hey, you know that guy over in publicity...?' "

The name *Gojira* would turn out to be a great choice, but in the beginning it was very confusing. "Very few people, even the cast, knew what Gojira would be," says actor Yoshio Tsuchiya. "Since the name was derived from *kujira* [whale] and gorilla, I imagined some kind of giant aquatic gorilla."

GETTING STARTED

Since the scenes using human actors were filmed separately from the special-effects monster footage, Honda didn't have to wait for Tanaka to work out the monster details before beginning to film. And he didn't: "Honda would direct me to act surprised that Gojira was coming," recalled actor Yu Fujiki, who played a sailor in the film. "But since I didn't know what Gojira would look like, it was kind of weird. So I asked Honda what Gojira would be like, and he said, 'I don't know, but anyway, the monster is coming!'"

For Part II of How to Make a Monster, turn to page 271.

First president to shake hands in greeting: Thomas Jefferson. Earlier presidents bowed.

DUMB CROOKS

With crooks like these, we hardly need cops.
Here's proof that crime doesn't pay.

GIVE ME ALL YOUR COUPONS

OSWEGO, New York—"His *name* may be Jesse James, but that's where any similarity ends. Jesse Clyde James IV was arrested last week after he used his shopper's bonus card to get a discount…just before allegedly robbing a grocery store.

"Police said James asked a market clerk if three pies would be cheaper if he used his card, police said. The clerk scanned the card. Then James and two accomplices pulled out a pellet gun and demanded money, police said. They made off with $600. James was arrested soon after."

—Medford, Oregon, *Mail Tribune*, June 8, 1999

MUG SHOT

"There are dumb criminals, and then there's the fellow who was found guilty of stealing Matthew Holden's car in London. In the glove compartment, the thief found a camera, which his girlfriend used to photograph him posing with the car in front of his own house. The vehicle was later recovered—with the camera and film still inside. Holden had it developed and brought the prints to the cops on the case…who recognized the crook, and arrested him."

—*Christian Science Monitor*, July 26, 1999

CAUGHT WITH HIS PANTS DOWN

"Knife-wielding James Boulder was caught in September 1993 when his [pants] fell down as he fled from a store in New Jersey that he'd just robbed. He then tripped over a fire hydrant and knocked himself out."

—*The Fortean Times Book of Inept Crime*

DUMB AND UNLUCKY

CARDIFF, Wales—"Mark Cason, 29, decided to rob a local post office. He purchased gloves and a mask but forgot to put them on.…

"Mark took more than $15,000 worth of British pounds, but his arms were so full he could not open the post office door to leave. So he asked two children to hold the door for him. They did, and jotted down his car license number as he pulled into traffic.

"Mark promptly got stuck in a traffic jam, so he ran to a train station, where he caught a train to a nearby town. He checked into a hotel using a fake name and said to the clerk, 'If the police ask for me, I'm not here.' He asked if he could put 'a large amount of money' in the hotel safe.

"When police arrived, Mark told them his occupation was 'armed robber.' He was sentenced to five years in prison."

—The *Portland Oregonian*

NO ANCHOVIES, PLEASE

"Christopher Kennedy, 36, and Johnny Poston, 26, allegedly ordered a couple of pizzas using their real names, phone number and home address. When the delivery man had trouble finding their house, he called and arranged to meet the two men nearby.

"'The delivery person got out carrying the pizzas and they put a gun to his face,' Lt. Julius Lee said. 'So the delivery person threw the pizzas at them, got back in his car and drove off.' He called the police, who had no problem finding the correct house. The pair was charged with armed robbery."

—*Dumb Crooks* Web site

HOW 'BOUT A BREAKFAST BURRITO?

YPSILANTI, Michigan—"The *Ann Arbor News* reported that a man failed to rob a Burger King because the clerk told him he couldn't open the cash register without a food order. So the man ordered onion rings, but the clerk informed him that they weren't available for breakfast. The frustrated robber left."

—*A Treasury of Police Humor*

RIGHTEOUSLY INDIGNANT

"A robbery suspect in a Los Angeles police lineup apparently just couldn't control himself. When detectives asked each man in the lineup to repeat the words, 'Give me all your money or I'll shoot,' the man shouted *'That's not what I said!'*"

—The *Edge*, April 12, 1999

Fast food: A bat can eat as many as 1,000 insects an hour.

THE REAL
POP ARTISTS

*The works of pop artists like Andy Warhol and Roy
Lichtenstein sell for millions of dollars…but what about the
artists who created images that are really part of popular
culture—do they make millions, too? Not quite.*

HARVEY BALL
Famous Work of Art: The smiley face
Compensation: $45

Inspiration: In 1963 the Massachusetts-based State Mutual Life
Insurance Company took over a small Ohio insurance company.
The transition was so rocky that State Mutual launched an internal
"friendship" campaign to improve staff morale. They hired Ball, a
freelance artist, to come up with a friendly graphic for a lapel button employees could wear. He came up with the smiley face.

State Mutual made up about 100 buttons and used the graphic in
a consumer ad showing President John Adams wearing one. That
was about it…until tens of thousands of people who saw the ad
wrote to the company asking for buttons. State Mutual Life took
advantage of the PR opportunity and distributed them until the
late 1960s. Then the symbol took on a life of its own and was used
on everything from clocks to underwear.

Note: Ball never filed for a copyright or a trademark, and never
made any more money off his creation. But he's angry now: In 1998
he learned that a Frenchman named Franklin Loufrani had trademarked the design in France…and owns the symbol in 79 other
countries. Loufrani, who's made millions from the smiley face,
claims he invented it in 1968 "to illustrate positive stories" after
student riots rocked France that year. However, there are photographs taken in 1964 that disprove this.

Ball says he's less concerned about the money than he is about
receiving credit for inventing the design. "Never in the history of
mankind or art," he says, "has any single piece of art gotten such

---

Mayonnaise is an excellent skin moisturizer.

widespread favor, pleasure, enjoyment, and nothing has ever been so simply done and so easily understood in art."

PHIL KRACZKOWSKI

Famous Work of Art: The original GI Joe head (see page 331)
Compensation: $600
Inspiration: In 1963 Hasbro was planning the first boy's doll ever. They spent most of their time creating a fully articulated body...then realized they still needed a head. So they contacted Kraczkowski.

"I asked them exactly what they wanted," Kraczkowski recalls, "and they said they would like a young, good-looking American man....It wasn't a big deal because I was used to doing faces....I did the Kennedy-Johnson inaugural medal, the Johnson-Humphrey inaugural medal. I had three sittings with J. Edgar Hoover for a life-size bust."

The executives didn't tell Kraczkowski the young man was going to be a soldier—that was top secret. "They said the head had to fit a certain doll," Kraczkowski says. "I said okay."

Ten days later, he turned in the head. "Apparently it was perfect," Kraczkowski says. "Does GI Joe look like John Kennedy? I'd done...full busts of him preceding the GI Joe project, so maybe the resemblance got in there subconsciously....I made six hundred dollars on the project —pretty good money. My first and last toy job."

CAROLYN DAVIDSON

Famous Work of Art: The Nike Swoosh
Compensation: $35
Inspiration: In 1972 the Portland, Oregon–based Blue Ribbon Shoe Company was looking for a new name and logo. They couldn't afford a big-time graphics firm, so the company's founder, Phil Knight, asked an art student from nearby Portland State University to design something. It was Carolyn Davidson's first "real job."

Knight wanted to imitate the Adidas logo—a stripe that was "functional" because it provided support, but looked "distinctive." "Try to make it reflect movement and speed," he told Davidson.

But, as J. B. Strasser and Laurie Becklund write in their book *Swoosh*, that wasn't so easy. "Davidson fretted for hours over her designs, coming up with, among other ideas, a thick stripe with a hole in the middle. After hours of frustration, she informed Knight that support and movement were hard to reconcile, graphically speaking. Support was static, movement was the opposite. She recommended he incorporate the support system into the shoe itself, and that he use the stripe to convey movement."

None of the shoe execs were particularly enthusiastic about Davidson's designs. But they flipped through her drawings and finally settled on "a fat, fleshy checkmark."

"I don't love it," Knight told Davidson, "but I think it'll grow on me." She named her own price for the work.

Note: The company's new name, Nike (the goddess of victory in Greek mythology), was selected a few days later. The term "swoosh" had been coined to describe the fabric of an early shoe; today no one remembers why or when it became associated with the logo.

GARY ANDERSON

Famous Work of Art: The recycling symbol

Compensation: $2,500

Inspiration: In 1970 Anderson, a 23-year-old college senior at the University of Southern California, entered an Earth Day contest to produce a universal symbol of recycling. It was sponsored by the Container Corporation of America (CCA), one of America's largest producers of recycled paper.

Anderson based his symbol on the Möbius strip, which is created by twisting a piece of paper once over and connecting the tips to create a continuous, single-edged, one-sided surface. CCA allowed Anderson's design to become public domain, and now it belongs to everyone. Anderson works at an "engineering, architectural, and planning firm" in Baltimore, and remains "environmentally concerned."

*   *   *

"Ever wonder if illiterate people get the full effect of alphabet soup?"

—John Mendoza

The Mayan Empire lasted six times as long as the Roman Empire.

VIDEO TREASURES

Ever found yourself at a video store staring at thousands of films you've never heard of, wondering which ones are worth watching? It happens to us all the time—so we decided to offer a few recommendations.

CHAN IS MISSING (1982) *Comedy (B&W)*
Review: "Two cab drivers try to find the man who stole their life savings. Wry, low-budget comedy filmed in San Francisco's Chinatown was an art-house smash. The first full-length American film produced exclusively by an Asian-American crew." (*VideoHound's Golden Movie Retriever*) *Director:* Wayne Wang.

THE YEAR OF LIVING DANGEROUSLY (1983) *Drama*
Review: "Indonesia, 1965: In the middle of revolutionary fervor, a wet-behind-the-ears reporter and a member of the British Embassy find steamy romance. This politically charged, mega-atmospheric winner has the romance and intrigue of a modern *Casablanca*." (*Seen That, Now What?*) *Stars:* Sigourney Weaver, Mel Gibson, Linda Hunt (won an Oscar for the role). *Director:* Peter Weir.

THE BIG SLEEP (1946) *Mystery*
Review: "One of the most stylish and satisfying film noir mysteries of the '40s. Lauren Bacall is at her sexiest and Humphrey Bogart is at his peak. The plot is exquisitely intricate, so don't blink—and DON'T MISS THIS MOVIE. The atmosphere and dialogue are impeccable." (*Mark Satern's Illustrated Guide to Video's Best*)

EUROPA, EUROPA (1991) *French-German/Drama*
Review: "Based on the death-defying autobiography of Solomon Perel, this stunning film traces the author's real-life adventures during World War II. A Jewish teenager accepted into the Nazi Youth Party, Perel sees the war from all sides in this ironic, spine-tingling story." (*Video Movie Guide*) *Director:* Agnieszka Holland

CHASING AMY (1997) *Romantic Comedy*
Review: "Winning, original comedy-drama about a comic book artist who lives with his dour work partner—until he meets an attractive up-and-coming female artist with a dynamic personality. He's seriously smitten—and stays that way even after learning that she's

---

An *anemophobic* person is someone who's afraid of high winds.

gay. Writer-director Kevin Smith hits all the right notes in this honest and appealing film, which refuses to take the easy way out (just like his lead character) right to the end." (*Leonard Maltin's 1998 Movie and Video Guide*) *Stars:* Ben Affleck, Joey Lauren Adams.

THE MAN WHO SHOT LIBERTY VALANCE (1962) *Western*
Review: "One of the greatest of director John Ford's westerns, a moving, bitter meditation of immortality and survival. Jimmy Stewart is cast as an idealistic lawyer who becomes famous for killing a notorious badman, played by Lee Marvin. John Wayne incarnates his own with subtle melancholy." (*Movies on TV*)

TAMPOPO (1986) *Japanese / Social comedy*
Review: "The tale of a Japanese widow who perfects the art of making noodles under the instruction of an urban cowboy truck driver is cleverly interspersed with amusing vignettes about food and social pretension. Funny, enjoyable, and you'll find yourself craving a bowl of hot ramen." (*Seen That, Now What?*) *Director:* Juzo Itami.

THE EMERALD FOREST (1985) *Adventure*
Review: "Captivating adventure about a young boy who is kidnapped by a primitive tribe of Amazons while his family is traveling through the Brazilian jungle. Boothe is the father who searches 10 years for him. An engrossing look at tribal life in the vanishing jungle. Beautifully photographed and based upon a true story." (*VideoHound's Golden Movie Retriever*) *Director:* John Boorman.

A GREAT WALL (1986) *Comedy*
Review: "A warm comedy about the clash of cultures that results when a Chinese-American family returns to its homeland. It is the first American movie to be made in the People's Republic of China. As such, it gives some fascinating insights into Chinese culture and often does so in a marvelously entertaining way." (*Video Movie Guide*) *Director/Star:* Peter Wang.

THE NASTY GIRL (1990) *German/Drama*
Review: "A teenage girl innocently decides to write about 'My Town in the Third Reich'...and her research reveals the truth behind the good citizens' official story. Based on a true story." (*Seen That, Now What?*) *Director:* Michael Verhoeven.

MYTH-SPOKEN

*We hate to say it (well actually, we like to say it), but some of
the best-known quotes in history weren't said by the people
they're attributed to...and some weren't even said at all!*

Line: "Go west, young man, go west."
Supposedly Said By: Horace Greeley, publisher of the *New
York Tribune*, in 1851
Actually: Even in 1851, big-city media had all the influence.
Greeley merely reprinted an article from the Terre Haute, Indiana,
Express, but ever since, people have identified it with him. The line
was really written by a "now forgotten and never very famous" news-
paperman named John Soule.

Line: "Taxation without representation is tyranny!"
Supposedly Said By: James Otis, a lawyer arguing in a Boston court
against British search warrants, in 1761
Actually: For years, schoolchildren were taught that this was "the
rallying cry of the American Revolution." But no one in Otis's time
ever mentioned him saying it. It wasn't until 1820, almost 60 years
later, that John Adams referred to the phrase for the first time.

Line: "This is a great wall!"
Supposedly Said By: President Richard Nixon
Actually: It's one of the lines used to denigrate Nixon...and he *did*
say it to Chinese officals in 1972 when he saw the Great Wall for
the first time. But it's a bum rap. As Paul Boller and John George
write in *They Never Said It*:

> This was not his complete sentence, and out of context it sounds
> silly. It is only fair to put it back into its setting: "When one stands
> here," Nixon declared, "and sees the wall going to the peak of this
> mountain and realizes it runs for hundreds of miles—as a matter of
> fact, thousands of miles—over the mountains and through the valleys
> of this country and that it was built over 2,000 years ago, I think you
> would have to conclude that this is a great wall and that it had to be
> built by a great people."

The fishing reel was invented around the year 300 A.D.

Line: "Let them eat cake."

Supposedly Said By: Marie Antoinette, Queen of France, when she was told that conditions were so bad that the peasants had no bread to eat

Actually: She was alleged to have said it just before the French Revolution. But the phrase had already been used by then. It has been cited as an old parable by philosopher Henri Rousseau in 1778—a decade or so before Marie Antoinette supposedly said it. Chances are, it was a rumor spread by her political enemies.

Line: "There are three kinds of lies: lies, damn lies, and statistics."

Supposedly Said By: Mark Twain

Actually: Twain, one of America's most quotable writers, was quoting someone else: Prime Minister Benjamin Disraeli of England.

Line: "Keep the government poor and remain free."

Supposedly Said By: Justice Oliver Wendell Holmes

Actually: Ronald Reagan said it in a speech. But it wasn't written by a speechwriter. Reagan's "speechwriting office" told a reporter, "He came up with that one himself."

*   *   *

CRÈME DE LA CRUD

The Portsmouth Symphonia was unique in that fully-two thirds of its members did not know how to play a musical instrument. Result: Their music (if you could call it that) was appallingly bad…but also "refreshingly original," one reviewer wrote. "Unhampered by preordained melody, the orchestra tackled the great compositions, agreeing only on when they should start and finish. The cacophony which resulted was naturally an immense hit."

Conductor Leonard Bernstein credited the Symphonia with "changing his attitude to The William Tell Overture forever." The Symphonia recorded two records, both of which "became very popular, demonstrating yet again the public's great appreciation of incompetence."

Fully grown, Argentina's falabella horses are only 16" tall. They're the smallest horses on Earth.

"SPEAK FOR YOURSELF, JOHN!"

Ever let someone speak for you? Sometimes it works, sometimes it doesn't. The other day Uncle John was in the...uh...reading room with nothing but a book of poetry. He opened it to Longfellow's "The Courtship of Myles Standish," and emerged wondering out loud how often "that sort of thing" happened. We took the hint and began looking for examples. Here's what we found.

MARRIAGE PROPOSAL
Who Said It: John Alden
Speaking For: Myles Standish

What Happened: As military leader of the pilgrims, Capt. Myles Standish was fearless. With ladies, however, he was the opposite. Standish was so afraid of expressing his love to Priscilla Mullens that he asked his young friend Alden to do it for him. The only problem: Alden was also in love with Mullens. Nonetheless, he went off to proclaim Standish's love to the woman, keeping his own a secret.

As it happened, Mullens harbored her own secret feelings for Alden. When Alden delivered Standish's proposal instead, legend has it she replied, "Why don't you speak for yourself, John?"

Note: Mullens married Alden. Standish supposedly went into the woods for a few days and sulked. He eventually got over it.

HISTORIC SPEECH

Who Said It: Norman Shelley
Speaking For: Winston Churchill

What Happened: A week after the demoralizing defeat of British and French troops by Germany at Dunkirk in 1940, Prime Minister Winston Churchill made one of the most stirring radio addresses in history. Speaking to the English public, he declared, in no uncertain terms, that the British would not fold.

> We shall fight on the beaches, we shall fight on the landing grounds, we shall fight in the fields and in the streets, we shall fight in the hills; we shall never surrender.

World's highest city: Lhasa, Tibet, at 12,087 feet above sea level.

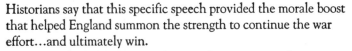

Historians say that this specific speech provided the morale boost that helped England summon the strength to continue the war effort...and ultimately win.

But Churchill didn't make the speech. He was "too busy to appear on the radio," so he asked Shelley to fill in—an actor who had perfected the Churchillian delivery to such a degree that few people could pick which voice was Shelley's and which was Churchill's.

PRESIDENTIAL QUOTE
Who Said It: Larry Speakes
Speaking For: President Ronald Reagan
What Happened: In 1985 President Reagan and Soviet premier Mikhail Gorbachev met for a summit in Reykjavik, Iceland. Afterward, Speakes told the press that Reagan had declared to the Russian: "There is much that divides us, but I believe the world breathes easier because we are talking together."

In truth, Reagan hadn't said it—or anything Speakes considered worth quoting that day. So the press secretary made it up. No one at the White House objected at the time. But when Speakes later admitted it in his 1988 book *Speaking Out*, all hell broke loose. The press was "outraged," and Reagan (who had to have at least implicitly condoned it at the time) strongly condemned the quotes as "fiction." Speakes paid for it: he was pressured to resign his job as senior public relations officer at Merrill Lynch, which had hired him after he left the White House. Speakes later apologized publicly for his "mistake."

PHILOSOPHICAL RAMBLINGS
Who Said It: Yoda
Speaking For: Obi-Wan-Kenobi (Alec Guinness)
What Happened: On the set of *The Empire Strikes Back*, Alec Guinness had an easy way of avoiding dialogue he didn't feel comfortable saying. Yoda was in nearly all of his scenes, so "if he didn't want to deliver one of his philosophical speeches," Dale Pollock writes in *Skywalking*, "he'd say to the director, 'Why doesn't the little green thing do this one?'" And Lucas would accommodate him.

WHAT SUPERMARKETS KNOW ABOUT YOU

This excerpt is from Jack Hitt's article in The New York Times *Sunday magazine, March 10, 1996.*

BACKGROUND. Ever wonder why toothbrushes are often at eye level, or why soup is not alphabetized? Perhaps you thought there was only one postulate in the world of supermarket design: put milk at one end, bread at the other and force the shopper to trek the length of the place. Friend, that was eons ago.

It turns out that each inch of space is scientifically calibrated to hold only what you will buy at the highest profit margin—a layout that is the culmination of complex experiments regarding displays, observational studies of the way customers move through stores, and intricate research on the effects of lighting, color and music.

Grocers now hire professional designers to shape a store's interior—its tables, stalls and shelves (known as gondolas), and the 30,000 products typically displayed—into a landscape that lures us in, moves us deliberately about and sends us back out the door with bulging grocery bags.

FIELD STUDY

When the [supermarket] doors open, the vision is of a cornucopia of bright fruit and vegetables spilling out into a lascivious spread. Many supermarkets begin with produce; others open with flowers. The idea is to introduce the consumer into a realm of freshness, color and beauty.

The choices can be bewildering: quince, gold tamarillo and horned melon; portobello, crimini, button, oyster and shiitake mushrooms; every combination of herb-flavored oils and vinegars.

But most people simply grab the five-pound of Florida navel oranges or the discount sack of McIntosh apples.

Supermarket designers know you. Their layout is a chaotic opera of flattery, making you feel that you're a chef picking over the finest in meats, the most delicate in fresh greens, the best in imported condiments, even as your cart fills with familiar hamburger meat and iceberg lettuce and prepared cake mixes.

127 people ran the first New York City Marathon in 1970; 32,000 ran in 1998.

Sure, here is a cooler overflowing with cheeses from every valley. But around the corner is a monster display of old standards—cheddar, American, Swiss, mozzarella—hung in handy packets.

SHOPPER'S STATS

To comprehend today's supermarket design, first know how well supermarkets comprehend you.

• The boys in the lab say you're probably female, although increasingly you're male. You shop on average 2.2 times per week in supermarkets, according to one of shopping's many think tanks, the Coca-Cola Retailing Research Council. A mere 31 percent of you arrive with a list, but it doesn't matter: only a third of your purchases are planned. The others, sometimes called "splurches," are nearly as predictable. The vast majority of you who sample a product will then buy it.

• The average "eye height" of a woman is 59 inches; a man's is 64 inches. And because the best viewing angle is 15 degrees below the horizontal, the choicest elevations on any aisle are between 51 and 53 inches off the floor. When you examine a shelf, you like to stand about four feet away, on average.

• Experiments show that if the store's layout encourages you to turn your cart in one direction, you will look the other way into the turn's "strong side." There, a cunning grocer will place what seems to be—but isn't—a good deal. The motive is to "push" you into making approaches ("shots") at a display or "facing." Other notorious locations include "in-aisle gondolas" (you may be robbed here) or "endcaps" (same chances).

• On any given visit shoppers spend an average of 35 to 40 minutes in a supermarket. For each minute beyond, you will spend about $2 more.

• If background music is slowed from a lively allegro of 108 beats per minute to a simple adagio of 60 beats, researchers report, then the speed of the average cart slows, more shots are taken and purchases soar by as much as 38.2%.

• According to packaging researchers, what brands you select will depend on your "need state" at the time—dieting, economizing, indulging, or impressing guests. Researchers have also learned that you buy more soup if it's not shelved in alphabetical order.

On average, grocery shoppers spend 8 minutes waiting in line at the supermarket.

If alphabetized, sales drop exactly 6 percent. If toothbrushes are placed at eye level, sales increase by 8 percent—no more, no less.

• Cereal arranged by type (brans, flakes) rather than by brand will fall 5 percent in sales. With roughly 150 brands competing for shelf space, one common strategy is the use of "flankers." These are simple variations of the highly profitable name brands—either outsized boxes or slightly altered flavors such as Apple Cinnamon or Honey Nut. The new products are dispatched to stand at the shoulders of the name brand. Their mission is to sop up precious shelf space. They may also complicate any effort on your part to make an easy price comparison with competing flagship brands.

SHIFT IN POWER

Power in a supermarket used to be held by the wholesaler, say, Campbell's Soup. Such brand-name companies were the only ones who knew what sold, judging from the shifts in warehouse inventory. So Campbell's could tell the supermarket that Turkey Noodle was hot that month, and relying on trust, the retailers responded. Now the power to know has been delivered to grocers by those familiar devices at the cash register that automatically record the price of each item as it is passed over a laser beam.

"The Universal Price Code (UPC) scanner put the retailer in charge," says Richard Rauch, a supermarket theorist and designer at Long Island University. "That device tells the retailer what customers are buying and at what price."

With such knowledge, retailers have found another source of profits. At the end of the day, a store manager can use a software program to crunch scanner information and create a landscape designed to wring the most splurches from each shopper.

BRAVE NEW SUPERMARKET

In the near future, data collection will become even more sophisticated. One manufacturer will have shopping carts that feature "promotronics"—a computerized screen to alert shoppers of nearby deals or new products. But it will also electronically generate a map of each cart's journey, culling information about which "shot" at what "facing" yielded a purchase.

…Slowly…More slowly… More time…More purchases…Lettuce… Slowly, now…Frozen popcorn shrimp…Sleepy, now…More slowly…

CARLINISMS

Irreverent thoughts from comedian George Carlin.

"The other night I ate at a real nice family restaurant. Every table had an argument going."

"If the shoe fits, get another one just like it."

"McDonald's 'breakfast for under a dollar' actually costs much more than that. You have to factor in the cost of coronary bypass surgery."

"Recently, in a public bathroom, I used the handicapped stall. As I emerged, a man in a wheelchair asked me indignantly, 'Are you handicapped?' Gathering all my aplomb, I looked him in the eye and said, 'Not now. But I was before I went in there.'"

"There is something refreshingly ironic about people lying on the beach contracting skin cancer in an attempt to acquire a purely illusory appearance of good health, while germ-laden medical waste washes up on the sand all around them."

"I think we should attack Russia now. They'd never expect it."

"Honesty may be the best policy, but it's important to remember that apparently, by elimination, dishonesty is the second-best policy."

"Some people see things that are and ask, Why? Some people dream of things that never were and ask, Why not? Some people have to go to work and don't have time for all that s**t."

"Who says life is sacred—God? Hey, if you read your history, God is one of the leading causes of death."

"A lot of times when they catch a guy who killed twenty-seven people, they say, 'He was a loner.' Well, of course he was a loner; he killed everyone he came in contact with."

"Whenever I hear about a 'peacekeeping force,' I wonder: If they're so interested in peace, why do they use force?"

"Most people work just hard enough not to get fired and get paid just enough money not to quit."

LET'S PLAY BALLBUSTER!

Millions of dollars were spent trying to make these toys work. But the only amusement they'll ever bring is a few bathroom laughs. Here are 6 classic toy flops.

BALLBUSTER

Product: No joke—the Mego Toy Co. introduced it in 1976 as "a family game that's loads of fun." It consisted of wire stalks attached to a gridlike base. Each was topped with a hinged red plastic ball. The object, according to Mego, was to "use your balls to bust your opponent's, if you can. Break 'em all and you're a winner!"

Problem: Somehow, Mego thought it could get away with the name. But the first preview of the Ballbuster TV commercial— shown to buyers from major toy and department stores—ended that illusion. The ad showed a family playing the game, after which the husband turned to his wife and said, "Honey, you're a *real* ball buster!" "The stunned silence that followed," Kirchner writes, "triggered the first suspicions that Ballbuster was not destined to displace Parcheesi in the pantheon of classic games."

FLUBBER

Product: Hasbro's Flubber was tied to Walt Disney's 1962 hit film, *Son of Flubber* (sequel to *The Absent Minded Professor*). It was similar to Silly Putty: "Flubber is a new parent-approved material that is non-toxic and will not stain," the company proclaimed. "Flubber acts amazing. It bounces so high. It floats like a boat. It flows and moves." Flubber was made out of synthetic rubber and mineral oil, so it was cheap to produce...but it was sold for a high profit. Hasbro, still a relatively small company at the time, was expecting a good year.

Problem: Flubber had one significant difference from Silly Putty— it made people sick. More than 1,600 kids and their parents came down with sore throats, full body rashes, and other reactions from handling the stuff. Hasbro had to recall Flubber...and then had to

---

Attention windsurfers: Wind speeds on Neptune can reach 1,500 mph.

find a way to get rid of several tons of it. Flubber floated, so they couldn't dump it in the ocean; they couldn't incinerate it, because it gave off "noxious black smoke"… so they buried it behind a new warehouse and put a parking lot over it. According to company legend, "on the hot summer days, Flubber oozed through cracks in the pavement—a primordial reminder of the vagaries of the toy business." Hasbro had been profitable in 1961, but Flubber almost put them out of business in 1963.

THE OOBIE

Product: It's the world's first—and so far, the last—hitchhiking toy, introduced by Parker Brothers at a time when hippies were bumming rides around the country and hitchhiking was still considered reasonably safe. Oobie was a clam-shaped plastic container with an address label and cartoon eyeballs painted on the lid. The idea was this: kids would write a note to a friend and put it inside, then put the friend's address on the outside and leave Oobie someplace where strangers would find it. If the stranger was headed in the direction of the address of the intended recipient, they could "help Oobie on his journey, hitchhiker style, across the street or across the country." With enough help, Oobie would eventually be delivered.

Problem: "Most parents," Paul Kirchner writes in *Forgotten Fads and Fabulous Flops*, "even in that more innocent age, did not like the idea that some pervert finding the Oobie would not only get their child's address, but be equipped with a splendid excuse to drop by. Parker Brothers quickly got the message—and Oobie was a dead letter."

ANGEL BABIES

Product: In the late 1970s, the Ideal Toy Corp. bought a product called "Fairies" from another toy company. They were tiny dolls with mechanical fluttering wings, and might have sold quite well… if an executive at Ideal hadn't insisted on changing the name to Angel Babies. They had to change the doll, too. "Now," says one toy industry insider, "they were these chunky little toddlers with halos and wings. They lived on clouds, played harps, very cute." Ideal introduced the toy at the annual New York Toy Fair in February, and waited for Christmas orders to pour in. They never came.

Problem: Ideal forgot something important. "The buyers said, 'OK, Angel Babies,'" recalls the toy industry insider. "'They're dead babies, right? Babies that died and now they're in heaven.' So of course, nobody would touch it." The product died an instant death (and went to…?).

THE ELVIS DOLL

Product: Hasbro made a fortune with New Kids on the Block dolls, so in 1994 they came up with another rock 'n' roll "sure thing"—a high-priced collector's doll of Elvis Presley. The Elvis stamp was a smash, and surveys showed that, 16 years after his death, the King was bigger than ever. Hasbro envisioned offering a new series of Elvis dolls every year, "enticing middle-aged women with memories and money to burn." Hasbro hired a top-notch sculptor to design the dolls, paid $1.5 million as an advance to Presley's estate, and put out the first three in the series.

At the end of December 1994, the company tried a limited sale of 16,000 dolls at Wal-Mart. With no advertising, they sold out in two weeks. It looked good for the big rollout in January, the anniversary of the King's birth.

Problem: It turned out that Elvis fanatics were the only ones seriously interested in the dolls—and once they finished snapping up their dolls in the first weeks, sales went into a freefall. Within a couple of months retailers had slashed prices from $40 to $19.99. Some retailers actually experienced *negative* sales, as angry shoppers who'd paid full price a week or two earlier returned to stores demanding a $20 refund. The Elvis doll, launched with one of the largest promotional campaigns in the history of the toy industry, ended up as one of Hasbro's biggest duds.

WORLD OF LOVE DOLLS

Product: Another Hasbro loser. World of Love Dolls were the company's response to the twin challenges of the astonishing success of Mattel's Barbie doll and the emerging hippie subculture. There were five dolls: Love, Peace, Flower, Adam, and Soul (an African American). Love, a longhaired blonde, was the doll that looked most like Barbie. "Love is today's teenager," the company's sales catalog read. "Love is what's happening."
Problem: Kids didn't want a World of Love—they wanted Barbie.

First hotel to stock Gideon Bibles: The Superior Hotel in Iron Mountain, Montana, in 1908.

CLASSIC HOAXES

The BRI library has a whole section of books on hoaxes and frauds. We've noticed that there are a few dozen hoaxes that appear in almost every book that set the standard for all hoaxers to come. Here are two of our favorites.

THE MANHATTAN ISLAND HOAX

Background: In 1824 a well-known retired carpenter and charismatic speaker named Lozier stood on a soapbox in Manhattan's busy Centre Market and announced to the crowd that because of all the buildings recently constructed, the southern tip of Manhattan Island had become too heavy and was in danger of sinking. The solution, he said, was to saw the island off at the northern end, tow it out to sea, turn it 180 degrees around, and reattach it.

Lozier claimed, that sawing Manhattan Island in half would be one of the biggest public works projects New York had ever seen, and that Mayor Stephen Allen had put him in charge of the project.

The idea sounded preposterous to most of Lozier's listeners; but then again, so had the Erie Canal, and that wonder of the world was nearly finished, wasn't it? Besides, if it wasn't true, why would he publicly declare that the mayor had authorized him to handle the project?

What Happened: Lozier began signing up hundreds of laborers for the task, offering triple wages to anyone willing to saw underwater. He directed blacksmiths and carpenters to begin designing the 100-foot saws and 250-foot oars needed to saw the island and row it out to sea. He also arranged for the construction of barracks and a mess halls for his laborers, and the delivery of 500 cattle, 500 hogs, and 3,000 chickens, so his workers would have plenty to eat.

After two months of planning, the date arrived for construction to begin. Scores of laborers, carpenters, blacksmiths, butchers, and animals—as well as a marching band and hundreds of onlookers—arrived at Spring Street and Bowery to see the historic project get underway. About the only people who didn't show up were Lozier and his accomplices, who'd suddenly left town "on account of their health."

They were actually holed up in Brooklyn, and although there was talk of having them arrested, Alexander Klein writes in *Grand Deception*, "no one seemed willing to make a complaint to the authorities or admit that he had been duped, and Lozier went scot-free."

THE WILD ANIMAL HOAX

Background: On November 9, 1874, subscribers to the *New York Herald* opened their morning papers to read an eyewitness account of the "escape" the night before of every wild animal from the Central Park Zoo. According to the *Herald* article, 49 people had been killed by the rampaging beasts, 200 more had been injured, and a Who's Who of New York notables, including future president Chester A. Arthur, were hunting the animals up and down Broadway and Fifth Avenue. At least a dozen of the animals were still at large, the story reported, the mayor had declared a "state of siege," and "all citizens, except members of the National Guard, are enjoined to keep within their houses or residences until the wild animals at large are captured and killed."

What Happened: "Much of the life of the city came to an abrupt halt," Carl Sifakis writes in *Hoaxes and Scams*, "and few ventured out, most cowering behind furniture that barricaded home doors and windows." Even James Gordon Bennett, owner of the *New York Herald*, collapsed in bed upon reading his own newspaper's story, and stayed there for the rest of the day. The *Herald*'s war correspondent, George Hosmer, showed up in the newsroom with two large Navy revolvers shouting, "Well, here I am."

What Bennett, Hosmer, and tens of thousands of other *Herald* subscribers failed to do that morning was read the story to the very end—where, in the last paragraph, managing editor Thomas Connery revealed that the story was "a huge hoax, a wild romance, or what ever epithet of utter untrustworthiness our readers may care to apply to it." Connery's motive for publishing the story: to "direct attention to the zoo's shortcomings," so that such escapes might never happen in the future. (So far, they haven't.)

More hoaxes on page 398.

"CARMEN, I BESMOOCH YOU!"

Here's one of the great mistranslations of all time, discovered by Stephen Pyle and reprinted in his book Heroic Failures.

BACKGROUND. In 1981 the Genoa Opera Company put on a production of Bizet's *Carmen*. For tourists in the audience, they translated the program into English. Here's an excerpt of what they printed.

ACT ONE

"Carmen, a cigarmakeress from a tobago factory loves Don Jose of the mounting guard. Carmen takes a flower from her corsets and lances it to Don Jose. (Duet: 'Talk me of my mother.') There was a noise inside the tobago factory and revolting cigarmakeresses burst onto the stage. Carmen is arrested and Don Jose is ordered to mounting guard on her but she subduces him and lets her escape."

ACT TWO

"The tavern. Carmen sings (Aria: 'The sistrums tinkling.') Enter two smugglers ('Ho, we have a mind in business.') Enter Escamillo, a Balls fighter. Carmen refuses to penetrate because Don Jose has liberated her from prison. He just now arrives. (Aria: 'Slop here who comes.') But here are the bugles singing his retreat. Don Jose will leave and draws his sword. Called by Carmen's shrieks the two smugglers interfere with her. Jose is bound to dessert. Final Chorus: 'Opening Sky Wandering Life.'"

ACT THREE

"A rocky landscape. Smugglers chatter. Carmen sees her death in the cards. Don Jose makes a date with her for the next Balls fight."

ACT FOUR

"A place in Seville. Procession of Ballfighters. The roaring of balls is heard in the arena. Escamillo enters (Aria and chorus: 'Toreador. Toreador. All hail the Balls of a toreador.') Enter Don Jose (Aria: 'I besmooch you.') Carmen repels him. She wants to join with Escamillio now chaired by the crowd. Don Jose stabbs her. (Aria: 'Oh, rupture, rupture.') He sings: 'Oh, my seductive Carmen.'"

If you're standing on a mountaintop and the conditions are just right...

A BRIEF HISTORY OF BUGS BUNNY

Who's your favorite cartoon character? Ear's ours.

IMPRESSIVE STATS

Bugs Bunny is the world's most popular rabbit:
- Since 1939, he has starred in more than 175 films.

- He's been nominated for three Oscars, and won one—in 1958, for "Knighty Knight, Bugs" (with Yosemite Sam).

- Every year from 1945 to 1961, he was voted "top animated character" by movie theater owners (when they still showed cartoons in theaters).

- In 1985 he became only the 2nd cartoon character to be given a star on the Hollywood Walk of Fame (Mickey Mouse was the first).

- For almost 30 years, starting in 1960, he had one of the top-rated shows on Saturday-morning TV.

- In 1976, when researchers polled Americans on their favorite characters, real and imaginary, Bugs came in second...behind Abraham Lincoln.

THE INSPIRATIONS

Bugs was born in the 1930s, but cartoon historians say his ancestry goes further back. A few direct descendents:

- **Zomo.** You may not have heard of this African folk-rabbit, but he's world-famous. Joe Adamson writes in *Bugs Bunny: Fifty Years and Only One Grey Hare:*

  > Like jazz and rock 'n' roll, Bugs has at least some of his roots in black culture. Zomo is the trickster rabbit from Central and Eastern Africa who gained audience sympathy by being smaller than his oppressors and turning the tables on them through cleverness—thousands of years before Eastman invented film. A con artist, a masquerader, ruthless and suave, in control of the situation. Specialized in impersonating women.

- **Br'er Rabbit.** Slaves brought Zomo to America and in the New World, he became Br'er Rabbit, whose stories were retold by Joel

Chandler Harris in *Tales of Uncle Remus* (1880). Typical plot: Br'er Fox catches Br'er Rabbit, who begs not to be thrown in the briar-patch (which is exactly where he wants to go). Br'er Fox falls for it, tosses him in, and the rabbit laughs all the way home. Occasionally, you'll see Bugs pull the same trick.

Closer to home, a few comedic geniuses helped mold Bugs:
- **Charlie Chaplin.** "It was Chaplin who established that 'gestures and actions expressing attitude' give a screen character life," Adamson writes. The Looney Tunes directors, all fans of Chaplin, even stole many of his gags. For example:

> The abrupt and shocking kiss Charlie plants [on] someone who's getting too close for comfort in *The Floorwalker* went on to become one of Bugs' favorite ways to upset his adversaries. [And] the walking broomstick in *Bewitched Bunny* does Chaplin's trademark turn, with one foot in the air, at every corner.

There are literally dozens of other Chaplin rip-offs. Bugs also lifted bits from silent comedians Harold Lloyd and Buster Keaton.
- **Groucho Marx.** "Bugs uses his carrot as a prop, just as Groucho used his cigar," points out Stefan Kanfer in *Serious Business*. "Eventually Bugs even stole Marx's response to an insult: 'Of course you know, this means war!' "

TIMELINE
1937: Warner Bros. animation director Tex Avery makes "Porky's Duck Hunt." Porky Pig hunted a screwball duck named Daffy—"who didn't get scared and run away when somebody pointed a gun at him, but leapt and hopped all over the place like a maniac." "When it hit the theaters," recalls another director, "it was like an explosion."

1938: Warner Bros. director Ben "Bugs" Hardaway remakes the cartoon with a rabbit instead of a duck, as "Porky's Hare Hunt." Says one of Bugs's creators: "That rabbit was just Daffy Duck in a rabbit suit."

1939: Bugs Hardaway decides to remake "Porky's Hare Hunt" with a new rabbit (as "Hare-um Scare-um"). Cartoonist Charlie Thorson comes up with a gray and white rabbit with large buck teeth. He labels his sketches "Bugs' Bunny."

1940: Director Tex Avery becomes the real father of Bugs Bunny with "A Wild Hare." Bugs is changed from a Daffyesque lunatic to a streetsmart wiseass. "We decided he was going to be a smart-aleck rabbit, but casual about it," Avery recalled. "His opening line was 'What's up, Doc?'...It floored 'em!...Here's a guy with a gun in his face!...They expected the rabbit to scream, or anything but make a casual remark....It got such a laugh that we said, 'Let's use that every chance we get.' It became a series of 'What's Up, Docs?' That set his entire character. He was always in command, in the face of all types of dangers."

• Bugs also gets his voice in "A Wild Hare." Mel Blanc, who did most Looney Tunes voices, had been having a hard time finding one for the rabbit...until Bugs Hardaway showed him the latest sketch for "A Wild Hare." Blanc wrote:

> He'd obviously had some work done. His posture had improved, he'd shed some weight, and his protruding front teeth weren't as pronounced. The most significant change, however, was in his facial expression. No longer just goofy, he was a sly looking rascal.

"A tough little stinker, ain't he?" Hardaway commented...and the light went on in Blanc's brain.

> A tough little stinker....In my mind I heard a Brooklyn accent....To anyone living west of the Hudson River at that time, Brooklynites were associated with con artists and crooks....Consequently, the new, improved Bugs Bunny wouldn't say jerk, he'd say joik.

• The rabbit is now so popular that he needs a name. According to some sources, he is about to be dubbed "Happy Rabbit." Tex Avery wants " Jack E. Rabbit." But when Thorson's year-old drawing labeled "Bugs' Bunny" is turned up, producer Leon Schlessinger chooses that. Avery hates it. "That's sissy," he complains. "Mine's a *rabbit*. A tall, lanky, mean rabbit. He isn't a fuzzy little bunny!" But the name sticks.

1941: Bugs Bunny becomes competitive. Four extremely talented directors—Avery, Friz Freleng, Bob Clampett, and Chuck Jones—try to top each other with new gags and aspects of Bugs's personality. It's the key to the character's success—he's constantly growing. "As each director added new levels to this character," Adamson explains, "it was picked up by the others and became a part of the mix."

First baseball team to pay its players: Cincinnati Redstockings.

1943: Animator Robert McKimson (later a director himself), working for Bob Clampett, refines Bugs's features into what they are today. "We made him cuter, brought his head and cheeks out a little more and gave him just a little nose," McKimson says. He looks more "elfin" and less "ratlike" now.

1945: During World War II, Bugs has become a "sort of national mascot." Critic Richard Schickel writes: "In the war years, when he flourished most gloriously, Bugs Bunny embodied the cocky humor of a nation that had survived its economic crisis [in surprisingly good shape], and was facing a terrible war with grace, gallantry, humor and solidarity that was equally surprising." By the end of the war, Bugs isn't just a cartoon character, but an American icon.

BUGS FACTS

Saved by a Hare. The inspiration for the original rabbit came from Walt Disney. In 1935 Disney put out a cartoon featuring a character called Max Hare. Hardaway's rabbit looks suspiciously like Max.

Trademarks. Where did Bugs's carrot-crunching and "What's up, Doc?" come from? No one's sure, but experts have suggested they might have been inspired by a couple of popular films:

• In Frank Capra's 1934 Oscar-winning comedy, *It Happened One Night*, Clark Gable nervously munches on carrots.

• In the classic 1939 screwball comedy *My Man Godfrey*, William Powell uses the line "What's up, Duke?" repeatedly.

On the other hand, Tex Avery had a habit of calling everyone Doc—so he may have inspired the phrase. (Mel Blanc also claims in his autobiography that he ad-libbed the line, but he seems to take credit for everything—so we don't believe him.)

Tough Act. Blanc, Bugs's voice, says that recording the "What's up, Doc?" line turned out to be the most physically challenging part of doing the voice:

"What's up, Doc?" was incomplete without the sound of the rabbit nibbling on the carrot, which presented problems. First of all, I don't especially like carrots, at least not raw. [Ed note: In another *BR*, we erroneously reported that he was *allergic* to carrots. Oops.] And second, I found it impossible to chew, swallow, and be ready to say my next line. We tried substituting other vegetables, including

When it was introduced in 1848, the modern golf ball was called a "gutta-percha" ball.

apples and celery, but with unsatisfactory results. The solution was to stop recording so that I could spit out the carrot into the wastebasket and then proceed with the script. In the course of a recording session I usually went through enough carrots to fill several wastebaskets. Bugs Bunny did for carrots what Popeye the Sailor did for spinach. How many...children were coerced into eating their carrots by mothers cooing..."but Bugs Bunny eats *his* carrots." If only they had known.

Eat Your Veggies. Actually, there were pressures to switch from carrots. "The Utah Celery Company of Salt Lake City offered to keep all the studio's staffers well supplied with their product if Bugs would only switch from carrots to celery," Adamson reports. "[And] later, the Broccoli Institute of America strongly urged The Bunny to sample their product once in a while....Mel Blanc would have been happy to switch...but carrots were Bugs's trademark."

Surprise Hit. To his creators, Bugs Bunny was just another character that would probably run in a few cartoons and fade unnoticed into obscurity. "We didn't feel that we had anything," Avery recounted years later, "until we got it on the screen and it got a few laughs. After we ran it and previewed it and so forth, Warners liked it, the exhibitors liked it, and so of course [the producer] ran down and said, 'Boy, give us as many of those as you can!' Which we did."

Bugs Bunny became so popular with the public that he got laughs even when he didn't deserve them. "He could do no wrong," remembers dialogue writer Michael Maltese. "We had quite a few lousy Bugs Bunnies. We'd say, 'Well we haven't got time. Let's do it.' And we'd do it, and the audience would laugh. They loved that rabbit."

*　　*　　*　　*

LOONEY TRIVIA

• The name "Looney Tunes" is a takeoff on Walt Disney's popular 1930s cartoon series, "Silly Symphonies."
• The real name of the Looney Tunes theme song is "The Merry-Go-Round Broke Down." It's a pop tune from the 1930s.
• The first Looney Tune, "Sinking in the Bathtub," appeared in 1930. It featured a character called Bosko.

Oldest American college sport still in existence: rowing.

RABBIT BRINGS FIRE TO THE PEOPLE

In honor of Bugs Bunny (see page 157), we've included this Native American folklore from the Creek tribe, explaining how they acquired fire. This adaptation was contributed by BRI mythologist Jeff Altemus.

In the beginning there was no fire and the earth was cold. Then the Thunderbirds sent their lightning to a sycamore tree on an island where the Weasels lived. The Weasels were the only ones who had fire and they would not give any of it away.

The people knew that there was fire on the island because they could see smoke coming from the sycamore, but the water was too deep for anyone to cross. When winter came the people suffered so much from the cold that they called a council to find some way of obtaining fire from the Weasels. They invited all the animals who could swim.

"How shall we obtain fire?" the people asked.

Most of the animals were afraid of the Weasels because they were bloodthirsty and ate mice and moles and fish and birds. Rabbit was the only one who was brave enough to try to steal fire from them. "I can run and swim faster than the Weasels," he said. "I am also a good dancer."

"Every night the Weasels build a big fire and dance around it. Tonight I will swim across and join in the dancing. I will run away with some fire."

He considered the matter for a while and then decided how he would do it. Before the sun set he rubbed his head with pine tar so as to make his hair stand up. Then, as darkness was falling, he swam across to the island.

The Weasels received Rabbit gladly because they had heard of his fame as a dancer. Soon they had a big fire blazing and all began dancing around it. As the Weasels danced, they approached nearer and nearer the fire in the center of the circle. They would bow to the fire and then dance backwards away from it.

When Rabbit entered the dancing circle, the Weasels

shouted to him: "Lead us, Rabbit!" He danced ahead of them, coming closer and closer to the fire. He bowed to the fire, bringing his head lower and lower as if he were going to take hold of it. While the Weasels were dancing faster and faster, trying to keep up with him, Rabbit suddenly bowed very low so that the pine tar in his hair caught fire in a flash of flame.

He ran off with his head ablaze, and the angry Weasels pursued him, crying, "Catch him! Catch him! He has stolen our sacred fire! Catch him, and throw him down!"

But Rabbit outran them and plunged into the water, leaving the Weasels on the shore. He swam across the water with the flames still blazing from his hair.

The Weasels now called on the Thunderbirds to make it rain so as to extinguish the fire stolen by Rabbit. For three days rain poured down upon the earth, and the Weasels were sure that no fire was left burning except in their sycamore tree.

Rabbit, however, had built a fire in a hollow tree, and when the rain stopped and the sun shone, he came out and gave fire to all the people. After that, whenever it rained, they kept fires in their shelters, and that is how Rabbit brought fire to the people.

*   *   *

LESSON IN STRESS MANAGEMENT

This arrived by Internet one day—we don't know who sent it, but it's become a favorite at the BRI offices, so we pass it on to you. Take a deep, gentle breath, relax...read this slowly and thoughtfully

Picture yourself near a stream. Birds are softly chirping in the crisp, cool mountain air. Nothing can bother you here. No one knows this secret place. You are in total seclusion from that place called "the world." The soothing sound of a gentle waterfall fills the air with a cascade of serenity. The water is clear. You can easily make out the face of the person whose head you're holding under the water.

The Pentagon spent $50 million on Viagra for American troops and retirees in 1999.

FABULOUS FLOP: THE "FREEZER ERA"

At the height of the Space Age, people seemed to believe there was no limit to what scientists could accomplish by 2000. Case in point: cryonics. Here's an excerpt from our book Uncle John's Indispensable Guide to the Year 2000. *Just when you thought you thaw it all...*

FREEZE-WAIT-REANIMATE. In the mid-1960s, a handful of people thought they'd found the key to immortality. Their secret: the "science" of *cryonics* (based on the Greek word *kryos*, "to freeze"). They planned to put people in a state of suspended animation by freezing them in liquid nitrogen...then bring them back to life when conditions in the world and medical knowhow were (presumably) better.

In the anything-can-happen atmosphere of the 1960s, it actually seemed plausible that scientists might be reanimating frozen humans in the near future. This belief was supported by the rumor that Walt Disney had been frozen after his death in 1966. After all, if Uncle Walt was involved, there *must* be something to it. (Note: It was just a rumor. Disney was cremated.)

A SYMBOL OF THE MILLENNIUM. The target year enthusiasts picked for the flowering of their art was 2000. By then, they believed, cryonics would usher in a new golden age for humanity: "The Freezer Era." In his 1964 book *The Prospect of Immortality*, Robert Ettinger declared: "The Freezer Era—if it develops into an age of brotherly love and a living Golden Rule, as I believe it will, may be accepted...as the embodiment of the Millennium."

A journalist reported: "Mr. Ettinger's followers propose to extend freezing throughout the world. By the year 2000 they would have several billion bodies in cold storage."

It didn't quite work out that way. In a widely publicized 1980s court case, a judge handed down a $1 million verdict against the Cryonics Society of California for allowing corpses to thaw. It's a cold world: the judgment permanently damaged their credibility. Few people took them seriously again.

LIFE AFTER DEATH

What do Sherlock Holmes, Davy Crockett, and Superman have in common? They were all popular characters whose creators killed them off...and then had to bring them back from the dead.

SHERLOCK HOLMES
Born: *1887 — Died: 1893 — Resurrected: 1903*

Background: Sherlock Holmes first appeared in 1887 but didn't become famous until 1891, when "A Scandal in Bohemia" was published in London's *Strand* magazine. Overnight, Holmes and his creator, Arthur Conan Doyle, became national celebrities. Over the next two years, Doyle turned out an average of one new story per month. But the more popular Holmes became, the less Doyle liked him. Doyle considered his historical novels to be his *real* work and felt that Holmes kept people from appreciating them. By 1893, Doyle loathed the detective.

Untimely Death: In 1893, at the end of *Strand*'s 24th Holmes story, Doyle placed Holmes on top of Switzerland's Reichenbach Falls, grappling with his arch-enemy, Professor Moriarty. Then he had both characters plunge to their deaths.

The author gleefully wrote to his mother: "The gentleman vanishes, never to return!" But others weren't so happy. Twenty thousand *Strand* readers (an enormous number for the time) cancelled their subscriptions; businessmen in London wore black bands to mourn Holmes's death; Doyle was inundated with letters. But he was unmoved, and snapped: "Holmes is at the bottom of Reichenbach Falls, and there he stays."

Resurrection: What could change Doyle's mind? Money. In 1903 *McClure's* (a U.S. magazine) offered him the astronomical sum of $5,000 dollars *per story* if he would resurrect the character...and *Strand* offered more than half that for the British publication rights. Doyle decided to "accept as much money as slightly deranged editors were willing to pay." Soon after, excited readers learned that Holmes hadn't died after all; he had merely gone into hiding.

The publisher couldn't print copies of the new Holmes stories fast enough. People waited in huge lines and mobbed bookstalls to

---

General Dwight Eisenhower owned a pair of pajamas with five stars on the lapels.

get them. Doyle continued writing about Sherlock Holmes until 1927, then retired the detective for good.

DAVY CROCKETT

Born: December 15, 1954 — Died: February 23, 1955
Resurrected: November 16, 1955

Background: Walt Disney's first TV program, "Disneyland," debuted in October 1954. A few months later, it featured TV's first miniseries—a three-part adventure about a real-life Tennessee politician and frontiersman named Davy Crockett (see page 459 for more about him). The Disney version was mostly fiction, but America took it to heart. One critic recalls, "Disney's Crockett instantly became the most popular hero television had ever seen. Just about every boy in the country owned a coonskin cap like Davy's." Coonskin caps sold so quickly that raccoons actually became hard to find...forcing hat makers to use foxes and rabbits instead. All Crockett items—coloring books, play sets, bubblegum cards, etc.—sold like wildfire. It was TV's first huge, merchandising fad, and it was making Disney a fortune.

Untimely Death: There was just one problem—when the three episodes had been filmed months earlier, no one at Disney had a clue the public would respond so enthusiastically. So they followed Crockett's standard biography, and killed him off at the end of the third episode (while defending the Alamo). Uncle Walt couldn't believe the blunder. "We had one of the biggest hits in television history," he moaned, "and there we were with a dead hero."

Resurrection: "This was the first time that a major hero had died in a television series," writes Jeff Rovin in *The Great TV Heroes*, "and many ·oungsters went into mourning for the noble warrior. More important, however, is the way in which television and the profit incentive were able to conquer death! Disney was not so foolish as to let a financial giant stay long expired."

The company went to work on new episodes, which they set before the Alamo. But it took too long to produce them. "We tried to come back with two more called *The Legend of Davy Crockett*," Walt Disney told a reporter, "but by that time the fever had run its course." The King of the Wild Frontier returned on November 16,

Q: What is a *gnomon*? The thing that casts a shadow on a sundial.

1955, in *Davy Crockett's Keelboat Race* and December 14, 1955, in *Davy Crockett and the River Pirates.*

"Those two never did catch on the way the original three did," Disney sighed. After that, Crockett stayed dead.

SUPERMAN

Born: 1938 — Died: November 18, 1992 — Resurrected: 1993

Background: DC Comics' Superman was the nation's first super-hero. He was introduced in 1938, took the nation by storm, and over the next three decades, became the most successful comic-book character in history.

Untimely Death: By the 1990s, comics had changed. They featured complex heroes who were tormented by angst and who killed their foes in vengeful bloodbaths. Comic fans delighted in "the smart-aleck snarl of Wolverine," and "the devilish depravity of Spawn." But Superman never killed his enemies; he preferred to turn them over to the proper authorities. Fans found his patriotism and politeness...boring. Superman's comic sales "plummeted faster than a speeding bullet," so DC Comics made plans to kill him.

The impending death was nationwide news. Social commentators lamented a society that could no longer find interest in a "decent" hero. Comic stores played up the hype, flying flags with the Superman "S" dripping blood, displaying Superman art, and having the "Death" issue delivered in hearses. Sales of *Superman* skyrocketed, but after a few issues that explored the world without Superman, DC stopped publishing the title.

Resurrection: But not for long. It turned out that Superman's death was a publicity stunt. Only four months later, the Superhero was back in a new form. It turned out his dead body had been taken to a space-age "regeneration center," which brought him back to life. Buyers of the "Death" issue who thought they were getting a collector's item were outraged, and loyal fans resented DC's toying with them. But the publicity did increase sales, at least temporarily—leading DC's executive editor Mike Carlin to happily proclaim death "good for Superman."

Makes sense: The giraffe has the highest blood pressure of any animal.

JEFF'S BRAINTEASERS

BRI member Jeff Altemus collected these puzzles and sent them to us via the BRI Web site (see page 521)...daring us to solve them. Naturally, Uncle John immediately took them to our "research lab." When he emerged, he pronounced them bona fide Bathroom Reading. Now, we "pass" them on to you.

1. A train enters a tunnel at 7 o'clock. Another train enters the exact same tunnel, also at 7 o'clock, on the same day. The tunnel has only one track, no passing places, and no other means for the trains to pass, around, under, or over. However, both trains make it to the other end of the tunnel, untouched.

How did they do it?

2. You have two hourglasses—a 4-minute glass and a 7-minute glass. You want to measure 9 minutes.

How do you do it?

3. If 2 hours ago it was as long after 1 o'clock in the afternoon as it was before 1 o'clock in the morning, what time is it now?

4. A donkey is tied to a rope 10 feet long. Twenty feet away is a field of carrots. How does the donkey get to the carrots?

5. If you were to put a coin into an empty bottle and then insert a cork into the neck, how could you remove the coin without taking out the cork or breaking the bottle?

6. You threw away the outside and cooked the inside. Then you ate the outside and threw away the inside.

What did you eat?

7. What is the easiest way to throw a ball, and have it stop and completely reverse direction after traveling a short distance without hitting anything?

8. Two boxers are in a boxing match (regular boxing, not kick boxing). The fight is scheduled for 12 rounds but ends after 6 rounds, after one boxer knocks out the other boxer. Yet no man throws a punch.

How is this possible?

9. In 1990 a person is 15 years old. In 1995 that same person is 10 years old.

How is this possible?

10. A man is lying dead in a field. Next to him there is an unopened package. There is no other creature in the field.

How did he die?

11. Uncle John was driving to the plumbing supply house the other day and saw a car with a license plate that read:

1 DIV 0

What kind of car was it?

12. A man lies dead in an alley with a tape recorder next to him and a gun in his hand. A police officer saw him and picked up the tape recorder in hopes of determining the cause of his death. He pushes play on the tape recorder and hears the man's voice say "I'm ending my life because I went bankrupt," followed by a gunshot. The policeman filed a homicide report instead of suicide.

Why?

13. A girl is running home. She sees a person with a mask and then runs back to where she started.

Why?

14. Captain Russo was out for a walk when it started to rain. He did not have an umbrella and he wasn't wearing a hat. His clothes were soaked, yet not a hair on his head got wet.

How could this happen?

15. A man takes his car to a hotel. As soon as he reaches the hotel, he is declared bankrupt.

Why?

For answers to Jeff's Brainteasers, turn to page 514.

KIDS ON MUSIC

From Fractured English *by Richard Lederer.*

• "Rock Mananoff was a famous post-Romantic composer of piano concerti."

• "Bach was the most famous composer in the world and so was Handel. Handel was half German, half Italian, and half English. He was very large."

• "Henry Purcell was a well-known composer few people have ever heard of."

The oldest person ever to be issued a driver's license in the U.S. was 109.

UNFINISHED MASTERPIECES

Uncle John was chatting by e-mail with BRI stalwart Jack Mingo, and this topic came up. "How many are there, do you think?" Uncle John asked…and Mingo sent back a list that was so long, he probably still hasn't finished it. Here are our favorites—so far.

THE UNFINISHED SYMPHONY. *Composed by Franz Schubert, this is perhaps the most famous unfinished modern masterpiece. Ironically, no one is sure if it really is unfinished.*

Background: Schubert grew up in early 19th-century Vienna. He was a prodigy who could dash off brilliant songs on the back of envelopes, but his genius was unrecognized. He was never able to attract the patronage that would have enabled him to concentrate exclusively on music…so he never heard many of his own works performed by a full orchestra (or even by professional musicians). He died of venereal disease in 1828, at age 31.

Unfinished Masterpiece: By 1865 Schubert was recognized as a master. A group of his ardent fans (The Schubert Society) heard a rumor that an old lawyer acquaintance of Schubert's had a copy of a lost symphony…and it turned out to be true. The piece was Schubert's *Eighth Symphony*, written in 1822. He had submitted it to an orchestra called the *Gesellschaft der Musikfreunde*, asking them to perform it. When it was rejected, he sent it to the lawyer…who held onto it for over 40 years. At the fans' request, he dug out the symphony…"but it was soon clear that the two last movements were missing. Only the first three bars of the third movement were found." What makes this particularly frustrating for music-lovers is that the symphony is generally considered Schubert's best work.

Update: The Schubert Society begged the lawyer to find the rest, but he insisted he'd only received two movements. True? Maybe. There are three theories:

1. Schubert wrote the first two movements as a sampler to see if any orchestras would be interested, then never bothered to finish it.

2. The last movement was incorporated into one of Schubert's later works.

3. The second half *had* to have been lost. Potential proof: The last page of the second movement was not blank— three bars of the third movement were at the bottom of the page, "strongly implying that it continued...somewhere," explains one Schubert expert. "Since then, a sketchbook apparently containing 250 bars of the third movement has been discovered. Fans hope that the rest of the papers are in an attic somewhere, waiting to be found."

KUBLA KHAN. *By Samuel Taylor Coleridge. One of the best-known poems in the English language, notorious as an unfinished piece because of the explanation Coleridge gave for not completing it.*

Background: Coleridge was sedated with opium and recovering from an illness one summer day in 1797 when he nodded off reading a book called *Purchas's Pilgrimage*. The last sentence he read before falling asleep was "Here the Khan Kubla commanded a palace to be built, and a stately garden thereunto. And thus ten miles of fertile ground were enclosed with a wall."

Coleridge said that he slept deeply for about three hours, during which he dreamed a complete 200- to 300-line poem about Khan.

Unfinished Masterpiece: When he awoke, Coleridge immediately started putting the words on paper. He had written the first 40 lines or so when a knock came at the door. But instead of sending his visitor away (some accounts say it was a salesman)—or refusing to answer the door altogether—Coleridge chatted for over an hour.

On his return to his room, Coleridge wrote, he found, to his "surprise and mortification, that though [I] still retained some vague and dim recollection of the general purport of the vision, with the exception of some eight or ten scattered lines and images, all the rest had passed away!" He managed to put a total of 54 lines to paper, but that was it—the rest of his 300-line poem was lost forever.

Update: Today scholars question whether Coleridge was being honest about his unfinished work. It's possible he simply wasn't sure what to write next, and never got around to working it out.

SPECIAL UNDERWEAR

At the BRI, we don't believe in keeping underwear innovations under cover. Here are three to take us into the next millennium.

SAFETY FIRST

"A Vermont inventor has figured out a way to prevent senior citizens from breaking bones when they take a spill: underwear air bags. Carl Clark, who also devised the first air bags for Lockheed Martin in the 1960s, says his emergency underwear has a sensor that automatically inflates two cushions around the wearer's hips when it detects the person starting to fall."

—*Los Angeles Times*

LARGER THAN LIFE

"A Tokyo man made international news recently when his inflatable underpants accidentally went off in the subway. He had invented the special underwear to allay his phobia of drowning. The good news is, they worked, inflating to 30 times their normal size. They had to be stabbed with a pencil to stop them from crushing other passengers."

—*The Edge*

THE ARMAGEDDON BRA

"Every Japanese has heard of Nostradamus, and millions lend credence to his prophecy that a terrible calamity will strike in July this year (1999)—a war destroying a third of the world's population.

"Now the lingerie firm, Triumph International Japan, is cashing in on the nation's doomsday boom with a hi-tech 'Armageddon Bra' that alerts its wearer to incoming missiles.

"Presented at a fashion show yesterday, the 'Armageddon Bra' includes a sensor on the shoulder strap, and a control box to warn of objects falling from the skies.

"Ideally the Armageddon Bra should be worn without outer garments to work efficiently."

—*The Times of London*

The island of Antigua and Barbuda issued Elle Macpherson postage stamps in 1999.

MY BODY LIES OVER THE OCEAN...

This section was inspired by an article in Harper's *about the fact that Albert Einstein's brain was removed when he died. We at the BRI wondered if other famous people "lost" a body part or two when they died. We did a little research...and were surprised by what we found.*

GALILEO'S MIDDLE FINGER

Where It's Located: Museum of the History of Science, Florence, Italy

How It Got there: In 1737, when Galileo's body was being moved from a storage closet to its final resting place in a mausoleum in the church of Santa Croce, a nobleman named Anton Francesco Gori cut off three fingers from Galileo's right hand for a souvenir. The middle finger was eventually acquired by the Museum of the History of Science; the other two surviving fingers "are in a private collection."

NAPOLÉON'S "NOBLE ORGAN"

Where It's Located: Columbia University's College of Physicians and Surgeons

How It Got There: In 1828 Abbé Ange Paul Vignali, the priest who administered last rites to Napoléon in 1821, was murdered. Among the many Napoleonic souvenirs found in Abbé Vignali's personal effects was the most personal effect of all—a tiny, "unpleasant looking piece of desiccated tissue" alleged to be Napoleon's private part—which was supposedly removed from the deposed emperor's corpse following his autopsy.

The artifact remained in the Vignali family until 1916, when it was sold to a London dealer of rare books. In 1924 it was sold to Dr. Abraham Rosenbach, who placed the withered item "inside a glass casket, in a tasteful case of blue morocco leather and velvet bearing Napoleon's crest," where it was displayed to friends, family, and just about anyone else who asked to see it. "Few so intimate portions of a man's anatomy," Rosenbach's biographer writes, "have ever been displayed to so many."

Each year, Americans use enough foam peanuts to fill ten 85-story skyscrapers.

In November 1944, the "shriveled short arm,"—which by now was said to look like "a maltreated strip of buckskin shoelace, or a shriveled eel"—was sold to a Philadelphia autograph dealer named Bruce Gimelson. He tried to auction it at Christie's, but withdrew it when it "failed to attract a $40,000 minimum bid." Seven years later, he sold it to a urologist named John K. Lattimer for a mere $3,000. Dr. Lattimer owns it to this day, and it's only one of the many odd but historically significant items in his collection. As Harvey Rachlin reports in *Lucy's Bones, Sacred Stones, and Einstein's Brain*, Dr. Lattimer also owns "Hermann Goering's suicide capsule container, a lock of Hitler's hair, and the nooses used to hang two of the conspirators for the murder of President Lincoln, Mary Surratt and Lewis Powell."

EINSTEIN'S BRAIN

Where It's Located: Lawrence, Kansas

How it Got There: When Einstein died in April 1955, he left a request that his friend and colleague Dr. Harry Zimmerman examine his brain. So Dr. Thomas Harvey, the pathologist who performed the autopsy on Einstein, removed the brain and had it cut into 200 pieces, some of which he gave to Zimmerman. The rest (representing about 75% of Einstein's brain) he took home and stored in formaldehyde-filled jars that he kept under his sink for nearly 40 years—occasionally doling out specimens to brain researchers upon request. (One such researcher keeps his section in his refrigerator, in a jar marked "Big Al's Brain.")

At last report, Harvey, who'd lost his medical license and was working in a plastics factory, was looking for a research lab or some other institution to take possession of Einstein's brain and preserve it for posterity.

OTHER CELEBRITY BODY PARTS

• **Walt Whitman's brain.** Donated to the Wistar Institute at the University of Pennsylvania, where it "was dropped on the floor by a lab technician and was discarded long ago." The Wistar Institute is no longer accepting new brains.

• **Lord Byron's lungs.** "Kept in a jar, somewhere in Greece."

More on page 280.

The Tour de France bicycle race is 2,300 miles long.

AMAZING LUCK

Sometimes we're blessed with it, sometimes we're cursed with it—dumb luck. Here are some examples of people who've lucked out...for better and for worse.

CELLULAR MEMORY

"In the Dent de Crolles region in France, shepherd Christian Raymond, 23, was rescued from a cliff from which he had been hanging by his fingers. He had called the emergency rescue operator on his cell phone earlier in the day and managed to make another call from the cliff by pressing 'redial' with his nose against the phone, which had fallen down the mountain with him but had landed right beside him."

—**The Edge, March 25,1999**

TRAIN KEPT A-ROLLIN'

"Participants in this tale of survival still can't believe it really happened. Thrown through the steel roof of his car in a head-on collision, a Denver man landed a hundred feet away—on railroad tracks, directly in the path of a speeding train. Too late to brake before passing over the body, the engineeer stopped as fast as he could and rushed back to the spot, certain he had killed the man. What he found was a guy limping, shaken, but very much alive. His only injury was the broken leg he suffered in the car collision."

—*Oops*

LUCK BE A LADY

"A mistake on a national Pick 7 ticket was worth $1.6 million to a bettor who selected the wrong number on Breeders' Cup Day.

"The 51-year-old engineer who bought the winning ticket said he punched 11 instead of 1 for his selection in the seventh race.

"'I liked the one and 11 horses in the sixth race, and I liked the No. 1 in the seventh,' the bettor said. 'But when I punched out my ticket for the seventh, I hit one and 11—the same numbers I had in the sixth—by mistake.'

"The 11 turned out to be Arcangues, the unknown French horse who won the Classic at odds of 133 to 1. It was the largest in Breeders' Cup history.

Poll result: 58% of schoolkids say pizza is their favorite cafeteria food.

"He had three other tickets with six winners, too, and collected a total of $1,152,317 after taxes."

—*San Francisco Chronicle,* November 11, 1993

BLESS THE TORPEDOES!

"A charmed life. That describes the experience of seaman Roy Dikkers during World War II. Sealed in a compartment when a German torpedo struck his tanker, he was freed by a second torpedo explosion. Racing on deck he found the sea around the floundering vessel ablaze with oil fires. He never had to make the fateful decision whether to stay with the sinking ship or risk the fiery sea. A third torpedo blew him far from the scene, beyond the oil slick. Landing near a floating raft, he crawled aboard and was found by a Norwegian freighter three days later."

—*Oops*

MY FORTUNE FOR A KISS

"Hauled before a Melbourne court in 1907 for hugging and kissing spinster Hazel Moore when she entered his shop, young Michael O'Connor defended himself by claiming it had been a lovely spring day and he was in high spirits. O'Connor had to serve a few months for breach of peace. So imagine his amazement ten years later when an attorney representing Miss Moore's estate gave him her bequest of 20,000 pounds! She left the fortune in memory of the only kiss she had received from a man in her adult life."

—*Oops*

AMAZING LOTTERY WINNERS

• "Randy Halvorson was one of 14 employees to share a $3.4 million jackpot in 1988. The Iowa resident then won $7.2 million with his brother in 1990."

• "In Wisconsin, Donald Smith of Amherst has won the state's SuperCash game three times: On May 25, 1993, June 17, 1994, and July 30, 1995. He won $250,000 each time. The odds of winning the SuperCash game just once are nearly one in a million."

• "Joseph P. Crowley won $3 million in the Ohio lottery in 1987. Six years later, he retired to Boca Raton, Florida, and played the Florida Lotto on Christmas Day of 1993. He won $20 million."

—*The Good Luck Book*

"BUT IT SAYS ON THE LABEL..."

You might assume that with all the regulations on labeling,
you can always tell what's in that product you just bought.
Well, guess again. Here are five examples that prove
it's still "buyer beware" in the marketplace.

FRESH IS FROZEN
The Label Says: "This Turkey Never Frozen"
You Assume: It's fresh.

Actually: Until 1998 any turkey that was stored at temperatures above 0°F could be called "fresh." Then, says the *Wall Street Journal*, the FDA changed the rules. Nowadays, to be called fresh, a turkey has to be stored at above 26°F—the freezing point for poultry. But the label still doesn't have to say *frozen* unless it was stored at 0°F or less. So a company can legally say it was never frozen, even if it was stored at 1°F.

YOUR LAWN OR YOUR LIFE?
The Label Says: "Pesticide Ingredients" and then lists them
You Assume: All the ingredients—particularly the toxic ones—are in the list.

Actually: According to a recent study, "more than 600 toxic chemicals included in pesticides aren't disclosed on the brand labels." Why not? "Under federal pesticide regulations, these chemicals don't have to be disclosed when they are *inert ingredients*, chemicals that assist in killing bugs and weeds, but aren't the active agent of destruction." And why aren't they listed? Pesticide companies say they need to protect trade secrets.

SOUNDS OFF
The CD Label Says: *Cape Cod...the Enchanting Sounds of the Surf*
You Assume: This "sounds of nature" CD was recorded off Cape Cod.

Actually: According to a report in the *Wall Street Journal*, the CD

When it was invented in India, badminton was known as *poona.*

was recorded in Naples, Florida. So was *Cocoa Beach...the Enchanting Sounds of the Surf* and the rest of the 200-title series. "I'd be an idiot to do separate recordings [for each title]," the producer told a reporter. "It's all surf."

Apparently, many (but not all) of the popular "sounds of nature" recordings are fakes. One "burbling stream" is really a toilet: "I wound up using a stereo recording of my toilet bowl filling up," a producer admitted. "It sounded more like a stream than the streams did." Another producer says he once "turned an 87-second roll of thunder into a 30-minute storm." Other tricks include "hosing down backyard pine trees to tape the drip of rain, or crouching in elevator shafts to catch the howl of wind."

DO IT AGAIN
The Label Says: "Recycled Paper"
You Assume: It's been used by a consumer, sent to a recycling center, and turned back into paper.
Actually: The only time you can be sure that's true is if the label includes the words "post-consumer." Otherwise, it could be something else. The government allows manufacturers to gather paper cuttings from the mill floor, dump them back into the paper pulp, and call the paper "recycled." The mills would do that anyway because it's cost-effective to save the scraps, so there's no savings of resources. But it sounds good...and it's legal.

DEM BONES
The Label Says: "Chicken Nuggets"
You Assume: It's chicken *meat*.
Actually: According to the National Consumer League, when "convenience foods such as chicken frankfurters, chicken nuggets, turkey salami and turkey bologna" are mechanically deboned, there's no telling what's in them. "The problem is that mechanically deboned poultry may contain bone fragments, marrow, skin, kidneys, sex glands, and lungs as by-products of the mechanical process. However, these by-products are not listed on the ingredients panel, so consumers do not know that they are both paying for, and eating, this extraneous material....Labelling requirements allow the poultry industry to hide behind a vague designation of product either as 'chicken' or 'chicken meat.'"

ANIMAL MYTHS

*Here are a few examples of things that some people
believe about animals…but just aren't true.*

Myth: Bats are blind.
Fact: Bats aren't blind. But they have evolved as nocturnal hunters, and can see better in half-light than in daylight.

Myth: Monkeys remove fleas in each other's fur during grooming.
Fact: Monkeys don't have fleas. They're removing dead skin—which they eat.

Myth: Male seahorses can become pregnant and give birth.
Fact: What actually happens is this: The female seahorse expels eggs into the male's brood pouch, where they are fertilized. And while the male does carry the gestating embryos until they are born 10 days later, he doesn't feed them through a placenta or similar organ (as had previously been thought). Instead, the embryos feed off of nourishment in the egg itself—food provided by the female. Basically, the male acts as an incubator.

Myth: Porcupines can shoot their quills when provoked.
Fact: A frightened porcupine tends to run from danger. If a hunter catches it, though, a porcupine will tighten its skin to make the quills stand up…ready to lodge in anything that touches them.

Myth: Whales spout water.
Fact: Whales actually exhale *air* through their blowholes. This creates a mist or fog that looks like a water spout.

Myth: Moths eat clothes.
Fact: Not exactly. Moths lay their eggs on your clothes, which eventually develop into larvae. It's the larvae that eat tiny parts of your clothes; adult moths do not eat cloth.

Myth: Bumblebee flight violates the laws of aerodynamics.
Fact: Nothing that flies violates the laws of aerodynamics.

What's another name for a roll of coins wrapped in paper? A *rouleau*.

TALKING HEADS

Who says talk show hosts don't have anything intellgent to say? Oh, never mind.

"Okay, our focus: 'Are Babies Being Bred for Satanic Sacrifice?' Controversial to say the least. Unbelievable to say the least. Disgusting to say the least. We'll be right back."

—**Geraldo Rivera, just before a commercial break**

"This is the 'Jerry Springer Show'....There is no such thing as class!"

—**Jerry Springer**

"That man is so repugnant. All of these satanic murderers are."

—**Geraldo Rivera, discussing Charles Manson**

"It's always difficult to be meaningful and relevant, because there's just not enough time."

—**Oprah Winfrey**

"Nobody differentiates between one show and another. It's all of us in the same trash can."

—**Sally Jesse Raphael**

"I'd rather be called sleazy than to be identified as intelligent."

—**Phil Donahue**

"There's nothing wrong with skipping your job to come to the 'Ricki Lake Show!'"

—**Ricki Lake**

"Your wife wants you to die. Your reaction, quickly."

—**Geraldo Rivera**

"My show is just plain STUPID!"

—**Jerry Springer**

"Tonight you'll be looking at some horrible scenes and meeting some horrible people."

—**Geraldo, introducing his TV special "Murder: Live from Death Row"**

"Wow! This story is beyond dysfunctional!"

—**Ricki Lake**

"Oprah's quitting in two years and I will be all you have, so you better be nice to me!"

—**Jenny Jones**

"If you think it was an accident, applaud."

—**Geraldo, speaking about Natalie Wood's drowning**

Top 5 U.S. soft drinks in 1998: Coke Classic, Pepsi, Diet Coke, Mountain Dew, Sprite.

THE ORIGIN OF BASKETBALL, PART II

Here's more on how the game of basketball
was invented. Part I starts on page 46.

P ROMISES, PROMISES...
As James Naismith admitted years later in his memoirs, the
new game he had in mind was an indoor version of an existing
sport, like baseball or rugby. And when Dr. Gulick put him in
charge of The Incorrigibles' physical education classes, he set out to
find one he could adapt.

Naismith spent two weeks experimenting with different games,
but something always seemed to get lost in the translation: Indoor
soccer, for example, was fun—but too many windows were broken.
And rugby turned out to be too dangerous on the gymnasium's hard-
wood floors. Other sports were safer...but they were so boring, The
Incorrigibles refused to play them.

Outdoor games were meant to be played outdoors, Naismith concluded, and that was that.

BACK TO THE DRAWING BOARD

Time was running out. With only 24 hours left till his deadline
for reporting to the faculty on the success of his efforts, Naismith
decided to try a different approach: he would analyze a number of
different games systematically, and figure out what made them
challenging and fun. Then he would incorporate many of those
elements into a new game that would be, as he put it, "interesting,
easy to learn, and easy to play in the winter and by artificial light."

Do Unto Others

Naismith's new game would also have to walk a political tightrope:
it had to be physically challenging enough to sustain the interest of
The Incorrigibles, but not so rough or violent that it would offend
conservatives within the YMCA movement. They had opposed getting involved with sports in the first place...and Naismith didn't
want to give them any excuse to declare the experiment a failure.

Shakespeare's *Hamlet* has been adapted into a film 49 times; Romeo & Juliet, 27 times.

HE GOT GAME

Amazingly, Naismith then sat down and, step-by-step, invented one of the most popular games in sports history.

Step 1. He figured that since nearly all popular sports have balls, his game should have one, too. But should it be small or large? Small balls like baseballs and lacrosse balls required bats, sticks, and racquets. Naismith was afraid players might use them to hit each other. He chose a big ball.

Step 2. Naismith felt that running with a ball would invariably lead to tackling the person carrying it—and tackling was too violent for the YMCA (not to mention too dangerous on a wood floor). So in the new game, the person who had the ball wouldn't be allowed to run with it; they wouldn't even be allowed to move. Instead, the player with the ball would have to stand in one place and pass it to the other players. That was the key to the game. "I can still recall how I snapped my fingers and shouted, 'I've got it!'" Naismith recalled years later.

Step 3. And what about the shape of the ball? It would either have to be round or shaped like a rugby ball (the predecessor of the football). Rugby balls were easier to carry under the arm, but that would encourage tackling. Round balls were easier to throw, which made them perfect for a passing game. Naismith decided to use a soccer ball.

Step 4. Naismith figured that there should be a goal at each end of the gymnasium…but what kind of goal? A huge one, like a soccer goal, would make scoring too easy—so the goal would have to be smaller. But a tiny goal would be easy to block…and blocking the goal would lead to pushing and shoving. So he decided to put the goal high over people's heads, where it would be impossible to block.

Step 5. This led to another consideration: if the goal was vertical, like the goalposts in football, players would throw the ball at it as hard and as fast as they could—which would be dangerous indoors. It would also reward force over skill, which was the antithesis of what Naismith wanted.

Naismith suddenly remembered a game he'd played as a child, called Duck on the Rock. The object was to knock a "duck" off of a rock by throwing stones at it. The best players always threw their rocks in an arc rather than directly at the duck, so that if they missed, they wouldn't have to run as far to retrieve the rock. That inspired Naismith to use a horizontal goal, parallel to the ground. That way, players wouldn't be able to score just by throwing the ball as hard as they could: they'd have to throw it in an arc to get it in.

SERENDIPITY STRIKES

Naismith figured a wooden box nailed to the balcony that ran around the gym would work pretty well as a goal, and asked the janitor if he had any boxes lying around.

"No," the janitor told him, "but I have two old peach baskets down in the store room, if they will do you any good." "Thus," Robert Peterson writes in *Cages to Jump Shots*, "did the game miss being called box ball."

Naismith nailed one peach basket to the balcony at one end of the gym, and one at the other end. The balcony of the YMCA in Springfield just happened to be 10 feet off the floor—which is why, today, a regulation basket is 10 feet high.

THE FIRST GAME

Naismith typed up a list of 13 rules and posted them on the gym's bulletin board. The following morning, he read The Incorrigibles the rules; then he divided the 18-man class into two teams of 9 and taught them to play the game.

He promised to change any rules that didn't work out. "It was the start of the first basketball game," he recounted in his memoirs years later, "and the finish of the trouble with that class."

Basketball still had a long way to go. Turn
to page 314 for the last part of our story.

Turn to page 314 for the last part of our story.

*   *   *

"Women want mediocre men, and men are working hard to be as mediocre as possible." —*Margaret Mead*

Until 1937, the referee tossed a jump ball after every basket in basketball.

HOW EN-LIGHTNING

Zap! BRI member Kurt Stark requested these facts about lightning.

Every second, there are 100 to 125 flashes of lightning somewhere on Earth.

A lightning bolt can be anywhere between 200 feet and 20 miles long, but the average length, cloud-to-ground, is 2 to 10 miles.

Lightning speeds toward the Earth at an average of 200,000 miles per hour.

The average flash of lightning contains 125 million volts of electricity—enough to light a 100-watt bulb for more than three months.

The chances of being hit by lightning in your lifetime are about 1 in 600,000. Still, anywhere from 500 to 1000 people are struck by lightning every year in the U.S.

The temperature of a lightning stroke can reach 50,000°F—hotter than the sun's surface.

Lightning bolts actually flicker—a *flash* is a series of strokes that follow the exact same path as the first one. The record number of strokes ever recorded in a single flash is 47.

When you see a lightning flash, count the seconds until you hear the bang of thunder. Divide by five—sound travels about one mile every five seconds—and this will give you an approximation of the storm's distance from you.

About one-quarter of all lightning strikes occur in open fields; 30% happen in July; 22% in August.

You can get struck by lightning while you're on the phone. It happens to about 2.5% of all lightning-strike victims.

Trees are lightning bolts' favorite targets—lightning is the largest cause of forest fires in the western U.S.

Estimated diameter of a lightning channel: 0.5 to 1 inch.

A charge of 100 million to 1 billion volts of electricity needs to be generated in a cloud to start a cloud-to-ground lightning strike.

For the last decade, an average of 20 million cloud-to-ground flashes have been counted over the continental U.S. each year.

THE DUSTBIN
OF HISTORY

*Think your heroes will go down in history for something they've done?
Don't count on it. These folks were VIPs in their time...but they're
forgotten now. They've been swept into the Dustbin of History.*

FORGOTTEN FIGURE: John "Bet-a-Million" Gates, a
compulsive gambler in the late 1800s, who once tried to bet
$1 million on a horse at Saratoga Race Track, "causing book-
makers to run for cover"

CLAIM TO FAME: Gates started out as a $30-a-month barbed-
wire salesman, but after a few years of skilled gambling, built a $50
million fortune. He was notorious for parting robber barons from
their money, taking millions from Andrew Carnegie and relieving
financier J. P. Morgan of $15 million on a single bet. Beating capi-
talists at their own game—making money—made him a hero with
the public.

Gates's luck eventually ran out and he lost everything in a bet
with J. P. Morgan...or almost everything. Gates reportedly got down
on his knees and begged Morgan not to bankrupt him; Morgan re-
lented—on the condition that Gates leave New York forever.

Gates had to accept. He moved to Texas and invested what little
money he had left in drilling for oil. Most of the wells he dug were
dry holes, but the few that weren't produced so much oil that John
D. Rockefeller offered to buy him out for $25 million. Gates refused,
returned to New York triumphantly, and by the time he died in
1911 once again had a fortune valued at between $50 and $100
million.

INTO THE DUSTBIN: Gates was buried in an opulent mausoleum near Wall Street. Still, hardly anyone remembers him today.

FORGOTTEN FIGURE: Anthony Comstock, an anti-vice
crusader at the turn-of-the century

CLAIM TO FAME: Known as "The Great American Bluenose,"
he was, for a time, one of the most powerful men in public life.

In 1873, at age 29, he founded an organization called the **New York Society for the Suppression of Vice.** A few years later he became the U.S. Post Office's special agent to enforce a federal anti-obscenity law…which he had created. Congress didn't even bother to define "obscenity"—they left that up to Comstock.

The problem was, Comstock seemed to think just about *everything* was obscene: He had Walt Whitman fired from the Department of the Interior for writing *Leaves of Grass* and had the George Bernard Shaw play *Mrs. Warren's Profession* banned after one showing because he found it "reeking" with sin. He even arrested a woman for calling her husband a spitbub (rascal) on a postcard. He was also notorious for personally dragging to jail any art dealer who refused to remove paintings with nudes in them from public display.

Comstock eventually developed a reputation as a kook: In 1915 he hauled some department-store window dressers into court for dressing their naked mannequins in full view of the shopping public—prompting the judge to exclaim partway through the trial, "Mr. Comstock, I think you're nuts." Comstock never lived the humiliation down, and died shortly afterward.

INTO THE DUSTBIN: About all that remains of Comstock today is the word *Comstockery,* which the *American College Dictionary* describes as "overzealous censorship of the fine arts and literature, often mistaking outspokenly honest works for salacious productions." The term was coined by a thankful George Bernard Shaw after Comstock's efforts to shut down *Mrs. Warren's Profession* turned it into a smash hit.

FORGOTTEN FIGURES: Daisy and Violet Hilton, two sisters who played jazz on the vaudeville circuit in the 1920s

CLAIM TO FAME: Daisy was an excellent alto saxophone player; Violet was an excellent pianist. But that isn't what attracted crowds to their performances wherever they went: Daisy and Violet were Siamese twins, joined at the hip. They made a fortune performing up and down the East Coast.

INTO THE DUSTBIN: By the late 1950s, the sisters had spent all of their performance money and were working at a supermarket in Charlotte, North Carolina. They died within hours of each other from influenza in 1960.

Top 5 holiday pies in the US: #1 pumpkin; #2 apple; #3 cherry; #4 lemon meringue; #5 pecan.

WE AIN'T LION: THE MODERN ZOO IS BORN

It wasn't that long ago that seeing an elephant at the London Zoo was about as shocking to the average person as meeting a Martian would be today. Here's the story of how zoos got their start.

OLD-TIME MENAGERIES
People have "collected" exotic animals for more than 5,000 years. Priests in ancient Egypt raised lions, tigers, and other sacred animals in and around temples, and as early as 1100 B.C., China's Zhou Dynasty established what was called the "Garden of Intelligence," a 900-acre preserve filled with deer, antelope, birds, fish, and other animals that were studied as well as hunted.

Exotic animals were also popular in ancient Rome, where they were collected by wealthy families and used in gladiator games. Sometimes the lions, tigers, bulls, bears, and other creatures fought each other to a bloody death for public amusement; other times they were pitted against Christians, heretics, or condemned criminals (or, if none were available, ordinary criminals). Sometimes the Romans even filled their coliseums with water, so gladiators in boats could hunt water animals like hippos and crocodiles.

These games were so popular—and killed so many animals—that by the time they finally came to an end in the 6th century A.D., numerous species in the Roman empire, including the elephants of North Africa, the hippopotami of Nubia, the lions of Mesopotamia, and the tigers of Hycrania, had all been driven to extinction.

THE DARK AGES

When Rome fell in the 5th century A.D., interest in animals declined, and it wasn't until the 13th century that nobles and other wealthy Europeans began collecting animals on a large scale again. They even exchanged them like trading cards.

Mugging someone on a subway in Britain can get you life in prison.

King Frederick II of Sicily was a typical collector of the era: his menagerie included hyenas, elephants, camels, lions, monkeys, cheetahs, and a giraffe…and when he got tired of the giraffe, he traded it to the sultan of Egypt for a polar bear.

THE LONDON ZOO

In 1235 King Henry III of England moved his grandfather's animal collection to the Tower of London. The collection included camels, lions, leopards, and lynx…and King Louis IX of France contributed an elephant—the first one ever seen in Great Britain. The animals were put on display for the royal family and its guests, but were also occasionally pitted against one another—tigers vs. lions, bears vs. dogs—to entertain royal visitors. However, the novelty eventually wore off, and the animals became neglected.

Then, in 1445, Margaret of Anjoy, wife of Henry VI, received a lion as a wedding gift…which inspired her to have the entire Royal Menagerie—what was left of it—restored. But when the royal family moved out of the Tower in the early 1700s, they left their animals behind. That created a problem: if the royal family wasn't going to support the menagerie, who was? Finally, someone came up with the idea of opening the collection to the public, and charging them admission. Price: three half-pence, or if you preferred, a dog or cat to feed to the lions.

CHANGING TIMES

As the British Empire expanded to the far corners of the globe in the early 1800s, interest in exotic animals grew beyond mere curiosity. In 1826 an explorer named Sir Stamford Raffles founded the London Zoological Society, which took its name from the ancient Greek word *zoion*, which means "living being."

Two years later, the Society moved the royal family's animal collection from the Tower of London to a new site in Regent's Park. It was a big hit with members of the royal family, many of whom contributed animals.

But unlike the Tower of London, the Zoological Park was closed to the public—the animals were "objects of scientific research," Raffles explained, "not of vulgar admiration." Only members of the Zoological society and their guests were allowed to visit. (A written

What do grape juice and the blesbok antelope have in common? Same color.

voucher would allow a non-member to enter, and these became very common and were even traded in pubs.)

The public was officially excluded from the "zoo," as it had become known, until 1846, by which time the novelty had worn off and attendance had fallen dramatically. So the Zoological Society opened its doors to anyone with a penny, and hundreds of thousands of new visitors streamed into the park. "For the city dweller," Linda Koebler writes in *Zoo*, "[it] provided a place of greenery that was a relief from the ugly, dirty cities of this period."

The term "zoo" entered mainstream culture a year after the London Zoological Garden opened to the public, thanks to the popularity of one particular song: "Walking in the Zoo is an Okay Thing to Do."

ZOOS IN EUROPE

In the early 1800s, having a public zoo became a status symbol for any European city that considered itself modern and sophisticated. If they still had royal collections of animals available, they quickly converted them to zoological parks. If they didn't, they created new zoos. Zoos in Dublin, Berlin, Frankfurt, Antwerp, and Rotterdam were among the best known.

Le Zoo

In France, however, the development of public zoos was slowed by the Revolution of 1789. Common people saw private collections of captive animals as a way for the rich to flaunt their wealth. According to one account, when a mob of revolutionaries arrived at the Ménagerie du Parc to free the animals, "The crowd wanted the animals set free so that others could catch them and eat them, outraged that these animals grew fat while the people starved. But once the zoo director explained that some of the creatures would eat the crowd rather than vice versa, the du Parc revolutionaries decided to 'liberate' only the more edible captives."

Cat got your tongue? Did someone call you a cheetah?
Don't monkey around, turn to page 407
for more wild facts about zoos.

ODD JOBS

*Looking for an exciting new job? Here's a list of the
most unusual-sounding occupations we could find.*

Killer Bee Hunter. Your mission: Track down Africanized "killer" bees, which are migrating north from Central America, and destroy them before they can take up residence in North America.

Chicken Shooter. Fire dead chickens out of a cannon at aircraft to see what kind of damage occurs.

Mother Repairer. It's not what you think. It actually entails repairing metal phonograph record "mothers" (the master from which records are pressed) by removing dirt and nickel particles from the grooves.

Anthem Man. A unique profession: King Alfonso of Spain was tone deaf...he employed one man whose job was to alert him when the Spanish national anthem was playing (so he would know when to salute).

Worm Collector. Get ready to crawl through grass at night with a flashlight, to catch the best worms for fishing. Tip: Grab them in the middle to avoid bruising.

Weed Farmer. If you like gardening, here's a change of pace: *grow* weeds...then sell them to chemical companies for herbicide research.

Pig Manure Sniffer. Workers try to recognize chemical markers in manure so researchers can determine which foods make pig manure so foul-smelling. Women only, because estrogen increases sensitivity to smell.

Sewage Diver. Put on a diving suit and plunge into a sewage-containment vat.

Animal Chauffeur. We've only heard of one—a guy named Stephen May. His "limousine" is equipped with, among other things: a blanketed floor, eight-inch color television, stereo speakers, and silk flowers.

Flush Tester. A gold star from Uncle John to the gallant professionals who test toilet-bowl standards by trying to flush rags down various toilets.

Armpit Sniffer. Enough said.

How did "venereal disease" get its name? From Venus, the Roman goddess of love.

RUDNER'S RULES

*Have you heard Rita Rudner yet? At the BRI, we
think she's pretty funny. Here are some of her lines.*

"Blondes have more fun, don't they? They must. How many brunettes do you see walking down the street with blond roots?"

"When I want to end relationships I just say, 'I want to marry you so we can live together forever.' Sometimes they leave skidmarks."

"Waiters and waitresses are becoming much nicer and more caring. I used to pay my check, they'd say, 'Thank you.' That graduated into 'Have a nice day.' That's now escalated into 'You take care of yourself, now.' The other day I paid my check—the waiter said, 'Don't put off that mammogram.'"

"I have to talk to my girlfriend every day on the phone. My husband says, 'Why do you have to talk to her again today? You just talked to her yesterday. What could you possibly have to tell her?' 'Well, for one thing, I have to tell her you just said that.'"

"My husband is English and I'm American. I wonder what our children would be like. They'd probably be rude, but disgusted by their own behavior."

"I'm afraid of planes—I don't trust the oxygen mask. The little orange cup—attached to that bag that's full of nothing. Maybe I'm cynical. I don't even think that it's an oxygen mask. I think it's more to just muffle the screams."

"We've begun to long for the pitter-patter of little feet—so we bought a dog. Well, it's cheaper, and you get more feet."

"I think men who have a pierced ear are better prepared for marriage. They've experienced pain, and bought jewelry."

"I have a friend who's so into recycling she'll only marry a man who's been married before."

What's the common name for the animal *anobium pertinax* ? Bookworm.

ARE YOU DYING TO WATCH TV?

Numerous scientific studies suggest that you may live longer—and be happier—if you trade in your TV Guide for an exercise bike and a copy of Uncle John's Bathroom Reader *(it's a great way to pass the time while you're working out, too).*

TV CAN GIVE YOU: High cholesterol

Evidence: In a study at the University of California, Irvine, scientists found that children who watch more than two hours of TV or video games each day have twice the blood cholesterol levels of those watching less than two hours.

Why is this true? Three things happen when kids sit in front of the TV: they snack more, they exercise less, and their metabolic rate drops even lower than if they were laying in bed doing *nothing.*

More Evidence: Advertisers know it, too. According to Dr. Thomas Starc of Columbia University, ads for high-fat foods (such as pizza and fast-food burgers) during children's cartoon shows rose from 16% of the total in 1989 to 41% in 1993.

TV CAN MAKE YOU: Violent

Evidence: A team led by Prof. Ronald Huesmann, University of Michigan, studied 1,300 children in the U.S., Europe, and Israel from the early 1970s on. Did the children who watched TV violence get in more fights, bully others, commit crimes, or get more traffic tickets? Yes—especially right after seeing violence on TV. There were exceptions, of course, but Prof. Huesmann insists that the correlation was statistically as strong as that between smoking and lung cancer. This outcome was enhanced if the TV perpetrator was attractive, if the violence was socially sanctioned, or if guns were used. The violent outcome was reduced if the resulting pain and suffering were shown, if the children talked with adults about TV violence being unrealistic, or if there were strong social sanctions against imitating the violence.

TV CAN MAKE YOU: Paranoid

Evidence: Prof. Barbara Wilson of the University of California-Santa Barbara, found that children who watch the news have an unrealistically fearful picture of crime, war, and natural disasters in today's world. In a survey of parents of kids in third through sixth grades, she found that 37% of the parents thought their children had reacted with fear to a TV news story within the past year. But when she asked the kids directly, 51% could describe a TV news clip that scared them. Her conclusion: Kids under eight years old aren't ready for news programs.

TV CAN MAKE YOU: Depressed

Evidence: In a study of 4,280 people conducted by Dr. Stephen Sidney at Kaiser Permanente Hospital, people watching more than four hours of TV daily were 54% more likely to score high on a test measuring depression. Sidney cautioned that the study does not prove TV causes depression, but insisted that there is a correlation.

TV CAN MAKE YOU: A poor reader

Evidence: According to a study by the National Assessment of Educational Progress, a large majority of heavy-TV-watching students fall in the "basic" reading level, just able to get the meaning of what they read. Around a quarter to a third of students, depending on age, are "proficient,"—which means reading at their grade level, and only 2% to 4% fall in "advanced," or able to make complex analyses from what they read.

TV CAN MAKE YOU: An addict

Evidence: As part of a scientific study in 1971, 184 German TV watchers agreed to quit TV cold turkey. According to the Society for Rational Psychology, the group showed a sudden increase in moodiness, child spanking, wife beating, extramarital affairs, and less interest in sex. Several of the subjects had to go back to TV after only a few days. Although they were being paid, no one lasted more than five months. However, once back at the tube, all of their behavior returned to normal.

* * *

Random Household Hint: For perfectly round pancakes every time, use a turkey baster to "squirt" the batter onto the griddle.

Theodore Roosevelt's boyhood friends called him Teedie, not Teddy.

UNEXPECTED HAZARDS OF TV

...And then there are risks in watching TV that no scientist can predict.

WATCH OUT FOR: Angry relatives
Detectives in Boynton Beach, Florida called it "the couch potato murder." The wife and daughter of Joe Grieco, 52, and the daughter's boyfriend conspired to shoot Grieco because he was "depressed and cranky all the time and all he wanted to do was lay on the couch and watch TV." They tried to give Grieco a heart attack by putting LSD in his chicken dinner and cocaine in his wine, but it didn't work. Finally Mrs. Greico shot him while he snored in bed.

WATCH OUT FOR: Burnout! (Not you, the set)
Charlotte Gardener, 86, of London, England, kept her TV on 24 hours a day. After two years a component burned out. The fumes killed her.

WATCH OUT FOR: Falling objects
In 1995 A 30-ton boulder fell 500 feet off a cliff, crashed through a mobile home roof and killed Jackie Johnson, 19, of Adams Beach, Kentucky while he was watching TV on the couch. The man's grandmother, who had been watching TV beside him, had just gotten up to let her dog in. His grandfather, who was also sitting on the couch, was thrown up in the air and got a broken shoulder.

WATCH OUT FOR: Just dropping dead and no one notices
• The fully-dressed skeleton of a man who died 10 months earlier while watching TV was discovered in Roubaix, France. The TV was still on. Neighbors thought the man, 55, was in the hospital.
• In Bonn, Germany, a landlord entered the apartment of Wolfgang Dircks when he fell behind on rent. He was found dead with the TV on...and a TV guide on his lap dated December 5, 1993. It was then November 1998. Police ruled he died around the date of the TV guide.

Write this one down: The typewriter was invented before the fountain pen.

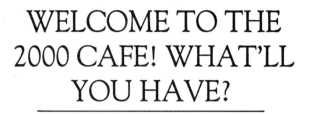

WELCOME TO THE 2000 CAFE! WHAT'LL YOU HAVE?

Burgers and fries? Pizza? Not in this joint. Even 20 years ago, experts figured that by now we'd be asking waiters to bring us worms & tofu. Here's a weird menu of predictions from our book, Uncle John's Indispensable Guide to the Year 2000

A BOTTLE OF FOOD PILLS

"By the year 2000, chemistry will replace agriculture. In the next century the day will come when everybody will carry his little gaseous tablets, his little ball of fatty matter, his little bit of sugar, his little bottle of aromatic spice, according to his personal taste."

—M. Berthelot, *Strand* magazine, February 1901

A SIDE ORDER OF UNDERWEAR

"By 2000, sawdust and wood pulp [will be] converted into sugary foods. Discarded paper table 'linen' and rayon underwear will be bought by chemical factories and converted into candy."

—John Smith, *Science Digest* magazine, 1967

A WORMS & TOFU PLATTER

"It's New Year's Day in the year 2001—the beginning of the 21st century. Claire and Sara are preparing a gala brunch. On tables in the living room are bowls of buffalo gourd seeds and cottonseed 'nuts' for guests to munch on. In the refrigerator, tofu pudding is chilling...

"Squid stew is bubbling on the stove...Sara is fixing scrambled egg substitute—special for guests who long for the foods mom used to make. But she's adding a modern touch—sautéed winged bean flowers.

Before Prohibition, the most common method of drinking beer at home was...

"Meanwhile, Claire nibbles a few fried meal worms (her favorite snacks) and rolls up the last of the Bee Won Ton. Just as she finishes, the doorbell rings. Happy New Year, everyone!"
—Paula Taylor, *The Kids' Whole Future Catalog*, 1982

PETROLEUM AND POOP

"A number of companies, both here and abroad, are looking into the use of petroleum as a source of edible protein.

"Then, too, our space activities have led to a lot of food science research. What we're really after here is some means of processing human waste so as to return it into food channels."
—John Smith, *Science Digest* (1967)

WATER FLEAS

"Man in [2000] may be eating 'water flea' steaks as a part of his daily diet [in 2000]. Dr. John R. Olive of Colorado State University said the 'water flea' Daphnia, is not really a flea at all but a bedbug-sized, soft-shelled crustacean that looks a bit like a tiny clam. Preliminary experiments have shown that a water flea-algae mixture is palatable as soup either cooked or uncooked. The mixture can also be dehydrated into a paste or into dried cakes.

"'It has a taste somewhat similar to shrimp,' Dr. Olive said. With just a small amount of flavoring, the mixture can be made to taste like eggs or steak."
—*Science Digest,* (1961)

EDIBLE CANS

"[By 2000], you may dump the contents of a can of beans into the saucepan—and then chop up the can and toss it in, too. If it were a corn-flavored can, [you] could have a tasty bowl of succotash…an edible whipped-cream-flavored can to go with preserved strawberries…And a tomato ketchup-flavored container to surround canned baked beans should appeal to a wide public. "
—Norman V. Carlisle & Frank Latham, *Miracles Ahead!* (1943)

drinking it straight out of a bucket filled at a local pub or brewery.

MOVIE STAR
FOR A DAY

Every actor hopes for that Big Break. But what if it comes...and nothing happens? Here are four examples of Hollywood's version of one-hit wonders, from Douglas Brode's book, Once Was Enough.

KATHERINE HOUGHTON
You're a Star! At age 21, shortly after graduating from college, Houghton won a lead role in the film *Guess Who's Coming to Dinner,* starring Spencer Tracy and Katherine Hepburn. Incredibly, she only had one year of acting under her belt...and didn't even have to take a screen test.

Just Kidding. Was she a prodigy? Nope—she was Hepburn's niece. And in the months leading up to the film's premiere, the movie studio and media hyped her as "another Hepburn." They built such high expectations that it was impossible for her to meet them. *Guess Who's Coming to Dinner* won an Oscar for best picture, but Houghton's performance was dismissed as "silly, shrill, and unsubstantial." It was the only blemish in an otherwise classic movie. There were no more film roles forthcoming, so Houghton retreated to regional theater.

NEIL CONNERY
You're a Star! In 1966 Italian film producer Dario Salsotello wanted someone who resembled Sean Connery to play the lead in a cheapo James Bond takeoff he was planning. A friend happened to mention that Connery had a younger brother who was working for $10 a day as a construction worker in Edinburgh. Astonished, Salsotello decided to hire Neil and make him the second big star in the Connery family.

Just Kidding. The movie, about "the younger brother of the world's greatest secret agent," was entitled *Operation Kid Brother.* Salsotello spared no expense to make it seem like an authentic part of the Bond series. He raided the casts of past 007 films, hiring Bond girls Daniela Bianchi (*From Russia with Love*) and Yashiko Yam (*You Only Live Twice*), and Bond villain Adolfo Celi (*Thunderball*) to reprise their roles. He even managed to hire Bernard Lee (M) and

---

What do people and lobsters have in common? Both like to eat lobster.

Lois Maxwell (Miss Moneypenny), although their characters' names weren't used, for fear of a lawsuit. All that was missing was big brother Sean. Brode writes:

> Neil was asked if his big brother might help out by making a cameo appearance; Neil admitted he and Sean were not particularly close. Sean had given him a Jaguar sports car that the superstar was ready to discard, but, Neil sighed, "I soon discovered the motor was shot." Sean Connery scoffed that the producers should "let Neil go back to plastering."

The movie, considered "the most expensive B-movie ever made" ($1.2 million) bombed...and Neil did go back to plastering.

GEORGE LAZENBY

You're a Star! Lazenby, a male model and onetime Marlboro Man, was handpicked by producer Albert "Cubby" Broccoli to play James Bond in the film *On Her Majesty's Secret Service* after Sean Connery quit the series in 1967.

Just Kidding. Broccoli offered Lazenby a second Bond film, but the actor turned it down and went sailing for 15 months, figuring he'd still be famous when he got back. Bad idea—while he was at sea, Connery returned to the Bond series and made *Diamonds Are Forever*. "When Lazenby returned home," Brode writes, "he was a forgotten has-been." Afterwards, he bounced from one bit part to another in bad kung fu movies and TV shows like *Hawaii Five-0*. His advice to Pierce Brosnan when Brosnan finished his first Bond film, *Goldeneye:* "Do two."

NICK APOLLO FORTE

You're a Star! Forte was an overweight, over-the-hill lounge singer in 1983 when a casting agent for Woody Allen saw his picture on an album in a record store bargain bin. The agent happened to be looking for an "overweight, over-the-hill lounge singer" to play a lead role in *Broadway Danny Rose*.

Just Kidding. Forte had never seen a Woody Allen film or acted in a movie, but he took the part. Allen even made Forte's song "*Agita*" (Italian for "indigestion") the movie's theme song...but the role had almost no real impact on Forte's life—though his lounge-singing rate went up from $100 to $150 per night. He never acted again.

THE GREAT "MARY" DEBATE

In Uncle John's Great Big Bathroom Reader, we mentioned the inspiration for the poem "Mary Had a Little Lamb." Little did we know that we were opening a Pandora's box of controversy and intrigue. We're not sure how this article from the Boston Globe came to us—one day it just appeared in our mailbox. We couldn't resist sharing it here.

WILD AND WOOLLY
It may not be the most weighty debate of the pre-millennial period, but the question of who wrote "Mary Had a Little Lamb" is sure consuming the folks in two small New England towns.

A century and three-quarters after the poem was published (give or take a few years, depending on which version of the story you believe), residents of Sterling, Massachusetts, and Newport, New Hampshire, are still arguing over ownership of the famous little ditty about a faithful lamb and unwelcoming schoolteacher.

The debate has at times gotten wild and woolly. Sterling (population 6,935) claims it was written by a schoolboy who witnessed an incident in that town involving a girl named Mary Sawyer. Newport (in the southwest corner of the state; population 6,110) insists it was written by a woman who had lived there, a prominent writer and editor. Proponents from both factions have produced what they say is definitive evidence for their case.

THE LION AND THE LAMB

Over the years, insults have been exchanged, allegations of plagiarism and lying tossed about. No one is backing down; in both cases, being known as the birthplace of the poem is a primary tourism draw.

"I've seen people go livid over this," says Lee Swanson, an historian with an interest in Sterling history. "They actually get red in the face."

Most recently (1999), passions have flared over the forming of the nonprofit Mary's Little Lamb Association, a preservation group of 12 Sterling residents who hope to parlay the Mary's lamb connection into a major fund-raising campaign. They would like to raise at least $250,000 to restore a farmhouse said to have belonged to the original Mary and make it a historical site.

HOMETOWN GIRL

"Everybody, including both sets of my grandparents, knew [the poem is part of Sterling history]," says Diane Melone of Sterling, a sixth-generation descendant of Mary Sawyer. Denying it is "like living in Gettysburg and saying the Battle of Gettysburg didn't happen there." Despite Melone's interest in all things Mary, she's never been to Newport to hear their side of things. "I'd probably get murdered," she says.

According to the official town source on the matter, "The True Story of Mary and Her Little Lamb," the Mary of the poem was a girl named Mary Sawyer born in 1806 in Sterling. One day in 1815 her devoted lamb followed her to school and up the classroom aisle when she was asked to recite a lesson. The teacher, alas, "turned it out," as the poem would have it.

The incident so amused and inspired a boy named John Roulstone, who happened to be visiting the classroom that day, that he took pencil to paper and dashed off the first three stanzas of "Mary Had a Little Lamb." Since then, the booklet states, three other stanzas have been added.

JUST THE FACTS...

The proof? "I don't have just one thing I wave under people's noses," says Melone, who...owns the Sawyer homestead. But evidence, she says, includes the fact that car magnate Henry Ford "believed it totally." Ford, who once owned the Wayside Inn in Sudbury, purchased the framework of the original schoolhouse in 1927 and had it moved to the inn, where it still stands.

It includes the corroboration of Judge Arthur P. Rugg of Sterling—a chief justice of the Massachusetts supreme court and Sawyer's next-door neighbor—who researched the poem's history and credited Roulstone with the first 12 lines. Plus, Mary Sawyer herself said Roulstone wrote it. The Historical Society archives contain a copy of an 1879 letter written by Sawyer in which she described the incident and confirmed Roulstone's authorship.

Supermarket news: The top 3 products for coupon redemption are cold cereal, soap, and deodorant.

TOURISTS WELCOME

Today, Sterling promotes itself as the home of Mary and her lamb. A small bronze lamb statue stands in tribute on the town common. The Sterling Historical Society sells Mary's lamb T-shirts and note cards and fuzzy lamb statuettes.

"Mary wasn't your simple country bumpkin," insists Mary's Little Lamb Association board member David Gibbs. "She went on to become matron of McLean Hospital. I believe if there is such credibility to the New Hampshire story, Henry Ford would have gone to Newport to obtain a schoolhouse."

ON THE OTHER HAND...

To Newport's proponents, it's uncomplicated: Every word of the poem was written by Newport native Sarah Josepha Hale.

Hale, easily Newport's most distinguished citizen, was editor of the publication called *Godey's Lady's Book* from 1837 to 1877, and author of 20 books and hundreds of poems. She is also credited with successfully advocating for Thanksgiving to be a national holiday and for the completion of the Bunker Hill monument.

The proof that she wrote "Mary Had a Little Lamb"? It was published in 1830 under her name, in a collection called "Poems for Our Children," says Andrea Thorpe, director of the Richards Free Library in Newport and chief proponent of the pro-Sarah side of the lamb debate.

Most important, Hale said she wrote it, in a signed statement that appeared in the *Boston Transcript* in 1889, written by her son on her behalf shortly before she died.

"She was shaping public opinion. Why would she stoop to plagiarize a lousy children's poem?" says Thorpe, administrator of the Sarah Josepha Hale award, given to writers with a New England connection. "Let's face it. Henry Ford...made good cars. I don't think he's a good historian."

A PLAQUE IN NEWPORT

Like Sterling, Newport proudly displays its link to the lamb. A memorial plaque to Hale states that "she composed the poem now called 'Mary Had a Little Lamb.'" Tour guides talk about it, and it's a subject of the Newport information guide produced by the Chamber of Commerce.

One in three dog owners say they've talked to their pets on the phone.

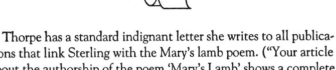

Thorpe has a standard indignant letter she writes to all publications that link Sterling with the Mary's lamb poem. ("Your article about the authorship of the poem 'Mary's Lamb' shows a complete disregard for literary history...and an ignorance of the contributions made by one of the most famous people to come from Newport.")

"It's getting so that every time (something is written), New Hampshire jumps in," snaps Ruth Hopfmann, curator of the Sterling Historical Society.

Meanwhile, the debate shows no sign of abating, although Sterling's Melone is willing to compromise and grant Hale authorship of the last three verses.

"Like she needs to be given the last three verses," says Thorpe. "We have no doubt that Sarah wrote it. Absolutely none.... Everyone except Sterling agrees with me."

THE PLOT THICKENS

Meanwhile, scholars Lee Swanson (historical coordinator of the Wayside Inn) and B. G. Thurston, who are collaborating on research on the history of "Mary Had a Little Lamb," say their research has led them to a nearly identical British version of the poem published earlier than Hale's about a "Lucy" and her little lamb. They are in the process of verifying the information.

Where would this leave Sterling and Newport? A little sheepish perhaps?

"I don't know," says Thurston. "I truly believe neither side is correct, though I don't have the full research to support it. It might be one of those mysteries that will never be solved."

*   *   *   *

A BAA-A-A-AD JOKE

Q: *Where do sheep get their hair cut?*
A: *At the baaa-baaa shop.*

Experts say: 46% of all violence on TV occurs in cartoons.

YEAH, WRIGHT

BRI members have been asking for more Steven Wright quotes—so here they are.

"For my birthday I got a humidifier and a dehumidifier...I put them in the same room and let them fight it out."

"I hate it when my foot falls asleep during the day because that means it's going to be up all night."

"I bought a dog the other day....I named him Stay. It's fun to call him...'Come here, Stay! Come here, Stay!' He went insane. Now he just ignores me and keeps typing."

"I stayed up all night playing poker with tarot cards. I got a full house and four people died."

"It doesn't matter what temperature the room is, it's always room temperature."

"A lot of people are afraid of heights. Not me—I'm afraid of widths."

"I just bought a microwave fireplace....You can spend an entire evening in front of it in only eight minutes."

"Last year I went fishing with Salvador Dali. He was using a dotted line. He caught every other fish."

"When I turned two I was really anxious, because I'd doubled my age in a year. I thought, if this keeps up, by the time I'm six I'll be ninety."

"I bought some land. It was kind of cheap. It was on somebody else's property."

"The guy who lives across the street from me has a circular driveway, and he can't get out."

"I bought some batteries, but they weren't included, so I had to buy them again."

"Babies don't need a vacation. But I still see them at the beach. It pisses me off. When no one's looking I'll go over to a baby and ask, 'What are you doing here? You haven't worked a day in your life.'"

"I went to a general store, but they wouldn't let me buy anything specific."

THE BEST BUSINESS DEAL IN U.S. HISTORY

The early days of the auto industry were like today's Internet boom—people could make huge fortunes by investing in the right car company. But no high-tech rags-to-riches story quite matched the return on investment that the Dodge brothers got for their $7,000 in auto parts and $3,000 in cash. It's a great, little-known business tale.

RAGS TO ROADSTERS
In 1901, the early days of the automobile, Ransom Eli Olds was looking for subcontractors who could manufacture parts for his Curved Dash Oldsmobile. The best machine shop in the Detroit area was a company called Leland and Faulconer, but they were already committed to supplying parts for the new Cadillac Automobile Company (see page 474). So Olds turned to the second-best machine shop in town, owned and operated by John and Horace Dodge.

Experience Counts
The brothers Dodge were only in their mid-30s, but they already had more than 20 years' experience working with internal combustion engines. Their father owned a machine shop on the river that connected Lake Huron with Lake Erie, and the brothers spent much of their childhood helping him repair and rebuild ship engines.

By the time John and Horace were in their 20s, both were working as machinists in Detroit. They spent the next several years perfecting their skills at various companies, and in 1897 opened a bicycle company to manufacture an "improved" bicycle they'd designed themselves. Two years later, they sold the company and used the money—$7,500 in cash and $10,000 worth of machine tools—to open the Dodge Brothers Machine Shop in Detroit.

SHIFTING GEARS
Dodge Brothers started out manufacturing parts for all different types of products, including firearms, bicycles, automobiles, and

steam engines. But they got so much business from Olds that they dropped everything else and began manufacturing auto parts exclusively. Olds sold 2,000 cars in 1902, more than any other carmaker in the country, and every one of them had a Dodge transmission. As production continued to climb, Dodge Brothers moved to a newer, larger shop and spent tens of thousands of dollars on new machine tools to keep up with the demand.

Then in 1903, the Dodge brothers took a huge risk: they dumped the Olds Motor Works account and agreed to begin manufacturing engines, transmissions, and chassis for the Ford & Malcomson Company—which, unlike Olds, had only recently opened for business had yet to manufacture a single car.

HARD BARGAIN

Why would the Dodge brothers abandon Olds for Ford–Malcomson? Part of the reason was that Henry Ford, the company's co-founder, had showed them the plans for his Model A "Fordmobile," and the Dodges were impressed. They thought it had a good chance of succeeding.

But there was an even bigger incentive: Ironically, Henry Ford's track record of failure (he had already run two companies into the ground) actually made doing business with him more lucrative for the Dodge brothers than if he had been a success. His credit rating was so bad that he had to offer the brothers a sweeter business deal than they could have gotten anywhere else in town.

Normally, in the machine parts industry, an auto company like Ford-Malcomson would have 60 days to pay for auto parts after delivery. But since the Dodges weren't sure if Ford would still be in business in 60 days, they demanded cash up front on the first shipment of parts, and payment within 15 days on each subsequent delivery. If Ford couldn't pay, ownership of all unsold parts automatically reverted to the Dodge brothers. The terms were tough, but Ford had to agree.

HOWDY, PARDNER

There was one more perk. When Henry Ford and Alex Malcomson, Detroit's leading coal merchant, set out to found an auto company together, they had hoped to finance the entire venture with their own savings. But they soon realized they didn't have enough

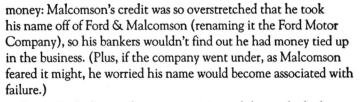

money: Malcomson's credit was so overstretched that he took his name off of Ford & Malcomson (renaming it the Ford Motor Company), so his bankers wouldn't find out he had money tied up in the business. (Plus, if the company went under, as Malcomson feared it might, he worried his name would become associated with failure.)

Henry Ford's financial position wasn't much better: he had very little money of his own, and had already alienated Detroit's business community with his two earlier business failures. Nobody wanted to invest in a company run by a two-time loser like Ford.

With so few people willing to invest in Ford, Malcomson pushed the company's stock onto friends and colleagues who owed him favors. He also pitched the shares to people who had a direct financial stake in the company's survival, two of whom were John and Horace Dodge. Malcomson offered them a 10% stake in the Ford Motor Company, in exchange for $7,000 worth of auto parts and $3,000 in cash.

Now you know what the deal is. Turn to page 295 for the rest of the story.

*   *   *

HOLY BAT FACTS!

• Most species of bats live 12 to 15 years, but some live as long as 30 years. Some species can fly as fast as 60 miles per hour and as high as 10,000 feet.

• Bats are social animals and live in colonies in caves. The colonies can get *huge:* Bracken Cave in Texas contains an estimated 20 million Mexican free-tailed bats.

• Vampire bats drink blood throw a "drinking straw" that the bat makes with its tongue and its lower lip. The bats' saliva contains an anticoagulant that keeps blood flowing by impeding the formation of blood clots.

• It's not uncommon for a vampire bat to return to the same animal night after night, weakening and eventually killing its prey.

Honeybees can fly as fast as 30 mph.

AESOP:
FACT OR FABLE?

*Chances are, you've heard of Aesop's fables—people have
been repeating them for thousands of years. But did you
know there was a real person named Aesop?*

BACKGROUND

If you were asked to name to the most influential writers in
Western history, you might include Aristotle...or Shake-
speare...or even Dr. Spock. But you probably wouldn't think of
Aesop.

Yet his works have been around for over 2,000 years, and he's
had an impact on everything from ancient Greek philosophy to
20th-century American culture. Adages such as "Don't cry over
spilled milk" and expressions like "sour grapes," for example, come
directly from his fables.

On the other hand, Aesop wasn't technically a writer. Nothing
was written down during his lifetime; it was oral tradition that kept
both his legend and his fables alive. Still, scholars are reasonably
certain he existed—and that he was a revered storyteller. "The best
evidence we have of Aesop's life comes from remarks about him in
early ancient sources like Herodotus, Aristotle, Aristophanes and
Plato," writes Leo Groarke Wilfrid of Laurier University. In fact,
Socrates, considered the greatest philosopher of ancient Greece, "is
said to have passed the time awaiting execution by putting Aesop's
fables into verse."

A BRIEF BIOGRAPHY

Scholars have established a few facts about Aesop's life:

• He was born a Greek slave in the sixth century B.C.

• He had a natural gift for fables and became famous in ancient
Greece because of it. Eventually his "learning and wit" earned him
his freedom.

• As a freed man he traveled widely until Croesus, the rich and
powerful king of ancient Lydia, invited him to become an ambassador. Aesop accepted and was sent to various republics of Greece,

---

What do tongue prints and fingerprints have in common? No two are alike.

trying to establish peace "by telling his wise fables."

• Aesop's last diplomatic mission was to Delphi. Croesus gave him gold to distribute to the citizens. However, Aesop was so offended by the Delphians' greed that he just sent the loot back to Croesus. Proving his point, the Delphians became so enraged that they accused Aesop of "impiety"—a major crime—and executed him as a public criminal. According to legend, they pushed him off a cliff.

• Following the execution of Aesop, a myth grew up around the incident. It was said that a series of calamities befell the citizens of Delphi. The disasters got worse and worse until, finally, the people confessed their crime and made reparations. After that, "the blood of Aesop" became a common reference to the fact that evil deeds will not go unpunished.

HOW THE FABLES CAME TO US

After his death, Aesop became a sort of mythical figure (like Mother Goose) to whom fables were automatically attributed, no matter who invented them. For a thousand years after his death, he was more famous than ever. But with the coming of the Dark Ages, he was forgotten.

Then, 600 years later, in the 1300s, a Turkish monk named Planudes assembled a collection of about 150 of Aesop's fables. When Italian scholars of the mid-1400s became interested in antiquity, Planudes' book was one of the first works they translated and printed, along with works by Homer and Aristotle.

Aesop's tales spread from Italy to Germany, where his popularity grew. The "great fathers of the Reformation" used his fables to inveigh against the Catholic Church; Martin Luther himself translated 20 of Aesop's fables and said that next to the Bible, he valued *Aesop's Fables* above all other books.

Finally, in 1610, a Swiss scholar named Isaac Nicholas Nevelet printed a version of Aesop's fables called *Mythologica Aesopica*. It was popular all over Europe and made Aesop a permanent part of Western civilization. "No book," wrote the compiler of a 19th-century collection, "with the exception of the Holy Scriptures, has had a wider circulation than *Aesop's Fables*. They have been translated into the greater number of the languages both of Europe and of the East, and have been read, and will be read, for generations by the inhabitants of all countries."

AESOP'S FABLES

Aesop's fables (see page 207) have been told and retold for thousands of years. Here are some of our favorites.

THE FOX & THE CRANE

A fox once invited a crane to dinner and served soup in a very shallow dish. He thought it was funny that the crane, with his long beak, couldn't drink any of the soup.

Then he said, "My dear crane, I'm so sorry to see that you're not eating anything. didn't you like the soup?"

"Oh, everything is just fine," the crane answered. "And now you must do me the honor of paying me a visit."

When the fox came to the crane's house and sat down to dinner, a very tall jar was placed in front of him. It was so tall and narrow that the fox couldn't get his snout into it.

"I'm so glad to be able to return your courtesy," said the crane as he reached his long beak into the jar. "I hope you enjoy your dinner every bit as much as I did mine when I visited you."

Moral: *What goes around, comes around. You get what you deserve.*

THE FIR TREE & THE BRAMBLE

A fir tree boasted to a bramble, "You're useful for nothing at all; while I am used for roofs and houses and all kinds of things." The bramble answered: "You poor creature, if you would only call to mind the axes and saws which are about to cut you down, you would wish you'd grown up a bramble, not a fir tree."

Moral: *Better poverty without care, than riches with a worried life.*

BELLING THE CAT

Long ago, a group of mice had a general council to consider what measures they could take to outwit their common enemy, the cat. Some said this, and some said that; but at last a young mouse got up and said he had a proposal to make, which he thought would meet the case. "You will all agree," said he, "that our chief danger consists in the sly and treacherous manner in which the enemy approaches us. Now, if we could receive some signal of her approach, we could easily escape from her. I venture, therefore, to propose that a small bell be procured, and attached by a ribbon round the neck of the cat. By this means we should always know when she was about, and could easily retire while she was in the neighborhood."

This proposal met with general applause, until an old mouse got up and said: "That is all very well, but who is to bell the cat?" The mice looked at one another and nobody spoke Then the old mouse said: "It is easy to propose impossible remedies."

Moral: *Talk is cheap.*

THE BUFFOON & THE COUNTRYMAN

At a country fair there was a Buffoon who made all the people laugh by imitating the cries of various animals. He finished off by squeaking so like a pig that the spectators thought that he had a porker concealed about him. But a Countryman who stood by said: "Call that a pig's squeak! Nothing like it. You give me till tomorrow and I will show you what it's like." The audience laughed, but next day, sure enough, the Countryman appeared on the stage, and putting his head

down squealed so hideously that the spectators hissed and threw stones at him to make him stop. "You fools!" he cried, "see what you have been hissing," and held up a little pig whose ear he had been pinching to make him utter the squeals.

Moral: *Men often applaud an imitation and hiss the real thing.*

THE DOG'S REFLECTION

Once there was a dog who was given a fine, meaty bone. With the bone firmly between his teeth, the dog trotted homeward, thinking of what a fine meal he was going to enjoy.

On the way, he had to cross a narrow bridge over a brook. As he looked over the side of the bridge, he caught sight of his own reflection in the water. Thinking it was another dog carrying a bone between his teeth, the foolish animal made up his mind that he would have that bone, too.

He leaned over and snapped at the dog beneath him. As he did, the bone fell into the water and was lost.

Moral: *Be careful that you don't lose what you have by trying to get more.*

ARMREST-LING

Don't you hate it when the person sitting next to you on an airplane or in a theater hogs the armrest between you? You're not the only one. This excerpt is from The Science of Everyday Life, *by Canada's favorite science-TV host, Jay Ingram.*

SPACE INVASION

We all carry around an invisible bubble of personal space. Its dimensions vary, but it extends about 70 centimeters (a little over two feet) in front, 40 centimeters behind, and 60 to each side. A wealth of social psychology research has established that we react negatively to violation of our personal space, because we reserve that area for ourselves. Obviously we can change the rules as we wish, allowing others into our personal spaces if we are fond of them, or if circumstances—such as a crowded subway—make it impossible to maintain the usual space. Scientific experiments have shown that the higher your social status, the larger your "personal space" (it must swell as your prominence grows)...that reactions to violation of personal space can range from flight to violence...and that men maintain larger personal spaces than women do.

SCIENCE AT WORK

It's hard to design experiments that measure exactly how much space we need, and how we react to personal "space invasions"...But one study, conducted by three social psychologists at St. Bonaventure University in 1982, did it brilliantly by posing the question: "What happens when men and women...have to fight for control of the armrests in the economy-class section of airplanes?"

• A total of 852 people—426 man-woman pairs of passengers sitting next to each other—on 20 different plane flights were watched to see who occupied the armrest.

• Then travelers were interviewed to get an idea of their attitudes towards possession of the armrest.

Economy-class seats may well have been designed by an experimental psychologist, because their narrowness ensures direct person-to-person conflict over the armrest. You know if you've sat in such a seat that your arms naturally fall over the armrests, and there's *nothing* natural about the position you have to adopt if those armrests are

That's ironic: Only U.S. president to head a labor union—Ronald Reagan.

denied to you. The armrest is actually an object that sits within the personal spaces of two individuals.

RESULTS

The results were clear-cut. Of the 426 co-ed pairs of passengers, 284 men and only 57 women used the armrest: that's 5 men for every woman. In 37 cases, both used it, and in a further 48, the armrest remained untouched. Even when the data were adjusted to ensure that only men and women of roughly equal size were considered, there were still three times as many men as women using the armrest. A questionnaire distributed to 100 air travelers of both sexes highlighted the male in-flight aggression. Sixty-eight percent of males interviewed claimed it "bothered" them to have a seat-mate use the common armrest, while only 42% of the females felt that way. And it's males under 40 who resent it most. Of 23 who admitted it bothered them not to have the armrest, 21 said they felt "very annoyed."

PERSONAL BIAS

I confess to some feelings of possession about the common armrest myself, but only if I feel I've been the victim of some hyper-aggressive, armrest-grabbing boor who seems to assume that it's theirs. Then I spend the next 10 minutes figuring out how to take possession. Sometimes I manage it gradually, resting just the tip of my elbow at the back and slowly pushing it onto the extreme edge, then pushing gently sideways. Sometimes an all-at-once seizure is possible (especially easy if the possessor has to go to the washroom). Of course meal-time becomes traumatic—how can you lift the lid off your dessert without relinquishing your territory, if only for a moment? Then there's the acute disappointment when it becomes clear that the other person isn't even aware of the armrest, makes no effort to reclaim it, and is totally oblivious to the fact that I've just spent the last 45 minutes stewing in my own hormones.

And you thought that it was only comfort that the extra-wide seating afforded business-class customers. It's much more: they are spared the stress of the constant battle for personal space that is waged in economy class. The airlines have it all wrong—economy class passengers should get the better meals and the high-grade cognac. They've earned it.

Why don't wolves bark like dogs? One theory: They don't want to.

CULTURE SHOCK

*Do you take it for granted that our culture is the "real" one...
and that other peoples' traditions are just sort of quaint? Some
Americans do and we wind up accidentally offending people
in other parts of the world. A few cases in point:*

P URELY COMMERCIAL
"Hindus are up in arms about Madonna's performance at the
MTV Video Music Awards. Madonna wore 'Vaishnava tilak,'
holy facial markings representing purity. But, says the World Vaishnava Association, 'wearing this sacred marking while wearing
clothing through which her nipples were clearly visible and gyrat-
ing in a sexually suggestive manner with her guitar player...offend-
ed Hindus...throughout the world.' The WVA seeks apologies."

—*USA Today,* **September 14, 1998**

DEJA VU
"Following weeks of protest from Hindu groups, Renaissance Pictures has agreed to pull out of worldwide circulation an entire episode of *Xena: Warrior Princess.* The story line involved the Hindu
deities Lord Krishna and Hanuman aiding Xena in her escape from
a demon king.... 'Not only does this make the viewing audience
think that Lord Krishna and other Hindu deities are fictional,' said
one protester, 'It makes Hindus themselves look foolish. After all,
nobody but a superstitious fool would worship a fictional god.'"

—*The Nation,* **June 7, 1999**

IT'S GREEK TO ME
"Disney's animated film *Hercules* has spurred a wrath in Greece
worthy of the mighty Zeus....Critics have lashed out at the Mickey
Mouse empire, accusing its creators of messing with ancient Greek
lore to a ludicrous degree....In the Hollywood film, the mighty
hero is born on Mount Olympus, the son of a happily wed Zeus and
Hera. He's kidnapped by wicked Uncle Hades, and on Earth takes
on more than a dozen tasks, including thrashing the Minotaur and
defeating the Medusa.

"One need not be a classics scholar to know that the Minotaur
was killed by Theseus, the Medusa by Perseus. Hades was not the

---

Experts say: If you're typical, your body contains about four ounces of salt.

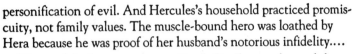

personification of evil. And Hercules's household practiced promiscuity, not family values. The muscle-bound hero was loathed by Hera because he was proof of her husband's notorious infidelity....

"To avoid further controversy, Greek distributors changed the film's title to *Beyond the Myth of Heracles*."

—*USA Today*, October 2, 1997

LOCAL HERO

"Nike Inc. agreed to scrap a billboard of an inner city Los Angeles basketball player nicknamed 'Allah' after an Islamic American group complained that the ads were offensive....The ad featured an L.A. Crenshaw High School graduate named John Williams, who was pictured hanging from the rim of a basket with the caption, '...and they called him Allah' and a Nike logo.

"The creative team that researched the ad found that, 'Whenever Williams stepped on the court, the crowd would chant "Allah," ' said Nike spokesperson Erin Patton. But he conceded Nike made a mistake in 'overlooking the spiritual relevance of the word.' "

—*Reuters*, 1995

IN THE TRASH

"McDonald's inadvertently offended thousands of Muslims by printing a Koran scripture on throwaway Happy Meal bags, then staged a retreat after Islamic leaders complained. The stir...began with a World Cup promotion that featured flags of the 24 competitors in this summer's soccer championship. The green and white Saudi flag contains an Arabic passage translated as 'There is no God but Allah, and Mohammed is his Prophet,' sacred words that Muslims say should not be crumpled up and thrown in the trash."

—*Fresno Bee*, June 8, 1994

FASHION STATEMENT

"In 1994 a dress that Karl Lagerfeld designed for Chanel was pulled from the season's line. The Arab world was up in arms after the sexy black item with Arabic words embroidered across it was modeled on the runway. The objectors complained that the words were from the Koran. Lagerfeld apologized, explaining that he was under the impression that the words were from a love poem. The dress was destroyed, along with all film and pictures of it."

—*The Business Disaster Book of Days*

Naturalists tell us: An adult crocodile can go two years without eating.

AMIMALS FAMOUS FOR 15 MINUTES

When Andy Warhol said, "In the future, everyone will be famous for 15 minutes," he obviously didn't have animals in mind. Yet even they haven't been able to escape the relentless publicity machine that keeps cranking out instant celebrities.

THE HEADLINE: *Vote for a Chimp, Not a Chump*

THE STAR: Tiao, a chimpanzee in Rio de Janeiro

WHAT HAPPENED: Before he entered political life, Tiao ("Big Uncle") was one of the main attractions at the Rio zoo, where he'd developed a reputation for "losing his temper, spitting, and throwing excrement at visiting dignitaries." Then in 1988, anti-establishment activists decided he was the perfect candidate to clean up the mess at Rio's city hall. They formed the Brazilian Banana Party and ran Tiao for mayor. He came in third, with more than 400,000 votes.

AFTERMATH: Tiao never ran for office again, but when he died in 1996, Rio's mayor declared a week-long mourning period and ordered that all flags at the zoo be flown at half-mast. "It is a great loss," the mayor said. "He demonstrated the joyfulness of Rio."

THE HEADLINE: *Dog Panics, Pig Stays Calm, Woman Is Saved*

THE STAR: Lulu, a 150-pound Vietnamese pot-bellied pig in Beaver Falls, Pennsylvania

WHAT HAPPENED: In August 1998, JoAnne Altsman was vacationing in a trailer with her dog, Bear, and her pig, Lulu, when she had a heart attack and collapsed. "I was yelling, 'Somebody help me....Call an ambulance,'" Altsman says. Bear could sense that something was wrong, but all he did was bark. Lulu, on the other hand, squeezed through the trailer's doggy door, pushed open a gate she'd never opened before, and ran into the street, where she lay on her back in front of passing cars.

The first driver who stopped was too frightened to get out of his car, but the second followed Lulu back to the trailer, found Altsman

---

Is your daughter engaged? Move to Thailand. The parents of the *groom* pay for weddings there.

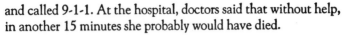

and called 9-1-1. At the hospital, doctors said that without help, in another 15 minutes she probably would have died.

AFTERMATH: Altsman underwent open-heart surgery and is recovering; Lulu, who received a cut on her belly trying to squeeze through the too-small doggy door, was treated by a veterinarian and released. For her bravery, Lulu was awarded a jelly donut.

THE HEADLINE: *Dog Emigrates to U.S., Master Doesn't*

THE STAR: Diana, a dog owned by Cuban refugees

WHAT HAPPENED: In the mid-1990s, a U.S. Coast Guard ship rescued 11 Cubans and one dog they found floating on a raft near Florida. It was U.S. policy to take Cubans rescued on the high seas to the U.S. Naval Station at Guantánamo Bay (instead of Florida), but dogs aren't allowed there. Normally that would have meant Diana would be shot...but on this day a CBS News crew was on board the Coast Guard ship. CBS producer Larry Doyle volunteered to take responsibility for the dog.

AFTERMATH: When CBS News broadcast the story of the rescue, it was deluged with calls from viewers (and even the Florida Humane Society) asking if Diana was okay. "She's better than okay," Doyle reported. "It turns out she's pregnant and will give birth to puppies soon." He placed the dog with friends living in Key West, Florida. Unfortunately, Diana's Cuban master wasn't so lucky—he was shipped back to Cuba.

THE HEADLINE: *Choking Kitten Calls 9-1-1, Saves Self*

THE STAR: Tipper, a cat in Tampa, Florida

WHAT HAPPENED: Tipper was home alone, chewing on her flea collar one afternoon in August 1996 when she began choking on it. As she struggled to free the collar from her mouth, the cat somehow hit the speed dial on the phone, which her owner, Gail Curtis, had programmed to dial 9-1-1. The emergency dispatcher, hearing only meows, sent paramedics...who arrived several minutes later. They found Tipper, removed the flea collar, and saved her life.

AFTERMATH: The story was featured on news programs all over the country. Tipper hasn't used the phone since.

"RUMORS OF
MY DEATH..."

While he was visiting England in 1897, Mark Twain received an inquiry from the U.S. about a report that he had died. "Rumors of my death," he cabled back, "are greatly exaggerated." He's not the only celebrity whose death has been erroneously reported. Here are three of our favorite "false death" stories, and their impact.

A PRIZE MISTAKE

Who "Died": Alfred Nobel, Swedish inventor of dynamite, blasting caps, smokeless gunpowder, and hundreds of other explosion-related items

Cause of "Death": Mistaken identity. On April 13, 1888, Nobel awoke in Paris, opened a newspaper, and was astonished to read his own obituary. But it was actually his brother *Ludwig* who'd died; the newspaper had goofed.

What Happened: As a result of this mistake, Nobel was given a rare gift—a chance to see how he would be remembered...and he didn't like what he saw. As David Zacks writes in *An Underground Education*:

> Alfred was shocked to see himself portrayed as the Merchant of Death, the man responsible for escalating the arms race....[Even though] he had made high-powered explosives much easier to use and was proud of how this power had been unleashed to mine precious minerals and to build roads, railways, and canals.

The obituary painted him as a "bellicose monster" whose discoveries "had boosted the bloody art of war from bullets and bayonets to long-range explosives in less than 24 years."

Determined to change his image and redeem the family name, Nobel hatched a shrewd plan. He used his wealth to create prizes in several areas—including peace. (Sort of like "the Exxon award for environmental safety...[or] the John F. Kennedy award for marital fidelity," Zacks says). It was successful spin control. Today, the Nobel Prizes are the most prestigious in the world...and few of us connect their creator to "the art of killing."

State with the highest percentage of people who walk to work: Alaska.

JUST A RUMOR

Who "Died": Vice President Thomas Jefferson

Cause of "Death": Dirty politics. America's first really nasty presidential campaign was underway in 1800 when, on June 30, the Baltimore *American* reported that Jefferson (running against incumbent president John Adams) had died suddenly at his Virginia home. The story was confirmed the next day by the Philadelphia *True American*.

What Happened: According to Bruce Felton and Mark Fowler in their book *The Best, Worst and Most Unusual*:

> Reports of the death of the vice president elicited no statements of sympathy, no words of grief from President Adams, vice presidential candidate Charles Cotesworth Pinckney, or any other prominent Federalist politician, which is a measure of the bitterness of the campaign. On the other hand, Jefferson's friends spent July 4 in somber mourning. News traveled slowly in that era, and reports of Jefferson's death did not reach some outlying areas until the middle of July. And the truth followed about one week behind.

What happened? *The Gazette of the United States* finally explained: "An old Negro slave called Thomas Jefferson, being dead at Monticello, gave rise to the report of the demise of the Vice-President—the slave having borne the name of his master."

But the whole episode "was no innocent misunderstanding," write Felton and Fowler. "The rumors and reports were cleverly calculated to underscore Jefferson's slave-owning status, and the gossip about his affairs with black women. Had the timing been better, it might have influenced the election."

WRITTEN IN THE STARS

Who "Died": John Partridge, best-known English astrologer of the early 1700s and publisher of the annual astrology almanac *Merlinus Liberatus*

Cause of "Death": A practical joke. Satirist Jonathan Swift, author of *Gulliver's Travels*, hated astrologers (he thought astrology was nonsense) but loved April Fools' Day jokes. In 1708 he pulled one on Partridge. Taking the pen name Isaac Bickerstaff and posing as a "true astrologer" who wanted to expose the "gross abuses...

nonsense, lies and folly" put out by "false astrologers" like Partridge, Swift published a penny pamphlet of bogus prophesies, titled *Predictions for the Year 1708*. He wrote:

> [My first prediction] relates to Partridge the almanac-maker; I have consulted the star of his nativity by my own rules, and find he will infallibly die upon the 29th of March next, about eleven at night, of a raging fever.

What Happened: On March 30, Swift—using a different pen name this time—published a second pamphlet: *The Accomplishment of the First of Mr. Bickerstaff's Predictions*. It supplied a graphic description of Partridge's supposed final moments, including a scene in which the anguished, repentant astrologer admitted in a deathbed confession that he was a fake. "All pretences of foretelling by astrology are deceits," Partridge supposedly said, "and none but the poor ignorant vulgar give it any credit." As and historian Rowse writes,

> Swift's plan succeeded beyond his wildest expectations. His own penny pamphlet sold in multitudes and pirate publishers were soon offering halfpenny reprints, replies, and imitations.... What had begun as a simple practical joke grew into a full-blown fantasy until more people knew of Partridge's death than had ever heard of him alive.

In the next issue of his almanac, Partridge protested that he wasn't really dead, and attacked Bickerstaff as an "impudent, lying fellow." Swift anonymously shot back with another pamphlet: *Vindication of Isaac Bickerstaff*, in which he provided several "proofs" that Partridge really was dead. He even accused Partridge of being an impostor of himself.

Result: People really came to believe that Partridge was dead and that the person claiming to be him—Partridge—was an interloper trying to take over the business. Because of this, sales of Partridge's almanacs plummeted, forcing him out of business. He never found out who was behind the hoax.

*   *   *

...DOES "ONE BAD APPLE" SPOIL THE BARREL?

According to apple experts, they do: When an apple starts to rot, it releases a chemical called ethylene that causes it to decay. The other apples in a barrel can sense this chemical reaction, and when they do, they start producing their own ethylene, causing all the apples in the barrel to spoil.

Til it's over: The decapitated jaws of a snapping turtle can keep snapping for about a day.

OOPS!

*More tales of outrageous blunders to let us know that
someone's screwing up even worse than we are. So
go ahead and feel superior for a few minutes.*

JUST DO IT

TICONDEROGA, New York—"A company is trying to erase an embarrassing mistake it made on pencils bearing an anti-drug message. The pencils carry the slogan: 'Too Cool To Do Drugs.'

"But a sharp-eyed fourth-grader in northern New York noticed when the pencils are sharpened, the message turns into 'Cool To Do Drugs' then simply 'Do Drugs.'

"'We're actually a little embarrassed that we didn't notice that sooner,' spokeswoman Darlene Clair told today's *Press-Republican* of Plattsburgh."

—Associated Press, December 11, 1998

WELL, NEVER MIND THEN

"We shall never know the identity of the man who in 1976 made the most unsuccessful hijack attempt ever. On a flight across America, he rose from his seat, drew a gun and took the stewardess hostage.

"'Take me to Detroit,' he said.

"'We're already going to Detroit,' she replied.

"'Oh...good,' he said, and sat down again."

—*Book of Heroic Failures*

STAMPS OF APPROVAL

WASHINGTON—"The Grand Canyon has been misplaced by the post office.

"A newly printed batch of 100 million 6-cent international stamps carry a picture of the canyon and, on the bottom of each stamp, the words 'Grand Canyon, Colorado.'

"The Grand Canyon is actually located in the state of Arizona."

—Associated Press, May 17, 1999

The London Zoo reportedly employs an "entertainment director" for the animals.

BEASTLY MISTAKE

"After Cody Johnston, 22, of Bozeman, Montana, was fined $195 for a traffic violation, a court computer error turned it into a conviction for deviate sexual conduct. That's the way it appeared in a crime report in the *High Country Independent Press*, where Johnston's parents read it. When he told them it wasn't true, his wife and his sister accused him of being in denial and urged him to seek counseling. Even though the *Independent Press* printed a correction, Johnston filed a libel suit against the paper and the court system, noting, 'I've heard every sheep joke you can imagine.'"

—*Weird News*

IF YOU DON'T COUGH, YOU MIGHT GET OFF

CARDIFF, Wales—"When a juror coughed, defendant Alan Rashid had a right to feel sick.

"The cough came just as the jury foreman announced a verdict of 'not guilty' in Rashid's trial on a charge of threatening homicide.

"The cough coincided with 'not,' Judge Michael Gibbon only heard 'guilty' and Rashid was sentenced to two years in prison.

"As the jury left the court Thursday, one inquisitive member of the panel asked an usher why Rashid was going to jail after being found innocent. So the jurors were herded back into court.

"Rashid was brought back to court, the jury confirmed its 'not guilty' verdict and Gibbon told the defendant he was free to go.

"'I am very relieved, as you would imagine,' Rashid said."

—Associated Press, April 16, 1999

HAPPINESS IS A WARM GUN

"Madison, Wisconsin, police chief Richard Williams turned on his oven to roast some turkey but forgot that was one of his favorite hiding places for his gun. "Shortly thereafter: boom!" police spokesperson Jeanna Kerr said, adding that Williams was given a one-day, unpaid suspension for violating his department's firearms policy."

—*News of the Weird*, November 1998

Rules of the road: Men are more likely than women to run stoplights...

CRÈME *de la* CRUD

Most celebrities are famous because they're good at what
they do…but a rare few are remembered as the
absolute worst. We at the BRI salute them.

THE CHERRY SISTERS, *world's worst variety act*

Background: In the mid-1890s, Broadway impresario Oscar
Hammerstein promoted a number of spectacular stage shows,
only to see them lose money due to lack of public interest. So he
decided to change gears. "I've been putting on the best talent and
it hasn't gone over," he groused to reporters. "Now I'm trying the
worst." He was referring to the Cherry Sisters.

Career Notes:
The four Cherry Sisters were from Cedar Rapids, Iowa. Tall, thin
Addie, Effie, and Lizzie were the singers in the group; short fat
Jessie "kept time," thumping intermittently on a bass drum.

• The sisters started by touring vaudeville houses in the Midwest
and were so awful—even to small-town audiences starved for entertainment—that wire screens had to be erected across the front of
the stages where they performed, to protect them from rotten vegetables and other garbage that audiences routinely threw at them.

• Hammerstein signed them to a $1,000-a-week contract to
play at his Olympia Theater. Their debut on November 16, 1896,
marked a turning point in their career: instead of being pelted
with garbage, they were met with a shower of bad reviews. In an
article titled "Four Freaks From Iowa," a *New York Times* reviewer
described the sisters as "genuine products of the barnyard," and
speculated that their performance might be due to poor diet. "It
is sincerely hoped," he wrote, "that nothing like them will ever be
seen again."

• Just as motorists slow down to look at traffic accidents, more
and more people went to see the Cherry Sisters perform. Their reputation for being the world's worst variety act grew, and soon they
were playing to sold-out crowds. Hammerstein made a small fortune off the act, and the Cherry Sisters became "the best-known,
if not the best-loved stage performers in America."

FLORENCE FOSTER JENKINS, *world's worst opera singer*
Background: There may have been worse opera singers, but none
who achieved fame for it. "She clucked and squawked, trumpeted
and quavered," said one observer. Another noted that she was
"undaunted by...the composer's intent." And in *The Book of Heroic
Failures*, Howard Pyle writes: "No one, before or since, has succeeded in liberating themselves quite so completely from the shack-
les of musical notation."

Career Notes:

• Singing opera was Jenkins's lifelong dream. But she was unable
to pursue it until 1909, at age 40, when her father died and left her
a fortune. Since no one in their right mind would finance Jenkins's
recitals, she paid for them herself, and developed an enthusiastic
following.

• "Different audiences reacted in various ways," writes Carl Sifakis in *Great American Eccentrics*. "Some roared with laughter until
tears rolled down their cheeks; others sat in utter silence, according
her unique voice an attention befitting the world's greatest
singers."

• Critics were at a loss as to how to describe her. Some called
her "The First Lady of the Sliding Scale." When she released a
record, *Newsweek* commented: "In high notes, Mrs. Jenkins sounds
as if she was afflicted with a low, nagging backache."

• Jenkins's trademark was outrageous costumes. Pyle writes:
"One minute she would appear sporting an immense pair of wings
to render 'Ave Maria.' The next she would emerge [as] a senorita,
with a rose between her teeth and a basket full of flowers." She often threw roses into the audience...then sent her accompanist to
gather them up so she could throw them out again. Once she became so excited that she threw the basket, too.

• On October 25, 1944, the beloved 75-year-old diva rented
out Carnegie hall...and performed to a sold-out crowd. "So great
was the demand for tickets," writes Sifakis, "that they were scalped
at the then-outrageous price of $20 apiece. More than 2,000 lovers
of music had to be turned away." La Jenkins took it in stride, as she
had over her 30-year career. "Some may say I couldn't sing," she
quipped, "but no one can say that I *didn't* sing." A month later,
she died.

THE BIRTH OF THE AMERICAN FLAG, PART I

How much do you know about the history of the American flag?
Much of Old Glory's history—who made it, what inspired it, or
when it first flew in battle—is shrouded in mystery. Here's
a look at what little we do know about the flag.

A SIGHT TO SEE

On January 1, 1776, George Washington announced the formal existence of the Continental Army. A huge ceremony was staged to mark the occasion on Prospect Hill in Somerville, Massachusetts, and Washington ordered a flag hoisted to the top of a 76-foot flagpole.

The flag that flew that day consisted of 13 alternating red and white stripes, with the British Union Jack as its canton (the design in the top left corner). The stripes represented the colonies, united in their struggle against tyranny. The Union Jack signified their loyalty to the ideals of the British constitution and the colonists' hope for reconciliation with England. The flag was known as the Grand Union flag and would serve as the official flag of the Continental Army until the signing of the Declaration of Independence that summer.

NEW GLORY

The Declaration of Independence, signed in July 1776, officially severed all ties with England, so the Grand Union had to go. But no one bothered to replace it for nearly a year. It wasn't until June 1777, when the Continental Congress met to plan defenses for an expected attack on Philadelphia and decide other pressing issues, that they got around to passing a resolution on the design of a new flag—which, it turns out, was very similar to the old one. They wrote:

> Resolved, That the flag of the thirteen United States be thirteen stripes alternate red and white; that the union be thirteen stars, white in a blue field, representing a new constellation.

Who introduced the resolution? What was the inspiration for the

---

A typical redwood tree's roots are only 5 to 6 feet deep...and spread out over an acre.

details of the flag? Was there a ceremony for the unfurling of the first stars and stripes? All of this has been forgotten. Apparently no one at the time thought it was important enough to record. However...

• Historians guess red, white, and blue were chosen for practical, not patriotic, reasons: Fabric-making and dying techniques were limited, and there were few other colors to choose from.

• The stripes were also practical. "There aren't many ways to incorporate the number thirteen into a flag," one historian writes, "at least not ways that are easy to sew by hand, as all flags were in the 1770s. Long, straight strips of cloth were as simple as it got, so a number of colonial flags had them."

LEFT UNSAID

The first flag resolution, important as it was, left out details of size, shape, and layout, so flag makers were free to interpret it any way they wanted. As a result, at least 18 different versions of the American flag came into use over the next few years. Stars on some flags had as few as four points; others had as many as eight. Some flags had the stars arranged in squares; others had them arranged in circles, rectangles, in an X shape, in an arch, or sometimes just in one long row.

HEAVENS TO BETSY

For all their variety, one thing that these early American flags had in common is that none of them were invented or first sewn by Betsy Ross—contrary to common belief. That story didn't even surface until 1870, when Ross's grandson, William J. Canby, delivered a paper before the Historical Society of Pennsylvania claiming that she was the first person to sew an American flag.

According to Canby (who claimed he'd heard the story from Ross herself): In early June 1776, George Washington and two representatives from the Colonial Congress paid a visit to Ross at her home in Philadelphia. Washington brought with him a crude sketch of the flag he wanted: 13 red and white stripes, and 13 six-pointed stars arranged in a circle on a field of blue. Ross suggested that five-pointed stars would be easier to cut out and sew, and Washington agreed. Ross made the flag, and it was taken to the Pennsylvania State House, where the Congress adopted it.

Queen bees only sting other queen bees.

Although this story immediately found a place in American mythology, there is no contemporary reference to the incident anywhere—not in the record of Congressional business transactions or in George Washington's diary. The record of the Committees of Congress from that time doesn't even mention a flag committee. In fact, the date of the "visit" was a month before the Declaration of Independence—before there even was a United States.

SETTING THE RECORD STRAIGHT

The Betsy Ross fable clearly filled a need in the late 1800s to turn the creation of Old Glory into a dramatic moment. But the truth is, it wasn't a top priority for many of the Founding Fathers.

For example:

• When Benjamin Franklin and John Adams were asked to describe the new flag during a diplomatic trip to Paris in 1778, they got it wrong, describing it as consisting of "thirteen stripes, alternately red, white, and blue."

• And despite his numerous requests for flags for his troops, George Washington did not receive his first flag from the Continental Congress until 1783, after the Revolutionary War had ended. Historians aren't even sure the flag he received that year really did have stars and stripes: it might have been a blue banner with an eagle on it, similar to the presidential seal today. So it's likely that the American flag, born of revolution, never flew in a single battle during the Revolutionary War.

"The Birth of the American Flag, Part II" is on page 433.

*   *   *

BIRTH OF A NICKNAME

"I had a dog named Duke. Every fireman in town knew that hound, because he chased all the firewagons. They knew the dog's name, but not mine, so the next thing I was Duke, too. I was named for a damn dog!"

—*John Wayne*

According to sleep researchers, only about 5% of people dream in color.

THE DISAPPEARANCE OF JUDGE CRATER

Every once in a while, somebody famous or controversial disappears and is never found, despite intense searches. How can a recognizable person vanish without a trace? It's probably more fun to speculate than to know. Here is one of the most-talked-about unsolved disappearances in American history.

JUDGE JOSEPH CRATER

Claim to Fame: Newly appointed justice of the New York Supreme Court—a shoo-in to win reelection in November, and a potential appointee to the U.S. Supreme Court

Disappearance: Crater and his wife were vacationing in Maine on August 3, 1930, when he received phone call from New York City. Clearly disturbed, he announced to her that he had to go "straighten those fellows out." Then he left for New York.

Crater was apparently taking a break from business when, on the evening of August 6, he bought a ticket for a show and arranged to pick it up at the box office. Then he went to Billy Haas's restaurant, where he ran into friends and joined them for dinner. Later, he took a cab to the theater, waving from the taxi as it disappeared. Someone *did* pick up the theater ticket...but no one knows if it was Crater—he was never seen again. Nine days later, his wife notified the police, and a massive manhunt began.

What Happened: Police searched Crater's apartment and found nothing suspicious. They offered rewards for information...but not even the taxi driver came forward. Even after interviewing 300 people—resulting in 2,000 pages of testimony—they still had no clues to his whereabouts.

But as the investigation continued, police—and the public—were astonished to see Crater's carefully constructed facade unravel. It turned out, for example, that he'd kept a number of mistresses and had often been seen on the town with showgirls. More surprising however, was his involvement in graft, fraud, and political payoffs. Crater was a player in two major scandals, which came to light after he vanished. It also seemed as though he'd be implicated

---

Henry VIII was the eighth English king called Henry and the first anywhere called "Your Majesty."

in the Ewald Scandal, which involved paying for a city appointment; there was even evidence that Crater had paid for his *own* appointment to the bench.

Crater's fate was hotly debated by the public. Some were sure he was murdered by gangster associates. Others—noting that the judge had removed files containing potentially incriminating evidence from his office just before he disappeared—speculated that political cronies had killed him to shut him up. Or maybe a mistress who'd been blackmailing him had done it. Then again, perhaps the judge had committed suicide rather than watch his career crumble because of scandal. Whoever was responsible, and whatever happened to the body, it was assumed Crater was dead.

Postmortem: Crater's wife suffered a nervous breakdown and didn't return to their New York apartment until January 1931. There, she found an envelope in the top drawer of her dresser. It contained $6,690 in cash, the judge's will, written five years before (leaving his entire estate to her), and a three-page penciled note that listed everyone who owed the judge money. It closed with the words, "Am very weary. Love, Joe." The police department had searched the apartment thoroughly, and had kept a 24-hour guard on it since the disappearance—so no one could imagine how or when the envelope had gotten there. But it gave rise to another possibility: Crater had intentionally disappeared.

Nothing more came of it. In July 1937, Judge Joseph Force Crater was declared legally dead, and his wife collected on his life insurance. By then, New York's police commissioner believed that "Crater's disappearance was premeditated." The famous file 13595 remains open to this day—no trace of Crater or his body have ever been found.

* * *

UGH!
"The Hotel Odeon in Paris is allegedly offering tourists the 'Diana Tour'—a personal reenactment of Princess Diana's last night alive. You dine at the Ritz, ride a black Mercedes along the route where she was chased by paparazzi to the tunnel where she crashed, and wind up at the hospital where she was pronounced dead." (*AM News Abuse*)

Extra-curricular activity: 80% of high school athletes—male and female—say they've been hazed.

AMAZING ANAGRAMS

We were thinking about doing a page of anagrams (a word or phrase that's made by rearranging the letters of another word or phrase), when amazingly, this list arrived from BRI member Ryan Kulkarni: "It's my Anagram Hall of Fame," he wrote. "These anagrams are freaky because when the letters are reordered, the basic meaning remains the same. Check them out for yourself!" (Your free book is on the way, Ryan!)

DORMITORY
becomes...DIRTY ROOM

CLINT EASTWOOD
becomes...OLD WEST ACTION

MOTHER-IN-LAW
becomes...WOMAN HITLER

ELEVEN PLUS TWO
becomes...TWELVE PLUS ONE

DAVID LETTERMAN
becomes...NERD AMID LATE TV

WESTERN UNION
becomes...NO WIRE UNSENT

THE COUNTRYSIDE *becomes*...
NO CITY DUST HERE

EVANGELIST
becomes...EVIL'S AGENT

ASTRONOMERS
becomes...NO MORE STARS

DEBIT CARD
becomes...BAD CREDIT

THE MORSE CODE
becomes...HERE COME DOTS

SLOT MACHINES
becomes...CASH LOST IN 'EM

CONVERSATION
becomes...VOICES RANT ON

STATUE OF LIBERTY *becomes*...
BUILT TO STAY FREE

CONTRADICTION *becomes*...
ACCORD NOT IN IT

TOM CRUISE
becomes...SO I'M CUTER

ANIMOSITY
becomes...IS NO AMITY

THE RAILROAD TRAIN
becomes...HI! I RATTLE
AND ROAR

THE HILTON
becomes...HINT: HOTEL

SNOOZE ALARMS
becomes...ALAS! NO MORE Z'S

THE DETECTIVES
becomes...DETECT THIEVES

A GENTLEMAN
becomes...ELEGANT MAN

Top four high school hazing sports: swimming, diving, soccer, lacrosse.

BRI'S FLATULENCE HALL OF FAME

It used to be that no one talked about farts...now, it's no big deal. You can't get way from it. Which is fine by us. Here is the very first section honoring people and institutions that have made an art out of passing gas. (By the way—if this is your favorite part of the book, we recommend a tome called Who Cut the Cheese?, *by Jim Dawson.)*

Honoree: Caryn Johnson, a.k.a. Whoopi Goldberg
Notable Achievement: First Hollywood star named after frequent farting
True Story: In her autobiography, Goldberg says she came up with the stage name Whoopi because she "frequently passed gas and sounded like a walking whoopee cushion."

Honoree: Taoism
Notable Achievement: Most interesting philosophy about farts
True Story: A 1996 BBC-TV program about the first Chinese emperor, reported that "Chinese Taoists believe everyone is allotted a certain amount of air at birth which it is important to conserve. Belching and farting are considered to shorten one's life. Taoists therefore carefully control their diet, avoiding foods which lead to flatulence."

Honoree: King Ahmose of Egypt
Notable Achievement: Most effective use of a fart as a political statement
True Story: In 568 B.C., King Apries of Egypt sent a trusted general named Amasis to put down a mutiny among his troops. But when Amasis got there, the troops offered to make him their leader instead...and he accepted.

King Apries couldn't believe it. He sent a respected advisor named Patarbemis to bring Amasis back. Amasis responded to the king's entreaties by raising himself from his saddle and farting. Then he told Patarbemis to "carry that back to Apries." Unfortunately,

---

In an average minute, 20,900 gallons flow from the Amazon River into the sea.

the king was so enraged by the message that he had Patarbemis's nose and ears hacked off. Committing such a barbarous act against such a respectable man was the last straw for many Egyptians—they turned pro-Amasis. With their support, Amasis's troops attacked and defeated Apries's army.

Note: Amasis became King Ahmose and reigned for 44 years, from 569 to 525 B.C., which modern historians call one of Egypt's most prosperous periods.

Honoree: Richard Magpiong, a career criminal
Notable Achievement: The ultimate self-incriminating fart
True Story: In 1995 the residents of a home on Fire Island (near New York City) were awakened by a noise. They got up and looked around, but couldn't find anyone. They were about to go back to bed when, according to the *New York Daily News,* "they heard the sound of a muffled fart." Magpiong was discovered hiding in a closet and was held until the police arrived.

Honoree: Edward De Vere, the seventh earl of Oxford and a courtier in Queen Elizabeth's court
Notable Achievement: Craziest overreaction to a fart
True Story: De Vere accidentally farted while bowing to the queen. He was so embarrassed that he left England and did not return for seven years. When he got back, the queen pooh-poohed the whole affair. "My Lord," she reportedly said, welcoming him back, "I had forgot the Fart."

Honoree: Spike Jones and His City Slickers
Notable Achievement: Bestselling fart record
True Story: According to *Who Cut the Cheese?*: "During World War II, Bluebird Records released a disc called 'Der Fuehrer's Face' by Spike Jones and His City Slickers (an orchestra noted for parodying pop tunes), only a few months after the U.S. joined the war. Jones's band, armed with rubber razzers to create flabby farting noises, [created] a zany gas attack on Adolf Hitler: "And we'll Heil! [*fart!*] Heil! [*fart!*] right in der Fuehrer's face!" It sold a million and a half copies in the U.S. and Great Britain.

LIBERAL JUSTICE

William O. Douglas was one of the most respected but controversial justices in the history of the Supreme Court. He was also one of the most liberal. Here are some of the thoughts that made him so well-known.

"We must realize that today's Establishment is the new George III. Whether it will continue to adhere to his tactics, we do not know. If it does, the redress, honored in tradition, is also revolution."

"If Nixon is not forced to turn over tapes of his conversations with the ring of men who were conversing on their violations of the law, then liberty will soon be dead in this nation."

"At the constitutional level where we work, 90 percent of any decision is emotional. The rational part of us supplies the reasons for supporting our predilections."

"I do not know of any salvation for society except through eccentrics, misfits, dissenters, people who protest."

"There is more to the right to vote than the right to mark a piece of paper and drop it in a box or the right to pull a lever in a voting booth....It also includes the right to have the vote counted at full value without dilution or discount."

"Political or religious dissenters are the plague of every totalitarian regime."

"Communism has been so thoroughly exposed in this country that it has been crippled as a political force. Free speech has destroyed it as an effective political party."

"It is better, the Fourth Amendment teaches us, that the guilty sometimes go free than the citizens be subject to easy arrest."

"Advocacy and belief go hand in hand. For there can be no true freedom of mind if thoughts are secure only when they are pent up."

"The great postulate of our democracy is confidence in the common sense of the people and in their maturity of judgment, even on great issues— once they know the facts."

"I have the same confidence in the ability of our people to reject noxious literature as I have in their capacity to sort out the true from the false in theology, economics, or any other field."

MR. CONSERVATIVE

Arizona Senator Barry Goldwater was defeated in a landslide when he ran as the Republican candidate for president in 1964. But at the same time, he started the modern conservative movement. Often outrageously blunt, he was widely respected as a man of honesty and principle.

"The income tax created more criminals than any other single act of government."

"Sometimes I think this country could be better off if we would just saw off the Eastern seaboard and let it float off to sea."

"The Democrats want to save more on defense so they can spend more money to buy votes through the welfare state."

"We cannot allow the American flag to be shot at anywhere on earth if we are to retain our respect and prestige."

"We are not far from the kind of moral decay that has brought on the fall of other nations and peoples."

"We should get back to the...doctrine of brinksmanship, where everybody knows we have the power and will use it."

"If they chased every man or woman out of this town who has shacked up with somebody else or got drunk, there wouldn't be any government left in Washington."

"I don't necessarily vote a straight ticket in my own state because there are sometimes Democrats out there who are better than Republicans. It's hard to believe but it's true."

"War is but an instrument of international policy."

"We can be lied to only so many times. The best thing that he [President Nixon] can do for the country is to get the hell out of the White House and get out this afternoon."

"No matter what you do, be honest. That sticks out in Washington."

"I don't want to see this country run by big business and big labor."

The U.S. Treasury mints about 37 million pennies a day.

SIT ON A POTATO PAN, OTIS

Palindromes are phrases or sentences that are spelled the same way backward or forward. Some people spend their whole lives making new ones up. Here are some of Uncle John's favorites.

So, Ida, adios!

Rats live on no evil star.

Go deliver a dare, vile dog.

Vanna, wanna V?

Man, Oprah's sharp on A.M.

(...Yawn.) Madonna fan? No damn way!

Too bad, I hid a boot.

Cain: A maniac!

Plan no damn Madonna LP.

Sex-aware era waxes.

Solo gigolos.

Sit on a potato pan, Otis!

Ah, Satan sees Natasha.

Cigar? Toss it in a can, it is so tragic.

A Toyota! Race fast, safe car. A Toyota

U.F.O. tofu.

Golf? No sir, prefer prison-flog.

Draw, O coward!

Egad! No bondage!

Lepers repel.

Flee to me, remote elf.

Sh...Tom sees moths.

Kay, a red nude, peeped under a yak.

Egad, an adage!

Must sell at tallest sum.

"Reviled did I live," said I, "as evil I did deliver."

No lemons, no melon.

Doc, note, I dissent. A fast never prevents a fatness. I diet on cod.

Gnu dung.

Lager, Sir, is regal.

Poor Dan is in a droop.

Sex at noon taxes.

Evil olive.

Flesh! Saw I Mimi wash self!

Sniff'um muffins.

Tuna nut.

Never odd or even.

The heaviest pumpkin ever recorded weighed 1,061 pounds.

SECRETS OF THE LAVA LAMP

It oozes, it undulates, it never stops…and it never goes away. Most people thought Lava Lamps had died and joined Nehru jackets in pop culture heaven. But no—they're still around. Here's a quick course in lava lampology.

EGG-STRAORDINARY HISTORY

Not long after he left the Royal Air Force at the end of World War II, an Englishman named Edward Craven-Walker walked into a pub in Hampshire, England, and noticed an odd item sitting on the counter behind the bar. It was a glass cocktail shaker that contained some kind of mucouslike blob floating in liquid.

Craven-Walker asked what it was, and the bartender told him it was an egg-timer. The "blob" was actually a clump of solid wax in a clear liquid. You put the cocktail shaker in the boiling water with your egg, the bartender explained, and as the boiling water cooked the egg, it also melted the wax, turning it into an amorphous blob of goo. When the wax floated to the top of the jar, your egg was done.

LIGHT DUTY

Craven-Walker saw a money-making opportunity floating in front of him—he could turn the egg timer into a lamp and sell it to the public. He set about tracking down its inventor—a man known today only by his last name, Dunnet—and found out he was dead. The good news was that Dunnet had died without patenting the invention, so Craven-Walker could patent it himself.

Craven-Walker spent the next 15 years perfecting Dunnet's invention so that it could be mass-produced. In the meantime, he supported himself by making "art-house" films about his other passion: nudity. (In those days, pornography was illegal in many places, and the only way around the law was by making "documentaries" about nudism. Whether Craven-Walker was a genuine nudist or just a pornographer in disguise is open to interpretation.)

Toto the dog was paid $125 a week for his work in *The Wizard of Oz*.

COMING TO AMERICA

In 1964 Craven-Walker finished work on his lamp—a cylindrical vase he called the Astrolight—and introduced it at a novelty convention in Hamburg, West Germany, in 1965. Two Americans named Adolph Wertheimer and Hy Spector saw it and bought the American rights to the lamp. They renamed it the Lava Lite and introduced in the U.S., just in time for the psychedelic '60s. "Lava Lite sales peaked in the late sixties," Jane and Michael Stern write in *The Encyclopedia of Bad Taste,* "when the slow-swirling colored wax happened to coincide perfectly with the undulating aesthetics of psychedelia....They were advertised as head trips that offered 'a motion for every emotion.' "

FLOATING UP...AND DOWN...AND UP...

At their peak, more than 7 million Lava Lites (the English version was called a Lava *Lamp*) were sold around the world each year, but by the early 1970s the fad had run its course and sales fell dramatically. By 1976, sales were down to 200 lamps a week, a fraction of what they had been a few years before.

By the late 1980s, however, sales began to rebound. "As style makers began to ransack the sixties for inspiration, Lava Lites came back," Jane and Michael Stern write. "Formerly dollar-apiece flea-market pickings, original Lava Lites—particularly those with paisley, op art, or homemade trippy motifs on their bases—became real collectibles in the late eighties, selling in chic boutiques for more than a brand new one." Not that brand-new ones were hurting for business—by 1998 manufacturers in England and the U.S. were selling more than 2 million a year.

LAVA LIGHT SCIENCE

Only the companies that make lava lights know precisely what chemicals are in the lamp, and in what combination—the recipe is a trade secret. But the principles at work are pretty easy to understand:

• When the lamp is turned off and at room temperature, the waxy "lava" substance is slightly heavier than the liquid it's in. That's why the wax is slumped in a heap at the bottom.

• When you switch on the bulb and it begins to heat the fluid, the

---

Sound travels a mile in five seconds through the air. Under water, it travels a mile in one second.

wax melts and expands to the point where it is slightly lighter than the fluid. That's what causes the "lava" to rise.

• As the wax rises, it moves further away from the bulb, and cools just enough to make it heavier than the fluid again. This causes the lava to fall back towards the bulb, where it starts to heat up again, and the process repeats itself.

• The lava also contains chemicals called "surfactants" that make it easier for the wax to break into blobs and squish back together.

• It is this precise chemical balancing act that makes manufacturing the lamps such a challenge. "Every batch has to be individually matched and tested," says company chemist John Mundy. "Then we have to balance it so the wax won't stick. Otherwise, it just runs up the side or disperses into tiny bubbles."

TROUBLESHOOTING

What if you have a vintage lava lamp, but can't get it to work right? No problem. The Internet is full of lava light lovers. Here are sample queries we found on the Web site www.OozingGoo.com:

Q: I have an older style lamp that I bought in the late '70s. It was in storage, but I came across it last year, and I've been using it from time to time. It was working fine, until it was knocked over (darned cats). Nothing broke, but now, the liquid has gone cloudy. Is there anything I can do? I don't want to get rid of it, but it's not as enjoyable any more.

A: Sorry. I'm afraid you can't fix it, but you *can* buy a replacement bottle in a range of colors. (Order through the Web site.)

Q: My son went to college, and his lava lamp was turned off for a year. Now it won't work. The red lava is lying at the base like a can of worms, and there seems to be some metallic substance/rings in the lava. There is also one-half inch of fluid missing from the lamp. Can this lamp be fixed?

A: STOP! DON'T MESS WITH IT! You may not even have a problem. The liquid is supposed to be about one-half inch down— gives room for expansion due to heat. Are you sure you have the right bulb? 40 watt frosted appliance. Leave the lamp on for long periods—4 hours each day for a week—sometimes they come back. Good luck!

MYTH-CONCEPTIONS

*Common knowledge is frequently wrong. Here are a few examples
of things that people believe...but that just aren't true.*

M **yth:** The captain of a ship at sea can perform weddings.
Fact: U.S. Navy regulations—and those of the navies of
many other nations—actually prohibit ships' commanders
from joining couples in marriage.

Myth: Your hair and nails continue to grow after you die.
Fact: They don't. Your tissue recedes from your hair and nails, making them appear longer.

Myth: Bananas spoil faster when you put them in a refrigerator.
Fact: This belief comes from an old ad jingle. The purpose of the jingle was to tell people to keep bananas out of the refrigerator...but only until they had ripened. Once ripened, bananas will last longer in the refrigerator.

Myth: You should never wake a sleepwalker.
Fact: There's no reason not to wake a sleepwalker. This superstition comes from the old belief that a sleepwalker's spirit leaves the body and might not make it back if the person is wakened.

Myth: Any American can make a citizen's arrest.
Fact: According to law enforcement officials, the concept of a citizen's arrest is pure fiction.

Myth: Shaving your hair makes it grow in faster and thicker.
Fact: The rate of your hair's growth is determined by hereditary factors. Shaving will have no effect on the rate of its growth.

Myth: During a flight, you'll sometimes hit an "air pocket."
Fact: What's often called an "air pocket" is actually a downdraft.

Myth: It's darkest just before the dawn.
Fact: Actually, it's darkest at about 2 a.m.

Poll result: 1 in 6 employees say they got so mad at a co-worker last year that ...

FAT CHANCE: THE WAR BETWEEN BUTTER & MARGARINE

These days, you expect to find both butter and margarine on grocery shelves...but did you know that margarine companies had to fight to get there? This article was written by Jack Mingo.

MARGINAL USE

"Oleomargarine" was a word coined in the late 1860s by a French chemist, Hippolyte Mège-Mouriès. The price of butter had soared, so Napoleon III, expecting shortages because of an anticipated war with Prussia, offered a prize at the Paris World Exhibition in 1866 to anyone who could come up with a cheap, plentiful butter substitute.

Mège-Mouriès did some research and discovered that even starving cows give milk containing milkfat. Since this fat isn't coming from their food, he reasoned that it must be coming from the cows themselves. Deciding that it must be possible to do the same thing mechanically, he invented a process to render oil from beef fat and combined the oil with milk to form a butterlike spread. He won Napoleon's prize, but lost the first marketplace skirmish—his margarine factory opened in 1873 near Paris, then had to close when peace unexpectedly broke out and ruined the expected butter shortages.

ACROSS THE OCEAN

Mège-Mouriès's process, however, found a home in the United States. The U.S. Dairy Company bought the rights to it in 1874 and licensed the process to 15 factories around the country. By 1882, it was making 50,000 pounds of the imitation spread every day. Soon, Armour and other meat-packing houses began producing margarine of their own, using fatty by-products left over from meat processing.

Farmers and butter manufacturers were beginning to get worried by this new product, especially those who made cheaper, lower-grade butter. Margarine was roughly comparable in price, but it was often of better quality.

In 1877 the dairy industry engineered the passage of laws in New York and Maryland requiring that oleomargarine "be marked, stamped, and branded as such, under penalty of $100 and imprisonment for thirty days." Even the margarine manufacturers agreed that these laws were reasonable, and didn't object when other states followed suit. In the words of a spokesman in 1880, "Of course, this had for a time its effect upon the sale of the product; but as oleomargarine is a pure and wholesome article of food, possessing all the qualities of good dairy butter, the people have overlooked the name and have decided to eat it."

GOING FOR THE JUGULAR

But that wasn't enough for the dairy interests. Ironically—since farmers of the time were notorious for extending and whitening milk and cream with water, chalk, magnesia, and even plaster of Paris—the dairy concerns created new organizations like the National Association for the Prevention of Adulteration of Butter, to combat the "adulteration and risk to health" supposedly posed by margarine. In lurid anti-margarine propaganda, the dairy interests featured slanderous tales of the repulsive ingredients used to make "bogus-butter."

"The slag of the butcher shop," they called margarine, "a compound of diseased hogs and dead dogs" that contained "the germs of cancer and insanity." They paid one Professor Piper, a mysterious researcher with dubious credentials, to do an imaginative "study" in which he found in samples of margarine "many kinds of living organisms, dead mould, bits of cellulose, shreds of hair, bristles, etc., doubtful worms, corpuscles from a cockroach, small bits of claws, corpuscles of sheep, the egg of a tapeworm, a dead hydra-virus..."

The margarine companies tried to defend themselves. But while the president of the New York Board of Health spoke of margarine's purity at their behest, dairy lobbyists in Maine, Michigan, Minnesota, New York, Ohio, Pennsylvania, and Wisconsin rammed through legislation that banned "any article designed to take the place of butter." By 1885, two-thirds of all margarine manufacturers in those states had gone out of business.

After court challenges in New York and Maine, courts ruled

The Mona Lisa has no eyebrows. Shaved eyebrows were the fad when she was painted.

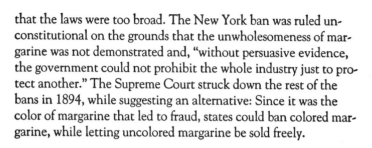

that the laws were too broad. The New York ban was ruled unconstitutional on the grounds that the unwholesomeness of margarine was not demonstrated and, "without persuasive evidence, the government could not prohibit the whole industry just to protect another." The Supreme Court struck down the rest of the bans in 1894, while suggesting an alternative: Since it was the color of margarine that led to fraud, states could ban colored margarine, while letting uncolored margarine be sold freely.

SLIPPERY MANEUVERS

Once again, dairy concerns rammed through laws—this time convincing 30 states, by the turn of the century, to ban colored margarine. (Ironically, the butter makers themselves routinely added annatto to their butter to make it more yellow.) Pallid off-white was an unappetizing color, and margarine sales went down again. But not down far enough for the butter lobby. They pushed harder, getting laws passed in five states that required margarine producers to dye their product pink. Not surprisingly, margarine sales in those states plummeted.

In 1902 the butter industry persuaded the federal government to get into the act as well, slapping a 10¢ tax on artificially colored margarine. This effectively increased the price to the consumer by 50%, making it more expensive than most grades of butter. In response, the margarine manufacturers began using vegetable oils for margarine—especially those with a natural yellow hue. It gave the margarine some color without incurring the tax. By World War I, vegetable-based margarine dominated the market.

In 1931 the government closed the loophole of allowing naturally colored oils by taxing all yellow margarines, whether colored artificially or not. Margarine makers found a way around that law, too. They discovered that it didn't prohibit consumers from dying their own margarine.

So they provided a yellow "color capsule" free of charge with every purchase of margarine. When consumers got the margarine home, they massaged the dye around inside the cellophane package of margarine until it was a uniform golden color. While this was a minor inconvenience for consumers, margarine sales began to creep up again.

The average American drinks 3.4 cups of coffee a day.

GOTCHA!

Finally margarine got a chance to fight back. During the financial insecurity of the Depression and butter rationing of World War II, consumers flocked to margarine, which was no longer perceived as a low-class, disreputable spread of dubious origin. Many consumers discovered that they preferred the economy and even the taste of margarine to that of "the high-priced spread," (as margarine ads called butter). And consumers began wondering why they had to put up with the mess of coloring margarine at home.

Finally in 1950, pushed by vegetable-oil producers, labor unions, and consumers, Congress narrowly passed a law to rescind the federal tax on colored margarine. States began following suit. Within five years, every state except Minnesota and Wisconsin had repealed such laws. (Minnesota held out until 1963; Wisconsin, "the Dairy State," until 1967.)

FAT IS FAT

In the 1960s and 1970s, the margarine market suddenly pulled ahead of butter as health-conscious consumers began avoiding animal fats, based on studies that concluded that margarine was less artery-clogging than butter.

But it turned out that the studies were wrong. More recent research showed that hydrogenating vegetable oil to make it semi-solid creates "transfatty acids" that act like saturated fats, raising blood cholesterol levels.

As that word got out to consumers, margarine sales dropped 8% in 1994, while butter sales went up 5.3%. Margarine makers, by now resigned to changing their product every few years to match the vagaries of life, law, politics, and consumer demand, scrambled to come up with formulations that tasted good and were free of transfatty acids.

After a century and a quarter, the war between butter and margarine isn't over yet.

*　　*　　*

...FOR THE BIRDS

The domestic turkey was domesticated by the Aztecs and the Incas, who used them as food and sacrificed them to their gods.

TRICK SHOTS:
MORE FAKED PHOTOS

*A few more historic photographs that people chose to
believe, even though they were pretty obvious phonies.*

FICTIONAL NEWS
Famous Footage: The "California Election Report"

Trick Shot: In 1934 Upton Sinclair, legendary muckraker
and author of *The Jungle*—an exposé of Chicago's meatpacking industry—ran for governor of California. Sinclair's candidacy
marked one of the best chances a socialist had ever had of winning
a statewide office in the U.S. That's when newsreels like the "California Election Report" appeared. It featured interviews in a railyard with one hobo after another, each saying that "he rode the
rails to the Golden State just as soon as he heard that the new governor would be handing out free lunches."

The Real Picture: The newsreels were pure Hollywood, put together by director Irving Thalberg with the support of Samuel
Goldwyn. Both considered Sinclair "a dangerous red who wanted
to rob the rich to support the poor." The hobos were just actors
(Thalberg and his crew wanted real hobos, but couldn't find any in
the L.A. railroad yard), and the "railyard" was a set on the MGM
back lot. Other newsreels were just as phony.

Development: In the days before television, newsreels were a primary source of news for the public, and this negative coverage—
shown repeatedly in California theaters—helped ensure Sinclair's
defeat.

ON TOP OF THE WORLD
Famous Photos: Frederick Cook at the North Pole

Trick Shots: On September 6, 1909, an exhausted Robert Peary
wired from Labrador, "Stars and Stripes nailed to the Pole—
Peary." Peary, 53, had apparently realized a goal he'd set 23 years
earlier—to be the first person to reach the North Pole. But it
turned out that he was too late: On September 1, explorer Frederick Cook had wired from the Shetland Islands that he'd made it

---

If you weigh 120 pounds on Earth, you'll weigh about 20 pounds on the moon.

to the North Pole the year before. Cook's proof: photographs of
him and his Eskimo companions at the Pole. Cook's photographs,
which were published all over the world, marked the completion
of one of the last great exploratory challenges on earth...or did
they?

The Real Picture: As it turned out, it was another of Cook's "ac-
complishments" that got him into trouble. Cook had previously
claimed he'd been to the summit of Mount McKinley. "On the day
Cook received the keys to New York City for his North Pole trek,"
write the editors of *Reader's Digest* in *Strange Stories of America's
Past*, "the man who'd supposedly climbed McKinley with him admitted they'd never really been *near* the 20,320-foot peak."
The Explorer's Club investigated and found that the McKinley
'summit' picture had been taken from a 5,300-foot ridge.

Development: The scandal brought Cook's North Pole claims
into question but, amazingly, he so charmed the public that many
people sided with him over Peary. His spurious North Pole
pictures weren't totally discredited until 1918, two years before
Peary's death. (Dr. Cook later served four years in Leavenworth
prison for promoting stock in a company owning oil he "discovered" in Wyoming.)

WHO'S WHO IN THE REVOLUTION?

Famous Photos: Spanish Loyalists committing atrocities in the
Spanish Civil War (1936–1939)

Trick Shot: In 1936, "when the Spanish Civil War broke out,
U.S. newspaper baron William Randolph Hearst jumped into the
fray. He ran photos showing atrocities...being committed by the
pro-democracy Loyalists against Fascist followers of Francisco
Franco."

The Real Picture: The Spanish picture was actually *Franco's men*
committing atrocities against the Loyalists.

Development: The controversy helped turn public opinion against
the Loyalists and hastened World War II. Without more support
from the U.S. and other Allied powers, the Loyalists faltered and
the Nazi-supported fascists were able to defeat their enemies—
providing momentum for Hitler and Mussolini.

THE PETTICOAT WARS

The sex scandal involving Monica Lewinsky (the first, and last, time we mention her name in one of these books) helped create a crisis in Washington that most Americans think was unparalleled. Actually, in the early 1800s, there was a worse one, that did measurable damage: an entire cabinet was overturned. Newspapers called it "The Petticoat Wars." Never heard of it? That's what we're here for.

FORGOTTEN FIGURE: Peggy O'Neal, a beautiful barmaid, tavern-keeper's daughter and "woman of easy morals" who worked in her father's Washington, D.C. tavern and lodging house in the 1820s.

CLAIM TO FAME: The most famous and controversial Cabinet wife of the 19th century—inspiration for the "Petticoat Wars" that rocked Washington in the 1820s

BACKGROUND: O'Neal was also the longtime mistress of Senator John Eaton, a wealthy young widower from Tennessee. On January 21, 1829, she and Eaton finally married. That was scandal enough in its own right; but not long after they were married, President Andrew jackson made Eaton Secretary of War, catapulting the former barmaid into the status of Cabinet wife, the pinnacle of Washington society.

Other Cabinet wives resented the new Mrs. Eaton's sudden elevation in social status. At the instigation of Vice President John C. Calhoun's wife Floride, they began freezing her out of their social functions. President Jackson was livid about it, and called a special meeting of the Cabinet to defend Eaton's virtue. When the Cabinet wives continued to ostracize Eaton, Jackson purged the entire Cabinet, replacing every appointee except Postmaster General William Barry.

Perhaps the biggest casualty in the Petticoat War was Vice President Calhoun, a southerner who had hoped to ride into the Presidency on Jackson's coattails. His wife's intransigence put an end to those dreams, and Jackson threw his support to Secretary of State Martin Van Buren, a bachelor whose immunity from the pressure of the Cabinet wives, enabled him to remain friendly with the Eatons throughout the crisis.

Van Buren replaced Calhoun as Vice President during Jackson's second term, and succeeded Jackson to the presidency in 1837. Some historians speculate that had Calhoun, a Southerner, become president instead of Van Buren, a Northerner, he might have been able to sooth the North-South tensions that led to the outbreak of the Civil War in 1860.

INTO THE DUSTBIN: When John Eaton became Minister to Spain, he and Peggy became the toast of Madrid. After Eaton died, Peggy, now in her sixties, married a twenty-something Italian dance instructor, only to watch him run off with her granddaughter and most of her money.

*   *   *   *
DON'T MISS THESE!

EXOTIC WORLD
Location: The desert town of Helendale, California, half-way between Los Angeles and Las Vegas.
Background: Probably the only museum in the world run by strippers for strippers. Tours are conducted by Dixie Evans, the "Marilyn Monroe of Burlesque," whose most famous act is an interpretive dance that highlights the major events in Monroe's life.
Be Sure to See... The Exotic World Rolls-Royce, Jayne Mansfield's couch, and thousands of 8x10 photographs of strippers covering the walls in each room. There's also a gift shop that sells T-shirts, lapel pins, and other baubles.

THE MUTTER MUSEUM
Location: Philadelphia College of Physicians
Background: Although intended primarily for medical professionals, it's chock-full of oddities that appeal to the average person.
Be Sure to See: The preserved liver of Chang and Eng, the original Siamese twins; and the Chevalier Jackson Collection of swallowed objects that had to be surgically removed.

UNFINISHED MASTERPIECE: LEONARDO'S HORSE

Here's an unfinished masterpiece from one of the Renaissance's greatest geniuses.

THE HORSE STATUE. *Created by Leonardo da Vinci. Would have been the largest equestrian monument on earth…if it had ever been built. Leonardo considered it a crowning achievement.*

Background: In the 1480s, the Duke of Sforza commissioned Leonardo to build a huge statue of a horse to honor his father, Francesco Sforza. Da Vinci worked on it for nearly 17 years, studying horses exhaustively and then making a series of models, including a full-sized clay model that was 24 feet tall. Next step: Completing the molds, into which more than 50 tons of molten bronze would be poured to create the final horse. Then a war broke out.

Unfinished Masterpiece: On September 10, 1499, before da Vinci could cast the horse, the French captured Milan. Some soldiers camped nearby…and a company of them used the clay model for target practice, riddling it with holes. Afterwards, the model was totally destroyed by exposure to the weather. When Leonardo died 20 years later, in 1519, he was "still mourning the loss of his great horse."

Update: In 1977 an American named Charles Dent happened to pick up a copy of *National Geographic* magazine, which contained an article on Leonardo and his horse. Dent was an Italian Renaissance buff and decided that completing Leonardo's horse would be a fitting way to honor the greatest mind of the period.

Leonardo had left no detailed drawings or other notes that indicated what the final horse was supposed to look like; all that survived were preliminary sketches. No matter—Dent decided to wing it, and on September 10, 1999, exactly 500 years to the day that Da Vinci was forced to abandon his dream, his horse (or at least an approximation) was unveiled in Milan. It was intended, Dent explained, as a gift "to all the Italian people from the American people." But, ironically, few Italians attended the unveiling—mostly Americans showed up (not Dent, though, he'd died a few years earlier).

According to one study, 85% of parents use child car-safety seats incorrectly.

DRAT, SHE'S DEAD!

*You don't always get a Hollywood ending when you're
making a Hollywood film. Sometimes the star dies or
becomes incapacitated during filming. It happened
in these movies. Here's how they handled it.*

SARATOGA (1937), *starring Jean Harlow and Clark Gable*
The Situation: The 26-year-old Harlow, "Hollywood's original platinum blonde," died of kidney failure when the film
was only about half complete. MGM wanted to abandon production and scrap what they had...but Harlow's fans protested. So the
studio "and a very reluctant Gable" continued filming.

Body Double: Harlow's scenes were filmed with her stand-in, Mary
Dees, who was "carefully lit and photographed in long shots, over
the shoulder, from behind, looking through binoculars, or under
wide-brimmed hats." Ironically, the film, which grossed $3.3 mil-
lion, was the most successful of Harlow's career—and also the most
critically acclaimed (although the *New York Times* complained that
in the film, "Harlow was patently not her tempestuous self.")

THE CROW (1994), *starring Brandon Lee—son of martial-arts star
Bruce Lee*
The Situation: A horrible accident occurred just three days before
filming was to be completed. In the story, Lee's character is shot
and killed. In real life, that's what happened to Lee. The tip of one
of the blanks loaded in a .44-caliber handgun hit Lee, 27, in the
stomach when the gun was fired during a scene. He died shortly
after. Police said it was an accident.

Producer Ed Pressman says: "We weren't so sure if we wanted
to finish it. But Brandon's mother and his girlfriend, whom he
planned to marry just after it was finished, wanted it finished and
released. So we finished it."

Body Double: The producers altered some existing footage digi-
tally and made plans to film new footage using stuntmen who
would be wearing special face masks made from a plaster cast of
Lee's face. But the stuntmen refused to wear the masks, arguing
they were in bad taste. "No one felt good about wearing the

Bet on it: Horse jockeys are the only U.S. athletes legally allowed to bet on themselves.

masks," says make-up artist Lance Anderson. "The director finally got around that problem by filming long shots instead."

YOU CAN'T CHEAT AN HONEST MAN (1938), *starring W. C. Fields*

The Situation: Fields was one of Hollywood's legendary drunks. Most of the time that didn't interfere with his films, but *You Can't Cheat an Honest Man* was different—Fields, who was supposed to both write the film and star in it, was too drunk to do either.

Body Double: Director George Marshall compensated by hiring a writing "assistant" named Everett Freeman for Fields, and by casting other stars like Edgar Bergen and Charlie McCarthy in the film to take up some of Fields's screen time. He also hired a double for Fields and filmed him in long shots. That turned out to be a particularly smart move: one afternoon, in the middle of production, Fields shuffled off the set into his limousine (which had a wet bar in the back) and never returned.

Marshall still didn't have all the footage of Fields that he needed to finish the film…so he improvised. He combined what he had with shots of Fields's double and put Edgar Bergan and Charlie McCarthy onscreen even longer.

Despite its flaws—or more likely because of them—the movie was a hit and to this day is considered a W. C. Fields classic. "All the critics," says Everett Freman, "referred to the movie's daring innovations, its departure from formula, and its innovative use of the camera—especially on the long shots intercutting to the close-ups."

THE THREE STOOGES (1955)

The Situation: Shemp Howard replaced his brother Curly in the Stooges in 1949 and co-starred with them for six years. In 1955, while working on several Stooges films, he had a heart attack and died.

Body Double: Moe and Larry considered appearing as a duo, but Columbia Pictures wouldn't hear of it. They also wouldn't scrap the unfinished Shemp episodes. Instead, they hired Joe Palma as a double. His face was never seen—his back was always to the camera. The four episodes: *Hot Stuff, Rumpus in the Harem, Scheming Schemers*, and *Commotion on the Ocean*. Check them out sometime.

The average American kid catches 6 colds a year. The average American kid in daycare catches 10.

SNAP, CRACKLE...FLOP!

*For every successful cereal like Frosted Flakes or Wheaties, there are
hundreds of bombs like Banana Wackies and Ooboperoos. Flipping
through the pages of* Cerealizing America, *by Scott Bruce and
Bill Crawford, we found these legendary cereal flops.*

Kellogg's Kream Crunch (1963). Frosted-oat loops mixed
with cubes of freeze-dried vanilla-orange or strawberry ice
cream. According to a Kellogg's exec: "The product kind of
melted into gooey ice cream in milk. It just wasn't appetizing."

Sugar Smiles (1953). General Mills' first try at sugar cereal. A
bizarre mixture of plain Wheaties and sugar-frosted Kix. Slogan:
"You can't help smiling the minute you taste it."

Dinos (early 1990s). After the success of Fruity Pebbles, Post
tried naming a cereal after the Flintstones' pet dinosaur. "A question that came up constantly," recalls a Post art director, "was
'We've got Cocoa Pebbles and Fruity Pebbles...so what flavor is
Dino?'...It sounds like something Fred would be getting off his
lawn instead of something you'd want to be eating."

Day-O (late 1960s). "The world's first calypso-inspired presweetened cereal," from General Mills.

Ooops (early 1970s). General Mills had so many bombs, they
came up with a cereal they actually *said* was based on a mistake—
jingle: "Ooops, it's a crazy mistake, Ooops, it's a cereal that's great!"

Kellogg's Corn Crackos (1967). The box featured the Waker
Upper Bird perched on a bowl of candy-coated twists. An internal
company memo said: "It looks like a bird eating worms; who wants
worms for breakfast?"

Punch Crunch (1975). A spinoff of Cap'n Crunch. The screaming pink box featured Harry S., an exuberant hippo in a sailor suit,
making goo-goo eyes at Cap'n Crunch. Many chain stores perceived the hippo as gay and refused to carry the cereal. Marveled
one Quaker salesman: "How that one ever got through, I'll never
understand."

One study has concluded that if a woodchuck could chuck wood, it would chuck about 700 lbs.

FAMOUS UNSOLVED DISAPPEARANCES

Here are two more unsolved disappearances that have made the news.

JIMMY HOFFA

Claim to Fame: Ruled the Teamsters Union from 1957 to 1967; turned it into America's biggest, richest and most corrupt union—with overt connections to the Mafia. In a highly publicized 1967 trial, he was convicted of jury tampering and sent to federal prison. In 1971 he was released—on condition that he not hold union office until 1980.

Hoffa didn't stay inactive long: In 1972 he filed a lawsuit to overturn the arrangement and began a campaign to return to power. By 1975, he'd gained enough support in the union to pose a threat to the leaders who'd replaced him—if his lawsuit succeeded.

Disappearance: On July 30, 1975, Hoffa went to a meeting with two men—an Eastern Teamster official and a Detroit mobster. He never returned. Police dug up fields, ripped up cement floors, and dredged rivers, but besides Hoffa's car—which was discovered at a shopping center near his home—no trace of him was ever found.

What Happened: Most experts, including the FBI, say the Mafia had Hoffa killed. Why? The mob had switched allegiance to Hoffa's successors while he was in prison and didn't want him messing things up. Hoffa's bodyguard, however, insists it was the government that killed the union boss. The reason? They were still trying to cover up the fact that they used the Mafia to try to kill Fidel Castro, and Hoffa knew too much.

MADALYN MURRAY O'HAIR

Claim to Fame: America's most famous (and most vilified) atheist, O'Hair filed the 1963 lawsuit that resulted in the U.S. Supreme Court's decision to ban school prayer, and in the late 1960s founded an organization called American Atheists, Inc.

Disappearance: In 1995 O'Hair, her son Jon, and her granddaughter Robin headed to Virginia for a vacation...and were never seen again. Several days later, a note appeared on the front door of the American Atheists headquarters informing employees that they'd been laid off and that O'Hair, forced to leave on important business, would eventually return. She never did. The only trace ever found was Robin's abandoned car, discovered six months later in an airport parking lot.

What Happened: Some O'Hair loyalists believe she was assassinated by the CIA or the Pope. Others think the 77-year-old woman disappeared so she could die in private; she was obese and suffered from diabetes, heart disease, and chronic dizziness. She may have chosen to avoid the distasteful (to her) praying that her death would surely generate.

Her enemies, and at least one reporter, have a different theory: They think O'Hair and her family embezzled money and fled. O'Hair's organization was "beset with lawsuits, an IRS investigation, and diminishing membership." And an investigation by *Vanity Fair* magazine turned up circumstantial evidence that after transferring considerable assets to New Zealand, O'Hair and her companions moved there.

Postmortem: Her disappearance preserved her place as a part of contemporary culture. "She was looking for a new role," a biographer wrote, "and she found it: missing person. [Now] she'll be on the mind of the public for centuries."

*　　*　　*

WHY DO WE FLY FLAGS AT HALF-MAST?

In the days of sailing ships, when someone died on board or a national leader died, ships slackened their rigging, which gave the ship a disheveled look that was supposed to symbolize mourning, "the nautical equivalent of walking around in sackcloth and ashes." Lowering flags partway down the mast was another part of the practice, the only part that survives to this day.

Q: What sports celebrity appeared simultaneously on *Time, Newsweek,* and *Sports Illustrated* in 1973?

TO SLEEP...OR NOT TO SLEEP?

Here are some random facts about sleeping that you may not know. Complied for us by the BRI's own John Darling, who has never met Peter Pan and would like us to stop asking if he has, already. (He probably hasn't had enough sleep.)

T HE NEED FOR SLEEP
Newborn babies sleep about 16 hours a day—adults average half that. Teens, especially girls, are gluttons for sleep (10 hours average), but it's not because they're lazy, as many parents think. Stanford researchers found it was tied to the complex inner labors of puberty. This hunch is underlined by teen girls' need for extra Z's during their periods.

• We sleep best at certain times and if we stray from our required sleep needs, there's no telling what will happen. The nuclear disasters at both Chernobyl and Three Mile Island, as well as the Exxon Valdez wreck and Challenger shuttle explosion, have been linked to lack of sleep or altered sleep cycles among key people at key moments.

• "Jet lag" shifts our sleep cycle, often creating confusion, mental dullness and a desire to sleep at odd times. The Army was disappointed to find that troops flown overseas often require a week to overcome their disorientation. This phenomenon is the bane of passenger jet crews. In one instance, for example, all three members of a jetliner crew fell asleep as they reached the end of their overnight New York-to-Los Angeles flight. While air traffic controllers radioed them frantically, the jet flew 100 miles out over the ocean. Finally, one of the crew woke up and saw the sea in every direction. They had just enough fuel to make it back to LAX.

TO NAP OR NOT TO NAP?

• According to Stanley Coren, in his book *Sleep Thieves*, science has identified the two big peaks in our need for sleep—at 3 a.m. and 3 p.m. The first is dead in the center of our sleep cycle, but the second is smack in the middle of our workday. Shouldn't we be napping in mid-afternoon? At present, only 38% of us do.

A: Secretariat, the race horse.

- Who's getting the most sleep? Surveys find:
  - —In the U.S., Westerners and Southerners sleep longer than Easterners and Midwesterners.
  - —Women sleep more than men.
  - —Poor people sleep more than the rich.
  - —People who work evening or night shifts get far less sleep—about 5.6 hours—than day workers. No matter how hard they try, researchers say, people who sleep out of their normal cycle never fully adjust.

DOES LESS SLEEP = SUCCESS?

- A short sleep cycle is not inherently bad. Some people seek it out and sing its praises. Multi-millionaire magnate Donald Trump boasts of needing only three to four hours a night. Former junk-bond king Michael Milken gets only four to five hours.

- This raises the question: is there a link between sleep and success? Tufts University researcher Ernest Hartmann found that people who sleep less than 5.5 hours tend to be extroverted, ambitious and efficient, while people who sleep more than 9 hours tend to be anxious, insecure, introverted and indecisive. Other researchers think this is nonsense, noting that short-sleepers tend to be fast-paced, Type-A personalities (thus prone to heart disease), while long-sleepers include society's creative, alternate type thinkers and artists.

- Researchers hoped a survey of the CEO's and chairs of the Fortune 500 companies would settle the question of whether "the early bird really does get the worm." Apparently, it does. They found that 46% of the leaders they surveyed slept an hour less than the national average of 7.5 hours. Fifteen percent slept 5-6 hours and 2% slept 4-5 hours.

THE TRICK OF GETTING MORE SLEEP

Most of us, however, aren't looking for ways to sleep less—our focus is on how to get more. Here are some tips from the experts:
- Go to bed about the same time each night.
- Avoid nightcaps, except warm milk.
- Avoid illuminated clocks (they're a reminder you can't sleep).
- Exercise before going to bed.
- A dark and slightly cool bedroom is best (about 65°F).

New data: The average American male laughs 69 times a day; the average woman, 55.

MORE STRANGE LAWSUITS

Here are a more real-life examples of unusual legal battles.

THE PLAINTIFF: Janet R.

THE DEFENDANT: Kay-Bee Toys at Valley View Mall, Roanoke, Virginia

THE LAWSUIT: She claimed that while shopping in the mall in 1996, she was hit by a truck—a toy truck. Apparently a customer, playing with a radio-controlled 4 x 4, bumped Robinson in the ankle. She sued for $100,000, asking compensation for "pain, humiliation, aggravation and disability."

THE VERDICT: Suit dropped by plaintiff.

THE PLAINTIFF: Etta Stephens of Tampa, Florida

THE DEFENDANT: The Barnett Bank

THE LAWSUIT: In 1995 Stephens opened the envelope containing her monthly money market statement...and found the account balance listed as zero, instead of $20,000 as she expected. "Upon seeing this," says one report, "Stephens clutched her bosom and fell to the ground" with a heart attack. Officials of the bank said it was a mistake caused by a "printing error" and apologized. But Stephens still sued them for nearly killing her.

THE VERDICT: Unknown.

THE PLAINTIFF: Katherine Balog, 60-year-old Californian

THE DEFENDANTS: Bill Clinton and the Democratic Party

THE LAWSUIT: In 1992 Balog filed suit "to recover damages for the trauma of Clinton's candidacy." She claimed she was suffering "serious emotional and mental stress" because Clinton, a "Communist sympathizer" and "draft dodger," was about to be elected president.

THE VERDICT: Unknown.

The U.S. Postal Service owns 176,000 cars and trucks, the largest civilian vehicle fleet on earth.

THE PLAINTIFF: Bennie Casson
THE DEFENDANT: PT's Show Club, an Illinois strip joint
THE LAWSUIT: In 1997 a stripper named Busty Heart allegedly approached Casson during her act and "slammed" her 88-inch bust (a reported 40 pounds per breast) into his head and neck. He sued for "emotional distress" and claimed an old neck injury had been aggravated by the attack.
THE VERDICT: No lawyer would take the case, so the judge had to dismiss it.

THE PLAINTIFF: Debra Lee Benagh, 44, of Denver
THE DEFENDANT: Elitch Gardens, an amusement park
THE LAWSUIT: In 1997, according to Benagh's suit, she rode on the Mind Eraser roller coaster...and actually suffered memory loss. Benagh sued for negligence, contending that the park operators should have known of the ride's hazards.
THE VERDICT: Unknown.

THE PLAINTIFF: Swee Ho, a Chinese merchant in Thailand
THE DEFENDANT: Pu Lin, a rival merchant
THE LAWSUIT: As reported by Gerald Sparrow, once a judge in Bangkok: "Pu Lin had stated sneeringly at a party that Swee Ho's new wife, Li Bua, was merely a decoration to show how rich her husband was. Swee Ho, he said, could no longer 'please the ladies.' Swee Ho sued his rival for slander in the British Consular Court, claiming that Li Bua was his wife in every sense."
THE VERDICT: Swee Ho won...without a word of testimony. Swee Ho's lawyer "simply put the blushing Li Bua in the witness box. She was quite obviously pregnant."

*　　　*　　　*　　　*

IRONIC TWIST

The Ramses brand condom is named after the great Pharaoh Ramses II, who fathered over 160 children.

Princess Diana of Wales was buried in a plot of land once used as the Spencer family pet cemetery.

CELEBRITY MALPRACTICE

*Famous spokespeople sell us everything from underwear to cars.
We assume they really stand behind the product…but as history shows,
that's not necessarily the case. Here are four examples of what* Newsweek
*magazine calls "celebrity malpractice"—good reminders to think twice
before you trust someone just because they're well-known.*

Celebrity: Pat Boone, former teen idol and squeaky-clean Christian.

Company: Karr Preventative Medical Products Inc., maker of Acne-Statin, a mail-order pimple cream

Malpractice: In the 1970s, Boone appeared in TV, magazine, and newspaper ads, claiming that Acne-Statin "had been scientifically found to cure the most severe cases of acne by eliminating certain bacteria and fatty acid from the pores of the skin." But as one critic pointed out, the product actually had "the same facial efficacy as shoe polish." In 1978 Boone was found guilty of false advertising, along with the manufacturer, and was ordered to stop appearing in the commercials and provide refunds to thousands of customers. At the time, it was the stiffest FTC penalty ever given to a celebrity endorsing a product.

Celebrity: Johnny Unitas, legendary Baltimore Colts quarterback

Company: First Fidelity Financial Services, Inc., a second-mortgage broker in Hollywood, Florida

Malpractice: In 1981 Unitas appeared on radio ads assuring listeners: "I know what it's like to put your name on the line and make it count. That's where my friends at First Fidelity come in." When First Fidelity went bankrupt and its founder was jailed for fraud, two investors sued Unitas (who'd received only $7,000 for his endorsement) for the $78,000 they'd invested and lost in the company. Their lawyer explained: "They invested their money based upon the belief that someone like Unitas…would not be involved in misrepresentation. A celebrity has some obligation to…make

---

sure he is not being used in a scheme of fraud." Unitas's lawyer protested: "There is nothing in the law to require an endorser... to go through the books to make sure the product he is putting his picture on is sound." Unitas became the first pro-football player ever sued for "advertising a bum product."

Celebrity: Lloyd Bridges, veteran TV and movie actor
Companies: Diamond Mortgage Co. (which lent money at high rates to people who couldn't get mortgages anywhere else) and an affiliated company, A. J. Obie & Associates (which found investors to finance the mortgages)
Malpractice: In 1986 Bridges and another actor, George Hamilton, appeared in ads promising people that the companies' "secured investments" would "help them to a better life." According to court documents, however, the only people who got a better life out of the deal were the executives who looted the companies. They kept investors' money instead of putting it into more mortgages, then, facing claims of more than $40 million, eventually went bankrupt. Two of them went to jail. Meanwhile, both Hamilton and Bridges were prosecuted by the state of Illinois under its consumer fraud law. Hamilton immediately settled, but Bridges fought the suit, insisting he was merely a spokesman for Obie "with no special expertise in investments." When an appeals court rejected his contention, Bridges gave up the fight and settled the case.

Celebrities: Ed McMahon and Dick Clark
Company: American Family Publishers sweepstakes
Malpractice: The avuncular McMahon and ageless Clark appeared in 1990s ads telling consumers to watch for the mailing with Uncle Ed's picture on it. But more than 30 states said the mailings were outright fraud. For example: Some mailings indicated that a recipient was one of two people vying for the grand prize, and the first person to return the entry form would win. "In their zeal to sell magazines," said Florida's attorney general, "AFP and its high-profile pitchmen have misled millions of consumers. They have clearly stepped over the line from advertising hype to unlawful deception." States sued AFP, McMahon, and Clark. AFP settled, paying $50,000 to each state and agreeing to change its practices.

Some 19% of Amercan taxpayers say "avoiding an audit" is their #1 priority when filling out

PUN FOR THE MONEY

BRI member Erica Gordon keeps sending Uncle John her horrible puns.
Of course, he loves them—and then insists on "sharing" them with us.
So why are we including them here? Have you ever heard the saying
"Misery loves company?" Heh, heh. Feel free to groan out loud.

TWO ESKIMOS were sitting in a kayak. They got chilly, so they decided to light a fire in the craft. Unfortunately, it sank—proving once and for all that you can't have your kayak and heat it, too.

TWO BOLL WEEVILS grew up in South Carolina. One went to Hollywood and became a famous actor. The other stayed behind in the cotton fields and never amounted to much. The second one became known as the lesser of two weevils.

THERE WAS A MAN who entered a local paper's pun contest. He sent in ten different puns, hoping that at least one of the puns would win. Unfortunately, no pun in ten did.

A WOMAN HAD TWINS, but gave them up for adoption. One of them went to a family in Egypt and was named "Amal." The other went to a family in Spain who named him "Juan." Years later, Juan sent a picture of himself to his mom. When she got the picture, she told her husband wistfully that she wished she also had a picture of Amal. Her husband responded: "But they're twins—if you've seen Juan, you've seen Amal."

SOME FRIARS NEEDED TO RAISE MONEY, so they opened up a small florist shop. Since everyone liked to buy flowers from the men of God, the rival florist across town thought the competition was unfair. He asked the good fathers to close down, but they would not. He went back and begged the friars to close. They ignored him. He asked his mother to plead with them. They ignored her, too. Finally, the rival florist hired Hugh McTaggart, the roughest and most vicious thug in town to "persuade" them to close. Hugh beat up the friars and trashed their store, saying he'd be back if they didn't close shop. Terrified, they did so—thereby proving (are you ready?) that Hugh, and only Hugh, can prevent florist friars.

tax forms; 33% say "taking as many deductions as possible" is.

THE ORIGIN OF
THE SHOPPING CART

*Some modern conveniences seem so simple and logical that it's hard to
believe they actually had to be invented. Take the shopping cart, for example. You might guess it evolved from some sort of small wagon people were
already using. But it came from the mind of one man. Here's the story,
told in* The Cart That Changed the World, *by Terry P. Wilson.*

A BIGGER BASKET

In 1937 Sylvan Goldman owned two Oklahoma City supermarkets. Back then, shoppers carried their food in wick-
er baskets provided by the grocer. One day Goldman was standing
around, watching customers, when he realized that as soon as a basket was either full or too heavy, people stopped shopping. "The
thought came to me," Goldman recalled, "that if we could somehow give a customer two baskets and still leave them with a free
hand to shop, we could do considerably more business." He came
up with a plan:

> In my office I had some folding chairs that salesmen used when
> they called on me. I realized that if I put wheels on them, raised
> the seats so there was room to put another rack at the bottom of
> the chair, and let the back of the chair be the handle, customers
> could be shopping comfortably with two baskets.

Goldman worked with a carpenter to adapt the chairs. Their first
effort was a flop—it hit a wooden match on the floor and collapsed.
But several months later, they created a collapse-proof steel-framed
"basket carrier." Now Goldman was ready to introduce it to the
public.

IT'S NEW! IT'S SENSATIONAL!

Goldman ran newspaper ads all week, announcing that he would
introduce a brand-new shopping convenience on the weekend.
The ads said: "Can you imagine wending your way through a spa-
cious food market without having to carry a cumbersome shopping
basket on your arm?...Every customer who visits our stores this

week end will see the latest device conceived by the mind of man; and be able to shop with an ease never before known in any Food Store!"

There was no mention of the shopping cart—customers had to come to the store to find out what the new marvel was. And that weekend, plenty of customers came...but *no one* used the cart. As Goldman relates:

> I went to our largest store, and there wasn't *a soul* using a "basket-carrier." An attractive girl at the entrance was asking them to "please take this cart" to do their shopping with. But the house-wives...decided, 'No more carts for me. I've been pushing enough baby carriages. I don't want to push anymore.' And the men would say, 'You mean, with my big strong arm I can't carry a darn little basket like that?' And he wouldn't touch it. It was a complete flop.

CONSUMER PSYCHOLOGY

A few days later, Goldman hit on an idea to get people to use the carts.

> For each store, I hired a young lady in her late 20s, another in her 40s, and someone else in her late 50s. I also hired a couple of men about 30 and 50 years old. [I put them] right by the entranceway of the store with basket-carriers, shopping, pushing the cart around with merchandise in the top and bottom baskets. I told this young lady who was offering the carts to customers to say, "Look, everybody's using them; why not you?" And when people saw them in use, they started using them, and the carts immediately became a huge success.

Within a few weeks all of Goldman's stores were offering "basket-carriers," and the devices became extremely popular.

SELLING THE SHOPPING CART

Encouraged by the success of his invention, Goldman patented the design and formed the Folding Basket-Carrier Company to manufacture it. Then he hired his cousin, Kurt Schweitzer, to demonstrate the cart at a meeting of U.S. supermarket operators.

The expo went so well that when he returned, Schweitzer offered to quit his import-export job and sell shopping carts full-time. Goldman agreed, and Schweitzer set out to visit every major grocery store between New York and St. Louis.

He returned with disastrous news: almost no stores had ordered the cart. Managers were afraid that children would race basket-carriers up and down the aisles, knocking merchandise off shelves and into customers. Cart-related accidents would lead to lawsuits, they said, and the convenience wasn't worth the risk.

GROCER PSYCHOLOGY

Goldman put considerable thought into solving the problem and, once again, came up with an idea that was revolutionary in its time:

> We gathered a group of employees in one of our stores after closing hours and took a movie of them acting as customers shopping… [That way, store-owners could see] exactly how this worked—how easily and how well it was accepted, how the problems a lot of them feared didn't materialize at all….When the film was finished, I told Kurt, "Now when you go in to try to see the buyer, tell him…you have something new and [you have to] *show* it to them."
>
> He took his projector in with the film, shut off the light, closed the door, and showed it on a wall.…Before he got halfway back to New York, we had so many orders for carts, we couldn't have made them in God knows how long a time.

The Folding Basket-Carrier Company bought new equipment and went into mass production. Goldman's basket-carriers evolved into today's shopping cart and quickly became a fixture in nearly every grocery store in America.

*　*　*

UNUSUAL THEME RESTAURANT

Baked Pig Face (*Seven Locations in Mainland China*)

Theme: Western-style restaurant built around a traditional dish from Northeastern China—baked pig heads

Details: Waitresses wear caps with the restaurant's "Porky Pig-like logo." Main dish: "a whole pig's head, yellow teeth and all, cooked for 12 hours in 20 herbs and spices." The steaming heads are "split in half and laid split-side down on a platter…piping hot, with pig-let-shaped dumplings as a garnish." Vacuum-sealed heads available for takeout.

THE ULTIMATE TASTE TEST

According to Dr. Alan Hirsch's Smell & Taste Treatment and Research Foundation, the fruits and vegetables you prefer tell a lot about your personality. Want proof? Take this test that Dr. Hirsch has put together— no cheating!—then let us know if you think we should print more.

1. Which groups of fruits do you prefer?
- **a)** Oranges, Bananas, and Grapes
- **b)** Eggplant, Corn, and Tomatoes

Analysis: If you prefer the first group, this indicates a strong-minded, ambitious, aggressive, dominant individual, who is a natural leader. If you prefer the second group, this indicates an introspective, self-searching person who is sensitive to the needs of others. You tend not to be impulsive in your decision-making processes, but rather weigh all the alternatives in question before making your decision.

2. Of these pairs of fruits, which do you prefer? (Must choose one of each pair.)
- **a)** Applesauce or Fresh Apples
- **b)** Pineapple Chunks or Pineapple Glaze
- **c)** Creamed Corn or Corn on the Cob

Analysis: If at least two of the above are the first choice, then you are a passive, easy-going, agreeable sort, who tries to solve problems without raising a commotion. If at least two of the above are the second choice, you tend to be an aggressive "go-getter" who will not take "No" for an answer. You work hard and play hard.

3. Do you like spicy pickles?

Analysis: If YES, you tend to be pessimistic. If NO, you tend to be optimistic.

One mother shark can give birth to as many as 70 baby sharks per litter.

4. Do you like:

a) Bananas; b) Boiled fish; c) Fruit; d) Honey;

e) Tapioca; f) Celery; g) Nuts; h) Hot Curry

Analysis: If five or more is YES you a natural optimist and view life through rose-colored glasses. You are a pleasant co-worker and would make a good friend. If five or more is NO, you tend to be pessimistic. Before being involved in social intercourse, you tend to be careful, doubting others' intentions.

5. Which do you prefer?

a) Green olives or Black Olives

b) Pecans or Almonds

c) Pickles or Cucumbers

Analysis: If two or more are the first choice, you tend to be assertive in your relationships and enthusiastic in all endeavors. Although anxious at times, you are a decisive, resilient person, prone to action. If two or more are the second choice, you tend to take responsibility for your actions. You are self-confident and a natural leader.

6. Which do you prefer?

a) Lemons or Oranges

b) Potatoes or Yams

c) Grapefruit or Tangerines

Analysis: If two or more are the first choice, you tend to be reserved, quiet, and contemplative. You usually are not impulsive. You tend towards introspection. If two or more is the second choice, you tend to be an out-going, gregarious person who enjoys a sound relationship. Many consider you to have a good sense of humor. You would make a good disc jockey, used car salesman, or politician.

*   *   *

Random Animal Fact: A female lobster, called a hen or chicken, can lay as many as 100,000 eggs at one time. Most end up as "food for other marine life."

NO RESPECT!

All these years, and Rodney Dangerfield still can't win.

"My mother never breast-fed me. She told me that she only liked me as a friend."

"A girl phoned me the other day and said, 'Come on over, there's nobody home.' I went over. Nobody was home."

"We were poor....Why if I wasn't born a boy...I'd have nothing to play with."

"When I played in the sandbox the cat kept covering me up."

"I could tell that my parents hated me. My bath toys were a toaster and a radio."

"When I was born...the doctor came out to the waiting room and said to my father, 'I'm very sorry. We did everything we could, but he pulled through.'"

"My mother had morning sickness after I was born."

"My father carries around the picture of the kid who came with his wallet."

"I remember the time I was kidnapped and they sent a piece of my finger to my father. He said he wanted more proof."

"My wife made me join a bridge club. I jump off next Tuesday."

"I worked in a pet shop and people kept asking how big I'd get."

"When I was born the doctor took one look at my face... turned me over and said, 'Look ...twins!'"

"I remember when I swallowed a bottle of sleeping pills. My doctor told me to have a few drinks and get some rest."

"When I was a kid, I was so short I had to blow my nose through my fly."

"It's been a rough day. I got up this morning...put on a shirt and a button fell off. I picked up my briefcase and the handle came off. I'm afraid to go to the bathroom."

In Venice, Venetian blinds are known as "Persian blinds."

BEEN NOWHERE, DONE NOTHING

BRI member Debbie Thornton sent in this list of real-life bumper stickers. Have you seen the one that says...

SUBURBIA: *Where They Tear Down the Trees and Name Streets After Them*

I Have No Idea What I'm Doing Out of Bed

Been Nowhere, Done Nothing

Support Bacteria: It's the Only Culture Some People Have

I Used to Be Indecisive; Now I'm Not Sure

My Reality Check Just Bounced

No Sense Being Pessimistic—It Wouldn't Work Anyway

The More You Complain, the Longer God Lets You Live

Forget About World Peace—Visualize Using Your Turn Signal!

Warning: *Dates in Calendar Are Closer Than They Appear*

Consciousness: That Annoying Time Between Naps

Age Is a Very High Price to Pay for Maturity

I Doubt, Therefore I Might Be

The Older You Get, the Better You Realize You Were

Dyslexics Have More Fnu

Men Are from Earth. Women Are from Earth. Deal With It.

The Gene Pool Could Use a Little Chlorine

So You're a Feminist... Isn't That Cute!

Time Is What Keeps Things from Happening All at Once

Your Kid May Be an Honor Student but You're Still an Idiot

We Have Enough Youth, How About a Fountain of "Smart"?

What do gorillas and housecats have in common? Both purr.

CELEBRITY PSYCHICS

If you're reading this before 2000, watch out. If you're reading it after 2000…well, we hope you're enjoying a good laugh. From our book, Uncle John's Indispensable Guide to the Year 2000.

JEANNE DIXON (1918–1996)
Claim to Fame: Supposedly predicted both John and Robert Kennedy's assassinations. In 1965, her biography, *Gift of Prophesy*, was a bestseller. From then on she was the most famous psychic in America and the darling of tabloids like the *National Enquirer*.

Psychic Visions for 2000: Look out—the anti-Christ is "alive today in the Middle East," and will start World War III in 1999 or 2000. "He will be a military figure beyond anything the world has previously seen," Dixon wrote. "He will conquer the earth and hold it in complete mastery with the most modern weapons." There will be terrible times, but he'll be defeated when Christ returns.

Believability Factor: It's up to you—but remember, she also predicted that the South Vietnamese would win, we'd have a woman president in the '80s, and O. J. Simpson would be convicted. She once wrote a column saying Jackie Kennedy would never remarry. It went to press as Jackie's marriage to Aristotle Onassis was announced.

EDGAR CAYCE (1877–1945)
Claim to Fame: Called "the Sleeping Prophet" because he'd lay down on a couch and go into a trance before making predictions or medical diagnoses (which were often correct). He also gave "life readings," telling people about their previous lives in Rome, Syria, Atlantis, etc. There are dozens of books on Cayce and his prophesies and a foundation carrying on his work in Virginia Beach.

Psychic Visions for 2000: Nature will go on the rampage. The poles will shift, causing earthquakes that wipe out cities all over the world. "What is the coastline now of many a land will be the bed of the ocean." The quakes will also destroy part of the Midwest, after which the Great Lakes will flow directly into the Gulf of Mexico. Safe places include Virginia Beach (Cayce's home), parts of the Midwest, and southern and eastern Canada.

Believability Factor: Cayce made some impressive predictions—including the discovery of the Dead Sea Scrolls and the 1929 stock market crash. On the other hand, he apparently predicted some of these cataclysmic events for 1998, not 2000. But who knows—as one critic suggests, "If he knew some aspects of the future, he *could* know others."

HAL LINDSEY

Claim to Fame: Author of *The Late Great Planet Earth* and *Satan Is Alive and Well on Planet Earth*, two of the bestselling books of the 1970s. Both are full of apocalyptic Christian prophecies. They don't give any specific dates, but as one critic says, "Readers were left with little doubt that the end of the world was imminent—by the end of the eighties, at any rate."

Psychic Visions for 2000: In 1994, the earth was still alive and well, so he published updated versions of his prophecies in *Planet Earth 2000 A.D.* The plot: Russia joins forces with Islamic countries to invade Egypt and Israel. Europeans bomb the Russians, and 200 million Chinese cross the dried-up Euphrates River to attack the Europeans at Megiddo. Result: World war—leading to the battle of Armageddon and the second coming of Christ.

Believability Factor: If he was wrong about the 1970s and 1980s, why assume he's right about 2000?

POLLY THE COW

Claim to Fame: According to news reports, the Plainview, Minnesota cow predicted the winner of each presidential election from 1972 to 1988 "by relieving herself on a photograph of the eventual winner after equal numbers of the candidates' photographs were spread on the ground. The day before the 1992 election, after 10 photos each of Clinton, Bush, and Perot were spread out in a pen in a shopping mall parking lot, Polly's celebrated patty landed squarely on a photograph of Bill Clinton."

Psychic Visions for 2000: Unknown.

Believability Factor: Accurate or not, it's hard to think of a more appropriate way to predict the outcome of an election. Polly for president!

COINED BY SHAKESPEARE

Sure, Shakespeare is considered the best writer in the history of the English language. But did you know that he also helped create it? Uncle John didn't...until he found a book called Coined by Shakespeare, *written by Jeffrey McQuain and Stanley Malles.*

ALLIGATOR: Before the Bard, it was known in English as a *lagarto* or an *aligarto* (from the Spanish *el lagarto*). First Use: *Romeo and Juliet* (V.i.42-43)—"in his needy shop a tortoise hung, / An *alligator* stuff'd, and other skins."

DAWN: The verb *dawning*, for "daybreak," already existed; Shakespeare turned it into a noun.
First Use: *Henry V* (IV.i.274-275)—"next day after *dawn*, / Doth rise and help Hyperion to his horse."

LONELY: Shakespeare added the *-ly.*
First Use: *Coriolanus* (IV.i.29-30)—"I go alone, / Like to a *lonely* dragon."

DRUG: He changed it into a verb, and gave it the negative connotation it has today.
First Use: *Macbeth* (II.ii.6)—"I have *drugg'd* their possets."

EYEBALL: The words *eye* and *ball* already existed; Shakespeare was the first to put them together.
First Use: *A Midsummer Night's Dream* (III.ii.369)—"make his *eyeballs* roll with wonted sight."

UNDRESS: Shakespeare added the *un-.*
First Use: *The Taming of the Shrew* (Induction.ii.117)—"*undress* you, and come now to bed."

PUKE: The Bard spewed this one out all by himself.
First Use: *As You Like It* (II.vii.144)—"Mewling and *puking* in the nurse's arms."

A hibernating bear can go as long as six months without a bathroom break.

DOMINEERING: Shakespeare adapted this word into English from the Dutch verb *domineren*.
First Use: *Love's Labor Lost* (III.i.177)—"A *domineering* pedant o'er the boy."

INAUDIBLE: Shakespeare added the *in-*.
First Use: *All's Well That Ends Well* (V.iii.40-42)—"We are old, and on our quick'st decrees / Th' *inaudible* and noiseless foot of time / Steals ere we can effect them."

PANDER: From *Pandarus*, a character in Homer's *Iliad*. The Bard trimmed the name and added the *-er*.
First Use: *Hamlet* (III.iv.88)—"reason *panders* will."

AMAZEMENT: Shakespeare added the *-ment*, changing the word to a noun.
First Use: *King John* (V.i.35-36)—"Wild amazement hurries up and down / The little number of you doubtful friends."

LEAPFROG: Though the game was familiar to his audience, Shakespeare gave it its name.
First Use: *Henry V* (V.ii. 136-39)—"If I could win a lady at *leap-frog*....I should quickly leap into a wife."

BEDROOM: Shakespeare invented this word to mean "room or space *within* a bed."
First Use: *A Midsummer Night's Dream* (II.ii.51)—"Then by your side no *bed-room* me deny."

HINT: Shakespeare took the Middle English verb *hent*, and used it as a noun.
First Use: *Othello* (I.iii.165-66)—"I should but teach him how to tell my story, / And that would woo her. Upon this *hint* I spake."

SUBMERGE: The Bard combined the Latin prefix *sub-* ("under") with the Latin word *mergere* ("to plunge") to create this verb.
First Use: *Antony and Cleopatra* (II.v.94-95)—"Half my Egypt were *submerg'd* and made / A cestern for scal'd snakes."

When medieval Europeans burned witches, the witches' families had to pay for the firewood.

HOW TO MAKE A MONSTER, PART II

*Here's the second installment of our history of Uncle John's
favorite movie monster...Gojira,the original Japanese
name for Godzilla. (Part I starts on page 133.)*

DESIGNING A MONSTER

It took the model department three tries to come up with the right design for Gojira. The first model had fishlike scales for skin and a line of pointy spikes running down its back. Producer Tomoyuki Tanaka liked the spikes, but thought the head was too big and the scales too "fishy." Next they created a "warty" Gojira with a smaller head and large rounded bumps on the skin. Tanaka didn't like this treatment either, so they came up with "alligator" Gojira, this time with much smaller, linear bumps arranged in rows like bumps on an alligator's back. Alligator Gojira got the nod.

SUITS ME FINE

Now Tanaka had a name and a look for his monster—but what kind of special effects would he use? Stop-motion animation, (e.g. claymation) used tiny, moveable clay models, and was filmed frame by frame. It produced excellent results—*King Kong* was filmed with stop-motion animation—but was time consuming and expensive. Plus, it limited the amount of detail that could be shown—a big problem, since so much of the script involved the monster knocking down buildings. (It's almost impossible to make a building collapse realistically when filming frame by frame.)

The alternative: use a man in a monster suit. That could be filmed at a larger scale, making higher levels of detail possible. And because the footage would be filmed in "real time" instead of frame by frame, it could be finished in a few weeks instead of several months. The problem with such a low-tech technique was that if the filmmakers weren't careful, the man in the monster suit would end up looking like...a man in a monster suit.

In the end, it was scheduling that decided the issue—a monster

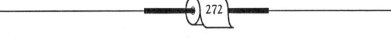

suit was quicker, and Toho studios had only a year to produce the film, so Godjira became a man in a costume.

The special-effects crew built a full-sized Gojira model, which they used to create plaster molds for the monster suit. Then they poured latex rubber into the molds to make Gojira's skin. The skin was then attached to a cloth "inner skin," made of cloth stuffed with polystyrene foam and bamboo to provide the monster's bulk. The fully assembled suit weighed more than 220 pounds.

The actor entered the costume via a zipper that ran along the dorsal fin; he was (barely) able to see out of the costume through four tiny holes in Gojira's neck. The monster's head was then mounted on a brace that rested on the actor's head; an offscreen technician used a radio-controlled mechanism to open and close the mouth.

SWEATY WORK

Gojira's action sequences were filmed at a high speed so that when it was slowed down for viewing, the buildings crumbled more realistically. But this meant that the set had to be lit twice as bright as when filming at normal speed, and the hot lights caused temperatures inside the suit to climb as high as 120°F, with the only ventilation provided by the eyeholes in Gojira's neck.

Under these conditions it was nearly impossible to film for more than a few minutes at a time. Typically, the actor inside the suit would spend 7 to 10 minutes rehearsing a scene in costume with the studio lights turned off. Then the lights came on and the scene was filmed for about 3 minutes, which was all the actor could take before he risked passing out from heat prostration and suffocation. Collapsing mid-scene was not unusual, and two actors who alternated as Gojira sweated so profusely that the crew drained as much as half a pint of sweat from the suit at the end of the day.

The on-screen result of filming in such difficult conditions was a slow, lumbering creature who shuffled and lurched across the tiny cityscapes…but that was just the look that Tanaka wanted: in the 1950s, paleontologists incorrectly assumed that most dinosaurs were huge, slow-witted, slow-moving creatures, and Tanaka's quest for dinosaur accuracy dovetailed nicely with the limitations imposed by the heavy suit and hot studio lights.

Most common phobia in the world: *odynophobia*—the fear of pain.

TINY TOWN

Entire city blocks of downtown Tokyo were reconstructed in elaborate detail for the film. For the scene in which Gojira destroys Tokyo's famous Ginza district, special effects man Eiji Tsuburaya's technicians reproduced a three-square-block section of the district in miniature, complete with interior floors and walls to make sure the buildings would crumble realistically when Gojira smashes them. Tsuburaya also insisted that the tiny automobiles, buses, and trains be hand made from cast iron to ensure that when Gojira stepped on them, the sturdy little vehicles would crush realistically.

MAKING NOISE

Finding a suitable roar for Gojira was one of the trickier aspects of creating the monster. The film's sound-effects team tried numerous actual animal sounds: grunts, growls, roars, and other noises. They played them backward, forward, individually, and in groups, but nothing seemed to work. Then composer Akira Ifukube tried rubbing the strings of a bass violin with the fingers of a resin-coated rubber glove, and reverberating the sound. That did the trick.

OPENING NIGHT

Finally, after 122 days of filming, *Gojira* premiered in Japan on November 3, 1954. The film had cost a fortune to make—the final tally was 60 million yen (about $65 million in 1999 dollars), about 250 times the average cost of a Japanese film at that time.

But it turned out to be a good investment: *Gojira* was one of the most popular films of the year and earned a fortune for Toho.

Gojira was also a critical success. "While American monster-on-the-loose films used radiation to get the monster up and running around," David Kalat writes in *A Critical History and Filmography of Toho's Godzilla Series*, "Honda saw his monster as a narrative device to discuss the terror of the nuclear age." Less than a decade after World War II, Japanese critics understood and appreciated the implicit message.

Turn to page 359 for Part III.

How do you know when a turkey is panicking? That's the only time it whistles.

MODEL CITIZENS

Some thoughtful commentary from the mouths of "babes."

"I don't have to fake dumb. I *am* dumb."
—Jerry Hall

"I don't wake up for less than $10,000 a day."
—Linda Evangelista

"Everywhere I went, my cleavage followed. But I learned I am not my cleavage."
—Carole Mallory

"I'm so naive about finances. Once when my mother mentioned an amount and I realized I didn't understand, she had to explain: 'That's like three Mercedes.' Then I understood."
—Brooke Shields

"Blah, blah, blah. I'm so tired of talking about myself."
—Elle Macpherson

"I don't think I was born beautiful. I just think I was born me."
—Naomi Campbell

"I've always been a bit more maturer than what I am."
—Samantha Fox

"Everyone should have enough money to get plastic surgery."
—Beverly Johnson

"I believe that mink are raised for being turned into fur coats and if we didn't wear fur coats those little animals would never have been born. So is it better not to have been born or to have lived for a year or two to have been turned into a fur coat? I don't know."
—Barbi Benton

"People think modeling's mindless, that you just stand there and pose, but it doesn't have to be that way. I like to have a lot of input. I know how to wear a dress, whether it should be shot with me standing up or sitting. And I'm not scared to say what I think."
—Linda Evangelista

"I look at modeling as something I'm doing for black people in general."
—Naomi Campbell

"I can do anything you want me to do so long as I don't have to speak."
—Linda Evangelista

"I wish my butt did not go sideways, but I guess I have to face that."
—Christie Brinkley

THE JOKE'S ON US!

*Americans tend to overlook an important side to our love affair
with celebrities—they're always trying to sell us something:
an idea, image, or product. And many of them don't
mind lying to us, either. Here are a few examples.*

FOR SALE: A Cherished Possession
In the early 1900s, Bat Masterson, legendary Wild West law-
man, became a New York sports writer. Because he needed the
money, he reluctantly agreed to sell his famous sixgun—the "gun
that tamed the West."

The Truth: He actually bought old guns at pawnshops or junk
stores, carved notches in them (one for each "kill"), and sold them
to admirers for a tidy profit. Each time, he swore it was the authentic gun he'd used in Dodge City.

FOR SALE: An Intellectual Image
In 1961 an article in *Time* magazine helped convince Americans
that they'd elected an exceptionally bright man as president. It reported that JFK had taken a course in something called "speed-
reading" and could zip through an amazing 1,200 words a minute. It
became common knowledge—and part of his mystique—that he
could read a whole book in one sitting.

The Truth: The number was concocted by Kennedy and *Time* reporter Hugh Sidey. First, JFK told Sidey he could read 1,000 words a
minute. Upon reflection, however, he decided that number sounded
too low. "How about 1,200?" Sidey asked. "Okay," Kennedy replied.
And that's what was printed. Actually, JFK never finished the
speed-reading course he took and, at best, could read 800 wpm (still
a lot, but not as impressive).

FOR SALE: A Folksy White House Tradition
It was a Yuletide tradition during the Reagan presidency. Gathering
with reporters, the Great Communicator would ceremoniously light
the National Christmas Tree on the Mall in Washington, D.C., by
pushing a button from inside the White House.

The Truth: The button wasn't connected to anything—a Park Service employee actually lit the tree. The press found out by accident in 1989, when President Bush went to the tree site and lit it in person. Bush's press secretary let it slip that, unlike the Reagan years, "that was the real thing." Cornered, he admitted that Reagan's button was a prop. "Then came the follow-up question," the *Washington Post* reported: "Were all the other buttons disconnected, too?"

FOR SALE: Ultimate Weirdness

In the 1980s, a number of strange stories about pop singer Michael Jackson were reported by the media—especially by the tabloids. The press reported, for example, that Jackson...

- had bought an oxygen chamber and was sleeping in it. The reason: he wanted to live to be 100.
- had offered to buy the remains of John Merrick, the "Elephant Man," for $500,000. (*Playboy* magazine jokingly responded that "descendants of the Elephant Man have offered $100,000 for the remains of Michael Jackson's nose.")
- was so obsessed with his chimp, Bubbles, that he was learning "monkey language" to communicate with him.

Even more than his music, the constant stream of reports on Jackson's weirdnesses made him a pervasive presence in pop culture. Everyone talked about him.

The Truth: The stories were all false—concocted, it turns out, by Jackson himself. According to one report, Jackson had "learned early how little truth means when seeking publicity" back when he was in the Jackson 5. In private, he even "began reading biographies of hokum-master P. T. Barnum for ideas."

*   *   *

...PROCEED WITH CAUTION

- A black widow's poison is 15 times more powerful than rattlesnake venom.

- Black widows like warm, dark places, and in pre-indoor plumbing days, were "fond of hiding in outhouses, where they often spin webs across toilet seats."

It takes 720 peanuts to make a pound of peanut butter.

RANDOM ORIGINS

*Once again, the BRI asks—and answers—the
question: where did this stuff come from?*

THE JOCKSTRAP

"Millions of male athletes can thank bicycling—and the cobblestone streets of Boston—for the truss that protects their masculinity....In 1897, those bumpy Beantown byways got too rough for the nether regions of bike racers. To address this unexpected need, the BIKE manufacturing company invented the "bicycle jockey strap"—eventually shortened to 'jock.'" (*Bicycling* magazine)

THE ROLODEX

Arnold Neustadter invented several devices (the Swivodex, the Clipodex, etc.) for clerical workers, but they were flops. In 1950, to clear his own desk clutter, he created the first Rolodex. It wasn't a big seller at $7.50. But then came Hollywood. The Rolodex was featured in films as the accessory of powerful men—"The bigger the Rolodex, the bigger the man," as Neustadter's son-in-law David put it. At one time, there were hundreds of Rolodex models, including the 6,000-card, triple-wheel Torque-a-Matic. Today only a few models are still offered, including a little, handheld, computerized version.

SNEEZING POWDER

In 1905 Sam Adams, a salesman for "a coal-tar product," noticed that it made people sneeze. *Scribner's* magazine wrote in 1940: "Adams began fooling with it for his own amusement....High spots included sprinkling the powder through hotel keyholes, in a cafe where a wandering brass band was serenading, and at a trapshooting contest where he unnerved his competitors by dusting it near them as they took aim....In 1906 he formed the Adams Novelty Company and marketed the powder as Cachoo....Cachoo divided the country like nothing since the Civil War. Town fathers passed ordinances, school principals preached sermons, editorial writers inveighed against Cachoo. But a laugh-hungry public demanded more." It was the beginning of the modern novelty industry. Adams went on to invent the Dribble Glass, the Joy Buzzer, and other classics. His biggest regret: in 1930 a Toronto company offered him exclusive rights to the Whoopee Cushion...and he turned it down. "The whole idea seemed too indelicate," said the man who invented the Bloody Finger, "so I passed it up."

THE ATLAS

"In the late 16th century French geographer Gerhard Mercator (1512-1594) published a book of maps whose frontispiece was a picture of Atlas holding the world on his back. Almost from then on any collection of maps has been called an *atlas*." (*Literary Life*)

THE FOOTBALL HUDDLE

"In 1924, Herb McCracken, the coach of the Lafayette College football team, discovered that his hand signals [flashed to players during the game] had been scouted and decoded by Penn, his upcoming opponent. On game day, McCracken countered by ordering his players to gather en masse, several yards behind the line of scrimmage, and talk over the plays in a whisper. It immediately became a ritual." McCracken later helped start the Scholastic publishing company, "but told family members that he was most proud of giving birth to the huddle." (*The New York Times*)

THE CASH REGISTER

In 1879 a Dayton, Ohio, saloonkeeper named James J. Ritty was vacationing on a transatlantic steamer when he took a tour of the engine room and saw a machine that counted the number of revolutions of the ship's propeller. He figured a similar machine might help him keep track of his saloon sales, and prevent dishonest bartenders from looting the till. When he got home, he and his brother invented "Ritty's Incorruptible Cashier"—a machine with two rows of keys with amounts printed on them, a clocklike face that added up the amount of money collected, and a bell that rang after every transaction. It was the first product from the business that would become the National Cash Register Company (NCR).

HAVE YOU HAD YOUR POLYSORBATE 60 TODAY?

Every day we consume things with ingredients whose names are impossible to pronounce and whose purpose we don't know. See if you can figure out which ingredients go with each of the 7 products in the list below.

MATCH THE PRODUCTS...

1. Frosting
2. Sweet 'N Low
3. Pepto-Bismol
4. CheezWhiz
5. Chocolate pudding
6. "Butter" spray
7. Marshmallows

...WITH THE INGREDIENTS

A. Nutritive dextrose, calcium saccharin, cream of tartar, calcium silicate

B. Xantham gum, soy lecithin, polysorbate 60, potassium sorbate, calcium disodium EDTA

C. Corn syrup modified food starch, dextrose, artificial color, tetrasodium pyrophosphate

D. Benzoic acid, magnesium aluminum silicate, methylcellulose, salicylic acid, sorbic acid

E. Partially hydrogenated soybean oil, modified food starch, cocoa (processed with alkali), sodium stearoyl lactylate

F. Dried corn syrup, sodium phosphate, whey protein concentrate, sorbic acid, oleoresin paprika

G. Monoglycerides, diglycerides, cellulose gel, polysorbate 80, sodium acid pyrophosphate

ANSWERS

1) G; 2) A; 3) D; 4) F; 5) E; 6) B; 7) C.

What do whales and buffaloes have in common? Both stampede.

MY BODY LIES OVER THE OCEAN...

More stories about miscellaneous body parts removed from famous people after they died.

EINSTEIN'S EYES

Where They're Located: Bank vault in New Jersey

How They Got There: It turns out Dr. Harvey wasn't the only sticky-fingered professional at Einstein's autopsy (see p. 174): at about the same time Harvey was absconding with the brain, Einstein's ophthalmologist, a doctor named Henry Abrams, was removing the eyes. He placed them in a jar and locked them away in a bank vault until 1994, when he reportedly began looking for a buyer. "When you look into his eyes, you're looking into the beauties and mysteries of the world," he told Britain's *Guardian* newspaper. "They are clear as crystal; they seem to have such depth."

JOSEPH HAYDN'S SKULL

Where It's Located: In Haydn's marble crypt in Eisenstadt, Austria, after being separated from the rest of the body for more than 145 years

How It Got There: Haydn's patron, the Prince of Esterhazy, saw to it that Haydn's body was buried intact following the composer's death in 1809. But some phrenologists (people who "read" skulls) wanted to see if they could divine the source of the composer's genius by looking at his skull. So they dug up his body, removed the head, took it away for study...and then refused to bring it back unless the Prince of Esterhazy paid them a ransom. The prince balked at paying the blackmail, so Haydn was reburied, without his head.

The head eventually ended up in the Musikverein museum in Vienna, Austria, where it was stolen, eventually resurfacing "in the home of an Austrian professor, who displayed it on his piano," and then returned to the museum in 1895. That year the village of Eisenstadt began lobbying for the head's return to Haydn's crypt. They negotiated until 1935, to no avail. Then, at the end of World War II, they tried again. Negotiations dragged on for nine years,

---

Medical term for earwax: *cerumen.*

and finally, in 1954, Haydn's head was reunited with the rest of his body.

SANTA CLAUS'S FINGERS

Where They're Located: "Now on display in the city of Antalya, Turkey"

How They Got There: Saint Nicholas, the Catholic bishop believed to be the inspiration for Santa Claus, died in the fourth century A.D. He was buried in his old church, in what is now the Turkish town of Demre, on the Mediterranean coast. But somehow, his remains ended up in a church in the Italian port of Bari (tradition has it Italian merchants from Bari stole them in 1087), and the town of Demre has been trying to get the bones back for 900 years. All they have left is "a finger or two," on display in a nearby city.

"One reason Christians aren't keen to send the bones back," the *Wall Street Journal* reports, "is because Turkey is now predominantly Moslem. In fact, some believe the 11th-century Christian monks in Myra allowed the Italians to remove the bones in order to save them from the advancing Turkish armies."

Muammer Karabulut, chairman of the Santa Claus Foundation, which seeks the return of the bones, says his group's mostly Moslem membership should not be an issue. After all, he insists, "Santa Claus is [a] universal figure."

STONEWALL JACKSON'S ARM

Where It's Located: The Chancellorville battle site near Fredericksburg, Virginia

How it Got There: On May 2, 1863, as he was returning to camp after engineering an important victory for the Confederacy, the legendary general was accidentally shot by his own troops. Jackson was hit in the right hand and in the left wrist and shoulder, and his left arm had to be amputated above the elbow.

Jackson's chaplain, B. Tucker Lacy, had a brother who owned a house near the hospital, so he took the severed limb to his brother's for burial. Confederate troops buried the arm in a nearby field, complete with a religious ceremony and a marble tombstone. When Jackson died from complications eight days later, he was buried in Lexington, Virginia.

At last count, Minnesota had 99 lakes named Mud Lake.

According to *Roadside America*, "The arm was exhumed in 1929 and reburied in a steel box on a plantation known as Ellwood. Around the field in which it now lays, there is only one gravestone: the one belonging to Jackson's arm."

OTHER CELEBRITY BODY PARTS

• **Thomas Hardy's heart.** "Hardy's heart was to be buried in Stinsford, England, his birthplace, after the rest of his body was cremated in Dorchester. All went according to plan until the great poet's sister's cat snatched the heart off her kitchen table and disappeared into the woods with it."

• **Emanuel Swedenborg's skull.** The famous Swedish philosopher's skull was stolen by a retired sea captain 50 years after Swedenborg's death. It turned up in an antique shop in Wales a century later. When Swedenborg's descendents learned of the skull's existence, they went to Wales and bought it…and then auctioned it off at Sotheby's for $3,200.

• **Buddha's teeth.** Tradition has it that two or three teeth (depending on who you ask) were found in Buddha's cremated remains following his death 2,400 years ago. Today the teeth are in temples in Beijing, China; Sri Lanka; and Taipei, Taiwan.

• **Percy Bysshe Shelley's heart.** When he drowned in 1822, Shelley "was cremated on the beach to which his body had washed. For some reason his heart would not burn and it was taken from the fire and given to his wife, Mary Wollstonecraft Shelley (author of *Frankenstein*), who carried it with her in a silken shroud everywhere she went for the rest of her life."

• **Chang and Eng Bunker's liver.** The two brothers, born in Thailand in 1811, were attached at the chest. P. T. Barnum made them world-famous (coining the term "Siamese twin"). One or both of their livers was apparently removed upon their death, and now sits in a jar at the Mutter Museum in Philadelphia.

* * *

Random Animal Facts: On average, cats spend 30% of their waking hours grooming themselves. They purr at 26 cycles per second, about the same frequency as an idling diesel engine.

HEY—THAT'S MY NAME ON THE BALLOT!

As people pay less attention to election issues, candidates have to focus more on name recognition. That can lead to some confusion, as it did in these elections.

RUSSO FOR CONGRESS!

In 1946 Joseph Russo, a popular Boston city councilman, decided to run for a seat in the U.S. Congress. At first his only opponent in the Democratic primary was a young World War II veteran named John Fitzgerald Kennedy. But at the last minute, another candidate appeared on the ballot: a *second* Joseph Russo.

Who was this new challenger? Turns out he was a family friend of the Kennedys. It's widely believed that JFK's father got Russo #2 into the race to confuse voters and ensure his son's victory.

Election Results: It worked. Joseph Russo and Joseph Russo split the Russo vote; JFK won the primary by a landslide.

CAROL MOSELEY-BRAUN FOR ALDERMAN!

In 1998, 21-year-old Lauryn K. Valentine asked a court to allow her to change her name to Carol Moseley-Braun. It had nothing to do with politics, she explained—it was a tribute to former U.S. Senator Carol Moseley-Braun, the first African-American woman to serve in the Senate. Valentine claimed that Moseley-Braun "had encouraged me to stay in school when I was considering dropping out." The judge granted her request.

Surprise! In December 1998, the new Moseley-Braun filed papers to run for Chicago city alderman. The real Moseley-Braun and another candidate for alderman both filed legal challenges.

Election Results: Unknown. (Anyone out there know what happened?)

JOHN F. KENNEDY FOR STATE TREASURER!

Future president John F. Kennedy had just been elected to the U.S. Senate in 1952; what was he doing running for State Treasurer in 1953? Answer: It was John *Francis* Kennedy. He was no relation,

---

Adolph Hitler had his own private train, complete with 15 railcars. It was named the *Amerika*.

wasn't rich, didn't attend Harvard—and wasn't even a high school graduate. This Kennedy had quit school at the age of 14 and was working as a stockroom supervisor at the Gillette Razor Blade Company when he decided to cash in on his popular name and run for office. The incumbent treasurer, John Hurley, resigned in 1953, and JFK ran in the special election to replace him. His qualifications? "I got a good name," he said in an interview, "I know a lot of people at Gillette to say 'hi' to, and I want to make money and get ahead in life."

Election Results: Kennedy lost the 1953 race…but never underestimate the power of a name. When he ran again in 1954, he won. Total campaign expenses: about $100, "most of which was spent to throw an election-night party." Kennedy served six years as state treasurer. In 1960—the year the other JFK was elected president—he ran for governor, and lost.

WARNER FOR SENATE!

In 1996 John Warner, the incumbent U.S. Senator from Virginia, ran for re-election against a multimillionaire businessman named… Warner. The challenger's first name was Mark, but under Virginia law, the ballot did not identify which Warner was the incumbent, or even which one was the Republican (John) or the Democrat (Mark). "Although some analysts figure the name problem will make no real difference in the end," the *Washington Post* reported, "others envision a chaotic scenario in which thousands of votes could be cast unwittingly for the wrong man. Mark Warner…figures, at least half seriously, that he could gain a couple of percentage points simply by winning the drawing to determine who will be listed on the ballot first."

Election Results: No contest—John Warner was re-elected.

OTHER RACES

Taylor vs. Taylor, 1886. "Two brothers named Taylor ran against each other for governor of Tennessee, a battle that became known as the 'War of the Roses' because their mother had given each candidate a different color rose." (*San Francisco Chronicle*)

Hansen vs. Hansen vs. Hanson, 1974. "George V. Hansen ousted incumbent Orval Hansen in a Republican primary for a House seat in Idaho, then topped Democrat Max Hanson in the fall."

In Athens, Greece, you can lose your driving license for being "poorly dressed" or "unbathed."

285

LOONEY LAWS

Believe it or not, these laws are real.

In Macomb, Illinois, it's illegal for a car to impersonate a wolf.

In Rumford, Maine, it's against the law to bite your landlord.

An ordinance in San Francisco bans picking up used confetti to throw again.

It's against the law in Atlanta, Georgia, to tie a giraffe to a telephone pole or street lamp.

It's against the law in Chicago to eat in a place that is on fire.

In International Falls, Minnesota, it's against the law for a cat to chase a dog up a telephone pole.

It's illegal to catch fish while on horseback in Washington, D.C.

It's illegal to take a lion to the theater in Maryland.

It's against the law to drive more than 2,000 sheep down Hollywood Boulevard.

Brawley, California, passed a resolution banning snow within the city limits.

In Tennessee, it's illegal to drive a car while you're asleep.

Anyone found underneath a sidewalk in Florida is guilty of disorderly conduct.

It's illegal in New Jersey to slurp your soup.

A Texas law states that when two trains meet at a railroad crossing, each must come to a full stop, and neither shall proceed until the other has gone.

It's illegal in Hartford, Connecticut, to kiss your wife on a Sunday.

It's against the law in Kentucky to remarry the same man four times.

In Marshalltown, Iowa, it's illegal for a horse to eat a fire hydrant.

In Tennessee, it's against the law to shoot game other than whales from a moving car.

It's illegal in Fairbanks, Alaska, for two moose to have sex on city sidewalks.

When pizza became popular in the U.S. in the 1930s, sales of oregano shot up 5,200%.

BIG, BAD BARBIE

She's the world's favorite doll, a friend to millions of little girls...
but don't mess with her—she's rough, she's tough, and she'll
sue the pants off you for just mentioning her name. How
scary can Barbie be? Just ask these former defendants.

BARBIE VS. PAUL HANSEN

Background: Hansen, a San Francisco artist, began selling "Barbie art" in the early 1990s. He took conventional Barbie dolls and turned them into social satire, creating characters like Exorcist Barbie, Tonya Harding Barbie, and Drag Queen Barbie.

Here Comes Barbie: Hansen had sold about 150 of the dolls and earned about $2,000 when Mattel filed suit against him, claiming $1.2 billion in damages.

Art is generally protected as free speech, but Hansen wasn't looking for a fight. He promised to pull his dolls from store shelves, sell them only in art galleries...*and* donate all of the profits to charities. Good enough? Nope. The *Wall Street Journal* reported: "Mattel's lawyer still wanted to go to trial to collect damages and win a stricter definition of 'art gallery.' After a year of litigation, even the judge lost patience...and granted a partial...judgement against Mattel 'for not having a sense of humor.'"

Outcome: Hansen eventually settled out of court and stopped making the dolls. "It was a year from hell," he says.

BARBIE VS. BARBARA BELL

Background: In 1992 Bell, a 44-year-old quiltmaker, claimed that she was receiving psychic messages from Barbie. (Barbie's first message: "I need respect.") For only $3 a pop, she offered to channel Barbie's spirit and answer personal questions from Barbie fans. She also published the *Barbie Channeling Newsletter*.

Here Comes Barbie: Mattel threatened a multimillion-dollar lawsuit against Bell if she didn't shut down her business and cease publication of her newsletter.

Outcome: Bell complied...but still doesn't see what all the fuss was about. "Look," she says, "for $3 nobody's getting hurt. I don't claim to be the only voice of Barbie. And I'm sure not taking any other channeler's business. I've carved out my own niche in the market. There are 700 million Barbie dolls in the world, with no voice."

BARBIE VS. AQUA

Background: In 1997 Aqua, a bubblegum rock band from Denmark, recorded "Barbie Girl" ("I'm a Barbie Girl / in the Barbie world / life in plastic / it's fantastic"). It became a Top 10 hit.

Here Comes Barbie: Mattel filed suit against MCA, the band's U.S. record label, in September 1997, claiming that the song infringed on Barbie trademarks and contained lyrics that "associate sexual and other unsavory themes with Mattel's Barbie products."

MCA fought back, claiming in a countersuit that Mattel had defamed MCA. They also threatened to introduce expert testimony that Mattel had based Barbie on a German "sexpot" doll called Lilli that was marketed to adults in the 1950s. "Mattel's idea in 1959," said their expert, "was to peddle a...grown-up sex doll to little girls by dolling it up in designer clothes. What Aqua has done in 'Barbie Girl' is not to make Barbie into a 'sex object'...but to point out...that she has been one all along."

Outcome: The judge dismissed both suits. Mattel is still appealing.

BARBIE VS. PAUL DAVID

Background: David, a Chillicothe, Ohio, Barbie collector and publisher of a Barbie catalog, remained in Mattel's good graces until the mid-1990s. That's when he wrote in one of his catalogs that "if there were an ugly contest, Elizabethan Queen Barbie would definitely win." He also forgot to put the registered trademark ® symbol on some Barbie photos.

Here Comes Barbie: Mattel swooped down and sued David for copyright infringement, accusing him of copying the company's packaging for his own use.

Outcome: According to the *Wall Street Journal*, "after a lengthy battle, he signed a settlement agreement...that stipulates that Barbie may only be portrayed in his catalog as 'wholesome, friendly, accessible and kind, caring and protecting, cheerful, fun loving, talented and independent.'" David then sold his entire Barbie collection in disgust.

BARBIE VS. MARK NAPIER

Background: Napier, a New York Web site artist, operated the Distorted Barbie Website, which featured such "repressed real-world Barbies" as Kate Moss Barbie, Fat and Ugly Barbie, and Dolly Parton Barbie.

Here Comes Barbie: Mattel sent Napier a cease-and-desist letter, telling him to shut down the site.

Outcome: Rather than shut down the site, Napier just blurred the doll's images and replaced the "B" in Barbie with a "$".

BARBIE VS. *HIM AND MEN'S HEALTH*

Background: In 1996 *Him*, a British men's magazine, and the German edition of *Men's Health* published a set of 10 photographs of Ken and Barbie in "improper...explicit and offensive positions." The British article promised a new "Position of the Month" in each subsequent issue, and the German magazine posted animated versions of the photographs on its Web site.

Here Comes Barbie: Mattel sued for unspecified damages, accusing the magazines of ruining Ken and Barbie's "wholesome and aspirational" image.

Outcome: Unknown.

* * * *

NEWSMAKER BARBIE

"Two former waitresses claim they witnessed the skewering, mutilation, and deep-frying of a Barbie Doll at Hoss's Steak & Sea House in Hampton Township, Pennsylvania.

"In March, the women filed a federal sex-discrimination lawsuit against the restaurant, alleging that the Barbie doll incident in September 1994 was a 'satanic ritual,' and that they had to work in a hostile environment. No trial date has been set....Both women seek reinstatement with back pay. They also want damages in excess of $25,000. The women contend that after the doll was fried, the grease in the fryer was not changed for seven days and was used to cook food served to patrons at the restaurant. Company officials have denied that the incident occurred or that either woman was harassed or subjected to a hostile working environment."

—**wire service report**

According to market research, if a girl owns one Barbie, she probably owns seven.

THE BIRTH OF FROSTED FLAKES, PART I

On page 82, you'll find Scott Bruce and Bill Crawford's tale of the birth of sugar-coated cereal, from their book Cerealizing America. *Here's another of their breakfast-food dramas.*

BATTLING IN BATTLE CREEK
Cereal flakes were invented by Dr. John Kellogg and his brother Will Kellogg (W. K.) in 1894, at their Battle Creek, Michigan, sanitarium. They were experimenting with wheat, trying to make "a digestible substitute for bread," when they accidentally left a batch soaking in water overnight. The next day, they discovered it could be formed and baked into little flakes.

After four more years of trial and error, the Kelloggs successfully applied the process to corn. However, they only sold cornflakes by mail as a health food, to patients and former patients; Dr. Kellogg wasn't interested in distributing it to the general public.

Post-al Service
On the other hand, C. W. Post, one of Kellogg's former patients, had no qualms about selling to the public. In 1896, using a stolen Kellogg recipe for faux coffee that he called Postum, he founded the fastest-growing business in America. In 1898 he created Grape Nuts, and in 1902 he brought cornflakes to market as Elijah's Manna.

Post was an advertising genius, but he couldn't keep up with the Kellogg Company. When W. K. finally bucked his brother and expanded the cereal business in 1903, he turned out to be every bit as good a promoter as Post was. He quickly grabbed the lion's share of the cornflake market, and never relinquished it. For 50 years cornflakes were the bestselling dry cereal. Kellogg's Corn Flakes were #1; the Post version of corn flakes, Post Toastie's were #2.

Both companies were located in Battle Creek, and over the years they fought tooth and nail for industry supremacy. People who worked for Post and Kellogg regarded each other as the enemy.

Given the opportunity, chimpanzees will hunt ducks.

HOW SWEET IT IS

In 1948 executives at Post (by then part of General Foods) noticed how well sugar-coated Ranger Joe Popped Wheat Honnies was selling in the Northeast [see page 82]. They envisioned it as the perfect way to overtake Kellogg, and secretly began developing their own sugar-coated wheat puffs.

This decision raised a serious moral dilemma for Post.

It was deeply ingrained in the corporate cultures of all major cereal makers that their products were healthy food...and sugar isn't especially good for children. Traditionalists (and nutritionists) feared that manufacturing sugar-coated cereal would violate the guiding principles of the company. But proponents of pre-sweetened cereal suggested that adding a controlled amount of sugar in the plant was preferable to kids adding an unlimited amount at the breakfast table. They also insisted that the company was merely "trading off sugar carbohydrates for grain carbohydrates—and sugar and starch are metabolized in exactly the same way." So the nutritional value of the product, they explained, wasn't changed.

In the end, though, the most convincing "argument" came from the marketing department. They were sure Post would make big bucks from sugar-coated cereal. And that was that.

THE SAGA OF SUGAR CRISP

Post came up with a product they figured could double as a breakfast food and a snack. They called it Happy Jax...but the Cracker Jack Company complained, so they renamed it Sugar Crisp. They packaged it in cellophane bags (like Ranger Joe) and in 1948, rolled it out from coast to coast.

To Post's great delight, Kellogg was blindsided by the new creation. "I remember going to a small department store in 1949 and finding Sugar Crisp there," recalls a Kellogg salesman. "Believe you me, it made the Kellogg people shudder."

Fortunately for Kellogg, however, Sugar Crisp was hit by the same problem that struck Ranger Joe the first time around. "The stuff used to turn into bricks," laughs an old-time Post employee. "It solidified so you couldn't pound it apart. You'd just rip the bag off and gnaw on a piece."

In 1951, Post improved the packaging and Sugar Crisp became a spectacular success. The moral argument conveniently forgotten, Post looked around for other products to cover with sugar. Six months later, they introduced "candy-kissed" Rice Krinkles, a caramel-coated rice cereal designed to steal market share from Kellogg's Rice Krispies. Once again, the product caught Kellogg flat-footed.

STILL MORE

Finally, Post moved on to the most important product—cornflakes. In 1951 they launched Corn Fetti, a sugar-coated flake designed to stay crispy and sweet in milk.

To support the product, Post advertised on TV with Captain Jolly, the first cartoon pirate of crunch. He sailed the video seas to sell Corn Fetti with the jolly bluster "Ho-Ho-Ho! No one can stay away from Corn Fetti. It never gets sticky, even in the box."

It was a crippling blow to Kellogg. "We were all a little bit shook up with Corn Fetti," a former Kellogg salesman says. "This wholesaler told me, 'Boy, Post's got Corn Fetti, they're really going to take you guys to the cleaners now!'"

And maybe Post could have...but they stumbled. It wasn't long before Kellogg realized that Corn Fetti wasn't selling. "It was a disaster," says an industry expert. "The flakes were hardened with this really beautiful, clear-candy coating. But it was so insoluble, it would cut your mouth all up like glass."

Instead of fixing the Corn Fetti formula and reintroducing it immediately, General Foods began an exhaustive, time-consuming product-testing process. "We were all so frustrated with the situation," recalls Post's art director at the time."While we had our sales force standing in line to reintroduce Corn Fetti, they continued to test market and test market...until finally, the competition stole the idea.

The competition was, of course, Sugar-Frosted Flakes.

For Part II, turn to page 384.

*   *   *

New Mexico has an official state question: "Red or green?"

An *exocannibal* is a cannibal who eats only enemies. An *indocannibal* eats only friends.

URBAN LEGENDS

We ran pieces on urban legends in our Great Big *and* Giant
Bathroom Readers. *Since then, we've found so many more
good ones that we just had to include them here, too. Remember
the rule of thumb: If a wild story sounds true, but also sounds
too "perfect" to be true, it's probably an urban legend.*

THE LEGEND: The Lego company has started to add a plastic homeless person to some of its kits. The reason: to make Legos more "relevant."

HOW IT SPREAD: By word of mouth in the early 1990s. It made the rounds of toy stores, where some employees apparently accepted the rumor at face value…and passed it on to customers. One Toys "R" Us salesperson explained to a reporter that the promotion was designed "to teach kids sensitivity and compassion."

THE TRUTH: In 1992 the *Chicago Tribune* asked the Lego Company directly about the rumors. A spokesperson insisted they were false. "You see, he said, "only happy, smiling people live in Legoland."

THE LEGEND: You can trade soda can pull-tabs for time on kidney dialysis machines. (Each pull-tab is worth one minute of dialysis for someone in need.)

HOW IT SPREAD: Word of mouth

THE TRUTH: This is just the latest version of a classic legend. For more than 40 years, people have been collecting worthless items —empty matchbooks, the little tags on teabags, and even cellophane strips from cigarette packs—as a humanitarian gesture, believing they will provide vital medical treatment (time in an iron lung was popular in the 1960s) or seeing-eye dogs. The definitive word: "There is no pull-tab/kidney dialysis donation program," writes Jan Brunvand in *Too Good to Be True*. "It never existed. Anywhere."

THE LEGEND: There's a slasher at the shopping mall near you. He lies in wait under shoppers' cars…and when they approach with

---

Al Capone's older brother Vince Capone was a policeman in Nebraska.

their packages, he reaches out from under the car and cuts their ankles and achilles tendons with a knife. When the shopper falls to the ground, he crawls out from under the car, grabs the merchandise, and runs away.

HOW IT SPREAD: Word of mouth. Supposedly it didn't make the news because your mall is bribing the police and paying off the victims to keep the story quiet.

THE TRUTH: The grown-up equivalent of the monster hiding under the bed has been around as long as shopping malls—about 50 years. It's especially popular during the Christmas shopping season. In fact, in 1989 the rumors about a mall in Tacoma, Washington were so pervasive that it had to set up police field stations in the parking lot to calm consumers who were too frightened to do their holiday shopping.

THE LEGEND: A man insured his expensive cigars, smoked them, then tried to collect on the insurance policy by claiming they were destroyed "in a series of small fires." The insurance company refused to pay up, so the man sued and won. But when he collected his money, the insurance company had him arrested for arson.

HOW IT SPREAD: The story was posted to the *alt.smokers.cigars* newsgroup on the Internet in 1996. It was identified as an urban legend and debunked at the outset; nevertheless, it has been circulating as a true story ever since.

THE TRUTH: The cigar story is an example of a classic theme in urban legends: a clever person finds a loophole in some kind of rule or regulation and exploits it, but gets nailed in the end.

*   *   *

JOB HUNTING:

Some entries from real-life job applications:

• "Note: Please don't misconstrue my 14 jobs as job-hopping. I have never quit a job."

• "I have become completely paranoid, trusting completely no one and absolutely nothing."

LIMERICKS

*Limericks have been around since the 1700s. Here are a few
of the "respectable" ones that our BRI readers have sent us.*

In the Garden of Eden sat Adam,
Disporting himself with his
    madam.
She was filled with elation,
For in all of creation
There was only one man—and
    she had'm.

There once was a pious young
    priest
Who lived almost wholly on
    yeast;
"For," he said, "it is plain
We must all rise again,
And I want to get started, at
    least."

There was a young woman of
    Thrace,
Whose nose spread all over her
    face.
She had very few kisses:
The reason for this is
There wasn't a suitable place.

There was a young fellow named
    Hyde,
Who fell through an outhouse
    and died.
His unfortunate brother,
He fell through another;
And now they're interred side by
    side.

A tutor who tooted the flute
Tried to tutor two tooters to
    toot.
Said the two to the tutor,
'Is it harder to toot, or
  tutor two tooters to toot?"

There was a young fellow from
    Dice
Who remarked, "Although
    bigamy's nice,
Even two are a bore;
I'd prefer three or four,
For the plural of spouse, it is
    spice."

Count Dracula said to his pal:
"Say, Frank, what you need is a
    gal,
And I know a young dear
Who's been dead for a year
So she'll surely improve your
    morale."

A famous bullfighter named Zeke
Pleased the crowds with his
    casual technique.
Each time he was gored
He just acted bored,
Pausing only to plug up the leak.

A canner, exceedingly canny,
One morning remarked to his
    granny,
"A canner can can
Anything that he can;
But a canner can't can a can, can
    he?"

There was a young lady named
    Munn
Who clobbered her boyfriend in
    fun,
Saying, "Don't worry, kid,
That's for nothing you did,
Just for something I dreamt that
    you done."

Most-used expression of any language on earth: "OK."

THE BEST BUSINESS DEAL IN U.S. HISTORY, PART II

When the Dodge Brothers put $3,000 in cash and $7,000 in parts into the Ford Motor Company, they made history. Here's what happened next. (Part I of the story is on page 204.)

TURNAROUND
Four weeks after the Dodge brothers made their deal with Malcomson, the Ford Motor Company was on the verge of bankruptcy. With $223.65 in the bank, not a single car sold, and payroll for the Ford workers due the next day, it looked like the company's stock would be worthless.

Then, on July 15, 1903, a dentist named Dr. E. Pfennig became Ford's first customer, paying $850 cash for a Model A. "Dr. Pfennig's payment of the full cash price through the Illinois Trust and Savings Bank represented a turning point in the fortunes of the Ford Motor Company," Robert Lacey writes in *Ford: The Men and the Machine.* "From $223.65 onwards, its cash flow went one way only."

UP, UP, AND AWAY
When it opened for business in 1903, the Ford Motor Company could only build a few cars at a time. But as orders increased, Henry Ford and his assistants knew that the key to success was to find ways to speed production.

They did. In the year ending September 1906, the company made 1,599 cars; the following year, production more than quadrupled to 8,000; and by 1912, Ford was manufacturing 78,000 cars per year. That was only the beginning: production more than doubled the following year and then more than doubled again in 1914, until Ford was manufacturing over 300,000 cars per year, or 1,000 cars for every work day, a production increase of 4,000% in just over a decade.

Oh, Brother
About the only thing that grew faster than the Ford Motor Compa-

ny's production and sales figures was the value of Ford stock, 10% of which belonged to the Dodge brothers. They'd earned back their entire $10,000 in the first year's dividends alone, and since then their Ford stock had paid out millions more.

In addition, since they were still manufacturing most of Ford's mechanical components at their own Dodge Brothers factory (at the time the largest and most modern such manufacturing plant in the world), they profited twice: first by supplying parts to Ford and second, by owning shares in the company.

T-TIME

That changed in 1914, when Henry Ford built his own parts manufacturing plant to replace the one owned by the Dodge brothers. Until then, the Ford Motor Company, like most other auto companies, had focused on assembling cars, leaving the actual manufacturing of the parts to subcontractors. Now that Ford could afford to finance his own manufacturing plant, he didn't need the Dodge brothers any more.

With their business relationship with Ford coming to an end, the brothers had to figure out what do with their plant. Henry Ford had offered to lease the plant and run it himself, and the Dodges gave it serious thought…but then they had another idea.

DON'T CHANGE A THING

When it went on sale in October 1908, the Ford Model T was the most advanced car of its day. As the years passed, automotive technology improved, but Henry Ford refused to make any changes to it, stylistically or even mechanically. Unlike other cars, you still had to start the Model T using a hand crank, and since it didn't come with a fuel gauge, the only way to tell how much gas you had was by dipping a stick into the gas tank. Having been with Ford from the beginning, the Dodge brothers knew all of the car's weaknesses, but when they suggested improvements, Ford ignored them.

In the end, the Dodge brothers decided to use their factory to manufacture the car that Henry Ford refused to build: one that was better than the Model T.

Turn to page 424 for Part III.

UNCLE JOHN'S PAGE OF LISTS

For years, the BRI has had a file full of lists. We've never been sure what to do with them...until now.

3 REAL EXCUSES USED IN COURT

1. "I was thrown from the car as it left the road. I was later found in a ditch by some stray cows."

2. "The indirect cause of the accident was a little guy in a small car with a big mouth."

3. "To avoid hitting the bumper of the car in front, I struck the pedestrian."

TOP 5 BILLBOARD SONGS ON APRIL 5, 1964

1. *Can't Buy Me Love* (The Beatles)

2. *Twist and Shout* (The Beatles)

3. *She Loves Me* (The Beatles)

4. *I Want to Hold Your Hand* (The Beatles)

5. *Please Please Me* (The Beatles)

3 CELEBRITIES WHO SAY THEY'VE SEEN A UFO:

1. Muhmmad Ali

2. Jimmy Carter

3. William Shatner

7 WEIRD PLACE NAMES

1. Peculiar, Missouri

2. Smut Eye, Alabama

3. Loudville, Massachusetts

4. Disco, Illinois

5. Yeehaw Junction, Florida

6. Slaughter Beach, Delaware

7. Humptulips, Washington

3 MEN KNOWN BY THEIR MIDDLE NAMES

1. James Paul McCartney

2. William Clark Gable

3. Ruiz Fidel Castro

5 MOST-HATED HOUSEHOLD CHORES

1. Washing dishes

2. Bathroom cleaning

3. Ironing

4. Vacuuming

5. Washing Windows
—*Gallup Poll*

4 WORDS NOBODY USES ANYMORE

1. Podge ("To walk slowly and heavily.")

2. Roinous ("Mean and nasty.")

3. Battologist ("Someone who pointlessly repeats themselves.")

4. Battologist ("Someone who pointlessly repeats themselves.")

3 MOST PRIZED AUTOGRAPHS

1. Shakespeare (6 *are known to exist*)

2. Christopher Columbus (8 *exist*)

3. Julius Caesar (*None are known to exist*)

WORD ORIGINS

Ever wonder where words come from?
Here are some interesting stories.

JACKPOT
Meaning: A huge prize
Origin: "The term goes back to draw poker, where stakes are allowed to accumulate until a player is able to 'open the *pot*' by demonstrating that among the cards he has drawn he has a pair of *jacks* or better." (From *Dictionary of Word and Phrase Origins, Vol. II,* by William and Mary Morris)

GRENADE
Meaning: A small, hand-thrown missile containing an explosive
Origin: "The word comes from the French *pomegrenade,* for pomegranate, because the military missile, which dates from the sixteenth century, both is shaped like the fruit and explodes much as the seeds burst out from it." (From *Fighting Words,* by Christine Ammer)

AMMONIA
Meaning: A potent, odorous cleaning fluid
Origin: "*Ammonia* is so called because it was first made from the dung of the worshippers' camels at the temple of Jupiter *Ammon* in Egypt." (From *Remarkable Words with Astonishing Origins,* by John Train)

HEATHEN
Meaning: An ungodly person
Origin: "Christianity began as primarily an urban religion; people in rural districts continued to worship older gods. The Latin word for countryman was *paganus*—whence, of course, pagan; the Germanic tongues had a similar word, something like *khaithanaz,* 'dwelling in the heath' (wilderness)—whence heathen." (From *Loose Cannons and Red Herrings,* by Robert Claiborne)

How about you? 50% of American adults attended an arts activity in 1997. (Up from 41% in 1992.)

CALCULATE

Meaning: Add, subtract, divide, and/or multiply numbers or money

Origin: "In Rome 2,000 years ago the merchant figured his profit and loss using what he called *calculi*, or 'little stones' as counters. So the Latin term *calculus*, 'pebble,' not only gave us *calculate* but...our word *calculus*...one of the most complicated forms of modern mathematics." (From *Word Origins*, by Wilfred Funk, Litt. D.)

MUSEUM

Meaning: Building or collection of art, music, scientific tools, or any specific set of objects

Origin: A shrine to the Greek Muses. "Such a shrine was known as a *mouseion*....When the *Museum* at Alexandria was destroyed in the fourth century...the word nearly dropped out of use. Three hundred years ago, a scholar rediscovered the word." (From *Thereby Hangs a Tale*, by Charles Earle Funk)

DOPE

Meaning: Drugs

Origin: "This word was originally a Dutch word, *doop*, meaning a sauce or liquid. Its first association with narcotics came when it was used to describe the viscous glop that results from heating opium. Then, by rapid extension, it came to mean any narcotic." (From *Dictionary of Word and Phrase Origins, Vol. III*, by William and Mary Morris)

RIVAL

Meaning: Competitor

Origin: "A *rival* is etymologically 'someone who uses the same stream as another.' The word comes from Latin *rivalis*, meaning 'of a stream.' People who use or live by the same stream are neighbors and, human nature being as it is, are usually in competition with each other." (From *Dictionary of Word Origins*, by John Ayto)

On average, people aged 24 to 35 worry less than adults of any other age group.

THE DISCOVERY OF PENICILLIN, Part I

*"A scientific experiment, briefly exposed to the air, became infected
with a fungus whose spores had blown in through an open door....And
left untended on a laboratory bench through the summer vacation, the fungus managed to destroy bacteria being grown as part of the experiment.
The improbable results could not have been duplicated." Fortunately,
they didn't have to be—they led to one of the most important medical
breakthroughs of the 20th century. This account of the discovery
of penicillin is adapted from Gilbert Shapiro's 1986 book,*
A Skeleton in the Darkroom.

THE BACTERIA ARTIST

Alec Fleming was playing with microbes again. One of his
favorite games was to make what he called "germ paintings."
He would sketch a scene within a four-inch glass petri dish: a landscape, a dancing ballerina, or a flag. Then he would carefully fill
each area to be colored with a culture medium and seed it with the
right strain of bacteria. By the next day the maturing colonies would
appear, each in its own characteristic color: red, blue, yellow, white,
pink, green, as Fleming had chosen. The whole "painting" would appear as if by magic on the floor of the dish.

Once the germ paintings had developed, they could be fixed by
spraying them with a chemical which killed the bacteria and protected the culture from deterioration. The paintings could be displayed to visitors to the laboratory or shown on public occasions,
such as the visit of royalty. They were shown to Queen Mary once
at the opening of a new building. She was rather puzzled, and as she
was leaving Fleming heard her say, "Yes—but what *good* is it?"

The answer to the queen's question was soon to be supplied.

A New Color?

Dr. Fleming was considered an expert on staphylococci, germs that
cause boils and carbuncles and other surface infections.

He had read a report about color changes in certain variations of
the germ that aroused his interest. The species called S. *Aureus* pro-

---

First baseball player to be named Rookie of the Year: Jackie Robinson, in 1947.

duces golden yellow colonies when grown in the usual way. But, the paper suggested, if you cut the incubation short and left the culture at room temperature for a few days, interesting color changes took place.

Fleming wanted to see these color changes for himself.

They might be useful in the clinic. At the very least, he might be able to add some new pigments to his palette for germ paintings. Accordingly, he began incubating the germs.

A SUMMER GIFT

It happened to be summer, and Fleming was planning to be away from London. While he was gone, his laboratory room would be used by Dr. Stuart R. Craddock. To make room for Craddock, some of Fleming's culture plates—including the latest—were piled in a corner, out of the sunlight and out of Craddock's way. Fleming wasn't concerned—there would be time enough to look them over when he returned form vacation.

In September, Fleming returned to London, reclaimed his room and set about cleaning up his bench. The old cultures were inspected. There had been a heat spell in London while he was gone, and some of the staph colonies had begun to grow again.... This subverted the color-change effect he was investigating, which was supposed to take place only at cool temperatures. There was nothing to do but drop the cultures into Lysol, an antiseptic that kills all the bacteria, so the dishes could be washed safely...and start over.

SERENDIPITY

Fleming had just placed a large pile of used culture dishes into the Lysol tray when a colleague stopped by to see how the experiments were going. The summer experiment had not gone all that well, as Fleming was ready to show. He reached for one of the discarded cultures at random.

The dish he selected was at the top of the pile, well above the level of the Lysol. The culture inside this particular dish had been contaminated by a fungus. (It was common for spores to be floating around in the air in such an old building, on a busy street, and one of them had obviously landed on the plate while the cover

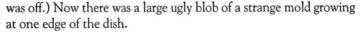

was off.) Now there was a large ugly blob of a strange mold growing at one edge of the dish.

There must be a better example to show his friend, Fleming must have been thinking, as he prepared to place the moldy culture back in the Lysol tank. But then something unusual about this plate stopped him. "That's funny," he muttered.

ONE IN A BILLION

Half of the dish was covered with yellow colonies of staphylococcus, like the other dishes. But at the edge of the moldy growth, the staph cells were colorless and translucent...and the cells at the edge of the mold looked as if they were *dissolving away*. Even stranger: inside a one-inch circle in the center of the mold, there were *no* staph cells visible at all.

There could be only one conclusion: something near the mold that had landed was killing the bacteria.

It was an extraordinarily lucky accident that brought that particular mold spore to that particular culture dish. But Fleming was prepared to take advantage of it. He immediately moved to preserve the mold. Fortunately, the contaminated dish had not yet been submerged in the Lysol—so the fungus was still alive. He scraped a sample from the dish and placed it in a test tube with a liquid used for growing fungi. Over the next 15 years, many generations of Fleming's mold would be grown in his laboratory and in other places where he sent samples.

Need antibiotics? Turn to page 426 for Part II.

*   *   *

BET YOU DON'T KNOW

The singer Engelbert Humperdinck's real name is Gerry Dorsey. Dorsey didn't make either name up, though: He borrowed it from a famous German composer. The original Engelbert Humperdinck wrote the opera *Hänsel and Gretel*.

Chameleon rule of thumb: If it loses a fight, it turns grey. If it wins, it turns green.

Q & A:
ASK THE EXPERTS

Here are some more random questions, with answers from America's trivia experts.

THE COLD, WET TRUTH

Q: *Why does your nose run in cold weather?*

A: "It is not necessarily because you have a cold. If very cold air is suddenly inhaled, the mucous membranes inside your nostrils first constrict, then rapidly dilate as a reflex reaction. This permits an excess of mucous to form, resulting in a runny nose or the 'sniffles.'" (From *The Handy Weather Answer Book*, by Walter A. Lyons, Ph.D.)

HAPPY TRAILS

Q: *Why do jets leave a trail of white behind them?*

A: "The white trail that you see is, in fact, a man-made cloud. At low altitudes, the air is able to absorb large quantities of water. But at high altitudes, water has a tendency to come out of the air, which can form a cloud. This only happens, though, if the air contains small particles—such as dust—on which the water can condense. It also helps the process if the air is agitated.

"Now enter the high-flying jet. Its exhaust fills the air with a huge supply of spent fuel particles, and at the same time it shakes or agitates the air...leaving a long, narrow cloud behind it." (From *Ever Wonder Why?*, by Douglas B. Smith)

EURASIA, EURASIA

Q: *Why are Asia and Europe considered two continents even though they appear to be one?*

A: "The ancient Greeks thought the Eurasian landmass was divided in two by the line of water running from the Aegean Sea to the far shore of the Black Sea.

"By the time they found out otherwise, Europeans were not about to surrender their continental status." (From *Why Things Are*, by Joel Achenbach)

Most common plastic surgery performed on American men: breast reduction.

YOU EXPECT ME TO SWALLOW THAT?

Q: *How do circus sword swallowers do it?*

A: Believe it or not, they really do swallow the sword. The main problem is learning how to relax the throat muscles and stop gagging. This takes weeks of practice....But it can be done.

"The sword doesn't cut the sword swallower's throat because its sides are dull. The point is usually sharp, but that's not a problem as long as the sword swallower doesn't swallow any swords long enough to poke him (or her) in the pit of the stomach." (From *Know It All!*, by Ed Zotti)

METHOD TO THE MADNESS?

Q: *How are interstate highways numbered in the U.S.?*

A: "Believe it or not, this is one government practice that is organized and logical. All east–west interstate highways are even-numbered and increase from south to north. Thus, east–west Interstate 80 is north of I-10. North–south interstates are odd-numbered and increase from west to east. City bypasses and spurs have triple digits and are numbered odd or even depending on their directional orientation." (From *Thoughts for the Throne*, by Don Voorhees)

YOU GET WHAT YOU PAY FOR

Q: *If you dropped a penny from the top of the Empire State Building (or any skyscraper) and it happened to hit someone on the head, would it easily pierce their skull?*

A: "Given that the Empire State Building is 1,250 feet tall and ignoring such factors as wind resistance, a penny dropped from the top would hit the ground in approximately 8.8 seconds, having reached a speed of roughly 280 feet per second. This is not particularly fast. A low-powered .22 or .25 caliber bullet, to which a penny is vaguely comparable in terms of mass, typically has a muzzle velocity of 800 to 1,100 FPS, with maybe 75 foot-pounds of energy.

"On top of this we must consider that the penny would probably tumble while falling, and that the Empire State Building...is surrounded by strong updrafts, which would slow descent considerably. Thus, while you might conceivably inflict a fractured skull on some hapless New Yorker, the penny would certainly not 'go through just like that.'" (From *The Straight Dope*, by Cecil Adams)

Speechless: When William Shakespeare moved into his new home, he named it New Home.

MONKEY SEE, MONKEY DO

Do television and movies influence our actions? Of course (see page 192), but unfortunately, some people take it to extremes. There's just no cure for stupidity.

MONKEY SEE: In the 1971 film *The Godfather*, Corleone family henchmen intimidate a Hollywood mogul by killing his prize race horse and sticking the horse's head in his bed.

MONKEY DO: In 1997 two New York crooks decided to use a similar method to intimidate a witness scheduled to testify against them at trial: "On the morning the witness was scheduled to testify, they left the head of a slaughtered animal as a death threat. 'We wanted to leave a cow's head because his wife was from India, and they consider cows sacred,' one said. 'But where do you find a cow's head in Brooklyn? So I went to some butcher in Flatbush and found a goat head. I figured it was close enough.'" One crook was sentenced to 4 years in prison; the other got 14 to 42 years.

MONKEY SEE: In the video for Joe Diffie's song "John Deere Green," a boy climbs a water tower and paints a green heart."

MONKEY DO: "This apparently gave some genius in Mississippi the bright idea of scaling his local water tower and painting 'Billy Bo Bob Loves Charlene' in green paint. Perhaps tuckered out from having to write all three of his first names on the water tower, the guy then lost his balance and was seriously injured when he hit the ground." (*Chicago Sun-Times*)

MONKEY SEE: In the 1993 film *The Program*, "drunk college football players lie down in the middle of a busy road to prove their toughness."

MONKEY DO: "A scene in the movie *The Program* will be deleted after one teenager was killed and two others critically injured while apparently imitating the scene, the Walt Disney Co. said Tuesday. ...Sources indicated it will cost $350,000 to $400,000 to re-edit." (*Daily Variety*)

The average person's skin weighs twice as much as their brain.

MONKEY SEE: In 1997 Taco Bell introduced a new advertising campaign featuring a talking Chihuahua that has since become known as the "Taco Bell Dog."

MONKEY DO: Since then, sales and adoptions of Chihuahuas have gone through the roof. "Before the Taco Bell commercials became popular, no one wanted Chihuahuas," says Marsha Teague of the Portland, Oregon, humane society. "Now people ask specifically for the 'Taco Bell Dog.'" The dogs, priced from $300 to $600, "sell within two days, faster if their coloration resembles the actual TV star. "We can't even keep them in stock," a pet-shop owner says. "Everybody always comes in and imitates the Taco Bell commercial." (*Portland Oregonian*)

On the other hand, it isn't necessarily all bad...

MONKEY SEE: The *Nancy Drew* series is about a strong-willed, independent teenage detective who constantly finds herself in danger, then has to think her way out of it.

MONKEY DO: In the early 1990s, an eleven-year-old Michigan girl was kidnapped and thrown into the trunk of a car. "Instead of panicking," *The Christian Science Monitor* reported, "she asked herself what Nancy Drew would do in such a situation. Then she found a toolbox, pried the trunk open, made a call from a nearby phone booth, and her assailant was arrested."

*   *   *   *

MORE MORE MORE!

• In 1997 an employee at a Bangkok hotel was sent to prison for robbing guests' safe deposit boxes. His method: he rubbed his nose on the buttons, making them oily so he could tell which ones the guests had pushed to open the safe. His inspiration: an episode of the TV show "MacGyver."

• In 1996, 17-year-old Steve Barone was booked for robbing a gun store. He claimed he did it "only because he was taken over by another personality, which was an amalgam of guys from the movies *Pulp Fiction*, *Reservoir Dogs*, and *Goodfellas*." (*News of the Weird*)

THE WORLD'S SIMPLEST QUIZ

Think the answers to this quiz are self-evident? They might not be as easy as you think. The questions are from The People's Almanac, *by David Wallachinsky and Amy Wallace.*

1. How long did the Hundred Years' War last?

2. In which month did Russians celebrate the October Revolution?

3. In which country are Panama hats made?

4. From which country do we get Peruvian Balsam?

5. Which seabird has the zoological name *Puffinus puffinus*?

6. From which animal do we get catgut?

7. From which material are moleskin trousers made?

8. Where do Chinese gooseberries come from?

9. Louis the XVIII was the last one, but how many previous kings of France were called Louis?

10. What kind of creatures were the Canary Islands named after?

11. What was King George VI's first name?

12. What color is a purple finch?

13. In what season of the year does William Shakespeare's *A Midsummer Night's Dream* take place?

14. What is a camel's hair brush made of?

15. How long did the Thirty Years' War last?

Answers on page 515.

* * *

RANDOM CAT FACT

World-record mouser: "Towser," a tabby who caught mice at a Scottish distillery. She lived to the age of 21, and caught an average of three mice a day. Estimated lifetime haul: 23,000 mice.

President McKinley's pet parrot was named Washington Post.

REEL DUMB

From Stupid Movie Lines *by Ross and Kathryn Petrus.*

"I am not here for your cold roast chicken. I am here for your love."
—**Vanna White,**
Goddess of Love

"I've had it with cheap sex. It leaves me feeling cheap."
—**John Travolta,**
Moment by Moment

"She was in great pain. We cut off her head and drove a stake through her heart and burned her, and then she was at peace."
—**Anthony Hopkins,**
Bram Stoker's Dracula

"Is it just me or does the jungle make you really, really horny?"
—**Owen Wilson,**
Anaconda

"You goddamned chauvinistic pig ape!…You want to eat me? Then go ahead!"
—**Jessica Lange,**
King Kong

"You may know about corpses, fella, but you've got a lot to learn about women."
—**Policeman to morgue worker,** *Autopsy*

"Your puritan upbringing holds you back from my monsters, but it certainly hasn't hurt your art of kissing."
—**Horror writer to woman,**
Orgy of the Dead

"There's a lot of space out there to get lost in."
—**William Hurt,**
Lost in Space

"The dead look so terribly dead when they're dead."
—**Tyrone Power,**
The Razor's Edge

Man: "I'd like to take you out in a monster-free world."
Woman: "I'd like that."
—*Gamera: Guardian of the Universe*

"I don't want to be killed! I just want to teach English."
—**Panicking teacher,**
Echoes in the Darkness

"War! War! That's all you think of, Dick Plantagenet! You burner! You pillager!"
—**Virginia Mayo,**
King Richard and the Crusaders

How did black sheep get such a bad rap? Their wool is harder to dye than that of white sheep.

I TAWT I TAW A PUDDY-TAT!

Sure, they're cartoon characters, but Tweety and Sylvester are still a classic comedy team—literally made for each other, right? Well, no. It actually took a few years before anyone thought of putting them in the same cartoon. Here's how it happened.

FIRST CAME TWEETY...

Created by: Looney Tunes director Bob Clampett

Inspiration: "In school I remember seeing nature films which showed newborn birds in a nest," Clampett recalled. "They always looked funny to me. One time I kicked around the idea of twin baby birds called 'Twick 'n' Tweet' who were precursors of Tweety."

• Tweety's basic design and "innocent stare at the camera" were copied from an even more unusual source: a nude baby picture of Clampett himself. That's probably why the original Tweety was pink.

Debut: "Tale of Two Kitties," a 1942 spoof of Abbott and Costello (who appeared as bumbling cats named Babbit and Cat-stello). The little nameless bird's opening line, "I tawt I taw a puddy tat!" made the cartoon—and the character—a hit. The voice was supplied by Mel Blanc (who also did Daffy Duck, Bugs Bunny, Porky Pig, et. al.). It was recorded at normal speed but played back faster.

• Tweety's next cartoon, "Birdy and the Beast" (1944), gave him a name and personality. In 1946 movie censors decided the pink bird "looked naked" and insisted Clampett put a pair of pants on him. The cartoonist refused; instead, he gave Tweety "yellow feathers and a slimmer body."

THEN CAME SYLVESTER...

Created by: Oscar-winning Looney Tunes director Friz Freleng

Inspiration: Freleng designed the cat "to look subtly like a clown. I gave him a big, red nose and a very low crotch, which was supposed to look like he was wearing baggy pants."

• According to Mel Blanc, the unwitting model was Looney Tunes' "jowly executive producer Johnny Burton."

Oregon has the most ghost towns of any state.

Debut: A 1945 cartoon, "Life with Feathers." The plot: "A love bird has a major fight with his wife and decides to end it all by letting a cat (Sylvester, before he had a name) eat him." The cat's first words, on finding a bird who wants to be eaten: "Thufferin' Thuccotash!"

• Sylvester's voice—also supplied by Mel Blanc—sounded more like Blanc's real speaking voice than any of his other characters. It was actually the same voice he used for Daffy Duck, but not sped up. Says Blanc in his autobiography, *That's Not All Folks*:

> Sylvester has always been a favorite of mine. He's always been the easiest character for me to play. When I was first shown the model sheet of Sylvester, with his floppy jowls and generally disheveled appearance, I said to Friz Freleng, 'A big sloppy cat should have a big *shthloppy* voice! He should spray even more than Daffy.' While recording Sylvester cartoons, my scripts would get so covered with saliva that I'd repeatedly have to wipe them clean. I used to suggest to actress June Foray, who played Tweety's vigilant owner Granny, that she wear a raincoat to the sessions.

Sylvester's first cartoon was nominated for an Oscar, and he appeared (still nameless) in two more before Clampett got permission to team Tweety with him in 1947. However, Clampett left Warners Bros. just as he began working on the project.

TOGETHER AT LAST

Freleng took over the cartoon. He gave the cat a name—Thomas (changed to Sylvester in 1948 by animator Tedd Pierce, who thought a slobbering cat needed a name that could be slobbered) —and made Tweety a little friendlier. "I made him look more like a charming baby, with a bigger head and blue eyes," Freleng explained.

In their first cartoon together, "Tweetie Pie," Thomas catches Tweety, who's freezing in the winter cold. But before he can eat the bird, Thomas's owner saves it and brings it home. Tweety then proceeds to terrorize the cat and take over the house.

"Tweety Pie" earned the Warner Bros. cartoon studio its first Academy Award and the pair made 55 more cartoons together.

MILLER'S RANTS

Some observations from America's premier purveyor of pseudo-intellectual humor, Dennis Miller.

"Is intelligence a liability nowadays? I think we can answer that with one word: *Duh.*"

"Remember—a developer is someone who wants to build a house in the woods. An environmentalist is someone who already owns a house in the woods."

"The easiest job in the world has to be coroner. You perform surgery on dead people. What's the worst that could happen? If everything went wrong, maybe you'd get a pulse."

"You know you're never more indignant in life than when you're shopping in a store you feel is beneath you and one of the other customers mistakes you for one of the employees of that store."

"The frightening reality is that every day this society seems to make its legal decisions in much the same way the Archies picked their vacation spots—blindfold Jughead, give him a dart, and spin the globe."

"Parenting is the easiest job to get—you just have to screw up once and it's yours."

"They have an amazing proliferation of TV channels now: The all-cartoon channel, the twenty-four-hour science-fiction channel. Of course, to make room for these on the dial they got rid of the Literacy Channel and What's Left of F***ing Civilization Channel."

"Bad day in the news. Michael Jackson and George Hamilton have officially crossed lines in the pigmentation flow chart."

"I know why we don't like to vote—marking your ballot nowadays is like choosing between the 3 a.m. showing of *Beastmaster* on Showtime and the 3 a.m. showing of *Beastmaster 2* on Cinemax."

"TV evangelists say they don't favor any particular denomination, but I think we've all seen their eyes light up at tens and twenties."

theorizing that his image might be recorded on their retinas.

THE MAN WHO INVENTED THE YEAR 2000

Why do we think it's the year 2000 (or 2001, or 2010)? Blame it on an obscure Ukranian monk named Dionysius Exiguus—"Dennis the Short"— who had the idea in the first place. Here are the details from our book Uncle John's Indispensable Guide to the Year 2000.

BACKGROUND

Until Dionysius Exiguus ("Dennis the Short") came up with the *Anno Domini* (A.D.) system, there was no uniform way to number years. Europeans measured time from any number of benchmarks—the founding of Rome (referred to as A.U.C.—short for the Latin *ab urbe condita*, or "from the founding of the city"), the reign of Emperor Diocletian, and other even more obscure dates.

The New Calendar

In 1278 A.U.C., Pope John I asked Dennis, the abbot of a Roman church and a respected scholar, to come up with a new calendar based on Jesus's birthday. This was no easy task: no one knew exactly when Jesus had been born.

Working from Gospel accounts, official Roman records, and astrological charts, Dennis finally settled on December 25, 753 A.U.C. Theoretically, December 25 should have been the first day of Dennis's new calendar. But he started the year eight days later, on January 1. The religious rationale was that it was the Feast of the Circumcision—Jesus's eighth day of life. But more likely, it was because January 1 was already New Year's Day in Roman and Latin Christian calendars.

Dennis called his first year 1 A.D. That made the current year 525 A.D.

NO IMMEDIATE IMPACT

The initial response to Dennis's calculations was silence. No one used the new system for centuries. In fact, even *he* didn't follow his own chronology (he continued to use the A.U.C system).

It took more than 1,000 years for many countries to accept Dennis's system (called *incarnation dating*). It was officially adopted by the Catholic Church at the Synod of Whitby in 664. But no one actually *used* it until late in the 8th century, when a celebrated English historian known as the Venerable Bede annotated the margins of a book with A.D. dating. This work was widely copied and is probably responsible for spreading knowledge of the system around Europe.

A.D. dating was made "universal" at the Synod of Chelsea in 816 A.D., but it still wasn't widely used by many Catholic countries until the 12th century—and even later for other nations. Britain, for example, didn't adopt the Gregorian calendar until 1752; China accepted it for civil use in 1911.

IMPACT NOW

Hardly anyone today has heard of Dennis, although his calendar is the international standard. In fact, the main reason he gets noticed isn't because of his achievements, but because of his screwups. Dennis made two fundamental mistakes: 1) he got Jesus's birthday wrong (Jesus was probably born between 11 and 4 B.C.), and 2) he started his calendar with 1 A.D. instead of zero.

Why did he do it?

It's easy to understand why Dennis got Jesus' birthday wrong—after all, he didn't have much to go on. No reference books, no computer searches.

But starting time with the year 1 goes against common sense. Logic dictates that we count a child's first birthday after a full year—when he or she is one year old—not when they're born. So why did Dennis do it?

Rushworth Kidder of the *Christian Science Monitor* speculates that "nobody wanted to describe the first year of Christianity as a zero." But Stephen Jay Gould says the answer is much simpler: "Western mathematics in the 6th century had not yet developed a concept of zero."

In other words, says futurist Josh Redel, "Dennis didn't really have any choice. He was a prisoner of history, like the rest of us."

THE ORIGIN OF BASKETBALL, PART III

We could go on and on about basketball, but we have to leave room for other subjects. So this is the last installment of our b-ball history…for this edition. (Part I starts on page 46.)

BY ANY OTHER NAME
In 1891, when James Naismith posted the rules to his new game on the YMCA bulletin board, he didn't bother to give it a name. He just called it "A New Game." One of The Incorrigibles suggested calling it "Naismith Ball"…but the phys-ed teacher just laughed.

"I told him that I thought that name would kill any game," Naismith recalled in his memoirs. "Why not call it Basket Ball?" The delighted player spread the word, and it's been basket ball (changed to *basketball* in 1921) ever since.

SCORE!
The Incorrigibles took to the game right away, and by the end of the week their games were drawing a crowd. Teachers and students from a nearby women's school started showing up on their lunch hour; a few weeks later, they began organizing their own teams.

When The Incorrigibles went home for Christmas a few weeks later, they brought copies of the rules—and their enthusiasm for the game—to YMCA chapters all over the country. In January, a copy of the Springfield school paper, complete with an introduction to basketball (including diagrams and a list of rules), was sent to each of the nearly 200 YMCAs in the U.S. "We present to our readers a new game of ball," the article read, "which seems to have those elements in which it ought to make it popular among the Associations."

In the months that followed, these chapters introduced basketball to high schools and colleges in their communities; YMCA missionaries to other countries began spreading the game all over the world.

"It is doubtful whether a gymnastic game has ever spread so

First movie ever shown in the White House: *Birth of a Nation,* in 1916.

rapidly over the continent as has 'basket ball,'" Dr. Gulick wrote proudly in October 1892, before the game was even a year old. "It is played from New York to San Francisco and from Maine to Texas by...teams in associations, athletic clubs and schools."

But just as soon as the rules for basketball began to spread, people began trying to change them. Sometimes they succeeded—even in the face of opposition from its founders—and sometimes they didn't. Overall, the game proved to be extraordinarily adaptable, a factor that has been instrumental in keeping it popular.

THE INVENTION OF DRIBBLING
One of the first rules to come under attack was the no-running-with-the-ball rule. When he invented the game, Naismith wanted the person with the ball to stand still and throw it to another player...who then had to stop moving and either shoot or pass.

But players quickly found that when they were cornered and couldn't pass, they could escape by either rolling or throwing the ball a few feet, then running to get it themselves. From there it was just a matter of time before they realized that by repeatedly throwing the ball in the air, they could move across the court alone—even though they weren't supposed to be moving at all. "In the early years," Paul Ricatto writes in *Basket-Ball*, "it was not uncommon to see a player running down the floor, juggling the ball a few inches above his hand. This so closely approximated running with the ball [travelling] that a rule was inserted saying that the ball must be batted higher than the player's head."

Down to Earth
Players also discovered that it was easy to move with the ball if they repeatedly bounced, or "dribbled," it with both hands. The idea is believed to have been born on the urban playgrounds of Philadelphia; from there it spread to the University of Pennsylvania and beyond. Eventually it became the preferred method of advancing the ball down the court (beating out juggling the ball over one's head).

Dr. Gulick and other basketball powers were not amused. In 1898 they inserted a rule into the official basketball rulebook outlawing two-handed dribbling. "The object of the [new] rule," Dr. Gulick wrote, "is largely to do away with dribbling....The game must remain for what it was originally intended to be—a passing game. Dribbling has introduced all of the objectionable features that are hurting the game."

Gulick assumed that the issue was dead, since one-handed dribbling was obviously too difficult for anyone to try. But players confounded the doctor. In fact, one-handed dribbling proved so effective that it became the standard.

HOW MANY PLAYERS?

Naismith originally recommended using nine players per team, but said the game could be played with almost any number—depending on the size of the court and how many people wanted to play.

Some teams took this advice to extremes: in the early 1890s, Cornell University played a game with 50 people on each side! So many spectators complained about losing sight of the ball at such games that most university teams began scaling back. Then in 1896, the University of Chicago and the University of Iowa played the first collegiate basketball game with only five players on a team. It worked so well that within a year, nearly every college team in the country used five players.

OUT-OF-BOUNDS

In his original list of rules, Naismith wrote that the first player to retrieve a ball after it had gone out-of-bounds got to throw it back into play. But he wasn't sure that rule worked; it seemed to encourage dangerous play: "It was not uncommon," Naismith wrote in his memoirs, "to see a player who was anxious to secure the ball make a football dive for it, regardless of whether he went into the apparatus that was stored around the gym or into the spectators in the bleachers."

The rule ended for good one day while Naismith was supervising a game in Springfield. As occasionally happened, the ball ended up in the balcony that circled the gym. Normally, the teams would race up the stairs to get to the ball first. But on this day, while one team scrambled upstairs, the other showed it had been practicing in secret. They used an acrobatic maneuver, boosting one player up onto the shoulders of another until they were high enough to jump over the railing onto the balcony. Naismith immediately changed the rule to what it is today (the last team to touch the ball before it goes out-of-bounds loses it).

NOTHING BUT NET

The wooden peach baskets broke easily when players threw balls at them, and within a year the YMCA replaced them with sturdier wire mesh trash cans. But these were a problem, too: every time someone scored, the action had to stop until the referee climbed a ladder and retrieved the ball by hand. (Apparently, nobody thought of removing the bottoms of the baskets.)

Over the next few years, the trash cans were replaced by specially made baskets with trapdoors that opened when the referee pulled a string...and then by bare metal hoops, which let the ball drop to the ground by itself.

But the bare hoops went a little too far. When nobody was standing near the basket, it was difficult to tell whether the ball really had gone in. So the YMCA suspended a rope net under the hoop to catch the ball. Believe it or not, these nets were closed at the bottom—the ball was pushed out with a stick. It wasn't until 1912 that they finally cut off the bottom. From then on, the "swish" made it obvious whether the ball had gone in or not.

THE ORIGIN OF BACKBOARDS

It's hard to imagine shooting a basketball without a backboard. But the backboard wasn't created to help players score—it was created to keep fans out.

In gyms like the one at Springfield, the only place for fans to sit was in the balcony. It became common for them to gather near the basket during the game. From there, Robert Peterson writes,

> It was easy for a fervid spectator to reach over the rail and guide the shots of his favorites into the basket or deflect those of his opponents. So for 1895–96, the rules called for a 4-by-6-foot wire or wood screen behind the basket to keep fans from interfering. Wire screens were soon dented by repeated rebounds, giving the home team an advantage because the players knew...their own backboard. So wood gradually supplanted the wire mesh boards.

ON THE MAP

From Dr. Gulick's point of view, basketball was an unqualified success. It had helped encourage interest in sports and physical fitness, increased attendance at YMCA chapters all over the country, and raised the profile of the YMCA in the communities it served. "One of the best solutions to the difficulty of maintaining the interest of the members has been the judicious introduction of the play element into the work," the journal Physical Fitness reported in the summer of 1894, "and in this line nothing has been so peculiarly and generally satisfactory as Basket Ball." Thanks in large part to the success of basket ball, Dr. Gulick's anti-sports critics were silenced and the YMCA became synonymous with sports and physical fitness.

WAR GAME

For all its successes, basketball was still just a game and might never have become a national pastime if it hadn't been for some bad publicity the U.S. Army generated for itself.

In 1916 Gen. John J. Pershing led the "Punitive Expedition" into Mexico in an unsuccessful attempt to capture Pancho Villa. "The newspapers had made much of the drinking and prostitution that had served to entertain an army with time on its hands," Elliott J. Gorn and Warren Goldstein write in A Brief History of American Sports, and when the U.S. entered World War I in 1917, it was determined that such embarrassing publicity would not be generated again.

"For the first time in American history," Gorn and Goldstein write, "sports were formally linked to military preparedness....As American troops were deployed overseas in 1917, they were accompanied everywhere by 12,000 YMCA workers who brought sports along with them"—including basketball. More than a million U.S. troops fought in World War I, and tens of thousands of them learned to play basketball while they were in Europe. By the time the war was over, basketball had become an inextricable part of American life.

* * *

OOPS

"In 1994, an Emergency Medical Service crew in New York rushed an abandoned bag of spaghetti to the hospital after they mistook it for a fetus."

—*Esquire,* **January 1995**

WHY ASK WHY?

Sometimes the answer is irrelevant—it's the question that counts. These cosmic queries are from BRI readers.

Why do we say something is out of whack? What is a whack?

If a pig loses its voice, is it disgruntled?

Why are a wise man and a wise guy opposites?

Why does the word "lisp" have an "s" in it?

Why do women wear evening gowns to nightclubs? Shouldn't they be wearing nightgowns?

If love is blind, why is lingerie so popular?

How does it work out that people always die in alphabetical order?

Why do "overlook" and "oversee" mean opposite things?

"I am" is reportedly the shortest sentence in the English language. Could it be that "I do" is the longest sentence?

If people from Poland are called "Poles," why aren't people from Holland called "Holes?"

If you ate pasta and antipasta, would you still be hungry?

How is it possible to "run out of space"?

If a vegetarian eats vegetables, what does a humanitarian eat?

Why is it that if someone tells you that there are 1 billion stars in the universe you will believe them, but if they tell you a wall has wet paint you will have to touch it to be sure?

If you mixed vodka with orange juice and milk of magnesia, would you get a Phillips Screwdriver?

If Barbie is so popular, why do you have to buy all her friends?

If Fred Flintstone knew that the large order of ribs would tip his car over, why did he order them at the end of every show?

If Superman is so smart, why does he wear underpants over his trousers?

If you jog backwards, will you gain weight?

Hot chocolate: In Japan, you can buy cocoa flavored with 2% chili pepper sauce.

IN MAYA OPINION...

Words of wisdom from Maya Angelou, one of our favorite poets.

"There is no agony like bearing an untold story inside of you."

"If you have only one smile in you, give it to the people you love. Don't be surly at home, then go out in the street and start grinning 'Good morning' at total strangers."

"The fact that the adult American Negro female emerges a formidable character is often met with amazement, distaste and even belligerance. It is seldom accepted as an inevitable outcome of the struggle won by survivors, and deserves respect if not enthusiastic acceptance."

"Children's talent to endure stems from their ignorance of alternatives."

"As far as I knew, white women were never lonely, except in books. White men adored them, Black men desired them and Black women worked for them."

"At fifteen life had taught me undeniably that surrender was as honorable as resistance, especially if one had no choice."

"Self-pity in its early stage is as snug as a feather mattress. Only when it hardens does it become uncomfortable."

"A bird doesn't sing because it has an answer, it sings because it has a song."

"I find it interesting that the meanest life, the poorest existence, is attributed to God's will, but as human beings become more affluent...God descends the scale of responsibility at a commensurate speed."

"One isn't necessarily born with courage, but one is born with potential. Without courage we cannot practice any other virtue with consistency. We can't be kind, true, merciful, generous, or honest."

"I love to see a young girl go out and grab the world by the lapels. Life's a bitch. You've got to go out and kick ass."

This year, Harvard University will deny admission to an estimated 1,600 high school valedictorians.

THE RIDDLER

What's white, and black, and read in the middle? This page of riddles. Here are some BRI favorites.

1. What unusual natural phenomenon is capable of speaking in any language?

2. A barrel of water weighs 20 pounds. What do you have to add to it to make it weigh 12 pounds?

3. Before Mount Everest was discovered, what was the highest mountain on Earth?

4. What word starts with an "e," ends with an "e," and usually contains one letter?

5. Forward I am heavy, but backward I am not. What am I?

6. He has married many women, but has never been married. Who is he?

7. How many bricks does it take to complete a building made of brick?

8. How many of each animal did Moses take on the ark?

9. How many times can you subtract the number 5 from 25?

10. If you have it, you want to share it. If you share it, you don't have it. What is it?

11. In Okmulgee, Oklahoma, you cannot take a picture of a man with a wooden leg. Why not?

12. The more you have of it, the less you see. What is it?

13. The more you take, the more you leave behind. What are they?

14. The one who makes it, sells it. The one who buys it, never uses it. The one who uses it, never knows that he's using it. What is it?

15. What can go up a chimney down but can't go down a chimney up?

16. What crime is punishable if attempted, but is not punishable if committed?

17. What happened in the middle of the 20th century that will not happen again for 4,000 years?

18. What is the center of gravity?

19. What question can you never honestly answer "yes" to?

20. You can't keep this until you have given it.

Answers are on page 515.

Pollination experts say: We can thank bees for apples, flies for chocolate, and bats for tequila.

LUCKY FINDS

Ever found something valuable? It's one of the best feelings in the world. Here's another installment of a regular Bathroom Reader *feature—a look at some folks who found* really *valuable stuff…and got to keep it. We should all be so lucky!*

LOTS OF LUNCH MONEY

The Find: Two paintings

Where They Were Found: At an estate sale

The Story: Carl Rice started buying paintings at thrift stores and garage sales in 1993, imagining they were worth a lot of money. Each time he found one that he thought might be valuable, he'd send a photograph to the famous New York auction house, Christie's. The reply was always the same: worthless.

By 1996 Rice owned a stack of 500 paintings and really couldn't afford to buy any more; his business was about to fold and he would soon be unemployed. But he was hooked. One day in 1996, as he roamed around an estate sale, he noticed a 6-by-12-inch picture of roses that he liked. He bought it for $10. On his way out, he saw a 15-by-24-inch floral picture on the wall and couldn't resist that, either. He bought it for $50. Rice tossed the paintings into his car trunk and headed home to an irritated wife. According to Rice, she said something like, "More of that s--t?"

But when they checked the artist's name—Martin Johnson Heade—in a price guide, they found out he was a well-known 19th-century painter. The excited couple sent photos to Christie's again, and this time there was no rejection letter—the auction house sent a New York vice president to authenticate the paintings. In 1998, the $60 investment was auctioned off for over $1 million. The Rices had to borrow money to attend the auction, but left with $600,000 after-tax dollars in their pockets.

BOOK BUYER'S BONUS

The Find: Three sketches

Where They Were Found: In a book

The Story: In 1999 a woman bought a book for $1 at a flea market in Amsterdam. While flipping through the book on her way home, she found three drawings that looked old.

She took them to an art expert to see what they were. His assessment: two were original drawings by Rembrandt and the third was by one of his students. She sold them to a German collector for $55,000, but oddly enough, didn't feel grateful. In fact, her agent told reporters, "When I asked for my 3% commission, [she] said I could have a beating instead."

OH, BABE-Y!

The Find: A baseball
Where It Was Found: In Grandma's attic
The Story: In 1997 a New Jersey boy named Chris Scala dressed up as Babe Ruth for a school project on famous Americans. When his 87-year-old grandmother heard about it, she remembered that she had an old ball that had been signed by Ruth, in her attic. It had been given to her husband back in 1927 "as a prize for making the New Jersey all-state high school baseball team."

Her son Mark had played in the attic many times as a kid, but had never seen the ball. Skeptical, he drove to his mother's house and looked around...and was surprised to locate it in an old box "with other discarded baseballs." He was even more amazed to discover an inscription that identified it not only as a Babe Ruth home run ball, but as the *very first* ball Ruth had ever hit for a home run in Yankee Stadium. He took the ball to the Baseball Hall of Fame in Cooperstown, New York. It was authenticated, and sold at auction in 1999 for $126,000.

LUCKY BUCKET

The Find: "An interesting rock"
Where It Was Found: In a mine in North Carolina
The Story: (From the Richmond, Virginia, *Times-Dispatch*, 1999)
"Ten-year-old Lawrence Shields was picking through a bucket of dirt at a commercial gem mine in North Carolina last week when he found an interesting rock. 'I just liked the shape of it,' he says.

"It turned out to be a 1061-carat sapphire. Lawrence and his parents say they've been told it could be worth more than $35,000."

SPECIAL UNDERWEAR

More important underwear innovations to keep abreast of.

SIX-DAY UNDERWEAR

"The Honda Motor Company's bi-annual inventiveness contest for employees has unearthed some unique innovations, but none to match 6-day underwear, the 1987 winner. According to the story in the *Wall St. Journal*, the underwear has three leg holes, which enables it to last for six days without washing. The wearer rotates it 120 degrees on each of the first three days, then turns it out and repeats the process."

—*Forgotten Fads and Fabulous Flops*

THE ALARM BRA

LONDON—"A newly developed techno-bra—the latest in personal alram systems—is the brainchild of Royal College of Art design student Kursty Groves. Targeted at young urban women, the bra uses miniature electronics and conductive fabric to monitor the wearer's heart rate. If it detects a sudden change in pulse—one that indicates panic—it radios a distress call to police and identifies the bra's location. And since the electronics are contained in jell-like cushions inside each cup, the bra enhances the wearer's figure. 'You can also have some lift and support if you like,' Groves says."

—*Wire Service Report, 1999*

SWEAT PANTS

Want to give off a manly, territorial odor without having to sweat for it? Japanese scientists have a new product—sweat-laced underpants.

Apparel and cosmetics maker Kanebo Ltd. says millions of tiny capsules in the fabric contain a synthesized pheromone found in the sweat of a man's underarms. Friction breaks the capsules, releasing the pheromone; an added musk scent intensifies the effect.

"Unfortunately, the power is fleeting—Kanebo estimates the pheromones are completely dissipated after ten washings."

—*Parade Magazine, 1998*

The world's first golf rule book was published in Scotland in 1754.

THE RETURN OF ZORRO

Here's the second part of our history of
"The Fox." (Part I is on page 121.)

THE MARK OF ZORRO

When Johnston McCulley created Zorro—the first "superhero" with a secret identity—in 1919, he didn't have any idea what mark he would leave on pop culture. "Zorro not only became a vehicle for stars such as Fairbanks," Sandra Curtis writes in *Zorro Unmasked*, "the character also directly inspired numerous dual-identity imitators, including the Phantom, the Lone Ranger, the Green Hornet, and Superman."

He was especially important to Batman. Creator Bob Kane saw *The Mark of Zorro* when he was 13, and credits Fairbanks with providing the inspiration for the Caped Crusader:

> [Zorro] was the most swashbuckling, derring-do, super hero I've ever, ever seen in my life, and he left a lasting impression on me. And of course later, when I created the Batman, it gave me the dual identity, because Zorro had the dual identity. During the day, he played a foppish count, Don Diego . . . a bored playboy, and at night became Zorro. He wore a mask and he strapped his trusty sword around his waist. He came out of a cave . . . which I made into a bat cave, and he rode a black horse called Tornado, and later on I had the Batmobile. So Zorro was a major influence on my creation of Batman.

THE NEXT ACTION HERO

McCulley went on to write a total of 64 Zorro short stories, many of which were the basis for the 10 feature films, 5 film serials, several TV series, and more than a dozen foreign films that have appeared over 70 years. Tyrone Power played Zorro in the 1940 remake of *The Mark of Zorro*, and nine years later Clayton Moore played the masked man—before going on to find fame as the Lone Ranger. In 1998 *The Mask of Zorro*, starring Antonio Banderas as the young protégé of the original, grossed over $90 million.

Highest denomination ever minted by the U.S. Treasury: $100,000 bill. Lowest: 5¢ bill.

THE TWO MOST UNUSUAL ZORRO FILMS:

• *Zorro's Black Whip* (1944). The only female Zorro. "Linda Stirling dons a black outfit and becomes the Black Whip, riding in the hoofprints of her crusading brother [Zorro], who was killed for his just beliefs." (*Video Movie Guide*)

• *Zorro, The Gay Blade* (1981). "Tongue-in-cheek sword play with George Hamilton portraying the swashbuckling crusader and his long-lost gay brother, Bunny Wigglesworth." (*Videohound's Golden Movie Retriever*)

ZORRO ON TV

The most popular post-World War II Zorro was Guy Williams, who played "The Fox" on the Walt Disney TV series from 1957 to 1959.

Disney bought the rights to Zorro in 1953, but spent so much money building Disneyland (which opened in 1954) that he didn't launch the Zorro series until 1957. Disney had been looking for an unknown actor to play the part of Zorro, and found his man in Williams—whose father and uncle were experienced swordsmen. Williams himself had studied fencing since the age of seven.

The Crockett Syndrome

A few years before (see page 165), Disney's "Davy Crockett" had created TV's first merchandising boom—every kid in America wanted a coonskin cap. Disney was caught off-guard and wasn't able to fill the demand. This time, he vowed not to make the same mistake. At the same time Zorro went on the air, the country was flooded with Zorro lunch boxes, puzzles, watches, pajamas, trading cards, Pez dispensers, and even sword sets—complete with a mask and chalk-tipped plastic sword, with which kids could mark "Z's" all over the house.

Disney had a hit on his hands, but cancelled the show after only two seasons when he couldn't agree with ABC on a price for it. Guy Williams was stunned by the decision, but went on to play Professor John Robinson on TV's "Lost in Space." (Special note to Zorro fans: We don't know what happened to Sgt. Garcia…but we're trying to find out.)

MORE "I SPY"
...AT THE MOVIES

*Here are more of the little in-jokes and gags that moviemakers
throw into films for their own amusement. The info comes
from* Reel Gags, *by Bill Givens, and* Film and
Television In-Jokes, *by Bill van Heerden.*

THE BLUES BROTHERS (1980)

I Spy... Steven Spielberg

Where to Find Him: He plays the Cook County small-claims
clerk. (Note: Spielberg returned the favor to co-star Dan Aykroyd
by giving him a cameo role in *Indiana Jones and the Temple of Doom.*
He played the English ticket agent at the airport.)

MAVERICK (1994)

I Spy... Actor Danny Glover

Where to Find Him: Glover, who appeared with *Maverick* star Mel
Gibson in the *Lethal Weapon* series, shows up in a cameo as a bank
robber. He and Gibson seem to recognize each other, then shake
their heads and say, "Nah." Glover even uses his line from the *Lethal
Weapon* films, "I'm too old for this s--t."

RESERVOIR DOGS (1992)

I Spy...A real-life act of revenge

Where to Find It: The scene in which actor Tim Roth shoots a
woman. The actress was his dialogue coach, who had apparently
made life difficult for him during the filming. He insisted the she
be cast in the role so he could "shoot" her.

TRADING PLACES (1983), TWILIGHT ZONE—THE MOVIE (1983), COMING TO AMERICA (1988), and other films directed by John Landis

I Spy... The phrase "See You Next Wednesday"

Where to Find It: Landis says it was the title of his first screenplay
and he always tries get it into a film somewhere. In *Trading Places*

Mercury is the only metal that is liquid at room temperature.

and *Coming to America*, for example, it's on a subway poster. In *The Blues Brothers*, it's on a billboard. In *The Stupids*, it's on the back of a bus. In *Twilight Zone*, someone says it aloud…in German.

TWISTER (1996)

I Spy…A tribute to Stanley Kubrick (Jan de Bont, *Twister*'s director, is a big Kubrick fan)

Where to Find It: In the characters' names; one is Stanley, another is called Kubrick. And when a drive-in theater is hit by a twister, the movie playing onscreen is Kubrick's *The Shining*.

BACK TO THE FUTURE (1985)

I Spy…A nod to "The Rocky and Bullwinkle Show"

Where to Find It: The scene in which Michael J. Fox crashes into the farmer's barn. The farmer's name is Peabody; his son is Sherman. Peabody and Sherman were the brilliant time-traveling dog and his boy in the Jay Ward cartoon show.

WHEN HARRY MET SALLY… (1989)

I Spy…Estelle Reiner, director Rob Reiner's mother

Where to Find Her: She's the woman who tells the waiter: "I'll have what she's having," when Meg Ryan fakes an orgasm in a restaurant.

RAIN MAN (1988)

I Spy…A reference to Dustin Hoffman's family

Where to Find It: When Hoffman recites names from the phone book. Two of them—Marsha and William Gottsegen—are his real-life in-laws.

NATIONAL LAMPOON'S ANIMAL HOUSE (1978)

I Spy…A way to get into Universal Studios free

Where to Find It: In the final credits, it says "Ask for Babs"—referring to a character in the film who supposedly became a tour guide there. For many years, if someone really did ask for Babs, they'd get free or discounted admission to the tour. Bad news: Universal doesn't honor the promotion anymore.

IN MY EXPERT OPINION...

Think the experts and authorities have all the answers?
Well, they do...but often the wrong ones.

"Animals, which move, have limbs and muscles; the Earth has no limbs and muscles, hence it does not move."
—Scipio Chiaramonti, professor of mathematics, University of Pisa, 1633

"Nature intended women to be slaves. They are our property. What a mad idea to demand equality for women! Women are nothing but machines for producing children." —Napoleon Bonaparte

"I must confess that my imagination refuses to see any sort of submarine doing anything except suffocating its crew and floundering at sea." —H. G. Wells, 1902

"You ain't goin' nowhere, son. You ought to go back to drivin' a truck." —Jim Denny, manager of the Grand Ole Opry, to Elvis Presley, 1954

"If excessive smoking actually plays a role in the production of lung cancer, it seems to be a minor one." —The National Cancer Institute, 1954

The horse is here to stay, but the automobile is only a novelty—a fad."—Marshall Ferdinand Foch, French military strategist, 1911

"With over 50 foreign cars already on sale here, the Japanese auto industry isn't likely to carve out a big slice of the U.S. market for itself." —*Business Week*, 1968

"We don't believe Jackie Robinson, colored college star signed by the Dodgers for one of their farm teams, will ever play in the big leagues." —Jimmy Powers, *New York Daily News* sports columnist, 1945

READ ALL ABOUT IT!

Two good reasons not to believe everything you read in the newspapers.

THE STORY: In the early 1920s, the *Toronto Mail and Empire* reported that two scientists named Dr. Schmierkase and Dr. Butterbrod had discovered "what appeared to be the fossil of the whale that had swallowed Jonah." The whale had a muscle that functioned like a trapdoor, giving access to its stomach.

The next day, evangelists all over Toronto read the story from the pulpit, citing it as confirmation that the Biblical story of Jonah and the whale was true....and the day after that, a rival newspaper ran a story reporting on the evangelists' speech.

THE TRUTH: Three days after the original story ran, the *Toronto Mail and Empire* ran a second story exposing the first one as a hoax, the work of a journalist named Charles Langdon Clarke.

Clarke liked to spend his free time cooking up news items based on Biblical stories, and then attributing them to fictional newspapers like the *Babylon Gazette* or the *Jerusalem Times* for added credibility. Anyone who spoke German would have had an inkling that the story was a joke—Dr. Schmierkase and Dr. Butterbrod translates as Dr. Cheese and Dr. Butter Bread.

THE STORY: In January 1927 the *Chicago Journal* reported that a "killer hawk" had been seen preying on pigeons in the downtown area. The next day other Chicago papers ran the story on their front pages, and continued doing so for five consecutive days, igniting considerable public hysteria in the process: A prominent banker offered a reward for capture of the hawk dead or alive; a local gun club sent shooters downtown to stalk the bird, with help of local Boy Scouts troops who joined in the hunt.

THE TRUTH: A week after the *Journal* ran the hawk story, it announced the start of a newspaper serial called "The Pigeon and the Hawk." The other papers, realizing they'd been tricked into publicizing a rival paper's promotion on their front pages for an entire week, never printed another word about the killer hawk.

Tigers can be taught to use litter boxes. Big litter boxes.

GI JOE: THE FIRST "ACTION FIGURE"

It's no big deal now to see a boy playing with dolls…er "action figures."
But until 1964, he might easily have been called a sissy…and his parents
probably would have been very worried. Then Hasbro came up with an all-
American, all-man version of Barbie called GI Joe, and used TV to sell it
directly to kids. Suddenly, parents' cultural biases became irrelevant.
Here's the story of another milestone of the gender-bending 1960s.

BY THE BOOK

In 1963 a freelance licensing agent named Stan Weston was hired by *Encyclopedia Britannica* to license the encyclopedia's name and content to other companies. During one meeting, Weston happened to mention that his family couldn't afford a set of encyclopedias when he was a kid. His client made note of the remark.

Three weeks later, a truck pulled up in front of Weston's house and dropped off three complete sets of encyclopedias—*Encyclopedia Britannica, Encyclopedia Britannica Jr.,* and *Compton's Encyclopedia.* Weston put the gift to good use: he dragged the books down to his basement and spent the next several months going through them, page by page, looking for new product ideas.

As it happened, one of Weston's regular customers was Elliot Handler, co-founder of Mattel Toys. Handler was making a fortune on the Barbie doll and explained on the basic philosophy behind it: "Elliot kept drumming into my head the so-called 'razor and razor blade' idea," Weston says. "Sell them Barbie the doll, which is the razor…and then sell them an awful lot of [accessories]—the razor blades. I never forgot that."

THE FRONT LINE

As he flipped through his encyclopedias, Weston was looking for a razor that would sell a lot of blades. And when he got to the section on the U.S. military, he knew he'd found it. Page after page was devoted to layouts of military uniforms, medals, flags, weapons, and equipment. He immediately imagined a male Barbie doll who was in the military…and all the accessories it would need to be a good soldier

Weston started making trips to a local Army-Navy store and to the United Nations souvenir shop, buying flags, military insignias, and other miscellaneous items.

THE ART OF WAR

About two weeks later, Weston met in Manhattan with Don Levine, the creative director of Hasbro. Levine didn't jump at the idea of the boy's doll, but spent some time discussing it with Weston. They agreed that if the doll was ever made, it would have to be fully articulated (movable), "so you can get him behind a machine gun or what have you."

After the meeting, Levine took a walk down 55th Street. As he was passing an art store, he noticed some wooden mannequins in the window. They were articulated so that artists could bend them to simulate just about any pose the human body was capable of. Not even Barbie was *that* flexible, and Levine was impressed. If there was some way to mass-produce a doll with that kind of flexibility—something that had never been done before—he'd have a product that was superior to anything else on the market.

In the weeks that followed, Weston's soldier doll continued to grow on Levine. He finally became hooked during a visit to the Soldier Shop on Madison Avenue, which specialized in handmade military figures for grown-up collectors. They sold for as much as $1,000 apiece—"Gorgeous stuff for the real aficionado," Levine says. "I started to go nuts in my own head. I became very interested in that colorful world of toy soldiers."

MILITARY SECRET

Even after Levine convinced the president of Hasbro (which had never made dolls) to give his project the green light, there was a huge problem to overcome—in the mid-1960s, boys did *not* play with dolls, and parents were likely to resist buying one. So Levine decided that they simply wouldn't *call* it a doll. As John Michlig writes in *GI Joe:*

> The offending "d" word would be banned from the language of everyone on the development team. "This is a moveable fighting man," he repeated as many times as possible. "An action figure." Once the new term was coined, anyone using the word "doll" in reference to the movable soldier was subject to Levine's wrath.

PUTTING IT ALL TOGETHER

Both soldiers and cowboys were popular with young boys in the mid-1960s, and Hasbro thought about making the first boy's doll a cowboy. But they settled on a soldier doll, for largely commercial reasons: a cowboy doll's accessories would be limited to what he could carry on his horse...but the amount of equipment you could sell with a solder doll was virtually limitless.

They decided from the very beginning that the *action figure* would be as lifelike and authentic as possible. The first GI Joe— the prototype—was actually a Ken doll "with some of the baby fat trimmed off his face." Then outside model-makers were hired to create a movable, muscular male body and a more realistic face (see page 138). Hasbro also decided that the figure should be just under 12 inches—tall enough to clothe and accessorize, but short enough to keep costs down. Also, not so coincidentally, that height would make Joe just a bit taller than Ken. For years, when kids inevitably compared the two, Joe would emerge as the "stud" of the toy world.

Meanwhile, members of Levine's creative team began fanning out to Army-Navy stores, military bases, and war museums in search of uniforms, weapons, and other accessories that could be taken back to Hasbro and reproduced in a very small scale.

Levine got blueprints for fairly advanced weapons from the military by pretending he was researching a line of child-size weapons and military gear that kids could use to play soldier.

HELLO, JOE

Initially Levine planned to make four different dolls—one for each branch of the military—and came up with three different names: "Rocky" for both the army and the marines, "Ace" for the air force, and "Skip" for the navy.

But when Hasbro's advertising agency learned about the soldier dolls, they advised using only one name for all of the dolls, because it would be easier to advertise. "You're shooting buckshot," they said. "You guys need a target and one direct hit."

Levine spent the next few days trying to think up a name that was strong enough and generic enough to apply to dolls representing every branch of the military. He finally found it (appropriately enough) on television. One night he decided to relax and watch a movie on TV. It turned out to be a 1945 film starring Robert Mitchum and Burgess Meredith called *The Story of GI Joe.*

SAVING FACE

The doll…er, action figure was just about complete, except for one thing: Hasbro needed a way to protect his image from copycats in the toy industry. The human form cannot be copyrighted. Any resemblance between Joe and another doll, no matter how blatant, could be explained away as a coincidence…unless some unnatural distinguishing feature could be added to his face. Levine decided that Joe should have a scar on the right side of his face. Not only would it make him look more masculine, writes Michlig, but "the small slash could not be considered a natural feature of the typical human face [and] therefore it would function as a trademark." Now, no other company could get away with manufacturing a doll that looked similar.

GREATEST AMERICAN HERO

In 1964 the toy business was still strictly seasonal; almost all new toys were introduced at Christmastime. The first Christmas orders were placed in February, to give manufacturers a chance to figure out how much inventory to stock, and the early orders for GI Joe were respectable. Chain stores like Sears were willing to stock enough of the product to give Hasbro's fall TV advertising a chance to be effective.

But Hasbro executives didn't want to wait until fall to see if Joe was a winner. So they decided to do something unprecedented: test-market him in the summer. Hasbro shipped about $50,000 worth of merchandise to some New York toy stores, then ran a few commercials on two New York TV stations. They used the ads to explain that GI Joe was *not* a doll (the theme song: "GI Joe, GI Joe, fighting man from head to toe"), and to show boys how to play with the new action figures.

The merchandise sold out by the end of the week. So Hasbro shipped another $250,000 worth to New York toy stores. It, too, sold out within a week. That's when Hasbro knew they had a hit.

How *big* a hit Hasbro had didn't become apparent until the end of 1964. "Five years earlier," Michlig writes, "Barbie was introduced with sales of 351,000 units; GI Joe had sold over

2 million," or about $5.3 million in sales for 1964. Sales peaked at $23 million in 1965 and remained strong through most of 1966, making GI Joe one of the most successful toy introductions in the history of the American toy industry…just in time for the Vietnam War.

For more on GI Joe, turn to page 484.

* * *

GI JOE FACTS

• One of GI Joe's distinguishing features started out as a goof: the sculptor who designed the prototype worked so fast that he'd accidentally transposed GI Joe's right thumbnail so it ended up where the thumbprint should be. Levine told him to leave it. "That thumbnail would act as our identifying mark," Levine says. "A mapmaker will sometimes add a nonexistent street with his name attached; if another map comes out with that same street on it, he knows he's been copied. Now we had a scar to protect the face and an error on the hand to individualize our body."

• As GI Joe was about to go to market, Hasbro and Stan Weston negotiated a royalty arrangement. Hasbro offered one half of 1% of sales as royalty; Weston wanted 5%. He eventually lowered his asking price to 3%, but Hasbro refused to go above 1%. Eventually, Hasbro offered Weston a choice between $100,000 up front or $50,000 up front, with a 1% royalty once sales passed $7 million. "I made my own personal decision, nobody counseled me," Weston says. "I said, 'I'll take the $100,000." The decision cost Weston millions of dollars in lost royalties over the next 30 years.

• The first big flop in the GI Joe line was GI Nurse, an "action girl" designed to bring American girls into the GI Joe universe. It didn't work—girls preferred Barbie, who wasn't subordinate to a male. Boys also refused to play with her, so Hasbro replaced her with a male medic. Today the doll, which sold for $4.99 in 1967, is so rare that it sells at auction for as much as $6,000.

"Acting is not an important job in the scheme of things. Plumbing is."
—*Spencer Tracy*

THE PRICE WAS RIGHT

You've heard people talk about how much things cost back in the "good old days"—heck, you might remember them yourself (Uncle John does). Talk about nostalgia—we found these prices in The Money Book, *by Peter Skolnick*

IN 1926:

1 lb. of steak: 37¢

1 dozen eggs: 45¢

Grand piano: $625

1926 Chevrolet: $510

Frigidaire Refrigerator: $395

RCA Radio: $150

Ticket from NY to Philadelphia on the Pennsylvania Railroad: $3.00

IN 1936:

FDR's presidential salary: $75,000 a year

Average starting salary for a college graduate: $20-25 a week.

First-class stamp: 3¢

Quart of milk: 12¢

Full dinner at New York's Roxy Grill: 75¢.

Six-pack of Coca-Cola (bottles): 25¢

13-day cruise from New York to Bermuda: $123

Three-minute call from NY to SF: $4.30.

IN 1946:

1 lb. of round steak: 41¢

One year's tuition at Yale University: $600.

Average wage for a registered nurse: $200 per month.

Average hourly wage at the Ford Motor Company: $1.38.

Dinner and show featuring comedian Sid Caesar: $2.75 per person.

IN 1956:

Median income for men: $3,400

For women: $1,100

Pound of steak: 43¢

The Detroit Tigers major league baseball team: $5.5 million (a record at the time).

RCA color TV: $795-895.

8-1/2 oz. box of Rice Crispies: 25¢.

Avis Rental Car: $5 a day, plus 8¢ a mile.

IN 1966:

Federal minimum wage: $1.25 an hour

Damages awarded to a New York lawyer "whose nose was bitten off by an angry litigant": $200,000

One-day stay in the hospital: $42

One year's worth of tuition at Yale University: $1,950

1966 Ford Mustang: $2,129

IN 1976:

National average annual family income: $14,000.

Average salary for an MBA working in New York: $20,000 a year.

Sylvania portable 19" color TV: $378.

One year's tuition at Yale University: $4,400

Top-selling doll in the country: Cher by Mego, $6.94.

Going down: Bottle-nosed whales can dive 3,000 feet in two minutes.

FAMILIAR PHRASES

Where do these familiar terms and phrases come from? The BRI staff has researched them and come up with some interesting explanations.

BUY A PIG IN A POKE
Meaning: Buying something sight unseen
Origin: "The poke was a small bag (the words pouch and pocket derive from the same roots), and the pig was a small pig. As related in Thomas Tusser's *Five Hundredth Good Pointes of Husbandrie* (1580), the game was to put a cat in the poke and try to palm it off in the market as a pig, persuading the buyer that it would be best not to open the poke because the pig might get away." (From *The Dictionary of Clichés*, by James Rogers)

TOUCH AND GO
Meaning: A risky, precarious situation
Origin: "Dates back to the days of stagecoaches, whose drivers were often intensely competitive, seeking to charge past one another, on narrow roads, at grave danger to life and limb. If the vehicle's wheels became entangled, both would be wrecked; if they were lucky, the wheels would only touch and the coaches could still go." (From *Loose Cannons and Red Herrings*, by Robert Claiborne)

KNOCK OFF WORK
Meaning: Leave work for the day
Origin: "[This phrase] originated in the days of slave galleys. To keep the oarsmen rowing in unison, a drummer beat time rhythmically on a block of wood. When it was time to rest or change shifts, he would give a special knock, signifying that they could *knock off*." (From *Dictionary of Word and Phrase Origins Vol. 2*, by William and Mary Morris)

DOES THAT RING ANY BELLS?
Meaning: Does that sound familiar?
Origin: "Old-fashioned carnivals and amusement parks featured shooting galleries, in which patrons were invited to test their marksmanship by shooting at a target—often with a bell at the center: if

---

Total combined population of the North American colonies in 1610: 350.

something was right on target, it rang the bell. Similarly, to say that something 'doesn't ring any bells' means that it doesn't strike any 'target' (evoke any response) in your mind." (From *Loose Cannons and Red Herrings*, by Robert Claiborne)

BEAT THE RAP

Meaning: Avoid punishment for a wrongdoing
Origin: "It is likely that this slang Americanism originated in another expression, *take the rap*, in which rap is slang for 'punishment,' facetiously, from a 'rap on the knuckles.' One who takes the rap for someone else stands in for the other's punishment. *Beat the rap*...often carries with it the connotation that the miscreant was actually guilty, though acquitted." (From *The Whole Ball of Wax*, by Laurence Urdang)

BE ABOVEBOARD

Meaning: Be honest
Origin: Comes from card playing. "*Board* is an old word for table." To drop your hands below the table could, of course, be interpreted as trying to cheat—by swapping cards, for example. "But if all play was *above board* this was impossible." (From *To Coin a Phrase*, by Edwin Radford and Alan Smith)

*   *   *

IRONIC DEATH

Thomas Par was thought to be England's oldest living man in the 17th century. He was supposedly 152 years old in 1635, when King Charles invited him to a royal banquet in hopes of learning the secret to his longevity. Parr's answer: "Simple meals of grains and meats."

Final Irony: According to one account: "'Marvelous,' said the King as he offered Parr goose livers and baby eels basted in butter and onions, followed by fried sheep's eyeballs. Throughout the banquet, Parr regaled the King with stories while the King saw to it that Parr's plate and glass were always full. Unfortunately, Parr, overwhelmed by the food, expired during the meal. The distraught King, feeling responsible, had him buried in Westminster Abbey."

In the 19th century, India imported ice harvested from ponds in the United States.

MYTH AMERICA: FROM BAD TO VERSE

In some instances, "common knowledge" about important moments in American history comes from poems that, though dramatic and inspiring, turn out to be complete fiction. Here are two examples.

THE LANDING OF THE PILGRIM FATHERS (1826)

The breaking waves dashed high
On a stern and rock-bound coast.
And the woods, against a stormy sky,
Their giant branches toss'd

And the heavy night hung dark
The hills and water o'er,
When a band of exiles moor'd their bark
On the wild New England shore…

Significance: According to Bill Bryson in *Made in America*, this poem is responsible for "forming the essential image of the Mayflower landing that most Americans carry with them to this day."

Background: It was written by Felicia Dorothea Hemans, who lived 200 years after the Pilgrims landed, never visited the United States even once, and "appears to have known next to nothing about the country" or the Pilgrims. So how did she come to write the poem? Bryson explains:

> It just happened that one day in 1826 her local grocer in Rhyllon, Wales, wrapped her purchases in a sheet of two-year-old newspaper from Boston, and her eye was caught by a small article about a founders' day celebration in Plymouth. It was probably the first she had heard of the Mayflower or the Pilgrims. But inspired as only a mediocre poet can be, she dashed off a poem.

Myth-understood: The Pilgrims eventually did land at Plymouth, but that was on their fourth trip to shore, not their first. And they didn't land at night, or anywhere near the rocks (including Plymouth Rock).

For that matter, the Pilgrims didn't even refer to themselves as

---

Attention employees: In a recent poll, 23% of workers surveyed said they'd work harder if…

"pilgrims"—they called themselves "saints," and would not become known as Pilgrims until 200 years later. (The sailors who brought the Pilgrims to the New World had another name for them: "puke stockings," Bryson writes, "on account of the Pilgrims' apparently boundless ability to spatter the latter with the former.")

PAUL REVERE'S RIDE (1861)

Listen my children, and you shall hear
Of the midnight ride of Paul Revere,
On the eighteenth day of April, in Seventy-five;
Hardly a man is now alive
Who remembers that famous day and year.
He said to his friend, "If the British march
By land of sea from the town to-night,
Hang a lantern aloft in the belfry arch,
Of the North Church tower as a signal light,
One, if by land, and two, if by sea;
And I on the opposite shore will be,
Ready to ride and spread the alarm
Through every Middlesex village and farm,
For the country folk to be up and to arm....

Significance: More than any other single source, this poem established the classic elements of the Paul Revere myth: that lanterns were hung in the church tower as signals and that Revere made the difficult journey alone, almost singlehandedly warning the nation of imminent British attack.

Background: Henry Wadsworth Longfellow wrote the poem to serve as an inspiration to Union soldiers fighting in the Civil War, and used considerable dramatic license to achieve that end. "He made the ride into a solitary act," says historian David Hackett Fischer. "Paul Revere for him becomes a historical loner who does almost everything by himself....The point was that one man, acting alone, could turn the course of history, and this was an appeal to individuals in the North to do it again in another crisis."

Myth-understood: Historians now believe that as many as 60 men rode that night to warn of the British attack. "That doesn't in any way take away from Paul Revere," Fischer says. "He, more than anybody, set those other people in motion." And while there may have been lanterns in the North Church tower, Fischer points out, Paul Revere wasn't the one who received the signal, he was the one who sent it to others, just in case he wasn't able to get across the Charles River to begin his ride.

In his book *Lies, Legends, and Cherished Myths of American History*, Richard Shenkman isn't so charitable about Revere. He writes:

> Paul Revere rode into the hero's spotlight only in 1863, when Longfellow wrote his famous poem...rescuing Revere from virtual obscurity. Historians say before the poem many Americans were not even familiar with Revere's name. In the early nineteenth century, not a single editor included Revere in any compendium of American worthies....[But] by the end of the century, his reputation had improved so immensely that the Daughters of the American Revolution put a plaque on his home in Boston.

And let's not forget, Paul Revere didn't even finish his famous ride—he was captured by the British.

*   *   *

AMPHI-FACTS

- The largest amphibian in the world is the Chinese giant salamander.

- The largest giant salamander on record: 5 feet—from the tip of the snout to the tip of the tail—it weighed nearly 100 pounds.

- The largest frog in the world is the rare Goliath frog of Africa.

- The largest toad in the world is probably the Marine toad, from tropical South America.

- The smallest known amphibian is the Arrow-poison frog, found only in Cuba.

- The smallest newt in the world—at about two inches— is the Striped newt, from the southeastern U.S.

- There will be a test in the morning.

If a grasshopper is hungry enough, it will eat the paint off your house.

FOR THE BIRDS

Here is a list of 10 of the world's most unusual birds, from
The Best Book of Lists Ever, *compiled by Geoff Tibballs.*

1. The **Hummingbird** is the only bird that can fly backwards. It achieves this feat by beating its wings up and down at great speed (some species have a wing-speed of 80 beats per second). Try it.

2. The home of the **Great Indian Hornbill** is a prison. When the female is ready to lay her eggs, she hides in a hole in a tree. The male then seals up the hole, leaving just a narrow slit through which he passes food. The female stays in there until the chicks are a few months old, when she breaks out and helps the male with feeding duties.

3. The **Secretary Bird** may have long legs but it can't run. Instead it hops along the African scrubland in search of its staple diet of snakes and lizards. The bird gets its name from the 20 black crest feathers behind its ears which are reminiscent of the old quill pens once favored by secretaries.

4. The eyes of the **Woodcock** are set so far back in its head that it has a 360-degree field of vision, enabling it to see all round and even over the top of its head.

5. The **Quetzal** from Central America has such a long tail (up to 3 feet) that it can't take off from a branch in the normal way without ripping its tail to shreds. So instead it launches itself backwards into space like a parachutist leaving an aircraft. The quetzal nests in hollow trees but has to reverse into the hole. Once inside, it curls its tail over its head and out of the hole.

6. The **Wandering Albatross** has the largest wingspan of any bird and can glide for six days without ever beating its wings. It can also sleep in mid-air.

7. The **Male Bower-Bird** from Australia attracts a female by building an elaborate love bower. After building a little hut out of twigs, he decorates it with flowers and colorful objects such as feathers, fruit, shells and pebbles or sometimes glass and paper if the nest is near civilization. One particular species (the atlas bower-bird) actually paints the walls by dipping bark or leaves into the blue or dark-green saliva he secretes. The entire bower-building procedure can take months and the bird will often change the decorations until he is happy with them. When finally satisfied, he performs a love dance outside the bower, sometimes offering the female a pretty item from his collection.

8. The **Young Hoatzin** of the Amazon forests has claws on its wings to help it clamber through the dense undergrowth. The bird is a throwback to the prehistoric archeopteryx, which also had three claws on each wing.

9. The **Kiwi** is the only bird with nostrils at the tip of its beak. Whereas other birds hunt by sight or hearing, the national bird of New Zealand uses its beaky nostrils to sniff out food at night. Although the kiwi is roughly the same size as a chicken, it lays an egg which is 10 times larger than a hen's.

10. The **Little Tailorbird** uses its sharp beak to pierce holes along the edges of two leaves. It then constructs a nest by neatly stitching the leaves together with pieces of grass.

*   *   *

CLASSIC TRIVIA

Alexander Dumas, author of *The Three Musketeers* and *The Count of Monte Cristo*, always wrote his novels on blue paper, his poetry on yellow paper, and his non-fiction on rose-colored paper. Always—to do otherwise, he explained, was "unspeakable."

• In one production of the opera *Carmen* at New York's Metropolitan Opera House, real horses were used to draw a coach carrying Enrico Caruso and co-star Maria Jeritza onstage. The bright lights and large audience so startled one of the horses that he "expressed his stage fright in a highly unsanitary fashion right on center stage."

• In a following scene, Caruso was supposed to stab Jeritza, and she was supposed to fall to the stage. But she refused to die, even when stabbed. So Caruso stabbed her again and shouted, "Die! Fall, will you!"…to which Jeritza screamed back, "I'll die if you find me a clean place."

When you use your car's brakes, they generate enough heat to warm your house.

STRANGE TOURIST ATTRACTIONS

The next time you're traveling across America, you might want to visit these unusual attractions. (From the hilarious book Roadside America.*)*

T HE NUT MUSEUM
Location: Old Lyme, Connecticut
Background: In 1973 an artist named Elizabeth Tashjian (now known as "The Nut Lady") crammed her antebellum mansion full of nuts, things made from nuts, things that are used with nuts, and things that are inspired by nuts, including the "Nut Anthem," which she wrote herself. "Oh nutttts," she croons, "have a bee-you-tee-ful his-tory and lorrrre…" Her Nut Museum is popular with tourists, despite the fact that the Connecticut Department of Tourism removed it from its official guide in 1988, claiming the house is overrun with squirrels. ("It's a plot," she says.)

Be Sure to See: Large nuts. Small nuts. Nut art. Nuts and nutcrackers living together in peace. "In the outside world, nutcrackers are the nuts' mortal enemy. Here," she says, "nuts and nutcrackers can be friends."

THE RICHARD NIXON LIBRARY AND BIRTHPLACE

Location: Yorba Linda, California

Background: Richard Nixon was born here in 1913; when he died in 1994, he was buried in the yard. Unlike most presidential libraries, the Nixon Library does not accept funding from the federal government, which means that Nixon's cronies (and Nixon himself when he was alive) were free to put their own alternate-reality spin on his failed presidency.

Be Sure to See: The Watergate: The Final Campaign exhibit, where you can listen to the "Smoking Gun" Watergate tape that forced Nixon from office, and then listen to the narrator distort the truth in your headphones: "It was Nixon's critics who call this 'the smoking gun.' But it is not what it once appeared to be….This conversation resulted in no obstruction of justice, and no cover-up resulted from the conversation."

What made the Dickin Medal for Valor unique during WWII? It was awarded to animals.

THE ANNUAL COW CHIP TOSS

Location: Beaver, Oklahoma

Background: Every year, dozens of contestants from as far away as Alaska and more than 2,500 spectators gather to see who can throw a cow chip farther than anyone else. Contestants pay $15.00 for two cow chips: The winner gets a jacket, losers get t-shirts, all of which say, "I Slung Dung." (The world record is 182.3 feet, set in 1979.)

Be Sure to See... The different cow chip-tossing techniques on display, including Frisbee, overhead baseball, and sidearm. "Throwing it like a discus above the head with a lot of back-spin works well," says contestant Brock Russell. "Licking your thumb before each toss helps too.

NATIONAL FRESHWATER FISHING HALL OF FAME

Location: Hayward, Wisconsin

Background: Opened in 1970, this Hall of Fame is housed inside the world's largest fiberglass fish (a muskie), half a city block long and standing four and a half stories tall at its highest point. The mouth doubles as an observation deck.

Be Sure to See: The Hall of Outboard Motors, the minnow bucket exhibit, the Examples of Poor Taxidermy wall, and the Primitive Fisherman and Primitive Fisherman's Son displays (fur-covered mannequins that are supposed to show how cavemen fished). If you'd like to honor the memory of a dead fisherman, you can bake their name into a ceramic brick and have it added to the hall's memorial wall.

*   *   *

KEEP ON TRUCKIN'

According to a poll by American Tours International the "most unexpected" (and unintentional) tourist attractions in the U.S. for foreign visitors are truck stops. Foreigners view truck drivers as "the last cowboys" and like to visit their eating places. Another big attraction: I-90 in South Dakota, "a blacktop with few towns for hundreds of miles."

Bug rule of thumb: Centipedes are carnivores, millipedes are vegetarians.

THE DEVIL'S DICTIONARY

Ambrose Bierce was one of the most famous newspaper columnists of the late 1880s—known as "the wickedest man in San Francisco" at a time when S.F. was a pretty rough-and-tumble town. Although not as popular as Mark Twain, his wit was just as satirical and biting. Case in point: The Devil's Dictionary, a caustic set of definitions for otherwise harmless words, written in installments for his column, then compiled in a book. Your library probably has a copy; if you like dark humor, it's great bathroom reading. Here's a sample of what you'll find in it.

Abstainer, *n.* A weak person who yields to the temptation of denying himself a pleasure.

Alone, *adj.* In bad company.

Bequeath, *v.t.* To generously give to another that which can no longer be denied to *somebody*.

Consult, *v.t.* To seek another's approval of a course already decided on.

Depraved, *p.p.* The moral condition of a gentleman who holds the opposite opinion.

Divorce, *n.* A resumption of diplomatic relations and rectification of boundaries.

Faith, *n.* Belief without evidence in what is told by one who speaks without knowledge, of things without parallel.

Fault, *n.* One of my offenses, as distinguished from one of yours, the latter being crimes.

Forbidden, *p.p.* Invested with a new and irresistible charm.

Governor, *n.* An aspirant to the United States Senate.

Heaven, *n.* A place where the wicked cease from troubling you with talk of their personal affairs, and the good listen with attention while you expound your own.

Homesick, *adj.* Dead broke abroad.

Hypocrite, *n.* One who, professing virtues that he does not respect, secures the advantage of seeming to be what he despises.

Impiety, *n.* Your irreverence toward my diety.

Impunity, *n.* Wealth.

Intimacy, *n.* A relation into which fools are providentially drawn for their mutual destruction.

If you count things compulsively, you're an *arithmomaniac*.

Jealous, *adj.* Unduly concerned about the preservation of that which can be lost only if not worth keeping.

Lawyer, *n.* One skilled in circumvention of the law.

Lecturer, *n.* One with his hand in your pocket, his tongue in your ear, and faith in your patience.

Marriage, *n.* The state or condition of a community consisting of a master, a mistress and two slaves, making in all, two.

Mythology, *n.* The body of a primitive people's beliefs concerning its origin, early history, heroes, dieties and so forth, as distinguished from the true accounts which it invents later.

Novel, *n.* A short story padded.

Once, *adv.* Enough.

Optimism, *n.* The doctrine, or belief, that everything is beautiful, including what is ugly, everything good, especially the bad, and everything right that is wrong.

Pantheism, *n.* The doctrine that everything is God, in contradistinction to the doctrine that God is everything.

Patience, *n.* A minor form of despair, disguised as a virtue.

Piety, *n.* Reverence for the Supreme Being, based upon His supposed resemblance to man.

Politician, *n.* An eel in the fundamental mud upon which the superstructure of organized society is reared.

Pray, *v.* To ask that the laws of the universe be annulled in behalf of a single petitioner, confessedly unworthy.

Rack, *n.* An argumentative implement formerly much used in persuading devotees of a false faith to embrace the living truth....

Reporter, *n.* A writer who guesses his way to the truth and dispels it with a tempest of words.

Road, *n.* A strip of land along which one may pass from where it is too tiresome to be to where it is futile to go.

Selfish, *adj.* Devoid of consideration for the selfishness of others.

Senate, *n.* A body of elderly gentlemen charged with high duties and misdemeanors.

Trial, *n.* A formal inquiry designed to prove and put upon record the blameless characters of judges, advocates and jurors.

Twice, *adv.* Once too often.

Year, *n.* A period of three hundred and sixty-five disappointments.

Zeal, *n.* A certain nervous disorder afflicting the young and inexperienced. A passion that goeth before a sprawl.

VEGETABLE NAMES

More vegetable facts from BRI member Jeff Cheek.

CABBAGE

Originated in Asia and introduced to Europe by Alexander the Great, about 325 B.C. The name comes from the Latin *caput*, meaning "head." It's high in vitamin C, but contains sulphurous compounds that, when cooked, give off odors similar to rotten eggs or ammonia.

SCALLIONS

These tiny green onions owe their name to the biblical city of Ashkelon. When the Romans conquered the city, they called the tiny onions *caepa Ascolonia* or "onions of Ashkelon." This became "scallions."

JERUSALEM ARTICHOKES

These sweet, starchy roots did not grow in Jerusalem and they are not artichokes. Native Americans used them as bread. The mix-up came when a Spanish explorer thought they were some kind of sunflower. *Girasol* (turn to the sun) is "sunflower" in Spanish. An American heard it as "Jerusalem." No one knows why he also added "artichoke."

BROCCOLI

The word comes from the Latin *bracchium*, or "branch." It was developed about 2,500 years ago on the island of Cyprus and was a popular dish at ancient Roman banquets. (The Roman emperor Tiberius, who ruled from 14 to 37 A.D., once publicly scolded his son for eating all the broiled broccoli at a state banquet.) It was popularized in the U.S. by Italian immigrants.

KIWI FRUIT

Originally from China, they were imported to New Zealand in the early 1900s and renamed "Chinese Gooseberry." They finally made it to the U.S. in 1962, and a Los Angeles distributor named Frieda Caplan named it after the New Zealand national bird, the kiwi. It took 18 years before the American public started buying it.

CANTALOUPE

A type of muskmelon brought to Italy from Armenia in the first century A.D., and grown in the town of Cantalupo, which is where it gets its name.

Second most-published playwright in history, after Shakespeare: Neil Simon.

STRANGE ANIMAL LAWSUITS

In the Middle Ages, it was not unusual for animals to be put on trial as if they could understand human laws. These lawsuits were serious affairs.

THE PLAINTIFFS: Vineyard growers in St.-Julien, France
THE DEFENDANTS: Weevils
THE LAWSUIT: In 1545 angry growers testified to a judge that the weevils were eating and destroying their crops. According to one source: "Legal indictments were drawn, and the insects were actually defended in court."
THE VERDICT: Since the weevils were obviously eating the crops, they were found guilty. In 1546 a proclamation was issued by the judge demanding that the weevils desist...and amazingly, they did. The farmers weren't bothered by weevils again until 1587. Once more, the insects were put on trial; however, the outcome is unknown.

THE PLAINTIFFS: The people of Mayenne, France
THE DEFENDANT: Mosquitoes
THE LAWSUIT: In the 1200s, a swarm of mosquitoes were indicted as a public nuisance by the people of the town. When the bugs failed to answer the summons, the court appointed a lawyer to act on their behalf.
THE VERDICT: The lawyer did such a good job pleading their case that the court took pity. The judge banished them, but gave them a patch of real estate outside town where they would be allowed to swarm in peace "forever."

THE PLAINTIFF: The city of Basel, Switzerland
THE DEFENDANT: A rooster
THE LAWSUIT: In 1474 the rooster was accused of being (or helping) a sorcerer. The reason, according to the prosecutor: it had laid eggs...and as everyone knows, an egg laid by a rooster is prized by sorcerers. On top of that, it was shown "that Satan employed

witches to hatch such eggs, from which proceeded winged serpents most dangerous to mankind."

The rooster's lawyer admitted it had laid an egg, but contended that "no injury to man or beast had resulted." And besides, laying an egg is an involuntary act, he said, so the law shouldn't punish it.

THE VERDICT: The judge refused to allow the lawyer's argument and declared the rooster guilty of sorcery. Both the unfortunate fowl and the egg it had allegedly laid were burned at the stake.

THE PLAINTIFFS: Barley growers in Autun, France
THE DEFENDANTS: Rats
THE LAWSUIT: In 1510 the rodents were charged with burglary, having eaten and destroyed the barley crop. A young lawyer named Bartholomew de Chassenée was appointed to defend them. When the rats failed to appear in court, Chassenée successfully argued that since the case involved all the rats of the diocese (the area under jurisdiction of one bishop), all of them should be summoned. When the rats failed to appear again, Chasenée argued that it was because they were scared by "evilly disposed cats which were in constant watch along the highways." Since, by law, the rats were entitled to protection to and from court, the plaintiffs "should be required to post a bond" that would be forfeited if the cats attacked the rats on their way to court.
THE VERDICT: Unknown, but the publicity from the case helped Chasenée to establish a reputation as a sharp lawyer. In fact, many historians now regard him as one of France's greatest lawyers.

THE PLAINTIFF: The Grand Vicar of Valence, France
THE DEFENDANTS: Caterpillars inhabiting his diocese
THE LAWSUIT: In 1584 the Grand Vicar excommunicated the insects for causing destruction to crops, and ordered them to appear before him. When they didn't appear, a lawyer was appointed to defend them.
THE VERDICT: The lawyer argued his case, but lost. The caterpillars were banished from the diocese. "When the caterpillars failed to leave, the trial continued until the short-lived caterpillars died off. The Vicar was then credited with having miraculously exterminated them."

POLI-TALKS

More quotes from (and about) our revered politicians.

"I think it's about time we voted for senators with breasts. After all, we've been voting for boobs long enough."
—Claire Sargent, Arizona senate candidate in 1992, on women candidates

"Elvis is in fact a Republican."
—John Kasich (R-Ohio) House budget chief, in 1995

"They told me to go for the jugular—so I did. It was mine."
—Bob Dole, on the 1976 failure of the Ford–Dole ticket

"Most people don't have the luxury of living to be 80 years old, so it's hard for me to feel sorry for them."
—Phil Gramm, opposing medical treatment for the elderly

"It's hard for somebody to hit you when you've got your fist in their face."
—James Carville, on the usefulness of negative campaigning

"If God had wanted us to vote, he would have given us candidates."
—Jay Leno

"Politics is show business for ugly people."
—Paul Begala, Clinton's campaign adviser

"Washington is Salem. If we're not lynching somebody 24 hours a day in this wretched town, we're not happy."
—Tom Korologos, Washington lobbyist

"That's a good question. Let me try to evade you."
—Paul Tsongas, presidential candidate, in 1992

"Look, half the time when I see the evening news, I wouldn't be for me, either."
—Bill Clinton, in 1995

"Democracy is the process by which people choose the man who'll get the blame."
—Bertrand Russell

"Unlike the president, I inhaled. And then I threw up."
—Christine Todd Whitman, governor of New Jersey

"If hypocrisy were gold, the Capitol would be Fort Knox."
—Sen. John McCain

IN 2000, YOU'LL WEAR...

Some predictions made by top fashion designers in 1981 about what you'd be wearing in the year 2000. Check your wardrobe to see if they were right. From our book, Uncle John's Indispensable Guide to the Year 2000.

SOLAR-POWERED CLOTHES
"Solar power packs, which will be designed into the shoulders of the garment, will draw energy from the sun and store it. Tubes to distribute this energy will extend from the shoulders through the entire suit. The retentive fibers will heat in the winter and cool in the summer by means of a control system."

—Larry Le Gaspi

DISPOSABLE CLOTHING
"A superb paper throwaway dress...will have all the texture and quality of silk or cotton. The elite will wear limited editions of paper dresses signed by the most outstanding artists of the time."

—Mary McFadden

PUSH-BUTTON WARDROBE
"We will press a button to formulate our clothing....Do we want it to be opaque, should it give off steam, do we want it to light up, do we want it to sparkle or do we prefer a matte finish, do we want it to glow in the dark?"

—Betsy Johnson

LOIN-CLOTHS
"In our own homes we will wear only the essentials; we will be Tarzan and Jane in a cushioned, caressing jungle."

—Chevali

FORMAL ATTIRE
"I envision a woman in a vaporous dress, entering a spatial gray-and-black Rolls-Royce which will cross the universe for a party on Venus, where all the men will be dressed in black tie."

—Jean-Baptiste Caumont

COLORED SKIN

"A person will be able to change the color of his skin at will."

—Louis Feraud

THE SAME OLD STUFF

"We will never lose the nostalgia for another era. By the year 2001, people may be nostalgic for the eighties."

—Bill Blass

*   *   *   *

RANDOM THOUGHTS ABOUT THE NEW MILLENNIUM

It's Our Party

"Time has no divisions to mark its passage. There is never a thunderstorm or blare of trumpets to announce the beginning of a new month or year. Even when a new century begins, it is only we mortals who ring bells and fire off pistols."

—Thomas Mann,
The Magic Kingdom

Post-Millennium Depression

"Someday soon, when the last millennial cookie has been eaten and the last deadline for the end of the world has passed uneventfully, we're going to wake up and find ourselves embarked on the 21st century, third millennium of the Common Calendar. It might not be so easy to handle. ...The odds are we'll see a sort of calendrical postpartum depression.

"After all, we were born in the 1900s. We're used to standing at the end of an era, looking backward...Now the curtain's going up on a whole new show, and we can only be around for the tiniest slice of the opening act."

—Gail and Dan Collins,
The Millennium Book

In 2000...

"Authors of self-help books will be required to provide proof that they have actually helped themselves."

—Jane Wagner, *Ms.* magazine, 1990

You can buy horseradish ice cream in Tokyo.

WEIRD DOLL STORIES

Maybe it's because they look human that dolls seem to inspire such bizarre behavior in people. Here are a few examples.

STAR TREK'S MR. SPOCK DOLL

In 1994, England, under the auspices of the European Union, slapped import quotas on all "nonhuman creature" dolls manufactured in China. The quota did not apply to human dolls, which meant that Captain Kirk dolls were allowed into the country. But the quota *did* apply to Mr. Spock, since he is a Vulcan and therefore a nonhuman creature (even though Spock's mother was human). "It seems very strange," said Peter Waterman, a spokesperson for the British toy industry, "that we should have customs officials involved in a discussion of whether Mr. Spock is an alien or a human being."

GROWING UP SKIPPER

Introduced by Mattel in the spring of 1975, Skipper—Barbie's little sister—really did grow up. When you cranked her arm, she grew one-quarter inch taller and sprouted breasts and an hourglass figure. The doll was attacked by feminists, who charged that the doll was "a grotesque caricature of the female body," and "caters to psychotic preoccupation with instant culture and instant sex object." The doll sold well anyway.

EARRING MAGIC KEN

In 1993 Mattel introduced Earring Magic Ken; a version of Barbie's boyfriend that came with a lavender mesh shirt, a lavender vest, and an earring. It became an instant camp classic in the gay community—which interpreted Ken's choice of clothing and jewelry to mean that there was a very good reason why, after more than 30 years of dating, Barbie and Ken had never gotten married.

Mattel insisted there was no hidden agenda. "The designers were amazed when all of this surfaced," they claimed. Then they took the doll off the market.

Chances are: 13% of the letters in this book are the letter "e".

TALKING BARBIE AND G.I. JOE DOLLS

In 1993 a group calling itself the Barbie Liberation Organization (BLO) claimed it switched the voice boxes on as many as 300 G.I. Joe and Barbie dolls in France, England, and the U.S. at the peak of the Christmas shopping season, to protest "gender-based stereotyping in children's toys." So when kids opened their G.I. Joes, they said things like, "I love school. Don't you?" and "Let's sing with the band tonight" in a female voice; Barbie said "Dead men tell no lies," in a deep, booming male voice.

TELETUBBIES

In 1998—shortly after televangelist Jerry Falwell attacked Tinky-Winky as a stalking-horse for gay culture—a woman who bought a Teletubby at a New York toy store claimed that when she got the doll home, it shouted obscenities like "bite my butt" and whispered anti-gay remarks. A spokesman for the manufacturer said that the doll, named Po, was actually bilingual—and was saying "Faster, faster!" in Cantonese.

THE CABBAGE PATCH SNACKTIME DOLL

The 1996 Snacktime doll came with a motorized set of gears that powered its lower jaw, allowing it to chew and "eat" plastic carrots and cookies. That, however, was not all it liked to eat—in 1997 the Consumer Produce Safety Commission received more than 100 reports of children getting their fingers and hair stuck in the mechanical mouth, "which would not stop chewing until the battery back was removed." Mattel later admitted that it had not fully tested the product, withdrew the doll from the market, and offered to buy back dolls for $40 apiece. Only about 1,000 of the 500,000 dolls sold were returned.

FURBIES

In 1999, the National Security Agency issued a Furby Alert, warning that the dolls—which come with sophisticated computer chips that allow it to record and mimic human speech—might "overhear secret information and 'start talking classified,'" inadvertently passing secret information along to America's enemies. Accordingly, Furbies were banned from sensitive areas in the Pentagon.

FAMOUS FOR 15 MINUTES

Here's more proof that Andy Warhol was right when he said that "in the future, everyone will be famous for 15 minutes."

THE STAR: Scott O'Grady, a U.S. Air Force captain
THE HEADLINE: *Downed Pilot Dodges Serbs, U.S. Media*
WHAT HAPPENED: In June 1995, O'Grady's F-16 was shot down over Serb-controlled Bosnian territory. He ejected safely...but as he parachuted to the ground, he could see Serb soldiers watching him float to earth. America held its breath as rescue operations took place. And somehow O'Grady evaded capture. He spent the next six days hiding under leaves, surviving on roots and bugs until the Marines were able to air-lift him to safety. His only injury: "trench foot," from wearing his boots for six days straight.
THE AFTERMATH: O'Grady made a few appearances on network news shows, and was guest of honor at President Clinton's State of the Union Address in 1996. He also wrote a book describing his experience, but generally avoided media interviews and kept a low profile. "He just wants his identity back," his father explained to *Time* magazine. "He wants to be a normal human being."

THE STAR: Greg Willig, 27-year-old toymaker from Queens
THE HEADLINE: *Toy Man Takes on Twin Towers*
WHAT HAPPENED: One afternoon in 1976, Willig noticed how beautiful the World Trade Center looked in the afternoon sun. "The light was reflecting off the building," he says, "and I thought of climbing it. It was like an epiphany—I was somehow irresistibly drawn to it."

On May 26, 1977, after about a year of preparation, Willig made the climb. Using handmade anchoring devices that he stuck into window-washing tracks, he scaled the 1,350 feet of the World Trade Center's South Tower in three and a half hours. Practically the whole time, news helicopters were circling, broadcasting the story.

In 1912 the Archbishop of Paris declared dancing the tango a sin.

When Willig got to the 55th floor, two policemen were lowered from the roof in a window-washer's bucket to talk him out of going any farther. When that failed, they quizzed him to see if he was insane. "Every response he gave was reasonable," one of the officers said. "The only thing unreasonable about it was that he was on the outside of the building."

THE AFTERMATH: Willig's brush with fame began the moment he made it to top, where police asked for his autograph before slapping on handcuffs and taking him to jail. Released on bail, he made appearances on the *Today Show* and *Good Morning America*. He also gave interviews to dozens of newspapers, magazines, and radio stations. But fearing he'd become "a sideshow attraction," Willig turned down offers to climb other buildings for money.

The city of New York charged Willig with criminal trespass, reckless endangerment, and disorderly conduct, and sued him for $250,000 (the cost of police overtime and the fuel used by the police helicopter), to discourage copycat "human flies"...but Mayor Abe Beame eventually reduced the amount to $1.10, a penny for each floor. Today Willig limits his climbs to mountains and rocks.

THE STAR: Wilhelm von Struensee
THE HEADLINE: *You've Got Mail! So Does Your Husband! And His Is Better Than Yours!*
WHAT HAPPENED: When Susan von Struensee moved to a new apartment in 1996, she listed both her husband Wilhelm and herself in the telephone directory. The only catch: she didn't have a husband—"Wilhelm von Struensee" was a name she added to her phone listing to discourage crank callers.

Susan didn't get crank calls, but Wilhelm got junk mail—lots of it—and Susan noticed that much of "his" junk mail was better than hers. For example: "I was thinking of joining AAA one winter," she says. "When Wilhelm got a free AAA membership and I didn't, I realized they assumed the men in marriages made all the decisions." Likewise, Cambridge Savings Bank invited Wilhelm (but not Susan) to a branch opening, and the Mt. Auburn Hospital sent him (but not her) a letter promoting its health services.

Susan filed a complaint with the Massachusetts Commission Against Discrimination.

No sweat: It takes twice as long to lose new muscle if you stop working out than it did to gain it.

THE AFTERMATH: When the story was picked up by wire services, newspapers all over the country published articles about Wilhelm. He became the most famous non-person ever listed in a Massachusetts telephone directory.

THE STAR: Joseph Hazelwood, captain of the Exxon *Valdez*

THE HEADLINE: *Captain's Career, and 1,500 miles of Alaskan Shoreline, Come to Oily End in Prince William Sound*

WHAT HAPPENED: On March 24, 1989, the Exxon *Valdez* oil tanker ran aground off the coast of Alaska, spilling 11 million gallons of oil over 10,000 square miles of water and 1,500 miles of shoreline. It was the worst oil spill in U.S. history. Hazelwood, who admitted to having consumed at least three drinks ashore before boarding the ship, had gone below and left his third mate and helmsman in charge of the ship. He was vilified by media all over the world as "a drunk who left his post."

THE AFTERMATH: Although he flunked the sobriety test administered 11 hours after the accident, Hazelwood was acquitted of operating a tanker while intoxicated. He was, however, convicted of misdemeanor negligence, fined $50,000, and sentenced to 1,000 hours of community service. He also had his captain's license suspended for nine months for leaving the bridge. Then he dropped out of the public eye. Although he was legally qualified to captain any ship on any ocean, he wasn't able to find work; no shipping company would risk the bad publicity. Instead, he worked as a lobster fisherman, boat transporter, and even as an instructor at New York's Maritime College, teaching students "how to stand watch on the bridge of a tanker."

*　　*　　*　　*

IRONIC DEATH

Lieutenant Andrew Bright. Credited as "the first Englishman ever to wear suspenders."

Final Irony: "Lieutenant Bright never quite got the hang of them, it seems. Forgetting he had them on one day, Bright tried to take his trousers off while still wearing his jacket. Tangled in the galluses, he knocked over a candle and perished in the ensuing fire."

Q: What's the average age kids begin to use a microwave? A: Seven.

HOW TO MAKE A MONSTER, PART III

Here's the third installment of the Godzilla
story. (Part I starts on page 133.)

COMING TO AMERICA
Gojira's box-office success in Japan caught the attention of American movie studios; in 1955 Joseph E. Levine of TransWorld Films bought the film's U.S. rights for $25,000. The spelling of the monster's name was changed to Godzilla, an approximation of how it was pronounced in Japanese (GO-dzee-la); and the title was changed to *Godzilla, King of the Monsters.*

Levine knew that if he released *Godzilla* with Japanese dialogue, it would appeal only to art-house film crowds—and he wouldn't make back his investment. A subtitled film would miss the youth audience entirely, since many kids were too young to read them. So Levine adapted the film for Americans by dubbing it into English.

MADE IN USA

It wasn't the only change Levine made: The plot was revised, scenes were rearranged or removed entirely, and brand-new scenes were filmed to insert an American character into the previously all-Japanese film. The American, played by Raymond Burr (of TV's *Ironsides* and *Perry Mason*), is a newspaper reporter named Steve Martin who happens to be on assignment in Japan when Godzilla goes on the attack.

Burr couldn't appear on screen at the same time as the Japanese actors in the original version of the film, but numerous scenes of Japanese actors talking to one another were re-edited to make it look like they were talking to him.

FROM A TO B

The effect of Levine's changes was to turn what had been a polished, serious film for adults into a monster movie made for drive-in movie theaters and kiddie matinees. But that was precisely what he wanted: In the mid-1950s, the American film industry was in a slump. The advent of television, combined with laws that had

---

Q: What, in 1952, did Einstein call "the most difficult thing to understand?" A: Income taxes.

forced the major studios to sell off their theater chains, caused a dramatic drop in movie attendance and movie profits. Major studios became extremely cautious, making fewer A-films than they had in the 1940s.

As a result, several companies sprang up to make cheapo B-movies for drive-ins and faded downtown movie palaces. Then, along came *Gojira*. "Though a big budget, major studio film in Japan," Stuart Galbraith writes in *Monsters are Attacking Tokyo!*, "the Americanized Gojira was released [solely] as an exploitation feature." Because it was intended for the B-movie market, the changes were done on the cheap, which lowered the quality of the American version of the film. The poor dubbing and sophomoric dialogue made it difficult for Western filmgoers, already used to clichéd American monster movies, to take the film seriously. And they didn't.

SON(S) OF GODZILLA

Say what you will about the changes Levine made to the original *Gojira*, he knew his audience. *Godzilla, King of the Monsters*, opened in the U.S. on April 26, 1956, and made more than $2 million at the box office, an astonishing sum for the 1950s. The American version did so well that it was exported back to Japan under the title *Monster King Godzilla* (Raymond Burr's dialogue was dubbed into Japanese), where it added to the profits already made by the original *Gojira*. And Burr's character was so popular with Japanese audiences that reporter characters became a staple of later Godzilla movies in the 1960s and 1970s.

Enthused by the success of the first *Gojira* film, Toho ordered up the first of what would become more than 20 sequels. *Gojira's Counterattack* (the U.S. version was called *Gigantis the Fire Monster*) was released in 1955. Toho made nine non-Gojira monster movies between 1955 and 1962, featuring such monsters such as the Abominable Snowman, and a robot mole named Mogera. But as J. D. Lees writes in *The Official Godzilla Compendium*, the release of *King Kong vs. Godzilla* in 1962 made Godzilla a superstar. "The pairing with the famous ape elevated Godzilla from the swelling ranks of interchangeable atomic monsters of the fifties and placed him among the classic pantheon of cinema creatures."

GODZILLA FLICKS

• **Godzilla Raids Again (1955).** The first cheesy Godzilla sequel, it was brought to America in 1959 as *Gigantis the Fire Monster*, to avoid confusion with the original. Plot: "Yearning for a change of pace, the King of Monsters opts to destroy Osaka instead of Tokyo, but the spiny Angorous is out to dethrone our hero. Citizens flee in terror when the battle royale begins." *Director:* Ishiro Honda (*Videohound's Golden Movie Retriever*)

• **King Kong vs. Godzilla (1963).** Developed from an idea by Willis O'Brien, creator of the original *King Kong's* stop-motion animation. O'Brien's story was about a fight between Kong and "the Ginko," a monster made by Dr. Frankenstein's grandson. But the only studio willing to make the film was Toho—and they insisted on using Godzilla. The Japanese played it as a satire, with the two monsters wrestling in Tokyo (where else?) and on top of Mt. Fuji. King Kong wins. *Director:* Ishiro Honda (*A Critical History of Godzilla*)

• **Godzilla vs. Mothra (1964).** Released as *Godzilla vs. the Thing*. "When the egg of giant monster Mothra is washed ashore by a storm, a greedy entrepreneur is quick to exploit it. Meanwhile, Godzilla reappears and goes on a rampage....Godzilla, who seems to be really enjoying his reign of destruction, shows more personality than in previous appearances....Excellent in all departments." *Director:* Ishiro Honda (*Cult Flicks and Trash Pics*)

• **Godzilla vs. Monster Zero (1965).** "Novel Godzilla adventure with the big guy and Rodan in outer space. Suspicious denizens of Planet X require the help of Godzilla and Rodan to rid themselves of the menacing Ghidra, whom they refer to as Monster Zero. Will they, in return, help Earth as promised, or is this just one big, fat double cross?" *Director:* Ishiro Honda (*Videohound's Golden Movie Retriever*)

• **Godzilla vs. Sea Monster (1968).** "This exercise in cardboard mayhem stars the saucy saurian as a crusty critter suffering a case of crabs when he's attacked by colossal crustaceans (notably Ebirah, a giant lobster) and does battle with the Red Bamboo bad-guy gang." *Director:* Jun Fukuda (*Creature Features Movie Guide Strikes Again*)

• **Godzilla on Monster Island (1972).** "In this harmless, toy-like movie, Godzilla talks, as he and spiny Angillus battle alien-summoned Ghidrah and new playmate Gigan, who has a buzzsaw in his belly." *Director:* Jun Fukuda (*Leonard Maltin's Movie & Video Guide*)

• **Godzilla vs. the Smog Monster (1972).** "A Japanese industrial city has an ecology woe; its bay of waste and rotting animal life breeds Hedorah, which shoots laser beams from its eyepods and flies at will....To the rescue comes the flat-footed Godzilla to indulge in a duel-of-the-titans." Godzilla flies in this one, and it looks really cheap—"the army consists of about 10 guys." *Director:* Yoshimitsu Banno (*Creature Features Movie Guide Strikes Again*)

• **Godzilla vs. Megalon (1973).** "The 400-foot-tall green lizard is aided by a jet-packed robot in fighting off Megalon (a giant cockroach with Zap Killer Beam), Baragon the stomper, and a race of underground Earthlings, the Seatopians." *Director:* Jun Fukuda (*Creature Features Movie Guide Strikes Again*)

• **Godzilla vs. the Cosmic Monster (1974).** Japanese sci-fi sukiyaki with the King of Monsters battling a cyborg Godzilla controlled by aliens bent on conquest. A huge rodent creature said to embody Asian spirits comes to the real Godzilla's aid when the languid lizard squares off against antagonistic Angorus." *Director:* Jun Fukuda (*Creature Features Movie Guide Strikes Again*)

• **Godzilla: 1985 (1984).** "After 30 years, the Big G recovers from his apparent death...and returns to destroy Tokyo all over again. Disregarding the previous fourteen sequels (most of which were set in "the future" anyway), the plot marches along much like a '70s disaster film." *Director:* Kohji Hashimoto. (*Cult Flicks and Trash Pics*)

• **Godzilla vs. Biollante (1989).** "Genetic scientist Surigama uses cells from Godzilla's body to create hardy new crop strains, while also splicing the cells' DNA to that of his dead daughter, using that of her favorite rose as a catalyst. His experiments result in the gigantic plant/animal monster Biollante, a nightmare of creeping vines, snapping teeth, and corrosive sap." *Director:* Kazuki Ohmori (*Cult Flicks and Trash Pics*)

• **Godzilla (1998).** Charmless big-bucks travesty starring Matthew Broderick. Bad career move.

their first trimester are: 1) frogs; 2) worms; 3) potted plants.

WORD ORIGINS

Here are some more interesting word origins.

PUNCH
Meaning: A fruity drink
Origin: "From Sanskrit *panca* or Hindustani *panch*, which means 'five,' the theory being that there were five ingredients—alcohol, water, lemon, sugar, and spice." (From *The Story Behind the Word*, by Morton S. Freeman)

EAVESDROP
Meaning: Secretly listen to someone else's conversation
Origin: "In Anglo-Saxon England, a house had very wide overhanging eaves…to allow rain to drip safely away from the house's foundation. So the *eavesdrip*, later the *eavesdrop*, provided a place where one could hide to listen clandestinely to conversation within the house." (From *Morris Dictionary of Word and Phrase Origins*, by William and Mary Morris)

CHEAT
Meaning: A dishonest person; the act of deceiving someone for gain
Origin: Comes from *escheat*—a medieval legal term for "the reversion of property to the state in the absence of legal heirs, and of the state's rights to such confiscation. The officer who looked after the king's *escheats* was known as the *cheater*….The dishonest connotations of the word evolved among thieves in the 16th century." (From *Wicked Words*, by Hugh Rawson)

SNOB
Meaning: A snooty person; someone who puts on airs
Origin: "It seems that Oxford freshmen were required to register 'according to rank.' Those not of noble birth added after their names the phrase *sine nobilitate* which was then abbreviated to 's. nob.,' thus creating…a perfect definition for the commoner who wishes to mingle with the nobles." (From *Dictionary of Word and Phrase Origins, Vol. III*, by William and Mary Morris)

Face value of a Titanic boarding pass auctioned in 1999: $8. It sold for $100,000.

ZANY

Meaning: Crazy

Origin: "Dates back to the commedia dell'arte in Italy of the 16th century. The *zanni* (as it was spelled in Italian) was a buffoon who mimicked one of the characters, usually the clown. The English changed its spelling to *zany* and used it to refer to any simpleton or bumbling fool." (From *Dictionary of Word and Phrase Origins*, *Vol. II*, by William and Mary Morris)

AMBITION

Meaning: Single-minded drive toward achieving a goal

Origin: *Ambitio* is the Latin term for "running around." The term originally referred to the way politicians in ancient Rome ran around "in search of voters to persuade or buy." (From *Loose Cannons and Red Herrings*, by Robert Claiborne)

ALCOHOL

Meaning: An intoxicating beverage

Origin: "The word comes from Arabic *al-kuhul*, a powder used as a cosmetic. Borrowed into English, *alcohol* came to mean any distilled substance. *Alcohol of wine* was thus the 'quintessence of wine'…by the middle of the 18th century *alcohol* was being used on its own." (From *Dictionary of Word Origins*, by John Ayto)

DIAPER

Meaning: A cloth used to capture a baby's waste

Origin: "From Greek *diaspros*, meaning 'pure white'.…Originally, a fabric woven of silk, sewn with gold threads, and used for ecclesiastical robes." (From *Thereby Hangs a Tale*, by Charles Earle Funk)

DOODLE

Meaning: Aimless, absent-minded scribbles on scraps of paper

Origin: "The word *doodle* comes from the German word *dudeln*, meaning 'to play the bagpipe.' The notion seems to be that a person who spends his time playing bagpipes would be guilty of other frivolous time-wasting activities." (From *Dictionary of Word and Phrase Origins*, *Vol. III*, by William and Mary Morris)

PLAYMATE IQ TEST

In 1997, two Playboy "Playmates of the Year"—Julie Cialini (1995) and Stacy Sanches (1996)—showed up on Howard Stern's radio show. Because playmates are role models for young girls everywhere, Stern asked a few questions to test the gals' grasp of current affairs. Here's the text of the quiz.

Q: *Who is the President of Russia?*
Julie: "Gorbachev."
Stacy: "Gretzky."
(CORRECT ANSWER: Boris Yeltsin.)

Q: *What is the center of our solar system?*
Julie: "The equator."
Stacy: "The moon."
(CORRECT ANSWER: The sun.)

Q: *Define the NAACP.*
Julie: "Something, something, something, for Certified Pianists."
Stacy: "It's some kind of police organization."
(CORRECT ANSWER: National Association for the Advancement of Colored People.)

Q: *Who invented the lightbulb?*
Julie: "I know Edison invented the telephone, but I can't remember the lightbulb guy."
Stacy: "I don't know."
(CORRECT ANSWER: Thomas Edison. Alexander Graham Bell was the telephone guy.)

Q: *Who's the Speaker of the House?*
Julie: "Gore or something-or-other."
Stacy: "Bill Clinton."
(CORRECT ANSWER [in 1997]: Newt Gingrich.)

Q: *Define the meaning of the letters CIA.*
Julie: "I don't know."
Stacy: "Certified Investigation Association."
(CORRECT ANSWER: Central Intelligence Agency.)

To give the playmates better odds, Stern tried a few "industry-related" questions.

Q: *What do the initials "DK" stand for?*
A: Both playmates knew it was fashion designer Donna Karan.

Q: *What car company has a model known as "911"?*
A: Both knew it was Porsche.

Q: *Whose face is on the $100 bill?*
A: Both knew it was Ben Franklin.

Drop off to sleep as soon as you go to bed? Sleep experts say that's a sign that you're sleep deprived.

A STRAIGHT FACE

Uncle John was reading a copy of Newsweek *magazine in the…
uh…library, and discovered this article, by Seth Stevenson. For
anyone who's ever wondered how some poker players can be so
consistently good at a game of "chance," here's the answer.*

WELCOME TO LAS VEGAS

The World Series of Poker: the Earth's greatest liars gathered together with millions of dollars on the line. In one sprawling room of Binion's Horseshoe Casino [in Las Vegas, Nevada], they duel for flat-out psychological domination. Cards fly to and fro, chips get stacked in strange architectures and cocktail waitresses glide by with coffee and bottled water. It's blur of action, but the educated spectator ignores these distractions and focuses on the players' mannerisms—it's all part of the science of "tells," reflexes a player can't control that, read right, give away his thoughts….Every eyebrow tic, every hand jitter, presents a clue to what cards they're holding. To play world-class poker is to read emotions in an instant, with a single glance; to intuit everything and give nothing away.

DON'T ASK, DON'T TELL

Binion's lies away from the Strip, in the slightly seedy old downtown. Outside, it's a glare-bright day as Mike Caro steers his car through the even seedier Vegas outskirts. The self-proclaimed "Mad Poker Genius," famed author and player, wants this above all to be clear. "Everything's a coin flip, a 50-50 bet, unless you've observed, and taken into account everything around you. It's the same with poker: the more you can take into account, the less the game becomes a coin flip, and the more you have an edge. Reading 'tells' is a huge edge."

We're headed to the Gambler's Book Shop—the resource for students of gambling in all its forms….The shop features the most comprehensive collection of gambling publications in the world. Howard Schwartz, curator of this little museum, takes us deep into the back rooms housing out-of-print horse-betting manuals and blackjack guides. "There's a long history of reading tells," he says, rooting through files for ancient clips. "The old fortunetellers, to find out if they were on the right track, looked at your pupils and your carotid artery to see if you got excited as they talked." Eventually, Schwartz finds studies on tells dating back to the turn of the century. Most gambling books dwell on the numbers—how to play the percentages, not how to read minds. "Of course the percentages are vital in poker," says Caro. "But just crunching the numbers isn't enough."

TELLING WHAT?

In general, weaker players subconsciously act aggressive when their hands are weak, and sad or indifferent when their hands are strong. Caro's long study has revealed several tells of this kind that appear universally in weak and mediocre players. A player who picks up a monster hand will instantly look away from the table: it's a reflex that implies indifference, hoping to cloak the massive excitement the player feels. Conversely, a player trying to win with a weak hand (to bluff) will stare right at opponents—a reflexive aggression masking weakness. Another tell is something Caro calls "pokerclack." If a player looks at his cards and instantly makes a soft clucking sound with his tongue, his hand is excellent. The cluck's a sad sound made subconsciously by an elated player. Hand gestures give you away, too. A flair, a tiny extra motion when placing chips in the pot, suggests a bluff: the player's bolstering a bet he knows is weak. Jittery hands during a bet signal a release of tension when a player thinks he'll win. The key to all these movements: the player doesn't realize he's making them.

DO TELL...

Any decent player will spot and exploit these tells. But excellent players control involuntary reactions in themselves. At the Bellagio poker room, topflight player Mori Eskandani takes me on a tour spanning all levels of play. In low-stakes games, weak players show classic tells—when they get good cards they reflexively touch or look at their chips, just raring to go. But up in the high-stakes room, the pros, playing for thousands of dollars a hand, are a blank slate. "There are about 400 great professional poker players in the world," says Eskandani, "and among them you won't spot 10 tells. Reading them is a much more subtle game."

Still, even among top players, tells show up. But no pro wants to divulge specific tells they have on opponents—then they'd lose that edge. Russ Hamilton, 1994 grand champ, had a tell—he won't say what—on his foe in the final competition. "At the last hand, with everything on the line, I looked over to see if I could spot the tell. But he was eating a cheeseburger so I couldn't use it!" Hamilton won anyway. At one World Series event this year, repeat champion Ted Forrest forces an opponent into a tell. Deciding whether to call a possible bluff, Forrest fakes a move to push all his chips in. His foe almost imperceptibly rocks back in fear. Forrest goes ahead and bets his chips, calling the bluff—and wins.

TELL ME TRUE...
Poker psychology is so complex that top players sometimes fake the tells. Then the decision becomes whether the tell you just saw was a reflex—or acting. Andrew Glazer, a poker scholar and player ...has feigned tells. "I had a monster hand. I wanted the other guy to bet so I could take his money. He stared at me, and I wasn't making a move, so finally I gave a tiny gulp, like I'd had to gulp the whole time and just couldn't hold it. He instantly bet, and I won."

I'm not a pro yet, but after hours of watching the best in the biz, I'm definitely set to bag a few tourist dollars. Moseying in to the low-stakes Hold 'Em game at the Plaza in downtown Vegas, I am quickly confronted with a large bet. My foe stares right at me. I touch my chips. He freezes. I call his bluff—and win.

COMMON POKER "TELLS"
Poker players' natural reflexes give away their hands. The most common "tells:"
- **The Look Away:** Players reflexively glance away from the table when dealt a monster hand, faking indifference.
- **The Stare Down:** Players who draw bad cards glare at opponents aggressively, implying a better hand.
- **The Freeze:** Bluffing players confronted with an opponent's big bet involuntarily cease movement and hold their breath.
- **The Flair:** Players who move chips with panache while betting signal that they're insecure about the hand.
- **The Chip Look:** Players with great cards immediately look at or touch their chips—they're raring to bet.

The largest of the Easter Island statues weighs more than 80 tons.

ON THE MARK

Quotes from America's great humorist, Mark Twain.

"Eloquence is the essential thing in a speech, not information."

"Good breeding consists in concealing how much we think of ourselves and how little we think of the other person."

"There is no sadder sight than a young pessimist."

"If you pick up a starving dog and make him prosperous, he will not bite you. It is the principal difference between a dog and a man."

"Irreverence is the champion of liberty and its one sure defense."

"Let us endeavor so to live, that when we die, even the undertaker will be sorry."

"Noise proves nothing. Often a hen who has merely laid an egg cackles as if she has laid an asteroid."

"All you need in this life is ignorance and confidence, and then Success is sure."

"Against the assault of laughter, nothing can stand."

"Whenever you find you are on the side of the majority, it is time to pause and reflect."

"You can't depend on your eyes if your imagination is out of focus."

"Golf is a good walk spoiled."

"Let us be thankful for fools. But for them the rest of us could not succeed."

"Everything has its limit— iron ore cannot be educated into gold."

"It is easier to stay out than to get out."

"It is noble to teach oneself, but still nobler to teach others—and less trouble."

"I find that the further I go back, the better things were, whether they happened or not."

"Do the thing you fear most and the death of fear is certain."

The average American uses 730 crayons by the age of 10.

BIRTH OF A GIANT, PART II

They never tell you things like this in school, but the father of the modern bathtub—a real bathroom hero—was also the father of General Motors. Or at least the grandfather. Here's Part II of the story. (Part I starts on page 101.)

ON THE ROAD

In 1904 William Crapo Durant became the head of the Buick Motor Company. Durant was so well known as a successful businessman that when he began his first official task, selling stock in Buick to the public, there was no shortage of takers. In a few short months, he had raised Buick's capital from $75,000 to more than $1.5 million.

Next, Durant set to work designing cars, setting up a network of Buick dealers, and building what was then the largest automobile factory in the U.S. The company grew by leaps and bounds: in 1904, Buick had sold fewer than 30 cars in its entire history. By the end of 1906, it had sold more than 2,000 cars, was building 250 new ones a week, and could not keep up with the new orders that were pouring in.

COME TOGETHER

In 1907 a financial panic rocked Wall Street, and although Buick emerged from the crisis even stronger than it had been before, Durant was convinced that the best way to weather future hard times was for the "Big Four" auto companies—Buick, Ford, REO (founded by Ransom E. Olds after he was forced out of the Olds Motor Works), and Maxwell-Briscoe (co-founded by the Briscoe Brothers with the money they made selling their Buick stock)—to merge into one large company. In Durant's vision, each company would swap its own stock for shares in the new company.

According to *A Most Unique Machine*, the scheme might have worked except that Henry Ford wanted $3 million in cash. Not to be outdone by Ford, Olds changed his mind and also insisted on $3 million in cash. Durant didn't have $6 million in cash, so the deal

The blood vessels of a blue whale are so wide that an adult trout could swim through them.

quickly collapsed. On September 1, 1908, Durant created his own new company and called it General Motors.

BOOM AND BUST

Two months after he founded General Motors, Durant bought the Olds Motor Works. The company had fallen on hard times since Ransom Olds had left to found a new company (REO); and as Durant soon learned, there weren't even any plans in the works for new Oldsmobiles. "We just paid a million dollars for road signs," he complained to an assistant.

A few days later, Durant came up with an idea for a quick fix: He showed up at the Olds plant with a new Buick and had workers saw the car's chassis into quarters. He moved the left and right sides of the car six inches apart and lengthened it by a foot.

"Make your new car a little longer, a bit wider, and with more leg room than my Buick," he told the workers. "It will look like an Oldsmobile when you put your radiator and hood on it. And there with paint and upholstery, is next year's Oldsmobile." The new car, priced at $250 more than the Buick, sold so well that the Olds division was making a profit by the end of the year.

Two months later, Durant bought the Oakland Motor Car Company, the predecessor to GM's Pontiac division; six months after that, he bought Cadillac, then one of the most profitable auto manufacturers in the country. In the meantime, he also snapped up a number of companies that supplied GM with auto parts.

BYE-BYE, BILLY

If Durant had stopped there, GM might have remained healthy. But he didn't. "Instead of consolidating his gains around the great Buick and Cadillac potential, and their suppliers such as Weston-Mott and AC Sparkplug," Richard Crabb writes in *Birth of a Giant*, "Durant brought into General Motors a long list of firms that held patents on devices which he thought might provide important improvements for future....He chased patents as some boys chase butterflies."

By the end of 1909, Durant had acquired 13 different auto companies and 10 auto parts companies, most of which were money losers that drained profits from his healthy divisions.

Home entertainment: 63% of American adults will rent at least one video this month.

Things came to a head in 1910, when sales at Buick and Cadillac slumped to the point where Durant didn't have enough cash to make his payroll and pay his bills.

Durant figured he would need about $7 million to weather the crisis, but he wasn't sure—he had acquired companies so fast and kept so many of the details in his head that GM's financial records were several weeks behind. By the time the records were sorted out, it turned out that Durant actually needed more than $12 million to meet his obligations.

Durant's bankers were aghast at the mess he had made of GM, but the company had grown so big so fast that they could hardly afford to let it fail: if GM crashed, it might take the entire Detroit economy with it. So they lent GM the money it needed...on the condition that Durant turn over control of GM to the bankers themselves, who would oversee the running of the company until the loans were repaid.

There was no other way out, so on November 15, 1910, Durant announced his retirement.

For Part III of the GM story, turn to page 401.

*   *   *

YOUR TAX DOLLARS AT WORK

"A Pentagon inspector general's report released in 1989 revealed that the Navy was sinking its surplus ships without first stripping them of valuable equipment. The report stated, 'We feel confident that public property valued in excess of $17 million was destroyed.' Among the items that could have been retrieved and sold were new mattresses (still in their plastic packaging), bandsaws, milling machines, motors, and lathes, as well as all types of furniture, gold and silver (in the communications equipment), brass, copper, ovens, radio equipment, cryptologic equipment, surgical equipment, and pumps. Investigators inspecting retired ships that were destined to be sunk noted the presence on board of numerous spare parts that were still being bought by the Navy."

—*Stupid Government Tricks,*
by John Kohut

WHAT'S IN A NAME?

*Product names don't necessarily reflect the product,
but rather the image that manufacturers want to
project. Were you fooled by these?*

CORINTHIAN LEATHER

Sounds Like: Fancy leather from some exotic place in Europe—specifically, the Greek city of Corinth. The phrase "rich Corinthian leather" was made famous by actor Ricardo Montalban, in ads for Chrysler's luxury Cordoba in the 1970s. (The seats were covered with it.)

The Truth: There's no such thing as Corinthian leather. The term was made up by Chrysler's ad agency. The leather reportedly came from New Jersey.

HÄAGEN DAZS

Sounds Like: An imported Scandinavian product.

The Truth: It was created by Ruben Mattus, a Polish immigant who sold ice cream in New York City, who used what the *New York Times* called the Vichyssoise Strategy:

> Vichyssoise is a native New Yorker. Created at the Ritz Carlton in 1917, it masqueraded as a French soup and enjoyed enormous success. When Mattus created his ice cream, he used the same tactic....He was not the first to think Americans would be willing to pay more for a better product. But he was the first to understand that they would be more likely to do so if they thought it was foreign. So he made up a ridiculous, impossible to pronounce name, [and] printed a map of Scandinavia on the carton.

The ice cream was actually made in Teaneck, New Jersey.

JELL-O PUDDING POPS

Sounds Like: There's pudding in the pops.

The Truth: There isn't. Family secret: One of Uncle John's relatives was involved with the test-marketing the product several decades ago. When John asked him about it, he laughed, "Our research shows people think that if it says 'pudding' on the label, it's better quality or better for you. They're wrong. It's really the

---

World's highest fast-food restaurant: McDonald's in La Paz, Bolivia, at 11,000 ft above sea level.

same." Anyway, we suppose that's why they still sell it with "pudding" on the label.

PACIFIC RIDGE PALE ALE, *"brewed in Northern California"*
Sounds Like: A small independent brewer in Northern California. The flyer says:

> Brewmasters Gery Eckman [and] Mitch Steele…always wanted to brew a special ale in Northern California just for California beer drinkers…so they created Pacific Ridge Pale Ale. It's produced in limited quantities, using fresh Cascade hops from the Pacific Northwest, two-row and caramel malts and a special ale yeast for a rich copper color.…Handcrafted only at the Fairfield brewhouse.

The Truth: In tiny letters on the bottle, it says: "Specialty Brewing group of Anheuser-Busch, Inc., Fairfield, California."

SWEET 'N LOW SODA
Sounds Like: The drink was sweetened with nothing but Sweet 'n Low.

The Truth: As Bruce Nash and Allan Zullo write in *The Misfortune 500*, "MBC Beverage Inc., which licensed the Sweet 'N Low name…discovered that consumers wanted the natural sweetener NutraSweet rather than the articifical saccharine of Sweet 'N Low. So they sweetened Sweet 'N Low soda with NutraSweet, a Sweet 'N Low *competitor*."

DAVE'S CIGARETTES
Sounds Like: "A folksy brand of cigarette, produced by a down-to-earth, tractor-driving guy named Dave for ordinary people who work hard and make an honest living." According to humorist Dave Barry, here's the story sent to the media when the cigarettes were introduced in 1996:

> Down in Concord, N.C., there's a guy named Dave. He lives in the heart of tobacco farmland. Dave enjoys lots of land, plenty of freedom and his yellow '57 pickup truck. Dave was fed up with cheap, fast-burning smokes. Instead of just getting mad, he did something about it…Dave's Tobacco company was born.

The Truth: Dave's was a creation of America's biggest cigarette corporation, Philip Morris, whose ad agency unapologetically called the story a "piece of fictional imagery."

Humdinger: Hawaii's state fish is the *humuhumunukunukuapua'a.*

ON BROADWAY

*Many Broadway hits started out with "no legs," but through the
perseverance, pluck, and luck, of people who believed in them,
managed to get on their feet and become runaway hits.*

SOUTH PACIFIC (1949)

When he first read James Michener's *Tales of the South Pacific*
in the late 1940s, director Joshua Logan knew it would make a
great Broadway show. He told producer Leland Hayward, and Hayward agreed—but warned Logan not to mention it to *anyone* until
they owned the rights. Too late: At a party, Logan tipped his cards
to Richard Rodgers—who, with partner Oscar Hammerstein, immediately purchased a controlling 51% interest and went on to write
the music and lyrics. (Logan wound up co-producing it with them.)

They cast Mary Martin, fresh from *Annie Get Your Gun*, and
famed opera singer Ezio Pinza in the lead roles. Martin was afraid
she'd be dwarfed by the Pinza's voice, so the composers avoided
duets. Martin had just cut her hair short and, realizing it would dry
in three minutes, suggested the song "I'm Gonna Wash That Man
Right Out of My Hair," which became a classic.

The play is considered one of the earliest entertainment vehicles
promoting racial tolerance in its portrayal of love between a Naval
officer and a Polynesian woman. *South Pacific* won Tonys in all the
acting categories, captured a Pulitzer Prize, and was the top-grossing
film of 1958.

LIFE WITH FATHER (1939)

The idea for this play comes from a series of autobiographical *New
Yorker* articles about growing up in a Victorian household in New
York City, written by Clarence Day.

At first, producer Oscar Serlin wanted to adapt it for a movie
starring W. C. Fields, but the author's widow was horrified at the
thought of the bulbous-nosed comedian playing the title role.

Serlin switched his sights to Broadway, but investors were ho-
hum about such tame fare on the eve of WWII. Serlin brought in
two writers, Howard Lindsay and Russel Crouse, who so loved the
concept that they worked without payment for two years developing

---

According to Pickle Packers International, the crunch of a pickle should be audible from 10 paces.

scenes for the play. When all major actors rejected the title role, writer Lindsay took it himself. And when the company didn't have enough funds to open in a Maine summer stock production, Lindsay and his wife, Dorothy Stickney ("Mother") mortgaged their home to get it going.

On the eve of the Broadway opening, Lindsay said to Crouse, "We've got a nice little comedy here. We might even get six months out of it." It turned out to be the longest-running of all non-musical shows in Broadway history to date (3,224 performances over eight years). In fact, it so engaged audiences that it was made into a movie in 1947 and a TV series that ran from 1953 to 1955.

THE WIZ (1975)

Producer Ken Harper got the idea of retelling *The Wizard of Oz* using African-American characters, and got 20th Century Fox to invest $650,000. But after disappointing tryouts in Baltimore, he was advised to close it. The director, Gilbert Moses, quit, so Harper replaced him with actor (and costume designer) Geoffrey Holder, who made big changes in cast and concept.

At its Broadway opening, the mostly white critics were disappointed because it "didn't measure up to the original movie." Closing notices were posted that night. But Harper got Fox to mount a huge advertising campaign—TV ads targeting bafrican-Americans. Word of mouth praised the dazzling choreography, staging, and costuming. "The Wiz" stayed open and went on to win seven Tonys, including Best Musical, and was made into a movie in 1978.

THE ODD COUPLE (1965)

"The idea came to me when I was at a party in California," playwright Neil Simon told the *Manchester Guardian*. "There were 24 people there; and do you know that every one of them was a divorcee? The men were either on their second marriage or recently divorced, and the women were in the process of getting divorced. All the men shared apartments because they had to be able to keep up their alimony payments and this was the cheapest method of living....I thought it was a good idea for a play" —and a movie...and a TV show...and a revival of the play...and a sequel to the movie...

Top speed of an abalone on the move: 5 yards per minute.

YOU'RE MY INSPIRATION

*It's always fascinating to find out who, or
what, inspired cultural milestones like these.*

STAR WARS. According to *Leonard Maltin's Movie Guide*, the 1958 Japanese film that was "acknowledged by George Lucas as a primary inspiration for *Star Wars*" is *Hidden Fortress*, directed by Akira Kurosawa. The comedy-adventure "deals with the adventures of a strong-willed princess—à la Carrie Fisher, in the space fantasy—and her wise, sword-wielding protector—Toshiro Mifune, in the role adapted for Alec Guinness," says *Video Guide*. The two other main characters, a pair of bumbling farmers, are said to have been models for C-3PO and R2-D2.

THE "MAN WITH NO NAME." The character in *A Fistful of Dollars* (1964), who made Clint Eastwood a movie star, was also inspired by Kurosawa. "It is almost a scene-for-scene remake of Akira Kurosawa's *Yojimbo*, the tale of a lone samurai (played by Toshiro Mifune) who comes to a town torn by two rival gangs of fighters. He plays them against each other...and in the end finishes off pretty much the whole town and leaves with all the money. Replace a samurai with a gunslinger and replace the Japanese village with a small Western town, and you have *A Fistful of Dollars*." (*Real Video*)

JAMES T. WEST. Robert Conrad, the original star of TV's "Wild, Wild West," fashioned James West's movements after a favorite actor—Toshiro Mifune.

DOLLY PARTON. Her famous "look" was inspired by a woman in her hometown. (No, not Toishiro Mifune.) Parton says: "There was this tramp that lived in our town, I better not say her name, 'cause she's probably got kids and grandkids now. But back then, she wore these bright-colored clothes and she had this peroxide yellow hair—yellow, not blonde—and she used to walk up and down the streets of our hometown and they always said, 'Oh she's just trash, she's just a whore.' But I thought she was beautiful."

Checkers used to be known as "chess for ladies."

IT'S A WEIRD, WEIRD WORLD

More proof that truth really is stranger than fiction.

¡YO QUIERO CASA SANCHEZ!

"A Mexican restaurant in San Francisco offered a lifetime of free lunches to anyone willing to get a tattoo of its logo, Jimmy the Corn Man, a sombrero-wearing mariachi boy riding a blazing corncob. Amazingly, 38 people have braved the needle for a permanent coupon at Casa Sanchez so far. 'I think people have gotten much stupider tattoos for much stupider reasons,' says tattoo artist Barnaby Williams, who created 30 of the 'body coupons.'"

—*USA Today*, **April 13, 1999**

TERRORIST VOGUE

"Carlos the Jackal was one of the world's most notorious and elusive terrorists, accused of 83 deaths worldwide and more than a dozen other charges stemming from a 20-year killing spree.

"After two decades of evading the law, he was arrested in a Sudanese hospital while undergoing liposuction and a tummy tuck."

—*San Francisco Chronicle*

NOSING AROUND

"Ruth Clarke, 23, of London, England, underwent surgery to correct a lifelong breathing problem in 1981. She was presented with a tiddlywink, which doctors had removed from her nose.

"Clarke vaguely recalled losing the disk as a tot, but she didn't dream it was right under her nose all the time."

—*Encyclopedia Brown's Book of Strange Facts*

THE POSTMAN RINGS MORE THAN TWICE

"From 1974 to 1976, a young man in Taiwan who wrote 700 love letters to his girlfriend, trying to talk her into marriage. He succeeded—she married the mailman who delivered the letters to her."

—*Weird News and Strange Stories*

Iron Age magazine once called Theodore Roosevelt "a drunk." He sued, and won 6¢.

THEY WENT THATAWAY

Malcolm Forbes wrote a fascinating book (They Went Thataway) about the deaths of famous people. Here are a few of the stories he found.

ALEXANDER THE GREAT

Claim to Fame: Greek conqueror who lived from 356 B.C. to 323 B.C.

How He Died: Complications stemming from a drinking contest

Postmortem: In 323 Alexander was in Babylon preparing to lead his troops into battle. One evening at a banquet, he got into a drinking contest with some of his soldiers and is believed to have consumed as much as a gallon and a half of wine. He woke up the next morning feeling miserable; a chill brought on by cold weather only made things worse. Ten days later he was dead.

W. C. FIELDS

Claim to Fame: Film comedian and legendary drunk

How He Died: Drank himself to death.

Postmortem: Excessive drinking was the hallmark of Fields's on-screen persona; with his bloated physique and enormous, fleshy red nose, he made a perfect movie buffoon. But if anything, he drank *more* in real life than in his films. He was notorious for polishing off two quarts of gin a day, and as early as 1936 spent a year in a sanatorium recovering from pneumonia and tuberculosis aggravated by drinking. He cut back on the booze…but only until his health returned.

By the early 1940s, decades of hard drinking had damaged Fields's health to the point where he no longer had the strength to appear in feature-length films; he was reduced to making short cameo appearances in heavy pancake makeup that hid the burst veins in his face. When his landlord raised the rent on his house in the fall of 1946, Fields just checked back into the sanatorium. He was failing fast—he had cirrhosis of the liver, cardiac edema, weakened kidneys, and stomach troubles—and the booze that friends smuggled into the sanatorium only made things worse. On Christmas Day in 1946, Fields suffered a massive stomach hemorrhage and died a few hours later. He was 67.

In the 1500s, England's Queen Elizabeth I outlawed wife beating after 10 p.m.

PLINY THE ELDER

Claim to Fame: Preeminent historian and scientist of the ancient Roman Empire. Much of what we know about life in ancient Rome comes from Pliny's numerous writings.

How He Died: Killed by his own curiosity.

Postmortem: One day in 79 A.D., Pliny's sister woke him up from a nap to tell him about a huge cloud of smoke that was rising from the top of a nearby mountain. Pliny, an admiral in the Roman Navy, ordered his ship to investigate.

The mountain was Mt. Vesuvius—an active volcano—and the cloud of smoke was part of an eruption that was burying the city of Pompeii, killing thousands of Romans even as Pliny sailed closer, paying no heed to the huge rocks that were raining down into the waters around his ship.

When his ship got close to the beach, Pliny waded ashore to walk along the base of Mt. Vesuvius and get an even closer look. His companions fled in terror when a huge, ominous-looking black cloud began to descend on the beach, but Pliny did not—and moments later he choked to death in a cloud of sulfurous gas.

MARIE CURIE

Claim to Fame: First woman to win the Nobel Prize (for the story of Alfred Nobel, turn to page 217), for discovering the element radium and pioneering the study of radioactivity

How She Died: Massive radiation poisoning

Postmortem: Although Curie helped discover radioactivity, she never understood its destructive power. She routinely handled radioactive material without any lead shielding, and as a result, suffered from radiation-induced exhaustion and even painful lesions on her hands.

When World War I broke out, Curie went to the battlefields of Europe and exposed herself even further, using primitive X-ray equipment to help surgeons find bullets and shrapnel in wounded soldiers. By the early 1930s, her immune system was so compromised by radiation poisoning that she could no longer fight off common illnesses. In July 1934, she died from anemia, a disease that normally would not have been fatal.

ZZZZ-Z-Z-Z-Z-z

According to experts we've been chatting with, horses, deer and giraffes sleep an average of only 3 hours a day…while cats get a whopping 15 hours. Humans fall between them, with an average of 7.5 hours. What happens during those 7 (or so) hours while you're sleeping? That will probably always be a big mystery, but we have more answers now than we did just half a century ago.

THE MYSTERY OF SLEEP

It wasn't until 1954 that science made a big breakthrough and recognized that REM (rapid eye movement) during sleep was caused by dreaming. Since then, the science of sleep has expanded rapidly, with over 100 distinct sleeping disorders now classified and many doctors devoting their careers exclusively to sleep problems.

Into the Waves

Scientists now recognize four stages of sleep

Stage 1) After your muscles relax, your brain produces smaller waves of 9-12 cycles per second. You think normal, everyday thoughts. Pulse and breathing are regular.

Stage 2) Brian waves get larger with sudden bursts. Your eyes go "off" and wouldn't register anything if they were opened. Eyes may roll slowly back and forth.

Stage 3) Brain waves get slower and bigger, about five times larger than in stage 1.

Stage 4) Profound unconsciousness, with the biggest, slowest brainwaves. It takes over an hour to reach this stage.

Most people only go to stage 4 once or twice, then come back to lighter sleep (generally stage 1), and experience REM (dream-state).

THE REM EXPERIENCE

Once you're in REM…

• The muscles of your middle ear begin vibrating (science doesn't know why).

• Brain waves resemble a waking state, but you're dreaming.

• Muscles are relaxed, but may twitch or move.

In France, it's considered good taste to spread your crackers with pig brain paté.

- Pulse and breathing speed up. But we breathe less oxygen and use fewer calories than in other stages of sleep.
- Blood flow and brain temperature accelerate.
- Eyes dart all over the place, "seeing" what we're dreaming.

The first REM episode averages 10 minutes; then episodes recur on a 90 to 100-minute cycle, with the deeper sleep stages (3 or 4) getting shorter in between. During REM, our bodily processes are not operated by the larger, evolved parts of our brain, but by the brain stem—the "ancient brain" we had millions of years ago when we were arboreal (living in trees) mammals.

REM FACTS

- We can dream without REM, but scientists have established that these dreams are simple and uneventful. REM dreaming, on the other hand, is the more exciting, dramatic kind. We do REM dreaming about two hours a night. In a lifetime, this adds up to 5 or 6 years of REM dreaming.

- You may think that because your body seems to go offline, your mind does too. Not so. Your brain spends the night integrating the info and experiences you've gained during the day, and most of this happens during REM sleep. Laboratory tests showed that if mice learned complex tasks and then were deprived of their REM time, they forgot what they learned. In tests on University of Ottawa students, researchers noticed that the faster students learned things, the more REM time they required. Slower learners needed less REM time.

- Life stresses and changes also increase the need for REM. Using a group of divorcing women in their early 30s as subjects, psychoanalyst Rosalind Cartwright conducted a study that demonstrated they needed more REM time to assimilate their big changes.

- Among people over 65, those who are mentally sharper experience REM more frequently.

- Most people don't reach REM until about an hour and a half after going to sleep; people with depression, however, get to REM in about half this time. They also experience it more intensely.

- REM occupies approximately 22% of sleeping time. Pleasant dreams.

BRITS VS. AMERICANS: A WORD QUIZ

People in both countries speak English, but we don't necessarily use the same words. For instance, the British call a raincoat a "mackintosh." See if you can match the British words to their American counterparts.

BRITISH
1) Knackered
2) Crumpet
3) Stone
4) Nick
5) Afters
6) Rubber
7) Lollipop lady
8) Berk
9) Pilchards
10) Chuffed
11) Redundant
12) Yob
13) Brolly
14) Spot on
15) Naff
16) Dodgy
17) Nappy
18) Nutter
19) Butty
20) Plonk

21) Doddle
22) Starkers
23) Tailback
24) Wally
25) Gormless
26) Wonky
27) Ladder
28) Daps
29) Argy-bargy

AMERICAN
a) Dessert
b) Heated argument
c) Moron
d) Umbrella
e) Sandwich
f) Pleased
g) An attractive woman
h) Sneakers
i) Easy task

j) Iffy, suspect
k) Stupid
l) Exhausted
m) Run (in stockings)
n) Crossing guard
o) Worthless, unfashionable
p) Diaper
q) Steal
r) Kook
s) Sardines
t) Cheap wine
u) Unemployed
v) Eraser
w) Perfect
x) Naked
y) Fourteen pounds
z) Traffic jam
aa) Nerd
bb) Unstable
cc) Hooligan

Answers

1) l; 2) g; 3) y, 4) q; 5) a; 6) v; 7) n; 8) c; 9) s; 10) f; 11) u; 12) cc; 13) d; 14) w; 15) o; 16) j; 17) p; 18) r; 19) e; 20) t; 21) i; 22) x; 23) z; 24) aa; 25) k; 26) bb; 27) m; 28) h; 29) b

What did all the passengers of the Mayflower have in common? None of them had middle names.

THE BIRTH OF FROSTED FLAKES, PART II

Hey, when you're done reading, how about a nice bowl of Corn Fetti?
Just kidding. Actually, we recently saw a cereal with that name on
our local grocery shelves. It's not the same product, though—just
the name is recycled. Here's the rest of the story, from
Cerealizing America. (Part I is on page 289.)

SUGAR IS SWEET, AND SO IS MONEY

The moral dilemma posed by sugar-coated cereal at Post was nothing compared to the debate it engendered at Kellogg. The argument about "presweets" and their impact on children's health had already been going on for years in Kellogg's Food Research Department.

It had a historic precedent. At the turn of the century, Dr. John Kellogg, who believed sugar was unhealthy, had argued vehemently against using it as an ingredient in cornflakes. But in 1902, while he was in Europe, his brother, W. K., unilaterally decided to add cane sugar to the formula. Dr. Kellogg was furious, but his medical concerns were less persuasive to W. K. than the opinions of consumers, who were buying more cornflakes than ever.

SOME THINGS DON'T CHANGE

By the mid-1950s, the battling Kellogg brothers had both passed away, but a large percentage of Kellogg stock was owned by the W. K. Kellogg Foundation, a charitable organization established to promote children's health and education. And they were dealing with the sugar controversy again. Was it right, they asked, for a children's health organization to promote presweetened cereals?

Well, maybe not...but never mind. It was still consumers' opinions that really mattered. Sugar-coated cereal was making money for other companies, so Kellogg was going to produce them too.

The company rushed to get out a product that would be competitive with Sugar Crisp. For their first effort, they picked Corn Pops, a puffed corn grit that had been developed back in the 1930s, and launched it as Sugar Corn Pops in 1950. It was so successful that

Kellogg had to run its Omaha, Nebraska, plant 24 hours a day just to meet demand.

BRING OUT THE FLAKES

Once Corn Fetti looked vulnerable, Kellogg went after the sugar-coated cornflake market, as one industry observer put it, "like it was their salvation." Initially there was some concern that tampering with the almighty cornflake might be a mistake. Corn Flakes, after all, were the cornerstone of the company. But Kellogg really had no choice; if they didn't do it, Post would have the market to itself.

Kellogg's marketing people learned from Post's blunders. Instead of using a crystalline coating, Kellogg developed a sugar-coating process that resulted (they said) in "the bright appearance of frost." And instead of a confusing name like Corn Fetti, Kellogg came up with the simple yet elegant "Sugar Frosted Flakes."

CRUNCHY CRITTERS

In 1949, Post's advertising agency had produced an animated TV commercial for Sugar Crisp featuring three identical bears named Candy, Dandy, and Handy. The furry trio scampered through commercial misadventures while an announcer declared: "For breakfast it's Dandy. For snacks it's so Handy. Or eat it like Candy."

The cartoon animals were crude, but effective, and Kellogg was focused on imitating them. "Sugar Crisp had the sugar bears," explained a representative of their ad agency," so Kellogg said, "We want animals, too."

But what animals?

The ad agency's task: come up with creatures that would help overcome the parental bias against a sugar-coated cereal but still attract kids. The admen turned to motivational research for answers. Then they got lucky: Behavioralist Konrad Lorenz happened to have just published his *Studies in Animal and Human Behavior*. In his book, Lorenz discussed the fact that the physical features of children triggered "innate mechanisms" for affection in adults. Big eyes, broad foreheads, and small chins made parents sigh. "Perhaps," thought the ad executives, "they also make parents *buy*." They decided to put Lorenz's theories to the test.

Cheap shrink: Sigmund Freud charged the equivalent of $8.10 an hour for his therapy sessions.

TONY IS BORN

The team of admen brainstormed until they'd narrowed the zoological field to four: a kangaroo, an elephant, a gnu, and a tiger. "The tiger was put in at that time because it was a symbol of energy," recalls an art director. Then they approached children's artists to create a "look" for each animal.

Once they had an artist's rendering, they brought in a TV expert to start writing commercials. He named them all: Tony the Tiger, Katy the Kangaroo, Newt the Gnu, and Elmo the Elephant. Two more admen wrote a jingle for each critter. Tony's four-line poem ended with one of the most memorable lines in ad history—"They're Grrr-eat!"

Elmo the Elephant and Newt the Gnu quickly disappeared, but Tony and Katy showed up on store shelves in 1952. Some folks in the ad industry couldn't see Tony's potential. "I am very fond of dry breakfast cereals," wrote ad critic James D. Woolf in *Advertising Age*, "but this Tiger concept completely fails to give me a hankering."

Consumers knew better. Tony's packages flew off the shelves while Katy's just sat there. Kellogg decided to retire the kangaroo and focus their energies exclusively on the tiger.

THEY'RE GRR-R-EAT

With a potential hit on their hands, Kellogg sent an agent to Los Angeles to find someone to animate their tiger for commercials. They picked Howard Swift, a Disney refugee who'd worked as the principal animator for *Dumbo*. He transformed the sketches of Tony into the character who has roamed the American cereal aisles and airwaves for the past forty years.

For Tony's voice, they cast a basso profundo named Thurl Reavenscroft. He rehearsed Tony's signature line until it was perfect. Today, all we have to do is print "It's Grr-r-eat!," and (admit it) you can hear his voice in your head.

Sugar Frosted Flakes immediately trounced the inedible Corn Fetti and went on to become America's most popular candy-coated cereal. Tony inspired other cereal-makers to create their own cartoon spokes-creatures, which then—as you know—took over kids' television.

Top three "problem" employees, according to the *Wall Street Journal*:

SPACED-OUT SPORTS

They give an awful lot of interviews, but sports stars—and even announcers—aren't always the most articulate people.

"Our similarities are different."
—Dale Berra, *on his father*

"Sutton lost 13 games in a row without winning a ball game."
—Ralph Kiner

"It's not so much maturity as it is growing up."
—Jay Milller, *hockey player, asked if his improved play was due to maturity*

"I've got a great repertoire with my players."
—Danny Ozark

"Three things are bad for you. I can't remember the first two, but doughnuts are the third."
—Bill Petersen

"There comes a time in every man's life, and I've had plenty of them."
—Casey Stengel

"Tony Gwynn was named player of the year for April."
—Ralph Kiner

"I just talked to the doctor. He told me her contraptions were an hour apart."
—Mackey Sasser, *on his wife's pregnancy*

"Noah."
—Barry Bonnel, *former Seattle Mariner, asked to name his all-time favorite Mariner*

"His reputation preceded him before he got here."
—Don Mattingly

"He slides into second with a stand-up double."
—Jerry Coleman

"Not true at all. Vaseline is manufactured right here in the U.S.A."
—Don Sutton, *on accusations that he doctored baseballs with a foreign substance*

"You have to be stupid, and this works out well for me."
—Bubba Baker, *on playing in the NFL*

"I'm going to cancel my prescription."
—Bob Stanley, *on being criticized in a Boston paper*

"What would I do that for? It only gets Spanish stations."
—Jeff Stone, *on why he wouldn't bring his TV back to the U.S. after playing in Venezuela*

#1 "The Non-Stop Talker"; #2 "The Screamer"; #3 "The Practical Joker."

LOST IN TRANSLATION

*Have you ever thought you were communicating brilliantly, only
to find out that others thought you were a lunatic? That's an especially
easy mistake to make when you're speaking a foreign language
or dealing with a foreign culture. A few examples:*

PRODUCT CONFUSION

• **Gerber Baby Food:** Gerber used the same packaging strategy in Africa that it used in America—a picture of the Gerber baby on the label. They apparently didn't realize that since many Africans don't read, it's standard practice to put pictures of the contents on jar labels. As you might guess, the product didn't go over well.

• **The Dairy Association:** Taking their "Got Milk?" campaign to Mexico, they translated their slogan into Spanish. Unfortunately, it came out as "Are you lactating?"

• **Johnson Wax:** When Johnson introduced their furniture cleaner Pledge into the Netherlands, they didn't know that, in Dutch, Pledge means "piss."

MEDIA TRANSLATIONS

• In the late 1970s, the TV sitcom "Laverne and Shirley" was shown in Bangkok, Thailand—where women did not act like the show's main characters. Each program was preceded by a disclaimer saying: "The two women depicted in the following episode are from an insane asylum."

• According to one source, audiences in Lebanon were going to see *Titanic* because the title in Arabic slang translates as *Let's Have Sex*.

MIXED-UP MENUS

These items are from real menus. Bon appétit.

- Horse-rubbish sauce (Rome)
- Torture soup (Djerba)
- Crab Meat Shaag and Botty Kebab (New York)
- Terminal soup (Istanbul)
- Farte aux Fraises (Turkey)
- Frozen soap with Peccadilloes (Madrid)
- Stewed abalone with 3 things and lucky duck (Bangkok)

Food for thought: The French eat an average of 200 million frogs each year.

SCREWED-UP SIGNS

• A street sign in London reads: "Dead slow children at play."

• When English/Spanish signs were first posted at Sky Harbor International Airport in Phoenix, Arizona, they were full of mistakes. One sign, meant to remind arriving travelers to declare fruits, vegetables, and meats, read "*Violadores Seran Finados,*" which translates as "Violators Will Be Deceased."

DIPLOMATIC SNAFUS

• A French ambassador, M. Cambon, once thanked a Chicago mayor for a tour of the city. "Thank you," he said. "But I am sorry so to cockroach on your time." The mayor replied, "But you don't mean 'cockroach,' Mr. Cambon; it is 'encroach' you mean." "Oh, is it?" Cambon asked. "I see, a difference in gender."

• An Englishwoman at a French dipomatic party asked a Frenchman for a light. What he heard instead was, "Are you a dunghill?"

CAMPING INSTRUCTIONS

These regulations were posted at a campground in Italy:

• Cars must enter or go away from the camp with motors out.

• THEN IS STRICTLY FORBIDDEN TO:
   a) Reserve box parking, spaces with chairs, fences, rape or other means
   b) Dainage of the plants and equipman
   c) Dig simples around tents
   d) Set to go into the camp, not authorized from the direction

• The above listed rules are inappellable. All of the camping personnel are authorized to send away anyone who does follow them.

IT'S JUST A TITLE, AFTER ALL

You have to wonder what Chinese movie audiences think they're going to see when U.S. films are shown in China as (for example):

Kindergarten Cop: *Devil King of Children*

Indecent Proposal: *Peach-Colored Transaction*

The Shawshank Redemption: *Excitement 1995*

A 4,500-year-old bristlecone pine named Methuselah is now the oldest tree on Earth.

GO, GO GOETHE

He's reluctant to admit it, but Uncle John does read things besides
The History of Parking Meters *and* Famous Movie Monsters. *He
even has a favorite philosopher—Johann Wolfgang von Goethe.*

"What is the best government? That which teaches us to govern ourselves."

"Legislators and revolutionaries who promise liberty and equality at the same time are either utopian dreamers or charlatans."

"Only law can give us freedom."

"If a man stops to ponder over his physical or moral condition, he generally discovers that he is ill."

"Preoccupation with immortality is for the upper classes, particularly ladies with nothing to do. An able man, who has a regular job and must toil and produce day by day, leaves the future world to itself, and is active and useful in this one."

"Never tell people how you are: they don't want to know."

"If youth is a fault, one soon gets rid of it."

"Fools and wise men are equally harmless. It is the half-fools and the half-wise who are dangerous."

"A clever man commits no minor blunders."

"Know thyself? If I knew myself, I'd run away."

"Whatever you can do, or dream you can, begin it. Boldness has genius, power and magic in it."

"Only the artist sees spirits. But after he has told of their appearing to him, everybody sees them."

"You can't understand something if you don't possess it."

"Nothing shows a man's character more than what he laughs at."

"Viewed from the summit of reason, all life looks like a malignant disease and the world like a madhouse."

A group of jellyfish is known as a "smack."

MR. TOAD'S WILD RIDE, PART II

Here's the second part of the story of Kenneth Grahame's classic,
The Wind in the Willows—*which has been adapted by everyone from
A.A. Milne, who wrote the play* Toad of Toad Hall *in 1930, to Walt
Disney, who animated it in 1949. (Part I starts on page 70.)*

SMEDLEY'S WILES

Magazines and publishers regularly begged Kenneth Grahame for articles...or perhaps a sequel to *The Golden Age* or *Dream Days*. But Grahame had become a notorious recluse; even getting an interview with him was nearly impossible.

In 1907 an American magazine called *Everybody's* put Constance Smedley on the job. The editors told Smedley to get Grahame to write something—anything. She was clever, and wrote to the author saying she was a relative of Governess Smedley—a fictional character in *The Golden Age* and *Dream Days*—who wanted to visit. Grahame was delighted. The two became good friends...but he still wouldn't write for her. Grahame said writing "was like physical torture," and "he hated it."

Smedley visited often. One evening, she overheard Grahame telling Mouse his bedtime story and, as one biographer put it, "moved in for the kill." She insisted that Grahame already had a story—he just needed to write it down. He even had much of the material for the book in the letters he'd written to Mouse. To his own surprise, Grahame agreed, and began expanding the letters into a book—the first professional writing he'd done in nine years.

He finished *The Wind in the Reeds* (as he called it) by Christmas 1907, "and packed it up and sent it to the eager Constance Smedley, who dispatched it to her editors, waiting excitedly in New York."

FALSE START

The New Yorkers were stunned. Grahame's other books had been about children—not wild animals. To Smedley's mortification, they turned the book down flat. The manuscript was sent back to Grahame, who gave it to his agent. But the agent couldn't find anyone in England who was willing to publish it, either.

The problem seemed to be that adults didn't understand *The Wind in the Willows* (now changed from *Reeds* to avoid confusion with an upcoming book by W. B. Yeats). It was a new genre—a novel-length animal fantasy that was not an allegory and had no human protagonist. "*The Wind in the Willows* had no clear generic predecessor," explains a Grahame biographer. "[It] shifted the identification of the reader to the animals themselves…and the first adults to read the work simply couldn't adapt to the change."

When Grahame finally did get his book published, he discovered that critics couldn't relate to his story, either. Some criticized it as a poorly thought-out allegory ("Grown up readers will find it monstrous and elusive"); others assumed that since it expressed such an "intimate sympathy with Nature," it was meant to be natural history. One newspaper commented that *The Wind in the Willows*—a book featuring a toad driving a car—would "win no credence from the very best authorities on biology." Even the *Times of London* wrote irrelevantly: "As a contribution to natural history the work is negligible."

One result of the confusion was that the book sold poorly. Another: Grahame couldn't find an American publisher.

THE PRESIDENT STEPS IN

This is where President Teddy Roosevelt figures in the story. Roosevelt was a big fan of Grahame's work. Years earlier, he had met millionaire book collector Austin Purves and learned that Purves knew Grahame. He sent Purves back to England with a request for autographed copies of *The Golden Age* and *Dream Days*.

Grahame, of course, complied, and Roosevelt wrote back, saying "No one you could have sent those books to would have appreciated them more than Mrs. Roosevelt and I." He invited Grahame to stay at the White House if he visited Washington, but Grahame never did.

When *The Wind in the Willows* was published in England, Grahame sent Roosevelt an autographed copy. But Roosevelt chose not to read it. He had recently written an article denouncing stories that confused animals with human beings, and after seeing the reviews of *Willows*, feared it would ruin his love of Grahame's other books.

However, Roosevelt's wife found the book at the White House and started reading it aloud to their children. Roosevelt overheard her and became fascinated with the story. He later wrote to Grahame:

> For some time I could not accept the mole, the water-rat and the badger....But after a while Mrs Roosevelt and two of the boys, Kermit and Ted, all quite independently, got hold of *The Wind in the Willows* and took such a delight in it that I began to feel that I might have to revise my judgement. Then Mrs Roosevelt read it aloud to the younger children, and I listened now and then....I have since read the book three times, and now all the characters are my dearest friends.

The Roosevelt children sent their copies of the book to England to be autographed by Grahame. Meanwhile, Grahame's agent was still trying to find an American publisher. He had just sent the manuscript to Scribner's—who informed him that they were not interested—when a note arrived at the publisher from President Roosevelt. It said: "*The Wind in the Willows* is such a beautiful thing, Scribner must publish it."

"With an apologetic cough, Scribner did." And never regretted it. The book sold slowly at first, but caught on and went through many printings. Its success in the U.S. made it a hit in England, too.

By 1908 Grahame (no longer with the bank) was living comfortably off the royalties from his books. *Willows* changed popular tastes and paved the way for the genre of animal fantasies, which includes everything from Mickey Mouse to *Charlotte's Web*.

NOTE: The story doesn't have a particularly happy ending, however. Like Peter, who inspired Peter Pan (see page 507), Mouse committed suicide. One day while he was at college, he went for a walk and never came back. He had been hit by a train. Officials called it an accident, but the wounds showed he had been lying on the tracks when the train came.

Q: What does an *algologist* study? A: Seaweed.

DUMB CROOKS

Here's more proof that crime doesn't pay.

NOTE-ABLY STUPID

"A 24-year-old man was pulled over outside of Buffalo, New York, for driving at night without headlights. When the patrolman asked to see his license, the driver began nervously searching in the car and eventually produced a handful of cards and papers. Among the various identification, the patrolman found a note which contained the message, 'I have a gun. Put all the money in the envelope quickly!' The note was linked to a heist [that occurred] two days earlier in which the man and a 25-year-old accomplice had robbed a Buffalo bank."

—Disorganized Crime

DRIVEN TO TEARS

SPRINGFIELD, Oregon—"On July 8, a teenage boy approached a 1995 Dodge Neon, pointed a handgun at the driver and ordered all of the passengers out of the car.

"The boy started to drive off, but the vehicle immediately stalled at the intersection…because he couldn't drive a stick shift.

"The would-be thief ran off, along with two other hidden accomplices. They were later arrested and charged each with three counts of robbery and kidnapping."

—Medford, Oregon, Mail Tribune, July 9,1999

RIGHT ON TIME

"Stephen E. Peterson, of Fort Collins, Colorado, was arrested for robbing the same 7-Eleven twice in one day. After the second holdup, he promised the clerk he'd be back in a few hours to clean the place out a third time. True to his word, Peterson returned, and the cops nabbed him."

—Maxim magazine

NO NEED TO DUST FOR PRINTS

"Cary L. Rider, 43, was recently arrested for burglary in Illinois after police found him in the hospital. The burglar had tried to move a safe, but it fell on his left hand—and his glove was found underneath it, still containing the top part of the burglar's middle finger....Said one officer: 'He admitted it. What can you do if your finger's there?'"

—The *Portland Oregonian*, November 21, 1997

RATS!

"An 18-year-old man walked into a store in Scotland and held a rat up to the cashier's face. The man then instructed the cashier to 'give me all your money or I'll sic my rat on you. The cashier just laughed.'"

—*Disorganized Crime*

NOT READY FOR HALLOWEEN

"J. Douglas Cresswell tried to rob a motel while disguised by a black garbage sack over his head. The trouble was that he had forgotten to cut eyeholes in the sack; his frantic efforts to punch holes in the sack with his fingers as he stumbled towards the door delayed his getaway and he was arrested by the police. He was jailed for twenty-five years."

—*Mammoth Book of Oddities*

TIME TO SPARE

"John William Howard, 45, fled Maryland, where he was wanted on sexual assault charges, and headed for Arizona. Passing through Brookshire, Texas, low on gas and cash, he tried to sell his spare tire to raise some money. A local merchant informed him about a police loan program for just such predicaments, so Howard went to the police station to apply. A routine check turned up his fugitive status, according to Police Chief Joe Garcia, who called Howard 'one of the world's dumbest criminals.'"

—*Dumb Crooks* Web site

NEW RECYCLING PROGRAM

"A [robber] in Mainz, Germany, got clean away with a bag of rubbish in April 1995. A clerk filled his carrier bag from the wastepaper bin rather than the cash drawer, and the thief dashed off without checking."

—*The Fortean Times Book of Inept Crime*

Laid end to end, the blood vessels in your body would wrap around the equator three times.

AESOP'S FABLES

Aesop's fables (see page 207) have been told and retold for thousands of years. Here are a few more we've picked to pass on.

THE FOX & THE GRAPES

A fox was walking along the road, when he spied some delicious-looking grapes growing on a high trellis. "My, they look good!" he said. He jumped up, but couldn't reach them. He tried again and again, but to no avail. Finally he looked angrily at the grapes and said, "Hmmm, who wants the old grapes? They're probably sour anyway."

Moral: *It's easy to despise what you can't have.*

THE SICK LION

A lion, unable from old age and infirmities to provide himself with food by force, resolved to do so by trickery. He returned to his den, and lying down there, pretended to be sick, taking care that his sickness should be publicly known. The beasts expressed their sorrow, and came one by one to his den, where the Lion devoured them. After many of the beasts had thus disappeared, a Fox, presenting himself to the Lion, stood on the outside of the cave, at a respectful distance, and asked him how he was. "I am very middling," replied the Lion, "but why are you standing out there? Please come in and talk with me." "No, thank you," said the Fox. "I notice that there are many footprints entering your cave, but I see no trace of any returning."

Moral: *The wise person learns from the misfortunes of others.*

THE FOOLISH TRAVELERS

A man and his son were walking along the road to market with their donkey. As they walked, they met a couple. "Did you ever see anything so silly?" the man said to his wife. "Two men walking when they have a donkey with them. What's a donkey for, after all, if not to carry a man?"

Hearing this, the man put his son on the back of the donkey and they went on their way. Soon they met two countrymen. "Did you ever see such a terrible thing?" one cried. "The strong young man rides while his poor father must walk." So the boy dismounted and the father got on instead.

They hadn't gone very far when they met two women. "Look at that heartless father!" exclaimed one of them, "His poor little son must walk while he rides." At that, the man said to his son, "Come up here with me. We'll both ride."

They both rode for a while until they reached a group of men. "Aren't you ashamed?" they called out. "Overloading a poor little donkey like that." So the man and his son both climbed off the donkey.

They thought and thought. They couldn't walk along with the donkey, or ride it one at a time, or ride it both together. Then they had an idea. They got a tree and cut it into a long pole. Then they tied the donkey's feet to it, raised the pole to their shoulders, and went on their way, carrying the donkey.

As they crossed a bridge, the donkey—who didn't like being tied up—kicked one of his feet loose, causing the father and son to stumble. The donkey fell into the water. Because its feet were tied, it drowned.

Moral: *If you try to please everyone, you'll end up pleasing no one.*

THE ASS & THE FOX

An ass put on a Lion's skin, and roamed around the forest amusing himself by scaring all the foolish animals he met. Finally, he met a Fox, and tried to scare him, too—but as soon as the Fox heard the ass's voice, he said, "Well, I might have been frightened...if I hadn't heard your bray."

Moral: *Clothes may disguise a fool, but his words give him away.*

THE THIRSTY PIGEON

A pigeon, overcome by thirst, saw a glass of water painted on a sign. Not realizing it was only a picture, she quickly flew towards it and crashed into the sign. Her wings broken, she fell to the ground...and was captured by a bystander.

Moral: *Zeal should not outrun discretion.*

THE SERPENT & FILE

A serpent wandered into a carpenter's shop. As he glided over the floor he felt his skin pricked by a file lying there. In a rage he turned and attacked, trying to sink his fangs into the file; but he could do no harm to heavy iron and soon had to give over his wrath.

Moral: *It is useless attacking the insensible.*

What do your body and an iron nail have in common? They contain the same amount of iron.

MORE CLASSIC HOAXES

Here are a few more of our favorite frauds.

THE PSALMANAZAR HOAX

The Set-Up: In 1703 a "converted heathen from Formosa" [now Taiwan] named George Psalmanazar was introduced to the Bishop of London by a local cleric (actually, his confederate). "In eighteenth-century London," as Laura Foreman writes in *Hoaxes and Deceptions*, "a Formosan was as great a sensation as a Martian would be today," and Psalmanazar became the toast of English society.

People were fascinated with his stories. They were shocked to learn, for example, that before he joined the Anglican faith, he was a cannibal—and that snakes, snake blood, and raw meat, including the flesh of executed criminals, were delicacies in Formosa. Divorce customs were similarly barbaric: If a Formosan man grew tired of his wife, "he had only to accuse her of adultery, and he then was entitled to cut off her head and eat her." Psalmanazar taught himself to eat raw meat, and whenever he dined with upper-class hosts, would insist on it.

The Bishop of London sent the "reformed savage" to Oxford University to study and to lecture on Formosan language and history. While he was there, the Anglican Church commissioned him to translate the Bible into Formosan (a language he promptly invented). The following year, Psalmanazar wrote his extremely popular *Historical and Geographical Description of Formosa*, complete with comprehensive descriptions of Formosan art, culture, diet, dress, and language. Among his disclosures: Formosan religion demanded that the hearts of 18,000 Formosan boys under the age of nine were sacrificed to the gods every year, "a population-depleting practice offset by the sparing of eldest sons, and polygamy."

Why It Worked: No one in England had ever been to Formosa, and Psalmanazar was so inventive that when a doubting missionary who really *had* spent 18 years in China challenged him publicly, Psalmanazar made him look foolish. Plus, the English of the time were incredibly gullible about other cultures. When, for example, they asked why he didn't he look Oriental, Psalmanazar explained that the ruling class spent all their time in underground houses—it was only the workers whose skin turned "yellow." The public bought it.

Perhaps the real reason Psalmanazar was so successful was religious chauvinism. He roundly criticized Catholic missionary work in Asia and embraced the Anglican Church—confirming as an outsider what many English felt was true anyway. And in 1700, it was considered a real feather in the English church's cap to have converted a cannibal when Catholics couldn't.

What Happened: Psalmanazar's graphic descriptions of life in Formosa were at odds with everyone else's, and skeptics kept attacking until he was finally exposed as a fraud by Dr. Edmund Halley (of comet fame) in 1706. Halley quizzed Psalmanazar on just how much sunlight those underground houses got—and Psalmanazar got this, as well as other phenomena, wrong. He finally admitted having made everything up—including the "language" he spoke— and confessed to being a Frenchman. But he never revealed his true identity...it remains a mystery to this day.

THE BARON OF ARIZONA

The Set-Up: In 1883 a man named James Addison Reavis filed legal papers claiming ownership of more than 17,000 square miles of territory in what is now Arizona and New Mexico.

This wasn't as far-fetched as it might sound: when the U.S. government purchased the Arizona Territory from Mexico in 1848, it agreed to honor all Spanish land grants, and according to Reavis, the land had been presented to Don Miguel de Peralta de la Cordoba in 1748 by the King of Spain. Reavis said he'd bought the land and title from the family that had inherited it, and now he was staking his claim.

If Reavis's claim was true, the thousands of people living and working in Arizona were there illegally...and could be forced to leave. At the time, there were thousands of land grants being processed and verified by the United States. Reavis's was just the biggest (and most outrageous). Government experts pronounced it real.

"The claim brought panic to the territory," writes one historian, "and an outpouring of riches to the new baron." Railroads, mines, and other businesses began paying him for the right to use his land. Over the next decade, he collected more than $10 million.

Why It Worked: Reavis was an extremely talented forger who had spent years laying the groundwork for his fraud. In particular, he had traveled to Spain where, after getting access to historic documents, he had skillfully altered them to create a record of the (nonexistent) Peralta family and their land grant. Then he produced impeccable copies of the grant itself.

What Happened: There are different accounts of how the hoax was eventually discovered. According to one source, a newspaper publisher noticed that the typestyle on one of the documents was too recent to be authentic, and that the watermark on the paper was from a Wisconsin paper mill that had not even been built when the document was supposedly drafted.

Another says that technology did Reavis in. When he planned his scheme, Reavis knew nothing of scientific innovations that would make it possible for investigators to test the age of paper and ink. By 1893, suspicious officials were able to have the tests done—and they revealed that the 135-year-old documents "were written in the wrong kind of ink on 10-year-old parchment." Reavis was sentenced to six years in prison for his crime, and died penniless in 1908.

*　　*　　*　　*

THAT'S ART!

• How slow a painter was Paul Cézanne? So slow that when he painted a bowl of fruit, it wasn't uncommon for the fruit to begin to rot before he finished painting. So he used waxed fruit for models.

• In the 19th century a 26-year-old painter named Richard Dadd went insane, killed his father, and was confined to an asylum. The asylum let him continue his painting…and his insanity actually *improved* his painting ability: *Oberon and Titania*, one of the works he painted at the asylum, is considered one of the greatest paintings of Victorian era.

BIRTH OF A GIANT, PART III

By now you know that the patent for the first modern bathtub spawned General Motors. But whatever happened to Billy Durant and David Buick? Read on. Here's Part III of the story. (Part II is on page 370.)

COMEBACK

The bank-appointed executives who took control of GM from Billy Durant made a number of moves that helped restore the company to health. They shut down all of the money-losing divisions and used the money they saved to improve quality at Buick, Oldsmobile, Cadillac, and other divisions that showed promise. In just a few years, they rescued the company from the brink of bankruptcy, paid back all bankers, and built GM into one of the most competitive auto companies in the U.S.

But the executives made a mistake that would cost them dearly: they discontinued the Buick Model 10, a low-priced Buick that Durant had created to compete against Ford's Model T. Shortsighted GM executives were skeptical that smaller, cheaper cars would ever make any money (the Model T would become the bestselling car in American automobile history). So they scrapped the Model 10, despite the fact that it was the most popular car in the Buick lineup, and concentrated on building bigger, more expensive cars.

The decision was a disaster for Buick: sales at the division dropped more than 50% in one year, forcing GM to shut down entire assembly plants and lay off hundreds of workers.

SEE THE U.S.A.

The crisis at Buick gave Durant an opening. In 1911 he bought an abandoned Buick factory, staffed it with Buick auto workers who'd been laid off during the sales slump, and announced that he was forming a new company to manufacture and sell cars designed by Louis Chevrolet, one of the most famous race car drivers of the day.

Some of the larger Chevrolets really were designed by Louis Chevrolet...but the new company's bestselling model, introduced in 1915, was basically a Buick Model 10 that had been rechristened the Chevrolet 490 (so named because it sold for $490). Priced just $50 higher than the Model T—but equipped with an electric starter and other features that the Model T lacked—the 490 was poised to give Ford a run for its money.

And thanks almost entirely to the 490, sales at Chevrolet nearly tripled from 5,000 cars to more than 13,500 cars in 1915, making Chevrolet one of the top auto companies in the country. Durant had done it again...and he was only getting started.

HE'S B-A-A-A-CK

Even as he was building Chevrolet into an automotive powerhouse, as early as 1913, Durant began secretly acquiring large blocks of General Motors stock. He encourged friends and associates to do the same, and even convinced the DuPont chemical company to acquire more than 25% of GM.

On September 16, 1915, Durant pounced. He showed up at GM's annual shareholders meeting accompanied by several assistants, carrying bushel baskets filled with the GM stock certificates that Durant either owned or controlled. "Gentleman," Durant calmly announced to the room, "I now control this company."

DÉJÀ VU

This time Durant managed to stay on at GM until 1920. He inherited a much stronger, more profitable company than the one he'd left in 1910, but as time passed he began to slip into his old habits. He bought the Sheridan and the Scripps-Booth auto companies and added them to the GM fold, but they did little more than steal sales from GM's other divisions. Durant also bought up several tractor companies and merged them all into what he named GM's Samson Tractor Division...which went on to lose more than $42 million before it was finally shut down in 1920.

Durant might have even managed to survive these debacles had the U.S. economy not fallen into a deep recession in 1920. As sales of automobiles dropped sharply, GM's stock price began to plummet, prompting Durant to buy shares in an attempt to keep the stock price from sliding further. It didn't work—by the time Durant exhausted his fortune in November 1920, GM's share price had dropped from a high of nearly $50 to under $12.

A *misodoctakleidist* is someone who hates practicing the piano.

But Durant wasn't just broke—he was deep in debt. He had purchased the stock using $20 million borrowed from 21 different stockbrokers and three different banks…and had no way to pay the loans back.

DuPont and the other major shareholders worried that if the extent of the company's insolvency became known, the value of GM's stock might collapse entirely. Once again, however, GM was too big to fail—DuPont feared that if GM collapsed it might drag the *entire country* into a depression, not just Detroit. Rather than allow that to happen, DuPont paid off Durant's loans on the condition that he hand over his GM stock and resign.

Once again, Durant had no alternative.

STRIKE THREE
But Durant was no quitter. He contacted 67 of his friends and told them he was starting another auto company. Forty-eight hours later he had raised more than $7 million in cash, and on January 21, 1921—less than two months after he was forced out of GM—he filed papers incorporating Durant Motors, Inc.

Next, he began taking orders for cars and selling shares in the new company. By January 1, 1923, he had collected cash deposits for more than 231,000 cars and had more stockholders than any other U.S. company except AT&T.

As it had been at Chevrolet, the most popular car of the Durant Motors line was the one designed to compete against the Ford Model T. The car was called the Durant Star and sold fairly well…until Henry Ford unexpectedly lowered the price of the Model T. Durant was not able to match him.

Two other cars, the Flint and the Durant Six, never caught on with the public, and although Durant Motors held its own through the 1920s, the company finally went under in 1933, during the Great Depression. Durant filed for personal bankruptcy three years later, listing more than more than $914,000 in debts and only $250 in assets (his clothes).

LAST STOP
A few months later, some reporters located Durant, washing dishes and sweeping the floor in a former Durant Motors sales-room that had been converted into a hamburger restaurant and a

Food Market grocery store. Durant owned them both, and he would later add some some bowling alleys to his holdings. It was his final attempt at empire building.

"Mr. Durant is just as enthusiastic over building up the Food Market as he ever was over automobiles," Durant's nephew told reporters. "In fact, he no longer can bear the thought of an automobile." Durant died 11 years later at the age of 86.

BYE, BYE BUICK

David Buick fared worse than William Durant. Although he sat on the Buick Co. board of directors, Buick was so deeply in debt that he owned only one share of Buick Co. stock. When he resigned from the company in 1908, Durant reportedly gave him a severance check for $100,000. Buick quickly burned through the money by investing in a new auto company, a carburetor company, shady oil deals, Florida real estate, and other get-rich-quick schemes. When he died in a Detroit hospital on March 5, 1929, Buick was so broke that, in the words of one reporter, "he could afford neither phone nor Buick."

*   *   *

THIS SPACE FOR GRAFFITI

HOMEMADE BESTSELLERS

Some books are published with high expectations but flop. Others have extremely modest beginnings...but turn into bestsellers. Here are three.

HOW TO KEEP YOUR VOLKSWAGEN ALIVE
Simple Start: John Muir was an ex-NASA engineer-turned-hippie-dropout living in Taos, New Mexico, in the mid-1960s. He supported himself by fixing cars, mostly Volkswagens. But when a friend's Volkswagen broke down while he was too busy to work on it, he typed up some instructions for the friend to follow herself. She got her Volkswagen running again, and Muir decided to turn his instructions into an auto repair manual. He "test-marketed" the book by reading it aloud to people working on their VWs and taking notes on how well they did.

Bestseller: Muir pitched the manuscript to a number of publishers, but they all turned him down, telling him there were already too many auto repair manuals on the market. "I knew there were no manuals like ours," Muir recalled in the 1970s, "so we sold the house in Taos, found a typist, and wrote to printers for bids. The plan was to sell mail order and directly to old book stores." Muir printed 2,500 copies using his own money, threw them in the back of his Volkswagen bus and began selling them store-to-store. Interest in the book began to build via word-of-mouth. "After that," says Steven Carey, president of John Muir Publications, "*Life* magazine ran a feature article on the book, and it just took off." To date, more than 2.5 million copies have been sold. Old-style Volkswagen Beetles and vans haven't been sold in the U.S. since 1977; even so, *How to Keep Your Volkswagen Alive* still averages sales of more than 30,000 copies a year.

THE CELESTINE PROPHECY
Simple Start: In the mid-1970s, a children's therapist named James Redfield was traveling through the Peruvian Andes when he heard tales of a lost ancient document that supposedly revealed the meaning of life. For some reason the story appealed to him, and remained in the back of his mind until 1989, when he quit his counseling job

The first thing Thomas Edison filmed with his movie camera was a person sneezing.

and began writing a novel about just such an ancient text. He wrote much of the book in a Waffle House restaurant. "That helped to keep the story simple," Redfield says.

Bestseller: Nobody wanted to publish Redfield's book, so he formed his own publishing company and spent his entire $13,000 savings printing up 3,000 copies, which he began selling to New Age bookstores across the American South. Redfield credits the book's success to independent bookstore owners, who recommended the book to their readers. *The Celestine Prophecy* bombed with the critics—*The National Review* called it "a tenth-rate melodrama joining Gnostic hubris with flower-child theology"—but it was a smash hit with the New Age crowd. Redfield self-published more than 150,000 copies before selling the rights to Warner Books, which went on to sell 5.5 million more.

LIFE'S LITTLE INSTRUCTION BOOK

Simple Start: When his son Adam was packing up to go to college, H. Jackson Brown decided to write down some observations and advice that he thought his son might find useful. "I started writing," Brown says, "and what I thought would take a few hours took several days." When he was finished, Brown put the notes into a binder and presented it to his son. A few days later, Adam phoned home. "Dad," he said, "I've been reading the book and I think it's one of the best gifts I've ever received. I'm going to add to it and someday give it to my son." Brown figured that if his son found the notes useful, other people would, too; so he made them into a book.

Bestseller: Brown self-published enough copies to sell to bookstores near his Nashville home, and they sold well enough that some bookstore owners encouraged him to sell the manuscript to an established publisher. He approached Rutledge Hill Press, but owner Larry Stone turned the book down. Brown gave him a copy anyway. "I left that copy on my desk for four or five weeks," Stone says, "and everyone who came in my office picked it up, flipped through it and even read a few things out loud. It caught up to me one day, and I thought hey, we probably ought to reconsider this book. So I called Jack up and asked if he'd found a publisher. He said, 'No' and I said, 'You have now.'" The book went on to sell more than 5 million copies.

Q. What do olives and tomatoes have in common?   A. They're both fruits.

THE MODERN ZOO, PART II

*Every year more than 120 million people visit zoos, aquariums,
oceanariums, and wildlife parks in the United States and
Canada —a greater attendance than that of football,
baseball, and hockey games combined! The story
of the origin of the modern zoo is on page 187.*

STATUS SYMBOL

In the late 1850s, Philadelphian Dr. William Camac visited the London Zoo. Inspired by what he saw, he founded the Philadelphia Zoological Society. His goal: To build a world-class zoological garden and the first scientific zoo in America.

By the late 1850s, major cities all over Europe either had zoos or were in the process of establishing them. They were status symbols: The citizens of Madrid, Hamburg, and Dublin, for example, regarded zoos as a means of communicating to the rest of world that their cities were to be taken as seriously as London or Paris.

Dr. Camac wanted the same thing for Philadelphia: "When we see cities such as Amsterdam, Frankfurt, and Dublin—cities not so large as Philadelphia—supporting first-class zoological gardens," he wrote, "we see no reason why Philadelphia, with all its taste, wealth, enterprise, and advantages, should not in time possess one of the finest institutions in the world."

SIDESHOW

The United States lagged far behind Europe in the development of zoos. Westward expansion brought pioneers in contact with animals they had never seen before...and many animals were captured and brought back to cities to be exhibited to curious crowds. But as late as the 1870s, most animal viewing was limited to spectacles like a bear chained up in the corner tavern, or traveling carnivals put on by sea captains to show off exotic animals captured overseas.

You can sweat as much as 3 gallons of water a day in a hot climate.

EARLY AMERICAN ZOOS

New York

By 1861 New York City had a menagerie in Central Park, but this jumble was little more than a dumping ground for private collections and carnivals, including a black bear, two cows, deer, monkeys, raccoons, foxes, opossums, ducks, swans, eagles, pelicans, and parrots. No rational thought was put into the collection; the keepers just accepted whatever animals people gave them.

Still, the menagerie was a popular attraction. "By the late 1800s," Linda Koebner writes in *Zoo*, "it was a center of entertainment both for wealthy Fifth Avenue strollers and for the poor who were looking for a break from their daily working lives. Newly arrived immigrants lived in dark, crowded tenements on the Lower East Side of New York. A trip up to the green of Central Park to see the menagerie was well worth the walk or the nickel fare on the trolley."

Chicago

The menagerie in Chicago's Lincoln Park wasn't much better than the one in Central Park. It got its start when the Central Park menagerie presented them with a gift of two swans. This prompted similar "gifts," and by 1873 the park had 27 mammals and 48 birds.

GENUINE ARTICLE

While these zoos were popular attractions, neither Central Park nor Lincoln Park knew anything about animals or bothered to hire anyone who did; care and feeding of the creatures was left to the parks department, whose main concern was picking up garbage and raking leaves.

As Dr. Camac proposed it, the Philadelphia Zoological Garden would be something completely different: a well-funded, intelligently planned collection of animals housed in permanent facilities and run by a professional, full-time staff. The public would be admitted into the zoo, but it would also serve a more serious purpose: scientists at the University of Pennsylvania, the Academy of Sciences, and other organizations would be able to study and observe the animals up close.

Planning for the facility began in March of 1859, but the outbreak of the Civil War interfered with construction, so it was not completed until 1873.

Big year: Dr. Pepper, Coca-Cola, and Hires Root Beer were all invented in 1886.

THE TOILET ERA

When it opened to the public on July 1, 1874, the Philadelphia Zoo was a state-of-the-art facility, complete with a monkey house, bird house, prairie dog village, and sea lion pool. But the early zookeepers had a lot to learn about caring for animals. Hunters and trappers who captured the animals knew next to nothing about how the animals lived in the wild or what they ate, and thousands died before they could be delivered to the zoo. The zookeepers didn't know much more, and animals that made it to the zoo didn't live much longer.

Because animal behavior was so poorly understood, animals that lived in social or family groups in the wild were often acquired one at a time and lived alone in bare cages—no attempt was made to simulate their natural environment. Animals frequently had nowhere to hide, and climbing animals like monkeys and wildcats had nowhere to go to get off the floor. The emphasis in cage design was on preventing disease by making them easy to clean: enclosures were usually made of concrete and tile and looked so much like bathrooms, Koebner writes, that "this manner of keeping the animals gave rise to the term 'the toilet era.'"

Visitors to the zoos were similarly shortchanged: displays did little to educate the public other than give the name of the animal and the feeding schedule. Scientific aspects of the zoo were played down; the garden's staffers themselves were poorly informed and so could do little to shed light on any of the exhibits.

Where the public was concerned, the emphasis was on entertainment. Elephants paraded, bears danced, and chimpanzees wore clothes and ate with silverware at dinner tables, part of the zoology garden's attempt to show how "humanlike" they were.

A NEW ERA

Things began to improve at the turn of the century, thanks in large part to a German circus trainer named Carl Hagenbeck, considered the "father of modern zoos." For years Hagenbeck had made his living catching and training exotic animals for zoos. In 1907 he expanded his business by opening his own zoo, which he named the Hagenbeck Tierpark.

As an animal catcher, Hagenbeck had seen animals in the wild and was determined that the animals in *his* zoo would never live in

John Scott Harrison's father, William Henry Harrison, was

cages that looked like restrooms. "I wished to exhibit them not as captives, confined to narrow spaces and looked at between bars, but as free to wander from place to place within as large limits as possible."

Hagenbeck put his experience as an animal trainer to work, testing the animals to see how high and how far they could jump, and then dug moats so deep and wide that the animals would not try to escape. He also tried to give the exhibits an authentic appearance so that the animals would be as comfortable as possible.

Optical Illusion

Hagenbeck also arranged the exhibits to give them as natural an appearance as possible; it even seemed as if predators and their prey were part of the same exhibit. The lion exhibit was located just in front of the zebra, antelope, and ostriches (safely separated by a moat that was concealed behind bushes and landscape.) All of the animals appeared to be together, just as they would be in their natural habitat in Africa. As a result, Koebner writes, "the public could see the interrelationship of animals, begin to picture what the African landscape looked like and learn about predators, prey and habitats."

The advantages of Hagenbeck's reforms were obvious, and most zoos began adopting his ideas to improve their exhibits. Still, his enclosures had drawbacks: They were expensive, took up more space than cages, and increased the distance between animals and the viewing public from 5 feet to as much as 75 feet. And some zoo directors felt they were too revolutionary. Dr. William Hornaday of the Bronx Zoo, for example, criticized the new enclosures as "a half-baked German fad." But Hornaday was in the minority. Zookeepers from all over the world began making pilgrimages to the Hagenbeck Tierpark to learn as much as they could.

CHANGING TIMES

Hagenbeck's reforms were part of a broader zoological trend: all over the world, zoos were beginning to take better care of their animals. In the old days, the supply of animals in the wild seemed inexhaustible—if an animal in a zoo died, they could just send a hunter into the jungle to get another one. Life was cheap, and animals were expendable.

a U.S. president. So was his son Benjamin Harrison.

By the early 1900s, zoos were already beginning to look different. Many animals had been driven to extinction or close to it. And foreign governments—realizing how valuable the surviving animals were—started charging zoos for the privilege of hunting in their territories. As the supply of animals went down and the cost of obtaining them went up, zoos became more interested in preserving and extending the lives of the animals they had.

But the practical aspects of running and maintaining a zoo didn't change as fast as the philosophy. "Even with increased difficulties in capture and export, it would still be many decades before capture in the wild slowed significantly," Koebner writes in *Zoo*. Until about the early 1960s, zoos still obtained the majority of their animals from well-funded expeditions into the wild, which amounted to little more than raids upon wildlife areas in Africa and Asia. Barbaric practices, such as killing a mother elephant or hippopotamus in order to capture its child, were still commonplace and widely accepted.

ZOOS TODAY

In the 1960s and 1970s, however, zoos began to make substantive shifts toward conservation—not just of the animals in the zoo, but also those still in the wild. And instead of competing against one another, they began working together to accomplish these goals. This is critical in the case of endangered species that are extinct, or practically so, in the wild...and survive only in zoos today.

In cases where only a few dozen animals survive and their numbers are scattered among several zoos, the only way to bring the species back from extinction is to manage the animals as one population.

"Today's zoos have a very specific message to preach," writes Allen Nyhuis in *The Zoo Book*. "By introducing the public to the world's enormous variety of animals and their native habitats, they hope that people will better appreciate the animals and want to help preserve them."

*   *   *   *

Since 1984, America's zoos have spent more than
$1 billion on upgrading and improvements.

Your fingernails are made from the same substance as a bird's beak.

HOT STUFF!

*In 1991 America turned a culinary corner—that's the first
year we spent more money on salsa than on ketchup.
If you love "hot" food, this chapter is for you.*

BLAME IT ON COLUMBUS
When Christopher Columbus arrived in the New World, he thought he'd landed in India. So he called the people he met there "Indians."

That wasn't the only mistake he made: When his hosts served a spicy food containing hot chiles, he assumed the chiles were related to *piper nigrum*, the plant that produces black pepper.

They're actually part of the *Solanaceae*, or nightshade, family and are more closely related to potatoes, tomatoes, and eggplants. But chiles have been known as chile "peppers" ever since.

MADE IN BOLIVIA

All varieties of chile peppers descended from prehistoric wild chile plants that originated somewhere near present-day Bolivia. Scientists believe that most animals avoided the painfully hot plants, but birds ate them—apparently because they can't taste chiles—and spread the seeds all over Central and South America. Humans began eating the wild peppers as early as 7000 B.C., and had domesticated them by 2500 B.C.

South American and Latin American peoples, including the Aztecs, revered the peppers. They were used for everything from treating upper-respiratory disorders to ritualistic morning beverages. Montezuma, the last Aztec emperor, drank a concoction of chocolate and hot chiles for breakfast. The Incas took their reverence a step further: *Agar-Uchu*, or "Brother Chile Pepper" in English, is one of the four brothers of the Incan creation myth.

Chiles remained exclusive to the New World until Columbus brought some to Europe. From there they spread via trade routes to every remaining corner of the globe, and within a century they were firmly established in the cuisines of India, China, and Africa. Today an estimated 75% of the world's population eats chiles on a

Coconut shells can absorb more impact than most crash helmets.

daily basis. Mexico tops the list—Mexicans consume, on average, one chile per person, every day.

CHILE SCIENCE

What Makes Them Hot?

• All chiles contain a powerful alkaloid called capsaicin (cap-SAY-a-sin), which gives chiles their heat—and which isn't found in any other plants. It's so potent that humans can detect it even when it's diluted to one part per million.

• The "capsaicinoids," as they're also known, are produced in the plant by the *placenta*—the part just below the stem of the chile. That's also where the seeds and the "ribs" grow. On average, these parts are 16 times hotter than the rest of the plant, so it stands to reason that one way to cool down a chile (if that's what you want) is to remove the placenta.

• How hot is capsaicin? It's so strong that it's the main ingredient in a product designed to drive grizzly bears away. It's also the "pepper" in pepper spray, which has replaced tear gas spray in more than 1,200 police departments around the U.S. According to *Smithsonian* magazine, when sprayed in the face, "it causes eyes to slam shut and creates a spasm in the respiratory system—an unpleasant experience that lasts 30 to 45 minutes."

What Makes Them So Good?

• When you eat chiles, capsaicin irritates the pain receptor cells in your mouth.

• Some scientists believe the receptors then release something known as "substance P," which rushes to "alert" the brain to the pain. In response, the brain produces chemicals called endorphins that kill the pain and elicit feelings of well-being. Does hot, spicy food taste less hot to you after a couple of bites? Chile enthusiasts say this is the endorphins at work.

• In fact, some experts theorize that it's the addictive nature of endorphins, not the taste of the chiles themselves, that makes the spice so popular.

One in every 5 potatoes grown in the U.S. end up as french fries.

Cooling Down

• Do you reach for ice water when you eat a hot pepper? It's not a great idea—it not only won't cool your mouth down, it will probably make things worse by spreading the capsaicin around. Beer might work (experts aren't sure), but the best way to put out the fire is to drink cold milk...or eat any dairy product (e.g., frozen yogurt) with lactic acid. They contain casein, which acts like a detergent to help wash away the capsaicin. Other recommended foods: sugar, salt, tortillas, brandy Alexander, hunks of bread, and corn.

THE SCOVILLE SCALE

In 1912 Wilbur Scoville, a pharmacologist with the Parke Davis pharmaceutical company, needed to test the potency of some chiles he was mixing into a muscle salve. He mixed pure ground chiles into sugar-water and had a panel of tasters drink the water, in increasingly diluted concentrations, until the liquid was so diluted that it no longer burned their mouths.

Next, Scoville assigned a number to each chile based on how much it needed to be diluted before the tasters tasted no heat. The "Scoville scale," as it's still known, measures potency in multiples of 100. Here's how some popular chiles are ranked:

Bell and sweet peppers:	0–100 Scoville Units
New Mexican peppers:	500–1000
Española peppers:	1,000–1,500
Ancho & pasilla peppers:	1,000–2,000
Cascabel & cherry peppers:	1,000–2,500
Jalapeno & mirasol peppers:	2,500–5,000
Serrano peppers·	5,000–15,000
De Arbol peppers:	15,000–30,000
Cayenne & Tabasco:	30,000–50,000
Chiltepin peppers:	50,000–100,000
Scotch bonnet & Thai peppers:	100,000–350,000
Habanero peppers:	200,000 to 300,000
Red savina habanero peppers (the hottest chiles ever recorded):	as much as 577,000
Pure capsaicin:	16,000,000

The average American eats 4 pounds of artificial flavorings, colorings and preservatives each year.

Today the potency of chiles is measured very precisely by machines that calculate the exact amount of capsaicin in each chile. But the scale that is used is still named the Scoville scale in Wilbur Scoville's honor.

HEALTH NOTES

Can eating chiles make you sick? Epidemiologists from Yale University and the Mexico National Institute of Public Health concluded that chile peppers may cause stomach cancer. However, peppers also contain quercetin, a chemical shown to reduce cancer risk in lab animals, so who knows?

Other maladies to watch out for if you're a hardcore chile eater:

- **Salsa sniffles.** "Sweating and rhinitis (runny nose) caused by eating hot peppers."
- **Hunan hand.** "The skin irritation that comes from chopping chiles."
- **Jaloprocitis.** "The burn jalapeños leave as they exit the body."

On the other hand, according to a book called *The Healing Powers of Chili:*

- A 1986 experiment at Oxford University in England found that eating chiles may assist in burning calories.
- The popular muscle salve Heet is made mostly of capsaicin.
- Chilies are low in fat, high in fiber, and loaded with beta carotene and vitamin C. One half cup of chopped chile peppers offers more than twice the vitamin C of an orange.
- Capsaicin is a natural antibiotic, slowing down bacteria's growth.
- A few more ailments that have been treated with capsaicin: indigestion, acne, alcoholism, arthritis, bronchitis, cramps, hemorrhoids, herpes, low blood pressure, shingles, wounds.

MORE CHILE FACTS

- *Chilli* is the Nahuatl, or Aztec, word for the plant.
- According to most accounts, chile peppers were introduced into what is now the United States by Capitan General Juan de Oñante, who also founded Santa Fe in 1598.

A runner consumes about 7 quarts of oxygen while running a 100-yard dash.

PARLEZ-VOUS DOUBLESPEAK?

In previous Bathroom Readers, we've quizzed you on the Orwellian speaking habits of politicians and buraeucrats. But you can find doublespeak in the real world, too. See if you can match the terms used by businesses, educators, and advertisers on the left (100% guaranteed real!) with the English on the right. From William Lutz's book, Doublespeak Defined.

Doublespeak

1. "Urban transportation specialist"
2. "Adverse weather visibility device"
3. "Renaturalize"
4. "Sea-air interface climatic disturbance"
5. "Judgmental lapse"
6. "Maximum incapacitation"
7. "Physical pressure"
8. "Nutritional avoidance therapy"
9. "Induce adverse reaction"
10. "Therapeutic misadventure"
11. "Natural amenity unit"
12. "Organoleptic analysis"
13. "Intuitively counter-productive"
14. "Data transport system"

Real English

A. Stupid
B. Smell
C. Torture
D. Briefcase
E. Crime
F. Cartel
G. Explosion
H. Undertaker
I. Mistake
J. Censor
K. Love
L. Outhouse
M. Cab driver
N. Windshield wiper
O. Medical malpractice

When you pop a champagne cork, it can travel as fast as 100 mph.

15. "Implement a lean concept of synchronous organizational structures"

16. "Human kinetics"

17. "Fee for quality"

18. "Producer cooperative"

19. "Suboptimal"

20. "Uncontained engine failure"

21. "Variance"

22. "Personal manual database"

23. "Weed"

24. "Creative altruism"

25. "Grief therapist"

P. Physical education

Q. Failed

R. Hunt

S. Wave

T. Fire someone

U. Death penalty

V. Calendar

W. Diet

X. Harm

Y. Tuition

Answers

18. F; 19. Q; 20. G; 21. I; 22. V; 23. J; 24. K; 25. H.
10. O; 11. L; 12. B; 13. A; 14. D; 15. T; 16. P; 17. Y;
1. M; 2. N; 3. R; 4. S; 5. E; 6. U; 7. C; 8. W; 9. X;

* * * *

ROCK GOSSIP

Wretched Excess. "Aerosmith liked to bring a chainsaw with them on tour so that they could chop up hotel rooms with greater efficiency. The musical group also traveled with extra-long extension cords. Why? So that the TVs they threw out of their hotel rooms would keep playing all the way to the ground…or the pool."

The Battle of Waterloo wasn't fought in Waterloo. It was fought in Pancenoit, 4 miles away.

KNOW YOUR BIBLE(S)

You've heard of the King James Version...the Revised Standard Version... and the New Revised Standard Version. Ever wonder why there are so many different versions of the Bible in the first place? Here's an explanation—as well as a look at some versions you've probably never heard of—from John Dollison's 1993 book, Pope-Pourri.

I N THE BEGINNING
Even by nonreligious standards, the Bible and its various translations are the most significant written works the Western world has ever produced. They are mileposts by which historians measure the progress of European civilization: The Gutenberg Bible (c. 1455), for example, was the first book ever printed on a movable type printing press; Martin Luther's 1534 German translation is considered the birthplace of the modern German language, and the King James Version of 1611 has been described as "the noblest monument of English prose," superior even to the works of William Shakespeare.

No one knows how many Bibles have been distributed over the centuries, but the number easily exceeds 100 million copies—making it by far the most popular book ever printed. (The second-best selling book in history? Dr. Benjamin Spock's *Common Sense Book of Baby and Child Care*.) So far the Bible has been translated into more than 260 different languages, including more than 20 different English versions—most of which are still in print. If there's one thing all of these editions and translations demonstrate, it's that as spoken languages continue to evolve, the Bible needs to be updated regularly so that it remains accurate, understandable, and relevant to the people who read it. Here's a look at some of the most important, most popular, and most unusual updates ever produced:

THE CLASSICS
The Vulgate Bible (405). Written by Saint Jerome (c. 342-420), the first person to translate the ancient Greek, Hebrew, and other texts that make up the Bible, into Latin. His version was named the "Vulgate" Bible because Latin was the language of the *vulgar* or common people, as opposed to Greek, the language of the upper classes and the nobility. The Vulgate is still in use today.

Bagpipes were invented in Iran and brought to Scotland by the Romans.

The Wycliffe Bible (1384). Shortly before his death, the English religious reformer John Wycliffe translated the Vulgate Bible into English. However, the Catholic Church forbade English translations, and denounced it as heretical. Wycliffe died before the Church got its hands on him, but in 1415 the Council of Constance ordered his body dug up, burned, and thrown into a river.

The Tyndale Bible (1526). William Tyndale, an English Protestant reformer, published the first English translation of the Bible taken directly from the ancient Hebrew and Greek texts. It too was condemned by the Church. In 1535 Tyndale was arrested on charges of "willfully perverting the meaning of the Scriptures"; a year later he was strangled and burned at the stake. (The first approved English translation, the Douay-Rheims Bible, was finally published in 1582.)

The King James Bible (1616). Commissioned by England's King James I, who wanted an official English translation of the Bible of Protestant Churches. It was translated from a 16th-century Greek text...which was later discovered to contain 14 centuries of copyists' errors. So in 1855 the Anglican Church published an update, the English Revised Version—and in 1901 released the American Standard Version, a special translation for U.S. Protestants. (Its revision, the Revised Standard Version, was published in 1946... which in turn was followed by the *New* Revised Standard Version in 1989.)

WEIRD BIBLES

The Geneva Bible (1560). Nicknamed the "Breeches Bible" because it was the first Bible to depict Adam and Eve wearing pants. Why? The editors thought Genesis 3:7 (the passage where Adam and Eve "sewed fig leaves together and made themselves *aprons*") was too racy...so they dumped "apron" and replaced it with "breeches."

Webster's Bible (1883). Published by Noah Webster, creator of *Webster's Dictionary*. He too thought the Bible was filled with smut: "Many words and phrases," he complained, "are so offensive, especially to females, as to create a reluctance in young persons to attend Bible classes and schools in which they are required to read passages which cannot be replaced without a blush." So he rewrote the entire Bible, removing the "filthiest" passages entirely and cleaning up the less offensive ones. Words such as "whore," "fornication," and "teat" gave way to milder expressions like "lewd woman," "lewdness," and "breast."

ULTRASPECIALIZED BIBLES

The Black Bible Chronicles. In 1993 African-American Family Press released *The Black Bible Chronicles: A Survival Manual for the Streets*, a street-language paraphrase of the first five books of the Old Testament. ("Thou shalt not steal" appears as "You shouldn't be takin' from your homeboys"; "Thou shalt not kill" translates "Don't waste nobody"; and "Thou shalt not commit adultery" emerges as "Don't mess around with someone else's ol' man or ol' lady.") The book was written by P. K. McCary, a Houston, Texas, Sunday school teacher who was having trouble reaching inner-city kids using standard Bible texts. "Over the years, I have found that kids just pick up on this language. For them, it's a kick. As my daughter would say, 'It's tight.'"

The Klingon Authorized Version. Ambrose Bierce once described faith as "belief without evidence in what is told by one who speaks without knowledge, of things without parallel." The folks at the Klingon Bible Translation Project are taking the concept one step further—they're translating the Bible into an imaginary language so that it can be read by a race of people who don't exist...except in the minds of "Star Trek" fans. Sample translation: John 3:16 ("For God so loved the world, that he gave his only begotten Son, that whosoever believeth in him should not perish but have everlasting life") reads: "toH qo' muSHa'pu'qu'-mo' JoH'a', wa' puqloDDaj nobpu' ghaH 'ej ghaHbaq Harchugh vay', vaj not Hegh ghaH, 'ach yln jub ghajbeh ghaH."

When finished, the Klingon Authorized Version may prove two things: 1) that the Word of God truly is universal; and 2) that "Star Trek" fans need to get out more often.

*   *   *

"The young have aspirations that never come to pass, the old have reminiscences of what never happened." —**H.H. Munro (Saki)**

UNCLE JOHN'S "STALL OF FAME"

More members of Uncle John's bathroom pantheon.

Honoree: Glen Dorenbush, formerly of San Francisco
Notable Achievement: Being flushed down the toilets of his favorite bars after he died
True Story: According to news reports, "When Dorenbush died in the summer of 1996, his cronies ended up with eight pounds of his ashes and an interesting predicament. The amiable eccentric left no will when he checked out, but had made it clear to those who knew him best what he wanted done with his remains: He wanted most of his ashes flushed down the toilets of his favorite bars."

The dilemma: "It's technically illegal in California to sprinkle cremated remains down the can, not to mention bad for the plumbing." His friends finally decided to "scatter some ashes on a beach in Puerto Vallarta where he loved to vacation and some more in the ocean off Stinson Cafe on Hyde Street. The rest, it was decided, would go down the latrines at several undisclosed locations."

Honoree: An unnamed homeowner in Fayetteville, Arkansas
Notable Achievement: Creative bathroom-based entrepreneurship
True Story: In 1995 the man bought Jimmy Johnson's former house and had a great idea while rennovating his bathroom. He took out an ad in a local paper, offering "a great for football fans": For only $250, they could own (and sit on) the toilet once used by the ex–Dallas Cowboys coach.

Honoree: Richard List of Berkeley, California
Notable Achievement: Creating a museum (and philosophical statement) featuring painted toilets
True Story: "New York has the MOMA," writes a San Francisco reporter, "Paris has the Louvre. Berkeley has the New Sense Museum, where art is strictly in the eyes of the beholder. The New Sense (say it fast) consists of a vacant, weed-strewn lot studded with weird ob-

jects, most notably a flotilla of commodes painted fluorescent pink, orange and green."

According to Richard List, the museum's guiding force, "People say, 'I don't get the message.' Well, that's the point. Life is a mystery."

Honoree: St. Louis circuit judge Edward Peek
Notable Achievement: Presiding over the first murder trial ever instigated by an argument about toilet paper
True Story: There's nothing funny about this, of course, but it's too weird to leave out. In the late 1980s, a 36-year-old man admitted to the judge that he had shot and killed his younger brother. The reason: He was angry that his brother had "used too much of a new eight-roll package of toilet paper." The man was convicted of second-degree murder.

Honoree: Barney Smith of San Antonio, Texas
Notable Achievement: Created the Toilet Seat Museum in his garage
True Story: Smith, a plumber, asked his customers if he could keep the old toilet seat every time he installed a new one. "Then," says the *Houston Post*, "he would decorate each seat with something special, things like keepsakes from a vacation or mementos from a historic moment....Smith has decorated and dedicated about 400 toilet-seat lids, artistically altering the functional commode covers to become hanging history. And he has generously hung them for the world to see."

Honoree: Nelson Camus of Hacienda Heights, California
Notable Achievement: Inventing the world's first urine-powered battery
True Story: The "Argentine-born electrical engineer," says John Kohut in *Dumb, Dumber, Dumbest*, "announced that his battery generates more power than standard acid-reaction batteries and is cheaper. His partner, Ed Aguayo, said 10 urine-powered batteries, each about half the size of a normal car battery, could power a normal house." No word on when the battery will become available.

IT'S A WEIRD, WEIRD WORLD

More proof that truth really is stranger than fiction.

PERFORMING UNDER PRESSURE

"On September 12, the Great Hurricane of 1938 devastated the New England states. That morning a man in West Hampton Beach received a barometer in the mail. The needle was stuck on "hurricane." Disgusted, and thinking it was defective, he marched back to the Post Office and mailed the instrument back to the store from which he had purchased it. When he returned, his home was gone."

—*Our Fascinating Earth*

DID HE CROAK?

"Doctors in a Mexican hospital were in the midst of open-heart surgery when a frog fell out of an overhead lamp and landed on the patient."

—*The Fortean Times*

ROCK YOUR WORLD

"For years, maps have shown that northern Germany's highest mountain, the Brocken, was 3,747 feet tall. But recently, more precise measurements revealed that the peak is only 3,741 feet tall. To avoid correcting the world's maps, a construction company trucked 19 tons of granite to the summit, stacking the rocks in a 6-foot pile."

—*Portland Oregonian*, February 28, 1998

NEXT COMES A *STRAIGHT* JACKET

"Despite 18 years working at a Florida fishing camp, Freddie Padgett was so terrified of water that he wore a life jacket to bed on stormy nights. Friends made fun of him, until a twister sucked him out of his RV while he was sleeping and dropped him into Lake Harney over a mile away. He suffered broken ribs and other injuries, but authorities say the life jacket probably saved his life."

—*The Skeptic*

Your teeth are 6 months older than you are—they start growing 6 months before you're born.

THE BEST BUSINESS DEAL IN U.S. HISTORY, PART III

Here's the last installment of the story. (Part II is on page 295.)

CAR WARS

On November 14, 1914, the first Dodge rolled off the assembly line. It had a bigger engine than the Model T and a modern stick-shift transmission, as well as features like a speedometer, an electric starter, electric headlights, a windshield, and a spare tire. And it only cost $100 more than the Model T.

THE EMPIRE STRIKES BACK

Naturally, Henry Ford was not amused that Ford dividends were being used to bankroll his competition. But when the Dodge brothers offered to sell him their Ford stock, he refused...and instead announced in 1916 that the Ford Motor Company would no longer pay dividends and would instead plow all of its profits back into the business.

The Dodge brothers sued to force Ford to pay dividends, and in 1919 they won: Ford was required to pay $19 million in back dividends (most of which went directly back to Henry Ford, since he owned the lion's share of the stock anyway), but Ford would not give in. On December 1918, he announced that he was "retiring" from Ford and turning control over to his son Edsel.

Henry left for an extended vacation in southern California. Then on March 5, 1919, the *Los Angles Examiner* broke a story that shook the automobile industry:

HENRY FORD ORGANIZING HUGE NEW COMPANY TO BUILD A BETTER, CHEAPER CAR

According to the report, while his old company had employed 50,000 workers, the new company would hire as many as 250,000 and would have automobile plants all over the world. The scale of production would make it possible to sell cars for between $250 and $350, cheaper than they had ever been sold before. No other auto manufacturer would be able to match the price.

In her entire life, Queen Berengaria of England never once visited England.

GETTING OUT

The Dodge brothers were in a bind—if Ford was serious, it would probably drive both Dodge Brothers and the Ford Motor Company out of business. Their own company and their Ford stock would be worthless.

"But the Dodge brothers and the other minority shareholders found themselves mysteriously approached in the following weeks by would-be Ford share purchasers," Robert Lacey writes. "It became clear that the threads all led back to Henry, working through Edsel in Detroit. The bidding started at $7,500 per share (the Dodge brothers owned 2,000 shares). The Dodge brothers responded with their $12,500 price—and $12,500, in the end, became the price that Ford had to pay." The "huge new company," it turned out, was just a ploy that Ford used to depress the value of the Dodge brothers stock so that he could buy them out on the cheap.

SO LONG, FELLAS

The Dodge brothers received $25 million for their Ford stock, which came on top of the $9.5 million they had received in dividends between 1903 and 1919, for a total return of $34.5 million on their original $10,000 investment. Even though Ford had gotten the better of the bargain, the Dodges (along with the other original investors in Ford) made so much money that business historians now consider it the most profitable investment in the history of American commerce.

Note: Less than a year later, the Dodge brothers were attending the 1920 New York Auto Show when Horace suddenly fell ill with pneumonia. His condition was so grave that John maintained a round-the-clock bedside vigil, only to catch pneumonia himself and die 10 days later. Horace lingered for just a few more months before he died. In 1925 their widows sold the Dodge Brothers Motor Car Company to a New York banking syndicate for $146 million in cash—at the time the largest cash transaction in auto history. In May 1929, the bankers sold Dodge Brothers to automaker Walter Chrysler for $170 million…just in time for the Great Depression.

Odds that you will become famous enough to merit mention in a history book: 1 in 6 million.

THE DISCOVERY OF PENICILLIN, Part II

Dr. Alexander Fleming thought he'd stumbled onto something important, but could never figure out how to make it really useful. Fortunately for us, he wasn't the only person paying attention. Here's the last part of our story about discovering penicillin. (Part I is on page 300.)

WHAT IS THIS STUFF?

For the next few days, an excited Fleming showed his moldy discovery to anyone who would listen, insisting that something really interesting had happened.

He was eager to identify it. What kind of mold was it? An expert on fungi—a Dr. C. J. LaTouche—had a laboratory on the floor below Fleming's, and LaTouche told him it was a species of *Penicillium*—green molds that grow on stale bread, ripening cheese, and decaying fruit. The man who originally named the mold thought that the tuftlike ends of its branches looked like paintbrushes; the same Latin root gives us the word *pencil*.

So Fleming decided to name his discovery "penicillin."

WELCOME TO...THE TWILIGHT ZONE?

The mold that Fleming preserved was similar to one of the species that LaTouche was keeping in his room downstairs. So it seems likely that one of its spores found its way into the air, up the stairwell, through the always-open door of Fleming's laboratory, and onto the historic culture dish.

What's truly astonishing is that *that specific mold* was the one to land in Fleming's petri dish. Because *none* of the other molds in LaTouche's laboratory—nor any that Fleming could come up with independently—was able to kill bacteria. Not one. In fact, in the years since then, intensive searches by many workers have not yielded *any species anywhere in the Old World* that produces penicillin. (In 1943, a strain of *Penicillium crysogenum* was found in Illinois that is even more potent than Fleming's, and this strain is

The "five golden rings" in the *Twelve Days of Christmas* weren't

now used in the commercial manufacture of penicillin.) Fleming's strain of *P. notatum* has never again been found outside the laboratory.

SO CLOSE...BUT SO FAR

Fleming began investigating what other bacteria were stopped by penicillin. He found that it can kill the germs that cause scarlet fever, pneumonia, gonorrhea, meningitis, and diphtheria, a roll call of the world's most dangerous infections. Penicillin had the potential of being the ideal antiseptic, provided he could show that it was safe for humans.

In Hollywood, that would be the end of the story—he would share his discovery, and people's lives would be saved immediately. But that's not what happened.

In Fleming's hands, penicillin proved to be quite unstable. When he stored it at room temperature, he could never make it last more than a week or two. And when he had a patient to try it on, he never seemed to have a fresh batch ready.

Fleming assigned two young researchers—Dr. Stuart Craddock and Dr. Frederick Ridley—to work on it. They did intensive research for four months, and made considerable progress toward isolating the active agent in the mold...but they still couldn't figure out how to use it as an effective antiseptic.

THE OFFICIAL NEWS

The announcement of the discovery of penicillin was made at a lecture at the Medical Research Club on February 13, 1929. The publication of the results appeared in the issue of May 10, 1929 of the *British Journal of Experimental Pathology*. The paper described the powerful antibacterial action of penicillin, and Fleming speculated on its use as an antiseptic. But he couldn't report any great clinical success in its use.

Fleming continued to experiment with it; he tried, for example, to use penicillin as an antiseptic on open wounds. But results were unspectacular. Ironically, he made no attempt to administer penicillin internally to clinic patients...or even to sick animals.

And then, strangely, the work came to a halt.

A great discovery had been made, and then its development

ceased for 10 years. How could it have happened? Why did it take the world so long to recognize the miracle that was penicillin? Why didn't Fleming continue to pursue the project vigorously?

THE HARD TRUTH

Part of the answer is that Fleming, like any researcher, was working on more than one project at a time, and didn't have enough resources to follow every possibility. He probably judged that he had done all he could with penicillin, and it was now time to pursue something else. His results were published where anyone could read them.

Meanwhile, the world around him was entering some desperate times. The Great Depression of the 1930s hit especially hard in Britain. When the concern of every person and every institution was centered on simple economic survival, the practice of research, even when it dealt with life-and-death matters like disease and its cure, must have seemed a great luxury.

Elsewhere in Europe, totalitarian governments had come to power. Soon a stream of refugees from their cruelty would be flowing westward. And after that there was the spectre of war.

IT AIN'T OVER 'TIL THE SCIENTIST SINGS

Fortunately for humankind, the story of penicillin did not end with Fleming's work. One of the important changes in medicine that took place during the 1930s was the discovery and use of the sulfa drugs—chemicals that kill or at least inhibit bacteria when taken internally. The success of these drugs alerted the medical community to the idea that safe chemical antiseptics were not only possible, but that they really existed.

The Other Heroes

The unsung heroes of the penicillin story are the group of pathologists at Oxford University led by Dr. Howard Florey, an Australian, and Dr. Ernst B. Chain, a Jewish refugee from Germany. In 1938 they started looking though scientific literature, examining all the antibacterial agents that had been reported, hoping to find something that would be effective against a wider range of diseases. Fleming's penicillin featured prominently on their list. Not only was it a promising germ killer, but it was available in their own laboratory. Descendants of Fleming's mold strain were being carefully tended and grown for their use as a reagent.

The Oxford team learned how to concentrate the penicillin and to keep it stable. They found that mice infected with deadly pneumonia were miraculously cured by penicillin. It was an experiment that Fleming might have been able to do, but he had not tried.

After this discovery the Oxford workers learned how to mass-produce penicillin until they had enough of it to test on human patients. By this time World War II had started, and bombs were falling on English cities. The work was transferred to chemical plants in the United States, which were able to produce enough penicillin to save the lives of thousands of wounded soldiers.

Miracle Drug

In peacetime the drug has been made available to wipe out the threat of diseases like pneumonia and scarlet fever. All of us have almost certainly made use of penicillin or some of the other antibiotics that have followed in its wake.

In December 1945, Fleming, Florey, and Chain shared the Nobel prize in medicine, Fleming for the discovery, Florey and Chain for the development of penicillin. The revolution in medical practice that these men began continues today.

*   *   *

...DEMOCRACY IN ACTION

• How did the Swedish town of Hurdenburg select its mayors during the Middle Ages? "All the candidates sat around a table, bending forward so that their beards rested on the table, and a single louse would be placed on the table's center. The man into whose beard the louse climbed would be mayor of Hurdenburg the following year."

• In the 1830s Congressman Davy Crockett—yes, *that* Davy Crockett—delivered a speech on the floor of the House of Representatives in which he declared that whiskey, the sale of which was banned in the Capitol building, should not only be legal but also free. "Congress allows lemonade to members and it is charged under the head of stationary," Crockett thundered, "I move that whiskey be allowed under the item of fuel."

Last animal in the dictionary: the zyzzyva, a tropical American weevil.

GREAT MOMENTS IN ADVERTISING

It may be hard to believe, but Americans weren't always concerned about bad breath, foot odor, dandruff, etc. It took a concerted effort by advertising agencies to focus our attention on these earth-shattering problems. The BRI salutes this contribution to our way of life by recognizing three memorable ad-chievements.

T HE DISCOVERY OF "HALITOSIS" (1926)
Product: Listerine
Story: Listerine antiseptic had been a product of the Lambert Company since the 1880s, but was never particularly successful. By the 1920s—the early years of Prohibition—its most attractive feature to consumers was its 25% alcohol content.

In 1926 the company decided to boost sales by creating an ad campaign around one special feature...but what could the product actually do? No one was sure, so they gave it to a chemist to find out. His list of Listerine's benefits included an unfamiliar term: "Removes halitosis."

"What's that mean?" the president asked.

"Bad breath," the chemist replied.

"Perfect!" said the president.

Armed with a scientific-sounding name, Listerine pioneered a new advertising approach: presenting bad breath as a crippling social disease that Listerine could (of course) cure. Their ads showed endless situations in which Halitosis spelled business and romantic ruin.

Sample Ad: (Photo of a woman staring into a mirror) *What Secret Is Your Mirror Holding Back?* "Night after night, she would peer questioningly into her mirror, vainly seeking the reason. She was a beautiful girl and talented, too...yet in the one pursuit that stands foremost in the mind of every girl and woman—marriage—she was a failure.

"Many men came and went in her life. She was often a bridesmaid, but never a bride. And the secret her mirror held back

---

Elvis was nearsighted. He owned $60,000 worth of prescription sunglasses when he died.

concerned a thing she least suspected—a thing people will not tell you to your face…Halitosis!"

Results: In a few years, the company's profits increased 4,000%. Roland Marchand notes in *Advertising the American Dream*:

> Not surprisingly, the company's style and strategy gave rise to a whole new school of advertising practice [of "scare" ads].… Phrases like "the halitosis style" and "the halitosis appeal" became standard advertising jargon. In unmistakable tribute, copywriters discovered and labeled over a hundred new diseases.

INVENTING "ATHLETE'S FOOT" (1928)

Product: Absorbine Jr.

Story: Until 1928 Absorbine Jr. advertised itself as relief for "sore muscles, muscular aches, bruises, burns, cuts, and abrasions." Then, inspired by Listerine's success, they looked for—and found— a new affliction they could cure: ringworm of the foot. Their masterstroke was making it *less* scientific sounding. They dubbed it "athlete's foot," and portrayed it as the secret worry of the upper-class.

Sample Ad: (Photo of a man relaxing on a yacht) *"You'd Like to Be in This Man's Shoes…Yet He Has* ATHLETE'S FOOT! A yacht, …a half dozen town houses and country seats…a flock of gleaming motors and a railroad or two—this man has everything the world has to offer—*and* ATHLETE'S FOOT! And he doesn't know what it is! A power among big men, he feels *furtive* about the dry, scaly condition between his little toes. But he will know soon what worries him. For now all medical authority knows that what he has is a form of ringworm infection caused by *tinea trichophyton* and commonly known as 'Athlete's Foot.'"

Results: Hardly anyone paid attention to it before Absorbine Jr.'s ad campaign. Today it's treated as a bona fide medical condition.

COINING THE TERM "B.O." (1928)

Product: Lifebuoy Soap

Story: In 1928 Lifebuoy, described by D. Allen Foster in his book, *Advertising*, as "a liver-colored cake smelling like a hospital after the morning cleaning," found its sales slipping badly. So Lever Brothers hired a new ad agency…which took the Listerine approach one step further—to "planned vulgarity." Foster explains:

B.O. (*body odor*) was its keynote....The copy hammered away at the deodorant theme—"How to play it safe"—with pictures of people practically holding their noses.

In *I Hear America Listening*, Stuart Flexner describes the Lifebuoy campaign as "the hallmark of scare ads against underarm and other body perspiration odors."

Sample Ad: (Picture of anguished office worker peering over his shoulder at two huddled co-workers) "*ONE LITTLE WHISPER SHATTERED MY PRIDE.* I'd given Dick and Bob a cheery good night! They merely nodded in reply—but I was getting used to their unfriendliness. Then, as I walked away—*came the whisper—* 'B.O.!' That explained it all. In a flash, I understood the coolness of others here at the office...my failure to land that promotion I looked forward to.

"*Nothing can ruin chances of social and business success as quickly as 'B.O.' Even the faintest hint of it is enough to turn others against you....*Tests prove that Lifebuoy not only stops 'B.O.' but that you can build increasingly better protection against 'B.O.' by using Lifebuoy every day!"

Results: Of course, it worked. By the early 1930s, "the two-note foghorn warning 'Beee-oohhhh' was known to everyone through radio ads—and Lifebuoy was the best-selling soap in America."

STILL MORE DISEASES!!!

Flexner writes: "With the success of Halitosis and B.O., modern advertising continued to coin and popularize terms for both real and imaginary ailments and embarrassing conditions." Some BRI favorites:

Accelerator Toe
Ashtray Breath
Acidosis ("sour stomach")
Bromodosis ("sweaty foot odor")
Cosmetic Skin
Dishpan Hands
Enlarged Pores
Homotosis ("lack of attractive home furnishings")
Incomplete Elimination
Middle-Age Spread
Office Hips
Pink Toothbrush ("bleeding gums")
Smoker's Fur
Summer Sluggishness
Tattletale Gray (dirt left on clothes by mild laundry detergent)
Tell-Tale Tongue

THE BIRTH OF THE AMERICAN FLAG, PART II

Here's the second installment of our history
of Old Glory. (Part I starts on page 224.)

GOING THROUGH SOME CHANGES
A flag with 13 stars and 13 stripes made perfect sense for a country with 13 states. In 1791, however, Vermont became a state, with Kentucky following a year later. Congress had to decide whether to change the flag, keeping in mind that it would be expensive. It was estimated at the time that the new flags would cost $60 each for every ship in the country—a cost that opponents warned would have to be borne again and again as new states entered the Union.

In the end, national pride won out over cost considerations. Both the House and Senate passed a bill stipulating that after May 1, 1795, "the flag of the United States be fifteen stripes, alternate red and white; and that the union be fifteen stars, white in a blue field."

A LONG STORY

By 1816 there were 19 states in the Union, with a 20th, Mississippi, on the way. Adding 4 or 5 more stripes would change the look of the flag considerably.

Making matters more confusing, there was little uniformity in American flags flown around the country. The official flag had 15 stars and stripes, but as new states entered the union, some states—the new arrivals in particular—had added new stars and stripes so they would be represented on the flag just as any other state. Some states flew flags with as many as 19 stars and stripes, while one government building in Washington, D.C., had a flag with only 9 stripes. Something had to be done.

In 1817 the Congress asked Capt. Sam Reid, a hero of the War of 1812, to come up with a lasting solution. He proposed returning to the original 13 stripes, but allowing a new star to be added to the blue field for each new state that entered the Union. Acting on his suggestion, Congress drafted and President James Monroe signed

---

Black sheep have a better sense of smell than white sheep.

into law the Flag Act of 1818. Once again, however, it was not a major issue for many Americans. Some politicians even resented having to "waste" time on the legislation. "A consummate piece of frivolity," huffed one on the Senate floor while the bill was being debated.

STAR SYSTEM

The bill passed by only four votes, and once again left significant details out. As in 1777, the new resolution did not specify the exact size of the flag or how the stars should be arranged. This time, no one did anything about it for 94 years. An investigation conducted in 1912 found that flags of 66 different sizes and proportions were adorning federal offices. President William Howard Taft responded by issuing an executive order that finally established official guidelines for the flag. It commanded that the stars on the flag, which by now numbered 48, be arranged in "six horizontal rows of eight stars each."

ONE MORE TIME

President Taft's 48-star flag remained the standard for nearly 47 years—until 1959, when both Alaska and Hawaii were on the verge of statehood. How would the 50 stars be arranged on the new flag? The House of Representatives introduced three different bills addressing the issue, but in the end President Eisenhower just issued an executive order directing that the stars be arranged in five rows of six, and four rows of five. The changes went into effect at 12:01 a.m. on July 4, 1960, with a special provision allowing existing 48-star flags to remain flying until they wore out, which saved the federal government from having to replace the more than 51,000 flags flown outside government buildings when the new flags went into effect. The flag has been unchanged ever since.

FLAG FACTS

• Capt. Sam Reid, whose flag design led to the Flag Act of 1818, received little recognition (Peter Wendover, the congressman who pushed the Flag Act through Congress, got most of the credit). Not only is the name Sam Reid almost completely unknown today, within a relatively few years after proposing the changes to

---

What do all of the characters in Shakespeare's plays have in common? None of them smoke.

the flag, he became a forgotten man in his own time. His death in the 1860s went almost unnoticed, and he was buried in a grave that remained unmarked until the 1940s, when Congress finally appropriated money for a tombstone and a flagpole for his grave.

• On June 14, 1777, the Continental Congress approved a resolution creating a national flag (which is why we now celebrate Flag Day on June 14). At the time, however, the resolution wasn't exactly the top news of the day. No one outside of the government knew about it until a Pennsylvania newspaper mentioned it in a brief article on September 2, 1777.

• On the other hand, on December 22, 1942, the Code of Flag Display and Use came into being. It more than made up for people's lack of interest in the past by describing, in meticulous detail, everything from what time of day to raise and lower the flag to how to drape it over a casket.

*   *   *

HOUSEHOLD TIPS

Here are some tips that B.R.I. member "Five2447" e-mailed to our Web site. We don't know if they work or not, but what the heck, we thought we'd pass them along:

• "To get the most juice out of fresh lemons, bring them to room temperature and roll them under your palm against the kitchen counter before squeezing."

• "If you accidentally add too much salt to a dish while it's still cooking, drop in a peeled potato. It absorbs the excess salt."

• "Wrap celery in aluminum foil when putting in the refrigerator—it will keep for weeks."

• "Stuff a miniature marshmallow in the bottom of a sugar cone to prevent ice cream drips."

• "Most Important: If your VCR has a year setting on it, which most do, you will not be able to use the programmed recording feature after 12/31/99. Don't throw it away. Instead set it for the year 1972 as the days are the same as the year 2000. The manufacturers won't tell you. They want you to buy a new Y2K VCR. Pass this along to all your friends."

WORD ORIGINS

Here are some more interesting word origins.

AMBULANCE

Meaning: A specialized vehicle for transporting the injured to a hospital

Origin: "The name comes from an invention of Napoleon Bonaparte's, *l'hôpital ambulant* (walking hospital), a litter fitted with bandages and other first-aid equipment that served as a field hospital for wounded soldiers. In time, the litters became elaborate and mechanized, yielding first to horse-drawn wagons, eventually to motorized ambulances." (From *Fighting Words*, by Christine Ammer)

TABOO

Meaning: A behavior or activity that is prohibited

Origin: "Originally a Tongan word, *tabu*, meaning 'marked as holy.' The first taboos were prohibitions against the use or even the mention of certain things because of religious belief that to do so would invoke the wrath of the gods. The word gradually was extended in use to cover all sorts of prohibitions or bans based upon social convention." (From *Dictionary of Word and Phrase Origins, Vol. III*, by William and Mary Morris)

BUMPKIN

Meaning: A loutish countryman

Origin: "From the Dutch *boomkin*, small tree—hence, a countryman thought to possess the tree's intelligence." (From *Loose Cannons and Red Herrings*, by Robert Claiborne)

SENATE

Meaning: A representative body in a republic or democracy

Origin: "Literally, 'a gathering of old men.' Like most cultures, ancient Roman society respected age. In the days before the Roman Empire, tribes would gather. The representatives from these clans were usually elders, whose experience led to wiser, more thoughtful deliberation. When the empire flourished, the tradition of the council of elders continued. To this day there are age requirements for our Senate." (From *Where in the Word?*, by David Muschell)

UNCLE JOHN'S TOP 10 AMAZING COINCIDENCES

We're constantly finding stories about amazing coincidences, so in this BR, Uncle John listed his 10 favorites. Send us yours, and next edition, we'll do a readers' Top 10.

10. WHAT GOES AROUND...

"In 1965, at age four, Roger Lausier was saved from drowning off a beach at Salem, Mass., by a woman named Alice Blaise. Nine years later, in 1974, on the same beach, Roger paddled his raft into the water and pulled a drowning man from the water. The man was Alice Blaise's husband."

—*The Book of Lists*

9. NUMBER NINE, NUMBER NINE...

BELOIT, Wisconsin—"Nicholas Stephen Wadle was born at 9:09 a.m. on the ninth day of the ninth month of 1999. But the string of coincidences doesn't end there. He weighed 9 pounds, 9 ounces.

"A spokeswoman for Beloit Memorial Hospitals said the mother 'couldn't believe it,' but 'the most surprised were the professionals involved....As the nines started to stack up, they were going crazy.'

"The baby was due Sept. 15, but complications with the births of Mrs. Wadles's two older children led her doctor to schedule a cesarean section for Thursday, to be safe. The delivery was set for 8:00 a.m. but there was an emergency, which allowed the 9:09 birth."

—Appleton, Wisconsin, *Post Crescent*, September 10, 1999
(*Contributed by Julie Roeming*)

8. ARE YOU MY DADDY?

"Wilf Hewitt, 86, a widower from Southport, wanted to look through a list of registered voters in the library, and asked the woman who had the list if she was going to be long. Vivien Fletoridis replied that she was looking for a man named Hewitt. She was his daughter, whom he had not seen for 46 years. Wilf had had a wartime love affair with Vivien's mother, who had died in 1983. Their daughter was adopted in 1941 and went to Australia with her foster parents. In July 1987 she traced her two brothers and sister through an agency, and then set out to find her father."

—*The Fortean Times*

7. REINCARNATED SURVIVOR

"On three separate occasions—in 1664, 1785, and 1860—there were shipwrecks where only one person survived the accident. Each time that one person's name was Hugh Williams."

—*The Book of Useless Information*

6. I DO, I THINK

"A woman in Kissimmee, Florida, should have no trouble remembering her new husband's name. But, following a bizarre chain of coincidences surrounding the couple's wedding, she *might* have trouble remembering what he looks like.

"Ronald Legendre married his girlfriend, Hope, in August 1995. The best man—who wasn't related to the groom in any way—was also named Ronald Legendre. And the ceremony was performed by someone who wasn't connected to *either* man: Judge Ronald Legendre."

—*Knuckleheads in the News*

5. SECRET-AGENT KID

"James Bond, 15, a pupil at Argoed High School, North Wales, and a candidate for examinations in 1990, was given the examination number 007 by a computer quirk."

—*The World's Most Incredible Stories*

4. HER NAME IS MY NAME, TOO

"A computer mix-up that gave two American women the same social security number was responsible for highlighting a further series of incredible coincidences. Patricia Kern of Colorado and Patricia di Biasi of Oregon were brought together by the blunder.

"The women discovered they had both been born Patricia Ann Campbell with fathers called Robert. They were born on the same date, too: March 13, 1941. Both Patricias married military men in 1959, within eleven days of one another, and had children aged nineteen and twenty-one. They also shared an interest in painting with oils, had studied cosmetics and worked as bookkeepers."

—*One in a Million*

3. AND HER NAME IS MY NAME, TOO

"Mother of two, Michelle Samways, was caught up in a spot of trouble—with mother of two Michelle Samways. The two women moved into numbers 5 and 6 Longstone Close, Portland, England, in Oct. 1994 and hardly a day goes by without a mix-up of some kind. They discovered that they share the same name only when they entered a raffle at a toddlers' group. The two Michelles, aged 26 and 27, were both named after the 1965 Beatles song. They are the same height and build, [and have] similar hair color."

—*The Fortean Times*

2. BABIES KEEP FALLING ON MY HEAD

"Joseph Figlock was passing an apartment block in Detroit in 1975 when he was knocked unconscious. A baby had fallen fourteen stories and landed on him. Both survived. One year later, Figlock was passing the same apartment block—and once again he was hit by a falling child…and survived!"

—*One in a Million*

And the #1 coincidence is…

1. CIVIL SERVANT

"One of the lesser-known figures of American history is Wilmer McLean, a Virginia farmer who took little interest in politics.

"In 1861, most of the Rebel army marched onto McLean's land. The Union forces attempted to bar their way, and the first full-scale battle of the Civil War (Battle of Bull Run), got underway—right on his farm. Thirteen months later, it happened again. The second battle at Bull Run destroyed McLean's land. McLean had had enough. He packed his wagons and moved two hundred miles away from the war.

"Three years later, in a weird twist of fate, two men confronted each other in Wilmer McLean's parlor. These two men talked and signed a document on McLean's best table; for he had moved to a little village called Appomattox Court House—where Robert E. Lee and Ulysses S. Grant negotiated the end of the Civil War."

—*Ripley's Believe It or Not*

Folk wisdom: More babies are conceived in December than in any other month.

ANYTHING FOR PUBLICITY

After Princess Diana's death on August 31, 1997, a Wall Street Journal reporter kept a watch on the press releases sent to newspapers. He was amazed at how quickly (and crassly) people tried to use her death as a PR "hook." Here are some of the press releases his office received.

August 31

PSYCHOLOGIST CALLS [FOR] SELF-EXAMINATION OF TABLOID VOYEURISM

Los Angeles, Entertainment Wire

A psychologist in Hollywood reacting to the tragedy in Paris today in which Princess Diana was involved in a serious automobile accident allegedly exacerbated by pursuing paparazzi said: "We are all to blame if this accident is a result of Princess Diana fleeing from tabloid photographers. The photographers are paid huge sums for these photos because we are addicted to them...."

Psychologist Robert R. B_____, Ph.D., has assisted radio, TV and print media since 1984 to find answers and provide insight to enhance understanding of psychological issues.

AMERICAN PHYSICIANS MOURN DEATH OF PRINCESS DIANA

Chicago, PR Newswire

Physicians of the American Medical Association are saddened at the tragic death of Diana, Princess of Wales....

Although we never worked with Princess Diana directly, the AMA is nevertheless proud of our mutual commitment to the campaign for a worldwide ban on anti-personnel land mines....As the world mourns this stunning loss, the AMA urges physicians everywhere to remember Princess Diana as a woman of courage, compassion and grace.

HOLLYWOOD PUBLICIST TO LEAD LAW CHANGE FOR PAPARAZZI STALKINGS

Los Angeles, PR Newswire

In response to the death of Princess Diana and producer Dodi Al-Fayed, Hollywood publicist Michael Levine has pledged to lead an effort to change laws to... punish the criminal behavior of stalking tabloid journalists.

Levine, who represented Hollywood producer Fayed for a year in the early '90s, expressed outrage at the "totally unnecessary loss of innocent life."

"I have witnessed the behavior of the tabloids go from obnoxious to criminal in the last few years," said Levine. "I'm frankly surprised that something like this didn't happen sooner."

DIANA'S DEATH—THE TRAUMA HER CHILDREN WILL EXPERIENCE

Los Angeles, Entertainment Wire

A psychologist reacting to the tragedy in Paris...says that another tragedy is just beginning. "The trauma faced by her two children and the psychological reactions they will face today and live with the rest of their lives."

"...There is no way we can begin to describe what these children are feeling but it's most likely a combination of shock, anger, denial, and depression. We might have lost a princess but they lost a mother and they need the help of experienced professionals to sort it out...." Contact: Robert R. B_____, Ph.D.

September 1
STATEMENT BY THE REV. BILLY GRAHAM ON THE DEATH OF DIANA, PRINCESS OF WALES

Minneapolis, PR Newswire

Like almost everyone else in the world, the unexpected death of Diana, Princess of Wales, came as a profound shock to my wife Ruth and me. I know that Her Majesty The Queen and the other members of the Royal Family especially [are] carrying a heavy burden during this time, and we are praying for them and for all those who were touched by this tragedy.

This tragedy should remind us again of how fragile life is, and how we should each be ready to enter eternity and meet God at any moment.

September 3
FTD ADDS OPERATORS TO HANDLE CALLS FOR FLOWER ORDERS IN MEMORY OF PRINCESS DIANA

Chicago, PR Newswire

[In] response to numerous calls regarding sending flowers for Princess Diana's London funeral this Saturday, FTD has added additional customer service representatives to process these international flower orders.

"Even given the extraordinary tragedy of the Princess's recent death, we are taken aback by the sheer volume of calls and inquiries we are receiving," said Bob Norton, President and CEO of FTD. "We are seeing to it that all orders received are processed with the utmost expediency and care."

September 4

PRINCESS DIANA TRAGEDY REINFORCES THE IMPORTANCE OF ESTATE PLANNING

Philadelphia, Business Wire

The recent tragedy involving the death of Princess Diana has left the world stunned and concerned for her two sons, Princes William and Henry.

It was reported that Diana has willed close to 90% of her $30 million dollar estate to her sons, which will include money, property and jewelry.

In light of this tragedy, the Pennsylvania Institute of CPAs suggests that everyone prepare a will for the sake of their heirs. Estate planning is important because it gives you control over how your wealth is distributed and can prevent unnecessary and expensive disputes about the disposition of your assets—as well as the caretaking of your children—upon your death.

September 5

MICHIGAN FOOD TRADE ASSOCIATION CALLS ON FOOD STORES TO STOP SELLING SLEAZE PUBLICATIONS EXPLOITING PRINCESS DIANA

Warren, Mich., PR Newswire

The Michigan Food & Beverage Association (MFBA) is asking all of its 2,900 members on a voluntary basis to refuse to sell certain supermarket tabloids or similar newspapers or magazines which exploit Princess Diana's death for a minimum period of four weeks effective immediately.

"Enough is enough," said Ed Deed, president of Michigan's largest food trade association.

"Exploiting Princess Diana's death is unconscionable."

*　　*　　*

JOB HUNTING

Some entries from real-life job applications:

- REASON FOR LEAVING LAST JOB: "I was working for my mom until she decided to move."
- PERSONAL INTERESTS: "Donating blood—14 gallons so far."
- REFERENCES: "None. I've left a path of destruction behind me."

AIR FORCE ONE

*You've heard of Air Force One, but what do you really
know about it? Here's a short history of what's now
considered the "flying White House."*

HOMEBOUND

Nowadays we take it for granted that traveling around the
world is part of the president's job. But that wasn't always
the case: As late as the 1930s, it was considered the president's duty
not to leave the country—he was expected to remain on U.S. soil
for his entire term of office…and wasn't even supposed to stray far
from Washington, D.C. This tradition was left over from the pre-
telephone age, when the only way a president could command the
government on a moment's notice in an emergency was to be physically in or near the nation's capital at all times. Leaving town literally meant leaving power, and presidents aren't supposed to do that.
For the first 130 years of the Republic, not a single American president left the United States while in office, not even once. (Well,
okay, once. Grover Cleveland briefly sailed across the U.S.–Canada
border in the 1890s.)

So in January 1943, when Franklin Roosevelt flew to North
Africa to meet with Winston Churchill and plan the Allied invasion of Southern Europe, he became only the fourth president to
leave the country (The others: cousin Teddy Roosevelt inspected
the Panama Canal in 1906 and Woodrow Wilson attended the Paris
Peace Conference at the end of World War I).

SMALL WORLD

FDR hated airplanes, but German submarines were patrolling the
Atlantic and sinking American ships, so the Secret Service forbade
him from traveling by sea. He flew in a chartered PanAm Flying
Boat seaplane called the *Dixie Clipper*. That changed everything.

When FDR's historic trip became publicized weeks later, it
turned out to be an important psychological boost not just for the
war effort, but also for the fledgling airline industry. If it was safe
enough for President Roosevelt to fly during the war, people reasoned, it would safe enough for anyone else to fly in times of peace.
Furthermore, Americans realized that with planes, the president

---

Napoleon's writing was so unreadable that many of his letters were mistaken for battlefield maps.

could travel almost anywhere in the world in a matter of days and return just as quickly if need be. And thanks to radio and telephone communications, it was possible to remain in fairly close contact with the government at all times. Within weeks of Roosevelt's historic journey, the U.S. Army Air Corps (precursor to the Air Force) began making plans to provide a custom-made plane for the president's exclusive use. Since then, each president has had an official plane, and today the president's airplane is considered an extension of the White House.

THE NAME

• Technically speaking, although there is a special presidential airplane, it doesn't have the radio call sign *Air Force One*. The call sign is attached to the president himself; it is given to whatever Air Force plane in which he happens to be flying. Likewise, any plane in which the vice president flies is known as *Air Force Two*.

• In fact, before JFK, each presidential aircraft had its own name: President Roosevelt's plane was nicknamed the "Sacred Cow" by the White House Press Corp; President Truman's plane was the *Independence* (Truman named it himself, out of fear that it might otherwise become the "Sacred Cow II"); and President Eisenhower's was the *Columbine*.

• Then, in 1962, President Kennedy took delivery of a Boeing 707, the first presidential jet airplane...and never bothered to name it. With no other name to go by, the media began referring to the plane by its call sign. The term *Air Force One* has been used for presidential aircraft ever since.

• In 1971 Richard Nixon renamed his plane *The Spirit of '76* in advance of the U.S. Bicentennial, but the name never took hold.

MADE TO ORDER

• One of the perks of being president is that you get to have *Air Force One* remodeled to suit your own tastes. President Truman had his plane painted to look like a giant eagle, with stylized blue feathers, cockpit windows that looked like eyes, and a nose painted to look like a big brown beak. (The nose was later repainted yellow, out of fear the White House Press Corps might nickname the plane "Brown Nose.")

Strom Thurmond was the only person ever elected to a U.S. Senate seat as a write-in candidate (1954).

• President Lyndon Johnson had all of the passenger seats unbolted and turned around so that they faced the rear of the plane—toward his compartment. He also ripped out the cherry wood divider separating his compartment from the rest of the plane and replaced it with clear Plexiglas, Jerry Ter Horst writes in *The Flying White House*, "so that he could keep an eye on everybody—and they on him."

• LBJ also installed a secret taping system, which, ironically, President Nixon ordered removed after he took office.

CODE NAME: PROJECT LIDA ROSE

The most extensive makeover for *Air Force One* came in the late 1950s and was proposed by Allen Dulles, director of the CIA. Not long after he inaugurated the super-secret, high-altitude U-2 spy plane program, Dulles proposed outfitting the president's airplane with hidden spy cameras for an upcoming trip to the Soviet Union.

Unlike U-2 spy planes, which flew at altitudes as high as 70,000 feet, President Eisenhower's plane would be flying under 5,000 feet, and was the only Western aircraft allowed into Russian airspace. Why not take advantage of the trip to take much closer pictures of Soviet defenses?

Whether or not Eisenhower was informed of the plan (many historians suspect he wasn't), it was approved, and his aircraft was fitted with a camera inside a hidden compartment in the fuselage. The controls were carefully disguised to look like the co-pilot's fresh-air vent, so that they would be undetectable even if a Soviet pilot was riding shotgun in the cockpit.

The cameras on board the presidential plane might well have provided the U.S. with the biggest intelligence coup of the Cold War...had they ever been put to use. But they weren't—on May 1, 1960, pilot Francis Gary Powers was shot down in his U-2 skyplane over Soviet airspace, and Nikita Khrushchev used the incident to scuttle Eisenhower's visit to the USSR. The cameras were removed when John F. Kennedy was elected president.

HELP YOURSELF

• Stealing objects stamped with the presidential seal has long been one of the perks of being invited to fly aboard *Air Force One*. Still,

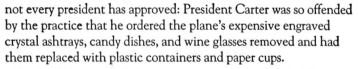

not every president has approved: President Carter was so offended by the practice that he ordered the plane's expensive engraved crystal ashtrays, candy dishes, and wine glasses removed and had them replaced with plastic containers and paper cups.

• Lyndon Johnson took the opposite approach—he filled the plane with expensive trinkets so that his guests would have something to steal. "It was useful to him to have people brag about flying with LBJ—and to have a souvenir with which to prove it," one aide remembers.

• True to form, when LBJ returned home to Texas on his last official trip aboard *Air Force One*, he reportedly stole everything that wasn't nailed down...and a few items that were, recalls pilot Ralph Albertazzie:

> When I took over the plane after it came back from Texas, I found an empty larder. We had no presidential china, no *Air Force One* silverware, no *Air Force One* cigarettes, no cocktail napkins, no towels—not even any paper products like toilet tissue. They were all gone. Even LBJ's special executive chair—the one we called "the throne"—was unbolted from the floor and taken away. The presidential stateroom was bare of pillows, blankets, and everything else that bore the presidential seal. I couldn't believe my eyes.

*   *   *   *

DRIVE-IN FOOD

The first drive-in restaurant was Kirby's Pig Stand, opened by J.G. Kirby on a highway between Dallas and Fort Worth in 1921. But it turns out that the idea of restaurant service to an automobile is almost as old as cars themselves.

It started as a way for the upper-class of Boston to show off. In 1904 Mrs. "Jack" Gardner of Boston, a social-climber famous for outrageous stunts like walking a lion around the city streets, organized a special "motoring event." She and four carloads of friends went to the Hotel Touraine, where, at her insistence, they were served oysters by waiters "compelled to run out with their trays to the autos." Next, the party motored to Adams House, where they were served soup in the street, and then to eight more establishments for eight more courses, the last of which was chop suey at a Chinese restaurant, for dessert.

THE "EXTENDED SITTING" SECTION

A Special Section of Longer Pieces

Over the years, we've gotten
numerous requests from BRI members
to include a batch of long articles—
for those times when you know
you're going to be sitting for a while.
Well, the BRI aims to please...
So here's another great way
to pass the uh...uh...time.

The English sparrow isn't a sparrow. And it comes from Africa, not England.

THE RAREST RECORD IN THE WORLD

If you collect old R&B or rock records, you know that the Holy Grail of collecting is "Stormy Weather," by the Five Sharps. Why is it so valuable? BRI fan Franklin Markowitz sent us this great article from the L.A. Times that gives the whole story.

THE LEGEND OF "STORMY WEATHER"

It's 1952. Five boys from the Jamaica housing projects in Queens, New York, like the way they sing together. They call themselves the Lovelarks, after tenor Bobby Ward's bird. Around the projects, they're known as the Bencholeers, because they practice on park benches. But those names don't stick. Neither is hip enough for a group known for its sharp harmonies and lush pink jackets. Someone suggests the Five Sharps.

They perform at school functions and any other place that will have them until they catch the eye of a local record producer.... [He] makes the usual promise of fame and success and sets up a recording session with Jubilee Records at a studio in...Harlem. For the Sharps, it's a dream come true. They're working for the same label as their idols, the Orioles, whose buttery sound influences every street-corner harmonizer in the country.

A Day to Remember

The Sharps receive no money for the daylong session. All they get to eat are a couple of wieners and orange soda. They bring two of their own songs: "Duck Butt Dottie," about Ward's girlfriend, and "Sleepy Cowboy," a humorous ode to bass singer Mickey Owens. They don't get to "Duck Butt Dottie," but they do record "Sleepy Cowboy" and a standard, "Stormy Weather."

It's a long day and the Sharps work hard. When Ward straggles in late, his dad hits the roof—it's a school night.

IT'S A FLOP!

Jubilee had a set routine for test-marketing records. "In those days we made the acetates [tapes of the record] at night," says Elliott

Blaine, who helped his brother, Jerry, run the company. They would take the acetate over to a bar called the Baby Grand on 125th Street, [which]...had a long bar and a live radio show dee-jayed by Wily Bryant, known as the Mayor of Harlem. "If you thought you had something, they'd play it," Blaine says. "You knew in 20 minutes if you had a hit."

The Sharps' record goes nowhere. They hear it on the radio twice. Sales are so poor, Jubilee makes the Sharps pay for their own copies. It gets so bad that the neighborhood record shop threatens to throw the records out unless the Sharps haul them away.

BACK TO REAL LIFE

After "Stormy Weather" fails, several of the Sharps go into the military. When they get out, they harmonize around the park bench, waiting for a break that doesn't come. Two Sharps, Clarence Bassett and lead singer Ronald Cuffey, eventually form a new group, the Videos, and record a song in 1958 called "Trickle, Trickle." Twenty-two years later, it becomes one of the Manhattan Transfer's signature tunes. After the Videos disband, Bassett joins Shep and the Limelites. They record one of the all-time doo-wop classics, "Daddy's Home," a song still played on oldies stations around the country.

The other Sharps fade back into their Queens neighborhood. Tommy Duckett, the piano player, changes bedpans in a nursing home. Ward marries and gets a job as a kitchen helper for KLM at Idlewild Airport. His life settles into a middle-class routine. He works his way up to supervisor of catering, buys a house, and raises three daughters. Sometimes he tells them about the record he made once, a damn fine record, too. But they're kids and he can tell they aren't buying it.

[ED. NOTE: Jump ahead to 1961. There's a dingy Manhattan record store called Times Square Records, run by a tall, cadaverous fellow called Times Square Slim. Uncle John visited it a few times when he was a kid, and he says it was literally underground, in the 42nd St. subway station. All the heavy-duty R&B record collectors hung out there, and UJ says they all looked as if they lived underground, too. "It was a very strange place," he recalls. Here's what happened next.]

Historic divide: If it happened before 476 A.D., it's "ancient." After 476 A.D., it's "medieval."

THE MAN

Irv "Slim" Rose prowled morosely behind the counter of Times Square Records, which was hidden away in a subway tunnel beneath Manhattan's 42nd Street. The light was terrible...and when trains rumbled into the station, [the hard-to-find rhythm and blues and vocal group] records fell off the wall.

...In those days, little was known about these records. When they were issued in the early '50s, they sold almost exclusively to an urban black audience. A hit shipped thousands, not millions, and [for performers], success was a hundred bucks in your pocket and the chance to make another record.

[Long ago], Slim had sold the records for a nickel each, but that changed after he bought time on radio station WHBI. The morning after the first broadcast of "Sink or Swim with Swingin' Slim," an outlandish misnomer since the dour Rose may have been the least swinging man in New York, the crowds outside his store were so thick he had to fight his way to open up. By 1961, records on the Rare Wall commanded as much as $10.

THE RAREST RECORD

One Saturday, a group of collectors was hanging around Slim's when a man walked in with a 78-rpm record nobody had ever heard. It was a version of "Stormy Weather" by the Five Sharps, on Jubilee Records.

The Ted Koehler–Harold Arlen composition is one of the most-recorded songs in pop history. Everyone from Frank Sinatra to Ethel Waters has interpreted it; Lena Horne's 1942 version remains the most famous. But the Five Sharps' rendition was something special. Cruder, rawer, it moved at a dirgelike pace, accompanied by thunderclaps and the sound of falling rain. Some who heard the record thought it was god-awful. Others declared it the greatest vocal performance ever recorded.

Here's where history begins to lose its way in the thickets of legend. Everyone agrees that Slim loved the record and asked to play it on his show. [But it never got that far, because it broke into pieces in the store.] According to one version of the story, Slim's pet raccoon Teddy plopped down on the 78. Others believe Slim dropped it. Whatever happened, the outcome was the same: the record shattered like a water glass.

Even if baboons wanted to, they couldn't play baseball. (They can't throw overhand.)

NOT AT ANY PRICE

Slim assured his angry customer that he would replace the record.
He put up a sign offering $25 in store credit for a 78-rpm copy and
$50 for a 45. He talked about it on his radio show. Weeks passed
and, to everyone's surprise, no record turned up. And none of the
regulars at Slim's could find one, either. Slim raised the offer, then
raised it again, until it became an obsession. Every collector in
New York was looking for it...then collectors in other cities joined
the hunt. It seemed as though the whole country was looking for
it...and no one could turn up a copy. It became a competition—
who would come up with this incredibly rare record first? As more
people sought it, the price kept going up.

Slim went to the Jubilee warehouse on 10th Avenue and asked
the company to dig the master out of its files. (The master is the
disc from which records are made.) But Jubilee reported that the
master for release No. 5014 was among 80 destroyed in a fire several years earlier. Or maybe it was a flood.

Thus was born the story of the rarest record in the world, a disc
so rare it might not exist.

THE 78s APPEAR

Years after Slim's wife left him and the record store closed down,
three copies of the Five Sharps' 78 turned up. One was cracked.
One had a half-inch chip. The other, found in a junkyard, was in
good condition.

The first "Stormy Weather" 78 turned up in 1972. Although it
was badly cracked, Ralph M. Newman, who edited a small fanzine
called *Bim Bam Boom*, was intrigued. After satisfying himself that
it was the real thing, he bought the record for a few hundred dollars and spent weeks making a tape and splicing the clicks out of it.
Then he reissued the song on the Bim Bam Boom label.

It didn't do much better than the Jubilee version. But it did get
airplay on oldies radio. Bobby Ward was in his basement tool shop
when he heard the song on the radio. He called upstairs for the
girls to come listen....

Then Ward tracked down Newman, who was stunned to hear a
ghost on the line. The mythic group on a faded record label that
has been bedeviling music enthusiasts for 20 years had finally become human, with faces and names.

In Tucson, Arizona, potholes are officially known as "pavement deficiencies."

INTRODUCING...THE FIVE SHARPS!

Ronald Cuffey and Mickey Owens had died of leukemia, but the other three were still around. There were twists and turns, details to be worked out, forms to be signed, all leading to a night in April 1975, when the Five Sharps took the stage for the first time in two decades. There were new members, but they hardly counted as new because they were original members of the Lovelarks.

Their appearance at the Academy of Music on 14th Street was promoted as "An Evening of Classic Doo-Wop Harmony." On the bill were some of the greatest vocal groups in history—the Five Keys, the Cleftones, the Tune Weavers—groups whose sound defined R&B harmonizing, groups with long careers, groups with hit records. The Sharps, on the other hand, were little more than a curiosity, a footnote. They were scared to death. The group took their places under a prop street light while sound-effect rain and thunder crackled offstage. They began singing, at first tentatively, but as they sang they gained confidence. Their voices, threading together, coiling and knotting and loosening to find new knots, took on a delicate power and desperate sadness: "Don't know why / There's no sun up in the sky / Stormy weather..."

How many in the crowd came because they knew the story of the most legendary failed musical group in pop history? How many came to hear them bring back another time? How many to support a music that was dying even then? You could read your own message into the audience response, but there was no mistaking it. The Sharps brought the house down. The other groups, the famous ones, the ones with hit records, come up afterward, shaking their heads.

"They had lost the lottery of life," Newman says. "But that night, they blew everybody away."

The group became a curiosity around New York for a while. They played some more shows, made a little money and then, once again, faded away....

BUT IS THERE OR ISN'T THERE?

In the legend surrounding "Stormy Weather," one mystery remains...the mystery that started it all, the mystery of the rarest record in the world: Was a 45 rpm copy ever pressed?

We may never know. In the early '50s, record companies serving the black market pressed records first on 78 and only shifted to the newer 45 format if the song sold. Blacks didn't adopt the technology as swiftly as whites because they didn't have the money to spend on another record player. Under that theory, the 45 version of "Stormy Weather" should not exist. But there is a strong case that it should. Its catalog number is 5104. Neither the record just before it—5103, "Kings Mambo" by the Five Kings—nor the record shortly after it—5106, "Why Don't You Believe Me" by Herb Lance—caused much of a splash. But Jubilee released both on 45. Why not 5104?

Bassett, the one Sharp to have a music career, believes there was a 45. He's pretty sure he has seen one. Ward, who possesses a large laugh and uses it readily, is doubtful. "Nobody liked that record. Nobody bought it. As far as we know there were only five copies of that record and they were bought by the Five Sharps."

The Eternal Quest

Val Shively [a well-known collector from Philadelphia] looked as hard for that record as anyone. Shively was at Slim's when the Wall was covered with rarities. He owns more than four million records, but the 45 of "Stormy Weather" has eluded him.

More than 30 years ago, he met a man whose job took him to all the record pressing plants in the New York area. I can get you anything, he told Shively. "What about 'Stormy Weather'" Shively asked.

No problem, the man said. He returned a few days later with 20 copies. But as soon as Shively played the song, he knew it was a remake done years later by a different group. Shively's contact then set out for Jubilee. He reported back that the company was grinding up all their old records to make room for new inventory. He grabbed what he could and handed Shively 100 records, all on the early Jubilee script label. Those records are now worth thousands of dollars, but "Stormy Weather" wasn't among them.

A decade later, Shively received a call from a friend in Columbus, Ohio. He said he was standing outside a tractor-trailer filled with records. He claimed to have a copy of "Stormy Weather" in his hand.

The owner of the truck made him put it back, but Shively's

More than 1,000 people belong to the Society of Jim Smiths. All of them are named Jim Smith.

friend said he would return in a few days to buy it. A week later, he called back: kids had set fire to the truck and everything was destroyed.

"I've heard it all with that record," Shively says. "I don't think it exists. By now, somebody would have found one."

Now you know the story of the rarest record in the world. And if you should happen to find the 45 in an attic or flea market somewhere, just remember who told you about it in the first place. Count us in, because today the original Five Sharps' version of "Stormy Weather" (not a bootleg—they're around, too, and they're phonies) could be worth as much as $50,000.

*   *   *   *

LAW AND ORDER

• In 1865, a counterfeiter named William Brockway printed some fake $100 bills. Like a lot of counterfeiters, he got caught. Unlike a lot of counterfeiters, his bills were indistinguishable from the real thing, and the Treasury Department was forced to withdraw all *real* $100 bills from circulation along with the fakes.

• A few years back an applicant for the Houston, Texas police force was asked if he had a police record. Figuring complete honesty would help his chances of getting the job, the applicant answered no, but admitted he'd once robbed a liquor store and had never been caught. The police arrested the man and charged him with 1) robbing a liquor store, and 2) illegal possession of a .32 caliber revolver, which the man had on him when he was frisked at the station house.

• In October 1971, Sir Peregrine Henniker-Heaton, a member of the British Intelligence Service, told his wife he was going out for a walk...and then vanished without a trace. Scotland Yard searched for him for three years, and found not even a clue to his whereabouts. They finally found his body, "in an unused room of his own home, where it had been all the time."

PAUL IS DEAD!

The biggest, most widely discussed rumor about rock bands and performers ever was—appropriately—about the Beatles. In 1969, millions of fans were convinced that Paul McCartney was dead, and spent months trying to prove it. Here's the inside story.

H AVE YOU HEARD THE NEWS?
Although no one knows precisely when or how it started, sometime in 1969 a rumor began circulating that Paul McCartney of the Beatles was dead. The idea really took off one Sunday that September, when an Eastern Michigan University student identifying himself as "Tom" called the "Russ Gibb Show" on WKNR-FM.

The caller told Gibb he'd heard that McCartney had been dead for some time, that the rest of the Beatles knew about it, and that they had started inserting "hints" of McCartney's death into their most recent record albums. Why were they keeping McCartney's death a secret? Maybe it was to let fans down easily…maybe it was to make as much money as they could before the death became public and the band had to dissolve.

But that was beside the point. The point was that Paul was dead, the caller told Gibb, and the proof was in the music.

GETTING IT BACKWARD

Gibb had been in the radio business for some time, and this wasn't the first dead-rock-star story he'd ever heard. Celebrity-death rumors were as common as they were unfounded, and Gibb initially dismissed this one as being just as ridiculous as the others…until Tom told him to play the Beatles' song "Revolution Nine" backward to hear one of the "clues."

When Gibb played back the part of the song where the voice says "Number Nine" over and over, he thought he could hear the words, "Turn me on, dead man." He began to wonder if Paul McCartney really was dead, and he shared his suspicions with his listeners. Within minutes the switchboard was lit up with calls. Everybody wanted to know if McCartney was really dead.

Worldwide, an estimated 85% of all phone calls are conducted in the English language.

PAPER TRAIL

The rumors might never have amounted to anything more, if someone named Fred LaBour hadn't been listening to the "Russ Gibb Show" that Sunday afternoon.

LaBour, a University of Michigan sophomore who wrote for his college newspaper, *The Michigan Daily*, was supposed to write a review of the Beatles' new *Abbey Road* album for an upcoming issue. But he was still looking for some kind of angle that would make the article more interesting.

As LaBour listened to Tom and Russ Gibb discussing whether Paul McCartney was dead, he knew he had his angle—turn the rumor into a full-length article, a satire that pretended to take the whole idea seriously. LaBour thought it would make an interesting and amusing read. He had no idea how right he was.

The next day, LaBour wrote up his "review" of *Abbey Road* and turned it in to John Gray, the arts editor for *The Michigan Daily*. Gray was so impressed that he decided to give it an entire page in the paper. "Just how long did it take you to come up with this masterpiece?" he asked.

"It only took an hour and a half," LaBour said, "and it's the best bull---- I ever wrote."

HOT OFF THE PRESSES

LaBour's article ran on page 2 of *The Michigan Daily* with the headline "McCartney Dead; New Evidence Brought to Light." The article claimed that Paul had been dead for nearly three years:

> Paul McCartney was killed in an automobile accident in early November, 1966, after leaving EMI recording studios tired, sad, and dejected. The Beatles had been preparing their forthcoming album, tentatively titled *Smile*, when progress bogged down in intragroup hassles and bickering. Paul climbed into his Aston-Martin, sped away into the rainy, chill night, and was found hours later pinned under his car in a culvert with the top of his head sheared off. He was deader than a doornail.

The article claimed that the surviving Beatles decided "to make the best of a bad situation," because "Paul always loved a good joke," LaBour quoted John Lennon as saying. The surviving Beatles decided to replace Paul with a body double and continue as if he hadn't died. To that end, the group held a "Paul Look-Alike Contest" and found a living substitute in Scotland, a man named William Campbell.

Thanks to extensive voice training, lip-synching, and a moustache (which John, George, and Ringo also grew), Campbell had somehow managed to pass himself off as Paul McCartney for more than three years, despite the fact that the band had been inserting clues into their songs and onto their album covers all along. The *Abbey Road* album cover, for example, shows the four Beatles crossing the street: McCartney is the only one walking out of step, the only one who's barefoot ("the way corpses are buried in Italy," LaBour claimed), and is holding a cigarette in his right hand, when everybody knows he is left-handed. On top of that, the license plate on one of the cars parked on the road reads "28IF"—which LaBour claimed was a coded way of saying that McCartney would be 28 if he were still alive.

CLUE ME IN

LaBour probably never intended for his joke to travel beyond the University of Michigan, but by the end of the day the story had spread to other nearby colleges, and from there to the rest of the country over the next several days. Wherever the rumor spread, people began studying the Beatles' recent album covers and listening to their albums backwards…and finding their own "clues," which only added to the story's credibility and caused it to spread even further.

"In terms of media coverage," Andru J. Reeve writes in *Turn Me On, Dead Man*, "the rumor reached an apex during the last two weeks of October. Major newspapers and network television had avoided comment up to this point, for they assumed that, like rumors of the past, the story would fade before the presses had a chance to warm up."

SILENT PARTNER

So did Paul McCartney: Recently married and burned out from the difficult *Abbey Road* recording session, McCartney was holed up with his wife and kids in Scotland and wasn't coming out for anything, not even to prove he wasn't dead. Like a lot of people, when he first heard the rumor, he figured it would soon pass.

Folk wisdom: If you refrigerate your rubber bands, they'll last longer.

But the rumor refused to die, and McCartney finally consented to giving Apple Records a written statement that he wasn't dead. But he still refused to make a public appearance. For many people, the fact that a written statement was all the Beatles' own record company could come up with was further proof that he really was dead.

WHEW!

It's probably fitting that *Life* magazine provided the most convincing evidence that death had not taken McCartney. *Life* sent a reporter and two staff photographers to McCartney's farm to "bring back any visual evidence of Paul's existence, even if he refused to be interviewed." McCartney not only refused, he heaved a bucket of water at them. Once he calmed down, however, McCartney let the photographers take some pictures of him with his family. *Life* ran one on the cover the next issue.

Amazingly, some skeptics saw the *Life* magazine article as further proof that McCartney was dead—when you hold the magazine cover up to a bright light, the car in the Lincoln Continental ad on the reverse side appears to be impaling McCartney. For most fans, though, seeing the pictures of Paul with his family was enough, and the rumor receded as quickly as it had spread.

FOR THE RECORD

The only unresolved question was whether the rumors were orchestrated or fueled by the Beatles themselves, perhaps to increase sales of *Abbey Road*.

"One undeniable fact became apparent," Andru Reeve writes: "sales of Beatles albums did increase." Priced $2 higher than earlier Beatles albums, *Abbey Road* sold slowly at first…until about the time that the rumors started circulating. Then, Reeve writes, it "rocketed to number one and the other albums germane to the rumor (*Sgt. Pepper's*, *Magical Mystery Tour*, and the "White Album") resurfaced on the Billboard Top 200 LP chart after absences of up to a year and a half."

*　　*　　*

"I did not attend his funeral, but I wrote a nice letter saying I approved it."
—**Mark Twain**

The average woman has 17 square feet of skin. It stretches to 18-1/2 feet during pregnancy.

HOW DID DAVY CROCKETT REALLY DIE?

On page 165, we wrote about the "death" of Disney's fictional Davy Crockett. Here is the story of how the real Crockett died, from Paul Aron's Unsolved Mysteries of American History.

BACKGROUND

To millions of Americans who remember Fess Parker in ABC's 1954 *Davy Crockett, Indian Fighter* series or John Wayne in the 1960 movie *The Alamo*, the answer to this [article's] question is no mystery: Davy died fighting at the Alamo, along with all its other defenders. In the television version, he is last seen swinging his rifle like a club, with the bodies of the Mexicans he has slain at this feet; in the movie version he is, if anything, more heroic, blowing up the fort's powder magazine to make sure a score of Mexicans die with him.

So clear was this image in Americans' minds that when historian Dan Kilgore presented evidence in 1978 that Crockett surrendered at the Alamo and was executed after the battle, Kilgore was branded un-American. Yet Kilgore's evidence was not new, nor were Hollywood's versions the first fictionalized accounts of Crockett's life and death. Crockett himself was famous as a teller of tall tales, and historians attempting to uncover the truth about his death had first to peel away many layers of legends, lies, and half-truths.

POLITICAL ANIMAL

Crockett's autobiography, *A Narrative of the Life of Davy Crockett,* presents a great hunter, a superman from the backwoods of Tennessee who killed 105 bears in a single season. So famed was he as a hunter that, so the story went, once a treed raccoon recognized him, it would yell, "Don't shoot, I'm a-comin' down!"

Above all, however, the real Crockett was a politician. Using his comic drawl and his log-cabin background as proof that he would fight for the interests of the common man, and of the westerner in particular, he was elected to the Tennessee House of Rep-

The average New Englander eats twice as much ice cream per year as the average Southerner.

resentatives in 1821 and 1823, and to the U.S. House in 1827, 1829, 1831, and 1833. At first he was an ardent supporter of the other "man of the people," Andrew Jackson [ed. note: seventh president of the U.S., and a member of the Democratic Party]. But Crockett broke with the president over his policies for disposing of Western lands and Indians, and was then embraced by the Whig party [ed note: at the time, the Democrats' main opposition]. The Whigs saw in Crockett someone who could match Jackson's image as the common man's protector—and who might even be able to challenge Jackson for the presidency. They began ghostwriting his speeches and books, including his *Narrative of the Life*, which was in one sense a campaign biography.

IMAGE VS. REALITY

The Whig propaganda made Crockett a national figure—a sort of western Poor Richard, uneducated but rich in common sense and experience. But Crockett's own constituents were less impressed …They noted that…in his entire congressional career he'd failed to get a single bill passed. With the Jacksonians mobilized against him, the 1835 congressional election promised to be a tight one. Crockett promised his followers that he'd serve them to the best of his ability if they elected him. And if they didn't "You may all go to hell," Crockett answered, "and I will go to Texas."

They didn't—and so he did.

TEXAS OR BUST

By the early 1830s, although Texas was a province of Mexico, Americans made up 75% of its population. Americans flocked there for land that was available at one-tenth the price of land in the United States. The Mexican government saw these increasingly assertive immigrants as a threat to its authority, and decided to outlaw new immigration. The more militant Americans responded by declaring Texas an independent nation and appointing Sam Houston commander in chief. Like Crockett, Houston was an ex-Tennessean and an ex-congressman; unlike Crockett, Houston remained tied to the Jacksonians [Democrats] in the U.S.

TEXAS POLITICS

By the time Crockett arrived in San Antonio in early February

---

If you never trimmed your fingernails, on your 80th birthday they'd be about 13 feet long.

1836, tensions were near the breaking point. Not only were Gen. Antonio López de Santa Anna and his 2,400 troops on the march toward the fort but the Texans at the Alamo were themselves split between those who acknowledged Houston's authority and those who did not. Houston, recognizing that the 183 men in the Alamo could not hold the fort against Santa Anna's troops, ordered its commander, Colonel William Travis, to blow up the Alamo and retreat. But Travis, as part of the [political] opposition to Houston, refused, thus setting up the fateful battle.

It is amidst these political maneuverings that Crockett's decision to stay at the Alamo—and the likelihood of his fighting to the death as opposed to surrendering—must be considered. Crockett had come to Texas because it was a land of economic and political opportunity, not so that he could fight and die. Moreover, Crockett was no soldier. But once he got to Texas he found his past political affiliations threw him in with the anti-Houston, anti-Jackson forces, and these were the forces defending the Alamo. He was stuck there.

LOOKING FOR EVIDENCE

Of course, that doesn't prove that Crockett surrendered, or that his heroic death scene is mere myth. Many have died heroically on the battlefield with less evidence of previous heroism than Crockett's life provided. What Crockett's past life proved was merely that he was the type of person who easily could have surrendered. To determine whether he actually did so, historians needed some actual witnesses.

The obvious problem with witnesses, at least on the American side, was that after 90 bloody minutes on the morning of March 6, 1836, they were all dead. (Not quite all: The Mexicans did spare the life of a woman, Susannah Dickinson, whose report of seeing Crockett's mutilated body has often been used to prove he died fighting. But she didn't see his body until well after the fighting had ended—and well after he might have been captured and executed.)

THE VIEW FROM THE OTHER SIDE

On the Mexican side, of course, there were many survivors. That their testimony was for so long ignored can only be attributed to American chauvinism. According to the narrative of José Enrique de la Peña, an aide to Santa Anna and an eyewitness to Crockett's death. Crockett most definitely did not go down fighting. Rather, he was captured along with six others and brought before Santa Anna. Drawing on his famous ability to tell tall tales, he attempted to talk his way out of his situation. He claimed he'd merely been exploring the country and "fearing that his status as a foreigner might not be respected," he'd sought refuge in the Alamo. Santa Anna didn't buy it. He ordered Crockett and the others killed.

Other Mexican witnesses offered similar versions of Crockett's death....In spite of efforts to discredit the testimony of these Mexicans, the sheer number of witnesses to his surrender, and the lack of any reliable eyewitness to his death in battle, clearly favors the surrender story.

At the time, many U.S. newspapers reported the surrender; in fact, the story of Crockett's execution was often used as evidence of Santa Anna's barbarity. Only after the Fess Parker/John Wayne versions were filmed did Crockett's death and battle become a part of American mythology. But mythology, not history, is almost surely what it was.

BETTER THAN DISNEY?

The revisionist view of Crockett's death, however, didn't mean he died in vain. Crockett's death focused the attention of the United States on Texas, and money and volunteers rolled into the territory. Six weeks after the Alamo, Sam Houston's army, crying "Remember the Alamo!" overwhelmed the Mexicans. A day later Santa Anna surrendered.

Nor should Crockett's surrender be confused with cowardice: faced with insurmountable odds, Crockett made the only reasonable choice. De la Pena's account of the execution concludes by telling how "though tortured before they were killed, these unfortunates died without complaining and without humiliating themselves before their torturers." Or, to put it another way, Davy Crockett died like a hero.

*   *   *

"Historian: An unsuccessful novelist" —**H. L. Mencken**

There are 250,000 sweat glands in a pair of human feet.

UNFINISHED MASTERPIECE: THE BEACH BOYS' *SMILE*

Today they're thought of as a golden-oldies pop band, but at their peak the Beach Boys were America's #1 rock band and considered the creative equivalent of the Beatles. Here's the story of the never-completed album that might have kept them on top.

UNFINISHED MASTERPIECE: *Smile,* by Brian Wilson, Van Dyke Parks and the Beach Boys

WHAT IT IS: An unfinished Beach Boys album. Considered by many who have heard bootleg tapes to be among the best albums in the history of rock 'n' roll, *Smile* might have had the same impact on the Beach Boys' career that *Sergeant Pepper's Lonely Hearts Club Band* had on the Beatles' (it was released a few months after Brian Wilson ended work on *Smile.*)

THE STORY: Before they'd even graduated from high school, the three Wilson brothers (Brian, Carl, and Dennis) their cousin Mike Love, and a friend named Al Jardine had hit it big with good-time pop music about Southern California surfing, cars, and girls.

The man behind the music was the oldest brother, Brian, who wrote most of their songs, arranged their harmonies, and worked with studio musicians to get exactly the right sound. In the Beatlemania mid-1960s, when it seemed like only British Invasion groups could make the charts, the Beach Boys successfully matched the Beatles, with hit after hit.

BATTLE OF THE BANDS

A rivalry developed between the Beach Boys and Beatles. When one group released a new album, it prompted the other to see if they could top it, a process that intensified as both bands' music became more serious and complex. Wilson, though, was at a disadvantage: The Beatles had two great songwriters, John Lennon and Paul McCartney (three if you include the less-prolific George). And they had a brilliant producer, George Martin. The Beach Boys essentially had just Brian. "From the point of view of his family," David Leaf writes in *The Beach Boys and the California Myth,* "Brian was almost a benefactor rather than an artist. He wrote the hits and

---

Worldwide, the average woman is 5 inches shorter than the average man.

made the records, and the group sang them and toured and were rich and lived in the manner they had become accustomed to, all thanks to Brian Wilson."

For several years, Brian managed to write virtually all the songs on the three albums a year the band released, while also performing in concerts all over the world. But with such an unrelenting schedule something was bound to give, and in December 1964, Brian had a nervous breakdown on an airplane while en route to a concert tour. He recuperated, but he and the band decided to hire a replacement for him for touring, so Brian could stay home and work full-time in the studio, creating songs that would be ready for the boys to add their voices to whenever they returned from the road.

Brian made the studio his instrument and created a unique pop sound. But the new songs began to take the Beach Boys in a new direction, away from the surfing, cars, and girls that had made them America's #1 rock 'n' roll act. It was a direction the other members of the band weren't sure they wanted to go.

PET SOUNDS

In May 1966, the group released an album called *Pet Sounds*, which many critics consider the best Beach Boys album ever. It served as a wake-up call to the Beatles, a warning that their rivalry with the Beach Boys was escalating to a new level. Paul McCartney was floored by what he heard. "No one is educated musically until they hear *Pet Sounds*," he said later. "It is a total classic record that is unbeatable in many ways....*Pet Sounds* was our inspiration for making *Sergeant Pepper's*. I just thought, 'Oh dear me, this is the album of all time. What are we going to do?'"

For all the praise it received, *Pet Sounds* was a commercial disappointment. "What many critics consider to be one of the best and most important albums in rock history never was embraced by American record buyers," Leaf writes. "It never sold enough to become a gold record....It took many listenings for a fan to finally appreciate and absorb what Brian had accomplished. In terms of record sales, this was damaging, because the fan underground quickly passed the word to 'stay away from the new Beach Boys album, it's weird.'"

Pet Sounds' weak sales took its toll on Wilson. "*Pet Sounds* was not a big hit," Brian's ex-wife Marilyn says. "That really hurt Brian

It takes 345 squirts from a cow's udder to get a gallon of milk.

badly. He couldn't understand it. It's like, why put your heart and soul into something. I think that had a lot to do with slowing him down."

GOOD VIBRATIONS

The rivalry continued. The Beatles' "All You Need Is Love" inspired Brian Wilson to piece together a complex single called "Good Vibrations." Today "Good Vibrations" is considered a pop oldie, but in its day it was a revolutionary piece of music, a "pocket symphony," as Brian Wilson called it, that took more than six months of recording time and 90 hours of recording tape to create. Brian created 11 different versions of the song before he finally found one he liked, a process that caused production costs to balloon to more than $50,000, a fortune in the mid-1960s.

The expense was worth it. Unlike *Pet Songs*, "Good Vibrations" was a huge hit. It sold 400,000 in the first four weeks alone and went on to become the Beach Boys' first million-selling single. "By the fall of 1966," Leaf writes, "the Beach Boys led by Brian Wilson, had musically gone past the Beatles....With 'Good Vibrations,' Brian surpassed everything current in popular music....It firmly established Brian as the foremost producer on the music scene."

"Jesus, that ear," Bob Dylan once remarked about Brian Wilson, "he should donate it to the Smithsonian."

SMILE

Brian Wilson's next project was an album tentatively titled *Dumb Angel*, which he told a friend would be a "teenage symphony to God." The album, a deeply personal statement, which was later renamed *Smile*, was poised to take the Beach Boys even deeper into the realm of "experimental" music, something that worried Brian Wilson's friend David Anderle. "I said, 'Don't have them as part of *Smile*. Do it on your own, man. Make it a Brian Wilson album.'" Perhaps out of loyalty to his brothers and his cousin Mike Love, Brian decided not to go off on his own. The band remained intact; *Smile* was slated as their next album.

By the time the other members returned from a concert tour of England, Brian had much of the background music for *Smile* finished; all the band would have to do was record the vocals. Lyrics for many of the songs had been written by Van Dyke Parks, a composer and lyricist known for his obscure, Bob Dylan-esque style.

The other Beach Boys were anything *but* Bob Dylan-esque, so they began arguing with Brian as soon as they got into the studio. "When they came back from England," David Anderle says, "the last thing they wanted to do was become experimental. From where they were coming from, the Van Dyke Parks influence was not a healthy influence for them lyrically. They were hearing things they'd never heard before. It was not Beach Boys lyrics."

Mike Love was the most resistant. "Don't f*** with the formula," he groused during one recording session. The other members of the band dreaded another commercial disappointment like *Pet Sounds*.

FROWN

"The group resisted the experimentation," Leaf writes, "and resented the way Brian treated them as a musical instrument, but most of all, they didn't like Van Dyke Park's words. It was the fighting over Park's lyrics that eventually made Brian, who loved what Van had created, begin to question the songs."

As the arguments continued, Brian began to lose confidence, and *Smile* fell behind schedule. Pressure was mounting. Then, suddenly in February 1967, Van Dyke Parks left to sign a solo contract with Warner Bros., leaving Brian to finish the remaining songs alone and fend for himself against the rest of the band. Rather than fight for his ideas, he began to withdraw. "He really did back away from it, just back off and go to the bedroom or whatever," Anderle says. "He just wouldn't face up to it."

Capitol Records pushed *Smile*'s release date back repeatedly; meanwhile, the Beatles, with much fanfare, came forth with *Sergeant Pepper's Lonely Hearts Club Band*. Brian bought a copy and put on the headphones. He played it over and over again into the night; and as he marvelled at the Beatles' accomplishment, what little self confidence he still had was shattered. He withdrew into his room and never finished his album. "*Smile* was destroying me," he explained in 1976.

"Had *Smile* been concluded and put out," David Anderle says, "I think it would have been a major influence in pop music. I think it would have been as significant if not a bigger influence than *Ser-*

---

geant Pepper was....That album was startling. And I think *Smile* would have been even more startling."

BEACHED BOYS

Within months after *Smile* bit the dust, the Beach Boys' reluctance to experiment caught up with them. The rock music world was changing all around them, and they weren't changing with it.

In June 1967, they cancelled their appearance at the Monterey Pop Festival at the last minute. The festival, which served as a springboard to superstardom for new artists like Janis Joplin, Jimi Hendrix, and The Who, was a major turning point in rock 'n roll, and the Beach Boys weren't a part of it. "Instead," Leaf writes, "they alienated the hip audience that had just begun to accept them because of music like *Pet Sounds* and 'Good Vibrations.' By not appearing, the Beach Boys quickly found themselves in exile as pop relics."

Within months of releasing "Good Vibrations," the Beach Boys had fallen so far out of step with where rock 'n' roll was heading that it had actually become fashionable to hate them. "In person, the Beach Boys are a totally disappointing group," *Rolling Stone* founder Jann Wenner wrote in December 1967. "The Beach Boys are just one prominent example of a group that has gotten hung up in trying to catch the Beatles. It is a pointless pursuit....Their surfing work continued for about ten albums with little progress."

While reproduced and rerecorded versions of some of the *Smile* material appeared on subsequent Beach Boys albums over the next five years, it wasn't the same. The magical moment for what might have been the greatest rock album of all time was lost.

POST-MORTEM

In the fall of 1989, I was working with a band who turned me on to the bootlegged recordings of Brian Wilson's legendary, aborted *Smile* sessions. Like a musical burning bush, these tapes awakened me to a higher consciousness in record making. I was amazed that one, single human could dream up this unprecedented and radically advanced approach to rock 'n' roll. How could a talent so great be so misunderstood and underappreciated?

—Record producer **Don Was**

There are no natural lakes in the state of Ohio. Every single one is manmade.

LAVATORY...OR LABORATORY?

Guys, has this ever happened to you? You're standing at a urinal ready to pee when someone walks up to use the urinal next to you. Suddenly, that raging urge has become a...well, let's just say nothing is happening. Why? Canadian TV host Jay Ingram's book, The Science of Everyday Life, *may give you the answer.*

THE PERFECT LABORATORY

Scientists who study behavior are always looking for the ideal place to observe their subjects—whether it's a crowded water hole on the Serengeti Plain or a treadmill in a cage. They work best in a location where animals perform obvious and repetitive behaviors—such as a public washroom. Public washrooms are also an ideal setting to witness human behavior free of the complications present in large social groups.

Sometimes investigators do not even need to enter the washroom. A researcher for the Washington State Department of Transportation, stopwatch in hand, watched people enter roadside washrooms and found that, on average, men spend forty-five seconds in the washroom, women seventy-nine.

However, while it's interesting to know that men spend, on average, thirty-four seconds less per visit than women, it's a bit like watching woodpeckers vanish into their holes and then emerge a short time later: you want to know what went on inside. Woodpecker researchers could probably resort to using a hidden camera, but washroom researchers usually have to enter the research site itself to record their observations. However, then they must be careful to maintain their role as observers and not confound the experiment by becoming part of the scene.

THE REAL DIRT

It's possible for clever observers to take advantage of the fact that their presence influences washroom behavior. In 1986 the journal *Perceptual and Motor Skills* published a paper entitled "Effects of an

Observer on Conformity to Handwashing Norm." The title means, "Do People Wash Their Hands More if They Think Someone Is Watching?" The hypothesis was that women using public washrooms would wash their hands if there were other women around, but wouldn't bother if they were alone. The study was conducted on "the campus of a large privately owned university in the western part of the United States."

• In the first part of the experiment, the observer was in a lounge adjoining the washroom, clearly visible to the subjects when they left their stalls. Of the twenty women who saw the observer in the lounge, eighteen washed their hands.

• In the second part, the observer hid in one of the stalls, with her feet up and an Out of Order sign on the door. Of the nineteen women who used the washroom, only three washed their hands.

This study seems to demonstrate that social pressure is a much more important determinant of handwashing behavior than concern about personal hygiene. (A majority of the people I've talked to claim not to be surprised by the results, while maintaining that *they* always wash their hands.)

Back to the Toilet

Psychologists again turned to public washrooms to study the effect on a man when his personal space is violated. All kinds of experiments have been conducted to try to define exactly what personal space is, how big it is, and most important, how we react if it's invaded. The problem in this latter instance has always been to find an experimental situation where someone's stress can unambiguously be traced to a violation of his space.

TO PEE, OR NOT TO PEE?

There's one particular setting in which a man's personal space is always invaded: when he's forced to stand next to a stranger at the urinal. The stress in this situation could be measurable, psychologists theorized, because research has confirmed that fear and anxiety can produce an inability to urinate. A fearful urinator is the victim of powerful opposing physiological forces: the bladder muscles contract, forcing urine into the urethra, but the sphincter muscles that must relax to let the urine out are paralyzed by fear. So if having someone stand at an adjacent urinal does invade your personal space, the stress that results might make it harder for you to start urinating and harder to continue, too. ("Delay in onset and decrease in the persistence of micturation," as it is phrased in psychological jargon.)

THE SCIENCE OF PEEING

The experiment to determine if personal space violation would actually cause men to stand and wait was conducted in a men's lavatory at a midwestern U.S. university (where all such experiments seem to be conducted). It contained two toilet stalls and three urinals. The unsuspecting experimental subjects were faced with three possible situations:

- They were alone, the other two urinals "out of commission" with Don't Use signs on them, or...
- There was one other man (a confederate of the experimenter) present, separated from the subject by an "out of commission" urinal, or...
- There was a man next to the subject, with the Don't Use sign occupying the end urinal.

So subjects experienced either no threat to their personal space, a minor trespass, or a major invasion.

I SPY...

For this experiment to work, it was necessary to time the subjects' urination—both the beginning and the duration. But researchers soon discovered that listening for splashing didn't work—the urinals were just too quiet. So the observer sat hidden in one of the stalls with a pile of books at his feet. Tucked in the pile was a periscope, positioned so that it was aimed up through the space below the stall wall and onto the "lower torso" of the urinal user (but not, authors of the study hastened to say, his face). Once in position, the observer waited for the subjects to come to him. [Ed. note: Another use for books in the bathroom!]

AN INTIMATE MOMENT

A student coming into the men's washroom found only one urinal available. As he stepped up to use it, the observer, watching through his periscope, started two stopwatches: one he stopped when the urine started to flow, the other when it stopped. So he knew how long it took to begin, and how long it lasted.

And the results? When the subject had the urinals to himself, delay in the onset of urination was, on average, 4.9 seconds, but the presence of a stranger one urinal away increased that time to 6.2 seconds. When the two men were shoulder to shoulder, the delay lengthened to 8.4 seconds. The results were, as they say, statistically significant.

Results...

To the experimenters' credit, their predictions were borne out, although not without some controversy. As you might expect, the psychologists who designed this experiment were accused of stretching the ethics a little by training periscopes on the groins of unsuspecting experimental subjects.

THE NOSE KNOWS

In 1987 psychologists brought one of the "hot" topics in animal behavior into the public washroom. Odors as messages are routinely used in the animal world, whether it's your dog sniffing the tree to see who's been there last, or a male moth flying hundreds of meters upwind to find the female who's emitting her scent. One of the big unanswered questions is "How important are these odoriferous molecules, technically called *pheromones*, in human communication? Not perfumes or aftershave, of course, but more subtle, naturally produced odors.

There are some hints that humans do indeed produce and respond to these odors. One chemical, called *androstenol*, that male pigs emit to persuade females to mate, is also found in human armpit sweat and urine. Of course, finding it there doesn't prove that we actually respond to it, and experiments designed to prove that we do have produced mixed results. But this murky picture changed in 1987 when a group at the University of Southern California had the bright idea of testing androstenol in a public washroom: they wanted to know if it might send the same message as the chemicals that dogs spray on fire hydrants—the "I have been here" declaration of territoriality.

PICKING A DOOR

During an experiment that ran for five weeks, researchers taped two-inch by two-inch Plexiglas squares, at about eye level, to each of the doors of the four stalls in the men's washroom. On weeks one, three and five, common lab alcohol was dribbled onto these sheets. The presence of a faint odor of alcohol had no effect on the pattern of usage and stalls. But on week two, a solution of androstenol in alcohol was deposited on the square on one of the walls. The use of that stall dropped dramatically, from around twenty visits per week to a mere four. (In fact, those four visits might all have been made by the same person.)

SOMETHING STRANGE IS GOING ON...

These results can't be explained simply by assuming that the men smelled the androstenol coming from the stall and chose another. It does not have an overwhelmingly powerful odor, nor is it easy to associate with urine or sweat. It's musky but faint. Andrew Gustavson, the scientist who designed the experiment, is trained to recognize the odor of androstenol, but even he couldn't detect it until he was halfway into the room. So how could this puny odor have somehow directed men away from the treated stall?

Further evidence that the deterrence was not caused by the presence of odor alone was provided in week number four. The Plexiglas square on the same stall was soaked this time not with androstenol but the closely related chemical *androsterone*. Even though it has the same sort of musky odor, it had no effect on stall choice. Only when androstenol was present on the Plexiglas square did most men avoid that stall, as if it were exerting a territorial "don't come near me" effect. (And it is a male phenomenon; a duplicate experiment run in the women's washroom had no effect whatsoever.)

MYSTERIOUS SMELLS

The experimenters reported that the men who avoided the androstenol stall did so in a very natural way. There was no walking right up to the test stall, pausing, sniffing, then backing off to go into another one. There weren't even sudden changes of direction. People just came in and headed smoothly for a stall—but never the one with the androstrenol.

Did any thoughts go through their conscious minds as they entered the washroom? Were they even aware that they'd chosen a stall without androstenol?

Unfortunately, we'll never know whether these men realized that anything unusual was happening. The ethics committee overseeing the experiment forbade the experimenters from quizzing washroom users about their thoughts and feelings. However, it would not be surprising if they weren't aware of anything unusual. Airborne androstenol could simply enter the olfactory nerve and exert its behavioral effect via nerve circuits that would not require thinking or considering. Whatever went on in the subjects' minds, it's clear that something very odd happened during the second week of this experiment.

Consider this...

Would you have believed that men coming into a washroom would unhesitatingly avoid a particular stall because of a barely perceptible odor emanating from the stall door? If these results can be substantiated, they'll go into the books as the first really solid evidence that we alter our behavior in response to extremely subtle odors. And they'll prove once again that as a setting for studying humans and the psychology of their everyday lives, there's no place like a public washroom.

*   *   *   *

Smile When You Say That

"One of Oscar Hammerstein's rarer finds was 'Sober Sue,' whom he introduced to audiences at New York's Victoria theater in 1908. During intermissions, Sue would appear on stage and Hammerstein would offer $1,000 to anyone who could make her laugh. There were lots of takers, but no one succeeded. What they didn't know: she *couldn't* laugh—her facial muscles were paralyzed." (*Felton & Fowler's Best, Worst, and Most Unusual*)

Living brain cells are bright pink, not gray. They're about the color of cotton candy.

THE BIRTH OF THE CADILLAC

Unless you're a car buff, you may not know that the Cadillac was first built by Henry Ford...or that it was considered the car that made driving safe for women...or that it was directly connected to the Lincoln. Here's the story, from John "I can't get my MG running" Dollison.

OH, HENRY

On October 10, 1901, Alexander Winton, a well-known race car driver, arrived in Grosse Point, Michigan, and challenged all comers to a race. The only man who took him up on the offer was a country boy named Henry Ford. Ford, whose Detroit Automobile Company had failed a year earlier, was racing a car he had designed and built himself.

Earlier that day, Winton had broken the world automobile speed record, driving a mile in 1 minute, 12.4 seconds—just under 50 miles per hour. Few people thought Ford, a local, had a chance to win...but when Winton's car developed engine trouble in the seventh lap, Ford shot past him to win the race. It was a significant victory.

As Robert Lacey observes in *Ford: The Men and the Machine*:

> It was a great and famous victory, thoroughly earned. A driver who wins a modern motor race through the mechanical failure of his rivals might feel less than satisfied. But on October 10, 1901...the ability of Henry Ford's racer to keep going reflected directly on each man's ability to address the problem that mattered more to early motorists than maneuverability and speed. Mechanical reliability was the real challenge...Henry Ford won hands down.

BACK TO WORK

The victory was so impressive that five local businessmen who had seen the race chipped in $10,000 each to set Ford up in a new auto company. They even named the firm the Henry Ford Company to capitalize on Ford's newfound fame.

As head of the company, Ford's first job was to design a passenger car that could be sold to the public. But he "did not seem inclined to settle down to a small car production plan," one

---

Metal shrinks when it gets cold. That's why the Eiffel Tower is six inches shorter in winter.

contemporary remembered. "He talked mostly about wanting to build a larger and faster racing car," and he began sneaking off to work on it.

A CHANGE IN PLANS

Ford's playing hooky was not a new problem—it was the same thing that had forced the Detroit Automobile Company to close its doors the year before. Rather than let that happen again, the investors hired Henry Leland, owner of Detroit's most respected machine shop, to supervise both the shop and Ford.

But Ford refused to take orders from Leland, and a few days later quit the company that bore his name, leaving Leland to take over. With Ford out of the picture, the investors renamed the company in honor of Antoine Laumet de Lamothe Cadillac, the French explorer and soldier of fortune who founded the city of Detroit. The Cadillac Automobile Company was born.

The investors who hired Leland "would not regret their decision," George S. May writes in *A Most Unique Machine*. "In a short time there could have been no doubt in their minds that in Henry Martin Leland they had found the man they had earlier hoped Henry Ford would turn out to be."

Today automotive historians consider Leland to be as important and indispensable a figure in the creation of the modern automobile industry as Henry Ford himself.

STRAIGHT SHOOTER

Leland had gotten his start in the firearms industry as a teenager in the 1860s. Too young to fight, he spent the Civil War years working in factories that mass-produced rifles for the Union Army, then after the war made revolvers at the Colt firearms factory. Whereas early firearms had been made and assembled one part at a time by highly skilled master craftsmen, the adoption of mass-production techniques and precisely engineered, fully interchangeable parts had made it possible for unskilled workers to assemble rifles by the thousands.

Just as Henry Ford was responsible for pioneering the use of the moving assembly line in automobile production, it was Leland, more than any other man, who introduced mass-production techniques to the automobile industry. When he arrived at Cadillac in

A *misomaniac* is someone "who hates everything."

1902, most auto parts were manufactured to a precision of no more than $1/16$ of an inch—which meant that even after parts were made, they still had to be filed, ground down, and sometimes even hammered by hand so they would fit properly into place. All this extra work was time-consuming and expensive, and added to the cost of a car.

Drawing from his experience in the firearms industry and in his own precision machine shop, Leland made automobile parts accurate to within 1/10,000 of an inch, something that had never been done before. Parts fit so well together that they could be assembled rapidly without special hand fitting. And because the parts were manufactured to such high levels of precision, the completed engines ran more smoothly, quietly, and reliably than had ever been possible before.

HIGH TECH

At first, Cadillac was marketed as a low- to mid-priced automobile; The first luxury Cadillac, the Model 30, wasn't introduced until 1905. Even so, thanks to Leland's manufacturing improvements, the company quickly acquired a reputation for offering higher quality than was available in any other car at any price.

The company also developed a reputation as a pioneer in automotive technology. Some of the most important innovations came about as the result of a tragedy. In 1910 a friend of Leland's named Byron Carter stopped to assist a woman motorist whose car had stalled. When Carter knelt down to start the woman's car using the hand-crank, the car backfired and the hand-crank shot out of Carter's hand, shattering his arm and his jaw. The injuries did not heal properly, and Carter later died from gangrene.

START ME UP

Devastated by his friend's death, Leland ordered his engineers to drop what they were doing and figure out a better way to start a car. "The Cadillac car," he told them, "will kill no more men."

A few months later, his engineers came back with a revolutionary electric self-starter powered by a battery so strong that it could also power an electric ignition system and electric headlights. From 1912 on, all Cadillacs started with the push of a button on the dashboard and featured headlights so bright that for the first

There are more than 5,500 islands in the British Isles.

time it was truly safe to drive at night. These improvements ushered in a new era in the automotive age, as Richard Crabb writes in *Birth of a Giant*:

> The self-starter and electric lights greatly extended the potential use of the motorcar. So long as it was necessary to crank the engine by hand and endure the hazards of either acetylene or magneto-powered lights, women could make only limited use of the motorcar. With the addition of these two features, introduced by Cadillac, women could drive, as well as men.

MOVING ON

When General Motors purchased Cadillac for $4.5 million in 1909, Leland agreed to stay with the company, but only after GM president William Durant promised that Leland could continue running the company with a free hand.

Leland stayed with Cadillac after Durant was forced into retirement...and though he'd grown wary of Durant's haphazard management style, even stayed with the company after Durant seized back control of GM in 1915. But when Durant, a pacifist, refused to allow GM to participate in the war effort at the outbreak of World War I, Leland resigned and formed a company to manufacture airplane engines.

TOP OF THE LINE

Leland, now in his mid-70s, had spent his career making cars better than anyone thought cars could be made. But he believed that his best cars were still ahead of him, and at the war's end, he returned to the auto industry.

Leland was the Grand Old Man of the auto industry, and his friends and colleagues urged him to finally put his own name on a car. But Leland would have none of it—his new car was going to be the greatest ever built, he explained, and should be named after the greatest American who ever lived. Leland named his car after Abraham Lincoln, the president for whom he'd cast his first vote, in 1864.

The 1921 Lincoln was an excellent car, but Leland had paid more attention to the car's engineering than to its styling, and it looked out of date. "Automotive writers were entranced by its ability to accelerate smoothly from walking speed to about 75 mph

---

Oldest vehicle in human history: a floating log. Second oldest: a sled.

without vibration, without fuss," Ralph Stein writes in *The American Automobile*. "Aesthetically, the Lincoln was a disaster. In 1921, people paying up to $6,600 for a new car did not wish to drive around in cars that looked like 1914, no matter how well they had been constructed."

THE END

That wasn't the only bad news: In the fall of 1920, just as Leland was bringing his Lincolns to market, the postwar boom petered out and the country slid into a deep recession. Sales stalled, and Lincoln filed for bankruptcy.

The situation at the Ford Motor Company was much different. Ford earned record profits in 1921, and when the Lincoln Motor Company was put up for auction in January 1922, he bought it for $8 million, barely half its estimated worth.

Ford publicly acknowledged Leland as "one of the greatest motorcar men in America," and when he bought Lincoln, he kept Leland on and promised that he would be allowed to run the company as freely under Ford ownership as he had before.

But less than 24 hours after Lincoln reopened for business, Ford executives began interfering in the running of the plant. Four months later, a frustrated Leland confronted Henry Ford personally and offered to buy the company back for the original $8 million, plus interest.

Ford refused. "Mr. Leland," he replied, "I wouldn't sell the Lincoln plant for $500 million. I had a purpose in acquiring that plant, and I wouldn't think of letting it go." Two weeks later, Ford, acting through intermediaries, forced Leland to resign. Leland spent the rest of his life battling Ford in court to win his company back, but never succeeded. He died in 1932 at the age of 89.

BOYTOY

What was Henry Ford's "purpose" in buying Lincoln at auction?

Ford's son Edsel had pestered him for years to get him to replace the Model T, which had been in production since 1908, with something more modern. Buying Lincoln and letting Edsel run it may have been Henry Ford's way of preventing Edsel from meddling with his beloved Model T—which remained in production until 1927.

PAYBACK

But the real motive may simply have been revenge:

Had Henry Ford really walked off the job at the Henry Ford Company in 1902, leaving Henry Leland to pick up the pieces at the company that would soon be renamed Cadillac? Or was Ford fired—by Henry Leland? "According to a story that has appeared in a variety of versions," George May writes in *A Most Unique Machine*:

> Henry Ford did not really resign from the Henry Ford Company. He had, in effect, been fired by his backers, whose growing suspicions regarding Ford's capabilities had been confirmed by criticisms of various aspects of Ford's work. They had received the evaluations from an unimpeachably qualified source, the brilliant mechanic, Henry M. Leland.

Twenty years later, Ford, by then the world's most successful and wealthiest automaker, bought Leland's precious Lincoln Motor Company at a bankruptcy auction...and then promptly reneged on his promise to allow Leland to continue at the helm. According to May: "This, it has been said, was Henry Ford's revenge for what Henry Leland had done to him in 1902."

*   *   *

7 EXCUSES FOR SLEEPING ON THE JOB
(*courtesy of the Internet*)

1. "They told me at the blood bank this might happen."

2. "Whew! I musta left the top off the liquid paper."

3. "This is one of the seven habits of highly effective people!"

4. "This is in exchange for the six hours last night when I dreamed about work!"

5. "Darn! Why did you interrupt me? I had almost figured out a solution to our biggest problem."

6. "Boy, that cold medicine I took last night just won't wear off!"

7. "I wasn't sleeping. I was trying to pick up my contact lens without my hands."

Mediterranean means "middle of the world." That's what people used to think it was.

THE GREAT PEDESTRIAN

Over the years, sports have changed. Back in the 1860s, before the NBA, NFL, or NHL, you might have been cheering for your favorite pedestrian! Here's the story of the Babe Ruth of professional walking.

WALKING FEVER

America's number-one pedestrian, Edward Payson Weston, walked his way to fame and fortune in the late 1860s and infected the sports world with a "walking fever" that raged for half a century. Largely because of Weston, walking contests for a time rivaled prize fighting and horse racing as an early big-money pro sport.

Foot racing had been common at country fairs, and distance walkers were setting records before he took up the sport, but Weston's endurance feats that attracted huge crowds of fans, filled the pages of sporting journals, and turned pedestrianism into an international craze.

AN HISTORIC WALK

Weston first gained attention at the age of 22 when he carried out a bet to walk 478 miles from Boston to Washington in 10 consecutive days, to attend Lincoln's inauguration. He started from Boston's State House on February 22, 1861, followed by a swarm of fans riding in buggies, and walked the first 5 miles in 47 minutes before settling down to a steadier pace.

Crowds cheered him town by town, and reporters covered every mile of his marathon. A snowstorm slowed him some, and he slipped and fell several times, but plodded on through New England and got as far as New York the morning of February 27. Most of the time he ate as he walked, although he did manage to sit down to one solid meal each day. Sleep was in catnaps by the roadside or in farmhouse kitchens, and he began each new walking day at midnight.

By the time he reached Philadelphia, Weston was ahead of schedule, so he bedded down for a day in a hotel room. He then walked all night from Philadelphia to Baltimore, had breakfast, and started out in pouring rain to hike the final lap over muddy roads. He made it to Washington at 5 p.m. on March 4, 1861, too late to see Lincoln sworn in as president but still in time to enjoy dancing at the Inaugural Ball that night.

A WALKING PRO

According to the terms of the wager, he collected only a bag of peanuts for his long walk. But he also collected reams of publicity and decided to turn professional. He got his first big fee as a pro, and also created an international sensation, by walking from Portland, Maine, to Chicago in 1867 for a prize of $10,000. To win he had to cover the distance of more than 1,200 miles within a month, not including Sundays, which were eliminated to prevent a public outcry against sporting on the Sabbath.

Nattily dressed in a short jacket, tight-fitting knee breeches, colored belt, silk derby, buff gloves, and red-topped brogans, he took off from Maine on October 29 and covered the distance in 26 walking days, with enough time to spare not only to attend church services but also to make speeches to crowds of admirers along the way. Weston carried a walking stick to chase away hostile dogs, and at one point had to use his fists to beat off a man who attacked him in an attempt to halt the contest. He received threatening letters from gamblers who had bet against him, two attempts were made to poison his food, and he was warned that the only way he would reach Chicago would be "in a coffin." But he arrived the morning of Thanksgiving Day, his feet hardly swollen, and was still fit enough to address a cheering crowd at the Crosby Opera House that evening on the benefits of walking as outdoor exercise.

THE MAIN ATTRACTION

For most of his long life, Weston crisscrossed the country's roads on endurance walks against time for fat wagers and big prizes. He also competed against hundreds of other pros in walking contests at race courses and indoor tracks, where he drew such crowds that he was often paid as much as three-fourths of the gate receipts. Some walkers beat him on level tracks in six-day matches, but few equaled his remarkable feats on the open roads.

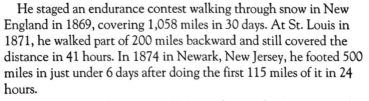

He staged an endurance contest walking through snow in New England in 1869, covering 1,058 miles in 30 days. At St. Louis in 1871, he walked part of 200 miles backward and still covered the distance in 41 hours. In 1874 in Newark, New Jersey, he footed 500 miles in just under 6 days after doing the first 115 miles of it in 24 hours.

Weston went to Europe in 1876 to cash in on his international fame and spent eight triumphal and profitable years there in crowd-drawing exhibitions, mainly in England. In London in 1879 he won the Astley Belt, emblematic of world supremacy, by defeating British champion "Blower" Brown in a 6-day "go as you please" match that allowed both jogging and heel-and-toe walking. He covered 550 miles in 141 hours, 44 minutes.

OLD MAN WESTON

At the age of 68 in 1907, after constant years of grueling competition, Weston repeated the walk he had made 40 years before, from Portland, Maine, to Chicago. He walked 1,345 miles in 24 days 19 hours to beat his own early record by some 29 hours. He celebrated his 70th birthday two years later with the longest endurance walk of his life, across the United States from New York to San Francisco.

Weston started from New York on March 15, 1909, hopeful that he could cross the country by "a rather devious route" that would let him cover more than 4,000 miles in 100 days. By then there was a motorcar instead of a horse-drawn carriage to transport the judges and supplies. But Weston disdainfully rejected most of the "modern" comforts offered him along the way and also held to his own ideas as to what was a proper diet.

He began his days at 3:30 each morning with a breakfast of oatmeal and milk, two slices of buttered toast, three poached eggs, three cups of coffee, a bowl of strawberries, two oranges, and half a dozen griddle cakes. On the road during the day he consumed 18 eggs, each beaten up in a pint of milk with a tablespoon of sugar. "If I want a piece of pie while I'm on a walk, I'll eat it, or griddle cakes or pudding," he said. "The stomachs that can't digest ordinary food are those that are spoiled by high living or no exercise."

STILL WALKING

Weston was still at it in 1914 when, at the age of 74, he tramped

1,546 miles from New York to Minneapolis in 51 days. Even after that he walked in some contests and exhibitions, but devoted more of his time to encouraging others to walk for health, competition, and the "joy of discovering the open road," warning that motorcars were making people more indolent than ever.

Ironically, the first great pedestrian was hit by a car while he was walking on a street in Brooklyn, New York, in 1927. He suffered injuries that kept him in a wheelchair most of the last two years of his life, and he died in 1929 at the age of 90.

*   *   *

OTHER GREAT PEDESTRIANS

• Daniel O'Leary was an Irish-born Chicagoan who did his first endurance walking as a door-to-door salesman. Inspired by Weston, O'Leary became his greatest rival. O'Leary's greatest performance was in 1907 in Cincinnati, where at the age of 63 he walked a mile at the beginning of each hour for 1,000 consecutive hours. During the 42 days it took to complete the test, O'Leary's longest period of uninterrupted sleep was 50 minutes.

• In 1910 John Ennis, crossed the country from New York to San Francisco. Ennis added a showmanly flair by taking time out for exhibition swims along the way. After a plunge into the Atlantic Ocean at a Coney Island amusement park, Ennis started walking on May 23, 1910. He swam in Lake Erie and later swam the Mississippi on a day he had walked 45 miles. As he made his westward way over the roads, he swam seven other rivers and lakes before reaching the Pacific at San Francisco on August 24. His total cross-country walking time was 80 days, 5 hours.

• A group known as the Kansas City Hikers made pedestrianism a family affair in 1913. Mr. and Mrs. Morris Paul teamed up with Mr. and Mrs. Gus Kuhn and their five-year-old daughter, Ruth, to walk from Kansas City, Missouri, to San Francisco. They took their time, stopping for as long as five days at some places, and spent a total of 227 days in walking the 2,384 miles.

WHATEVER HAPPENED TO GI JOE?

There was a time when GI Joe was considered a "staple" in the toy indus-
try—one that would be around for generations, like Barbie and Monopoly.
But check your local toy store shelves today—you won't find "America's
Fighting Man" there. It turns out that Joe was caught in a cultural
upheaval. When the traditional view of wars changed in America,
GI Joe lost his cultural footing...and never regained it. (For Part I
of the GI Joe story, turn to page 331. Here's Part II.)

(For Part I of the GI Joe story, turn to page 331. Here's Part II.)

MAN OF WAR

GI Joe may have been born in 1964, but in spirit he was born on D day, 20 years earlier. The post–World War II era was one in which American fighting soldiers were revered as heroes—as boys-next-door who answered the call of their country and, at great personal risk, battled evil and advanced the cause of freedom in nearly every corner of the globe.

GI Joe—and Hasbro—basked in this positive image. The company sold the dolls as fast as it could manufacture them, and that was only the beginning: in an average week, Hasbro received more pieces of mail addressed to GI Joe than the typical American adult received in 14 years, and by 1965 the number of kids in the official GI Joe fan club exceeded the entire population of Vermont.

THE TIMES, THEY ARE A-CHANGIN'

In 1966, however, the public mood began to change as a result of the intensifying war in Vietnam. As graphic images of that bloody conflict were broadcast into American homes on the evening news, the doll that carried an M-60 assault rifle, threw hand grenades, and shot a flamethrower came to be seen in a more sinister light. "By 1966," John Michlig writes in *GI Joe*, "the American public-at-large was beginning to express its distaste for the seemingly endless American military build-up in East Asia" by abandoning war toys.

Major retailers also began to act on the shifting public mood: in 1967 Sears announced that it would no longer carry "war toys" in its catalog, and other merchandisers began to scale back as well. By

---

If you have a compulsive urge to dance, you're a *dinomaniac*.

the end of 1967, Hasbro had sold only $8 million of GI Joe merchandise for the year, down from $23 million in 1965, and the outlook for 1968 was even worse. Something had to be done.

SPLIT PERSONALITY

Hasbro's research showed that although kids enjoyed the military side of GI Joe, they were just as interested in playing a male version of "house"—building forts and hideouts for him—and sending him out on nonmilitary adventures.

So Hasbro decided that, beginning in 1969, they would focus on the "adventurer" side of Joe. In effect, the company gave him an honorable discharge. "His hitch in the military was over," Michlig writes. "The soldier, sailor, pilot and marine converted to a contemporary adventurer, aquanaut, and astronaut—categories which maintained the 'air, sea, and land' configurations necessary for unlimited accessory potential."

JOE & CO.

Hasbro wanted to sell an "adventure team," but didn't want to add characters or change Joe's trademarked face. Their solution: hairlike spray-on fuzz. Hasbro executives realized that by using different combinations—brown, blond, black, or red hair, and with a beard or without—they could alter GI Joe's appearance so radically that it was possible to turn one doll into four different characters, each named GI Joe. The four-man GI Joe Adventure Team was born—now if a kid wanted to have the full GI Joe experience, he had to buy four dolls, not just one.

Last, But Not Least

Hasbro made one more substantive change to its action figures: it abandoned GI Joe's rectangular-shaped military dogtag in favor of a circular medallion with the letters "AT" (Adventure Team) inside the circle. "Upon presentation of the design," Michlig writes, "someone commented that the blocky 'A' and 'T' configuration looked suspiciously like a peace sign. 'I hope so,' the president of Hasbro commented.'"

The changes put GI Joe back on the map, halting his sales slide and, in fact, propelling the brand to a record $26 million in sales in 1973. But the success didn't last.

A *gozzard* is a person who owns geese.

BORN AGAIN...AND AGAIN...AND AGAIN

"Adventure teams succeeded as a short-term gimmick," writes
G. Wayne Miller in *Toy Wars*, "but something vital had been lost
in Joe's pacifist makeover." Sales started slipping again in 1974,
and Hasbro began looking for new ways to give GI Joe a makeover.
Most of the gimmicks piggybacked on various fads sweeping the
country:

• When the martial-arts craze appeared in 1974, GI Joe acquired
"Kung Fu Grip."

• When the TV series "The Six Million Dollar Man" became a hit
in 1975, Hasbro added "Mike Power, the Atomic Man," to the Adventure Team. He came complete with an "atomic" right arm and
"bionic" left leg. Sales were okay...until the real Six Million Dollar Man dolls (manufactured by a competitor) hit the market.
Then Mike Power was out.

• When superheroes became popular in 1976, Hasbro added Bulletman—a doll with metal arms, a removable metal helmet, a red
costume, and red boots—to the adventure team.

• In 1976 the company also introduced GI Joe's first enemies:
caveman-like space creatures known as The Intruders. "We made
them look like Neanderthals," says a Hasbro exec, "but instead of
being limited in intelligence, they're superintelligent beings from
another planet."

SAY IT AIN'T SO, JOE

Bulletman and space-cavemen were both dumb ideas, and kids
everywhere knew it: by the end of 1976 GI Joe sales were down
more than 75% from the glory days of 1973. Worse, a fivefold increase in the price of oil made a 12-inch-tall, petroleum-based
plastic doll prohibitively expensive to produce.

The hot new toys of 1977 were the *Star Wars* action figures—
which were only $3^3/4$-inches tall and had only a few moving parts
(as opposed to GI Joe's 21). They demonstrated that an action figure didn't have to be an engineering marvel to capture the hearts
of kids anymore. So in 1978 Hasbro introduced a stripped-down,
6-inch-tall action figure called Super Joe...which flopped immediately. When it did, Hasbro scrapped the entire GI Joe line.

SELLING JOE SHORT

Three years later, Hasbro reintroduced GI Joe—this time as a 3³/₄-inch figure, like the *Star Wars* dolls that had driven him out of the marketplace. But because America was becoming more pro-military under the Reagan administration, the company once again marketed GI Joe as a military toy. This time he was a member of a top-secret government "peacekeeping force" that was armed with futuristic weapons and equipment. Joe was in tune with the times again. The new doll was a huge hit, selling more than $186 million in 1986, a third more than the *Star Wars* toys sold during their peak. Joe looked like a winner.

By the early 1990s, he was in trouble again. Even the battles in real-life Iraq couldn't save him. Sales of GI Joe dolls went into another freefall, and once again Hasbro again tried to freshen up Joe's image by piggybacking on popular trends. They released Ninja Force Joe, Streetfighter II Joe, and even Drug Elimination Force Joe and Eco Warrior Joe. Nothing worked, and in 1994 Hasbro scrapped the entire product line for a second time.

TAPS

In 1996 Hasbro resurrected Joe yet again. Borrowing from current events, they introduced GI Joe Extreme, a soldier who battles "a band of superterrorists who have emerged from the ruins of a collapsed superpower."

GI Joe Extreme had his own animated TV show, but never caught on with kids. Hasbro cancelled the line within the year, and as of Fall 1999, the only GI Joes Hasbro made were limited-edition, 12-inch "classic" GI Joes marketed to adults—the same people who had played with the original GI Joe in the late 1960s and early 1970s.

Will Joe return in another incarnation? It's hard to keep a fighting man down, but only time (and current events) will tell.

*   *   *

...TOO MUCH TO ASK

When the Whig Party nominated Zachary Taylor for president in 1848, it took him several days to respond. Reason: "he didn't want to pay the 10¢ postage due on the official letter of notification."

A warthog has only four warts, all of them on its head.

THE STRANGE DISAPPEARANCE OF AUGUSTIN LE PRINCE

Why do history books credit Thomas Edison with inventing the movie camera and ignore Augustin Le Prince? That was our question...until Uncle John found a copy of The Missing Reel, *by Christopher Rawlence, which lays out the circumstances of Le Prince's life and disappearance. Believe us, you conspiracy buffs should have a field day with it. Is this story true? And if it is, why isn't it more famous?*

B ACKGROUND
Augustin Le Prince was a French inventor who studied with Louis Daguerre, one of the fathers of photography. In the early 1880s, Le Prince began experimenting with a new idea—a motion-picture camera. By 1885 he had a working prototype, and by 1886 he'd applied for a U.S. patent. In 1888 he received the first patents ever granted for a movie camera, in both France and the United States.

In March 1890, Le Prince demonstrated his camera to officials at the Paris Opera house. It was an amazing feat. For the first time ever, moving pictures were projected onto a screen. Recognizing Le Prince's genius, they encouraged him to show his invention to the public right away. But Le Prince was bothered that the picture was flickery and hard to make out. So instead of making a name for himself, he returned to his workshop in Leeds, England, to perfect his machine.

DISAPPEARANCE

In September of that same year, after a weekend visit with his brother in Dijon, Le Prince boarded a train for Paris to meet with his friends, the Wilsons. They planned to travel to England together, but Le Prince never arrived. The Wilsons waited awhile, then "assuming he had been detained on business, decided to go on to London without him."

Meanwhile, Le Prince's wife and children were living in New

York. Le Prince planned to visit them in October and promised to bring his single-lens movie camera and projector—which he felt were now completed and ready to patent.

But he didn't show up and didn't send any word of explanation. Le Prince's wife, Lizzie, frantically cabled their home in Leeds. When she got no reply, she contacted Richard Wilson. Wilson had no idea what had happened and went to Le Prince's house to investigate. He found it locked up and deserted.

Gone!

Lizzie called in Scotland Yard and the French Missing Persons Bureau. They searched "every morgue and asylum between Dijon, Paris, London, and Leeds. Every railway station along the route was visited. Messages were placed in all the French national newspapers. They even looked into the possibility that Le Prince had lost his mind and enlisted with the Foreign Legion. But no trace of Le Prince was ever found.

What became of Le Prince's work? Unfortunately, Wilson cleaned out Le Prince's studio. While he saved the more complete-looking items, he threw out the bits and pieces that may, in fact, have provided unqualified proof of Le Prince's great achievements. Three months after Le Prince's disappearance Thomas Edison applied for—and ultimately received—a patent for the first practical "motion-picture machine." Today he's considered the father of the movie camera.

SUSPICIOUS FACTS

• Le Prince had not yet patented the latest designs of his movie camera and projector—he was worried that if he went public with his discoveries before they were perfected, someone would find a loophole in the patent and capitalize on his invention before he could.

• As a result, he revealed it only to a close circle of friends... including his lawyer, Clarence Seward. Le Prince didn't know it, but Seward and his partner also worked for Thomas Edison—who, only months later, claimed to have invented the motion-picture camera.

• In the process of applying for a previous U.S. patent, Le Prince's lawyers (Seward & Guthrie)—without informing him—dropped a

---

Still life: Your body uses 300 muscles to balance itself when you're standing still.

crucial clause that would have given him broad protection. Le Prince never had time to correct it—he was too busy writing more-detailed British and French patents and perfecting his projector.

WHAT HAPPENED?

Theory #1: *Le Prince's patent lawer betrayed him. He was kidnapped and/or murdered to prevent him from filing for the patent on his newest camera (or so that others could steal the valuable patents he was presumed to be carrying)—which was at least a decade ahead of its time.*

Interesting points:

• Edison's invention (presented with great fanfare as a huge break-through but actually more rudimentary than Le Prince's machine) infringed on Le Prince's patents. But when Lizzie Le Prince tried to sue Edison, she learned she couldn't: under U.S. law, someone is not declared dead until seven years after they have dissappeared, and as long as the holder of a patent is living, only *he* can sue for infringment.

• Edison had a reputation for ruthlessness among fellow inventors. There were invariably bitter patent battles involving his inventions, with someone always claiming Edison had stolen them. Edison himself once said: "Everyone steals in industry and commerce. I've stolen a lot myself. The thing is to know how to steal."

• Le Prince, in fact, had wanted to collaborate with Edison—but had been strongly warned against it and decided to keep his distance.

• After Le Prince disappeared, Lizzie Le Prince accidentally found out that Seward's partner, Guthrie, had been in Europe at that time. He could have engineered the disappearance...and Lizzie suspected that he had.

On the other hand...

• Inventors are often involved in patent battles—because inventions are usually built upon the work of many people. And occasionally, two inventors turn out to have developed the same idea simultaneously but independently.

• Also: While Edison had a reputation for patenting inventions not clearly his own, he didn't have a reputation for violence. One modern investigator concluded after a thorough investigation that "not a shred of evidence [has been found] to suggest Edison...had anything to do with Le Prince's disappearance."

Theory #2: *Le Prince had lied—the camera and/or projector were not perfected. Depressed, nearly bankrupt, and out of options, he committed suicide.*

Interesting Points:

• Despite having a working model, Le Prince could not perfect the projector, and refused to demonstrate his invention until he could. (Ironically, Edison didn't have a projector either—people looked through a small peephole. Further irony: only months after Le Prince's disappearance, high-quality celluloid—the material that would have allowed Le Prince to perfect his projector—became available.)

• We have only Lizzie Le Prince's say-so that her husband claimed to have solved his projector problems.

• Le Prince was plagued by debt and constantly feared that his laboratory would be raided by creditors. Though his mother had recently died and left a considerable inheritence, there was a bitter dispute with his brother over his claim to the money. Le Prince had been visiting him in Dijon, trying to work things out. But it is believed that his brother thought Augustin had gotten all the money he deserved from the estate.

• Faced with failure after years of grueling work, Le Prince may have felt life was not worth the struggle anymore.

Some Possible Explanations

• Le Prince's lawers may have dropped the important part of his American patent application only because they didn't understand his revolutionary work—in fact, the patent office itself didn't understand Le Prince's patent until he went down and explained it to them in person.

• Though Seward, Le Prince's patent lawer, worked for Edison, it may have been plain coincidence—he was a prominent patent lawer of the day.

• It may have been just a lucky break for Edison that Le Prince—who could have challenged him for patent infringement—disappeared.

And then again...

Not surprising: An estimated 12% of U.S. businessmen wear their ties so tight...

THE TONIGHT SHOW, PART IX

The feature story in our Giant 10th Anniversary Bathroom Reader *was the history of the "Tonight Show." But we never finished it—it was interrupted by a guest host, Professor Pear, and then Johnny Carson went on vacation. Well, we finally got the rest of the story. For all of you BR fans who've been waiting for part IX, here, at long last, it is.*

NO CONTEST

By 1973 Johnny Carson was the undisputed king of late-night television. With the timeslot virtually to itself, the "Tonight Show" grossed an estimated $100 million a year for NBC. This gave Carson a lot of power. When his contract came up for negotiation, he used his heavyweight status to push for shorter work-weeks and huge salary increases.

The biggest battle came in 1979, when Carson announced he was quitting the show. NBC finally lured him back, but only after tripling his salary and cutting the length of the show from 90 minutes to an hour. Carson did make one concession: he agreed to go back to a four-day workweek. But from then on, he—not NBC—would own the "Tonight Show."

GROWING OLD

In its early years, the "Tonight Show" defined hipness for the viewing audience, but as the years passed, what had seemed so fresh and lively in 1962 inevitably began to show its age. The "Tonight Show" still got huge ratings, but there was little new about the show: same host, same sidekick, same bandleader wearing loud sport jackets, same guests, same formula jokes, same skits with Aunt Blabby, Ed Fern, and other stale characters.

Carson came under increasing criticism for being stale in the 1980s, but he sill managed to defeat all challengers without difficulty. Comedian Alan Thicke launched "Thicke of the Night" in the fall of 1983 (his sidekick: Arsenio Hall); he lasted nine months. In 1986, comedian David Brenner began a syndicated talk show called "Nightlife." It was dead within a year. In the fall of 1986, New York newspaper columnist Jimmy Breslin started an interview show on ABC called "Jimmy Breslin's People." Like the others, Breslin could not compete with Carson's ratings. He quit after four months.

The problem with the "Tonight Show" wasn't that it was losing established viewers, it was that it wasn't gaining any new ones. Younger viewers—the ones advertisers want the most—got their comedy elsewhere, including "Saturday Night Live" and "Late Night with David Letterman."

Because of this (and also because Carson had a penchant for talking about retiring whenever his contract came up for renegotiation), NBC spent a lot of time mulling over who would fill his shoes when he finally left the show.

CAN WE TALK?
In the mid-1980s, the leading candidate to take over Carson's chair was comedian Joan Rivers, who had signed on as Carson's "permanent guest host" in 1983. Rivers bested Carson's own ratings many nights, and she helped attract younger audiences to the show with guests like Cher, Elvis Costello, and Pee Wee Herman.

Things changed in 1986, when Carson (once again) hinted to NBC that he was thinking of retiring in 1987, marking 25 years on the job. The network circulated a secret memo listing possible replacements...and Rivers found out she wasn't on the list.

Jumping Ship
Meanwhile, TV executive Barry Diller had been hard at work trying to create a "fourth network" for Fox Broadcasting. Diller played poker with Carson occasionally...but that didn't stop him from going after Rivers when he heard she was unhappy at NBC.

Diller needed a flagship show to launch the Fox network, and he figured a late-night talk show hosted by Rivers would have a good shot at stealing Carson's crown. He offered the job to Rivers, and she took it...without telling Carson beforehand. It was the biggest mistake of her career.

The day after she signed the contract with Fox, Rivers called Carson with the news. But word had already leaked out, and Carson was furious. He refused to speak to Rivers when she called, and he hung up on her a second time the next day.

If you feed beer to a laboratory rat, it will live six times longer than a rat that drinks only water.

Doc Severinsen and others have speculated that Carson would have been supportive *if* Rivers had told him about the move sooner. "He probably would have plugged her show, or even done a walk-on for her," Severinsen says. "But he and others were disappointed nothing was said to them until the last minute."

The Carson–Rivers split was on the front page of newspapers all over the country, but Carson—who immediately tore up Rivers's "Tonight Show" contract—maintained an icy silence on the show. He never brought the subject up again, except for the occasional joke in his monologue. "I hope Reagan runs again," he joked in June 1986, "If he doesn't, he'll probably start his own talk show." But things continued to happen behind the scenes, Bill Carter writes in *The Late Shift*:

> In a demonstration of just how powerful Carson still was, Rivers found herself one step removed from leper status in Hollywood. Guests had to risk the wrath of the "Tonight" show to go on with Joan. She did herself no favors by trying to turn into a hipster, booking rock-and-roll acts half her age and singing "The Bitch is Back" with Elton John. The show was doomed and disappeared in months.

FADING AWAY

Not long after Joan Rivers left the "Tonight Show," comedian Jay Leno replaced her as permanent guest host. Like Rivers, Leno's ratings matched and many nights even bested Carson's ratings, and he attracted younger, more ethnically diverse viewers to the show—just what the advertisers wanted.

Carson was still the undisputed King of the Night and the "Tonight Show" was the biggest moneymaker in the history of television, but his hold was slipping. The show's audience dropped 47% between 1978 and 1992, and the viewers who kept watching were mostly older than the 20- and 30-somethings advertisers increasingly coveted.

HEAD START

It was just a matter of time before Carson retired...or was pushed aside for a younger, fresher face. Other networks smelled blood. They figured that if they could get a talk show up and running by the time Carson finally did retire, they'd have a shot at capturing the late-night audience for themselves.

CBS struck first by luring Pat Sajak away from "Wheel of Fortune" to host the "Pat Sajak Show" in January 1989. They were sure he'd bring his 43-million-strong "Wheel of Fortune" audience with him to late-night TV.

They were wrong—Sajak appealed to the same audience that watched the "Tonight Show," but those viewers were perfectly happy with Carson. Sajak actually beat Carson in ratings his first week on the air, but that lead evaporated and the show went into a death spiral. In the months to come, Sajak's staffers had trouble even finding a *studio* audience, let alone a television audience, and by the end of the year, more than 50 CBS stations around the country dumped him in favor of the "Arsenio Hall Show," an independently produced program which had also premiered in January 1989.

Arsenio appealed to the younger viewers who'd abandoned the "Tonight Show" over the years, and as Pat Sajak went into the tank, Arsenio began building an audience.

TAKING IT ON THE CHIN

Things were so bad at CBS that the network approached Jay Leno about starring in a "Jay Leno Show" that would keep the affiliates from defecting to Arsenio Hall. Sure, they said, Leno was guest hosting the "Tonight Show," but who knew when Carson would retire...or if Leno would still be on the job when he did.

Leno mulled the offer for a couple of months...then turned CBS down. Why take over Sajak's failing show when he was so close to inheriting Carson's? Leno wanted to follow in Carson's footsteps, not Joan Rivers's, so he stayed put. The "Pat Sajak Show" went off the air in April 1990.

But that didn't stop Leno from using the CBS offer to cement his position at NBC. He already had a "penalty payment" in his contract that paid him a large settlement if Carson left the show and Leno wasn't named as his replacement; now he renegotiated for a higher salary and an unwritten promise from NBC that he would take over "Tonight" when Carson retired.

In May 1991, the network made it official—they signed a contract guaranteeing that Leno would be named Carson's successor when he finally retired...but how long away was that? Weeks? Months? Years?

Breakfast food: Americans eat 4 million pounds of bacon and 175 million eggs every day.

BATTLING THE SYNDICATES

Nobody at NBC knew it at the time, but it would take exactly seven days. Leno signed the new contract on May 16; on May 23, Carson announced he was quitting.

The announcement came as a total surprise to NBC—Carson hadn't told anyone at the network. In fact, he timed it to embarrass NBC, announcing his decision at the annual NBC affiliates' convention as stunned network officials sat openmouthed in the front row. "This is the last year that I am doing the "Tonight Show," he said simply, "and it's been a long, marvelous run....My last show is going to be May 22, 1992."

WHAT ABOUT DAVE?

When NBC gave Leno the nod for the "Tonight Show," it did so with the expectation—or at least the hope—that David Letterman would stay put in the 12:30 a.m. slot, where "Late Night With David Letterman" had been since 1982. But Letterman wanted the "Tonight Show" job...and he felt that his 11 years on NBC had earned him the right. Hosting the "Tonight Show "had been his goal since childhood. "I've had one dream in my life," he later explained to his agent, "All I want is the 'Tonight Show.' "

But as Letterman himself admitted, he had never told anyone at NBC how badly he wanted the job. He later recalled,

> When Johnny was still there, it would have hurt my feelings if he'd thought that I was politicking for his job...So what I did was take every opportunity, if asked, to go on the record as saying, "Yes I would like to be considered for the job." I wasn't comfortable with anything more than that.

Letterman had hoped that his success with his own show would be enough to get him the job. It wasn't.

SECOND CHANCE

Letterman spent the next few months after Carson's announcement in a funk, convinced that his entire career had boiled down to playing second fiddle to Jay Leno...or getting out of show business entirely. "My market value is zero," he complained to his friends.

But his mood began to improve late in the summer of 1991, when he hired Michael Ovitz, chairman of Creative Artists

---

Reports say the average American spends two years of their life waiting for meals to be served.

Agency (CAA) and then the most powerful agent in Hollywood. Letterman's NBC contract kept him at the network through April 1993, and forbade him from considering other offers until that February, still 17 months away. But Ovitz began sounding out networks and syndication companies behind the scenes to see who would be interested when Letterman finally became available.

THE SEDUCTION OF DAVE

Everyone wanted Letterman: CBS, ABC, Fox, Paramount, Columbia Television, Walt Disney, Viacom, and others all made pitches to Ovitz. But Letterman refused to consider any timeslot later than 11:30, which knocked out ABC (it wasn't about to move "Nightline"), and Fox, which had committed to creating a late-night show starring Chevy Chase. The syndicates, which sell shows to one television station at a time, were out too because they had no control over when or where a show would air. That left CBS and NBC, which had the right to keep Letterman at the network by matching the highest offer.

CBS offered Letterman a contract paying a $12.5 million-a-year salary, plus an $82 million budget for the show over three years. Like Carson, Letterman would retain ownership of the show, plus production rights for an hour-long show that would run from 12:30 a.m. to 1:30 a.m.

NBC had until January 15, 1993 to match CBS's offer. But to do so, they had to fire Leno, who was finally settling into the job and earning decent ratings, after months of turmoil. The company split along regional lines: executives in Burbank, where the "Tonight Show" was taped, sided with Leno; New York wanted Letterman.

GUY NEXT DOOR

In the end, reputation—Letterman's for being impossible to work with, and Leno's for being a team player—played as big a role in deciding their fates as any other factor. While Letterman was insulting NBC executives—by *name*—on the air, banning them from "Late Night" staff parties and squabbling over control of "Late Night" reruns, Leno, on his own initiative, was making appearances at affiliates all over the country to shore up support for his show.

NBC ultimately decided that even if Leno's ratings dipped a

little when he went up against Letterman, he was a team player; Letterman, on the other hand, was a pain in the ass. As Bill Carter writes in *Night Shift*,

> Jay had done his groundwork exceptionally well. All that campaigning through affiliates and advertisers, every appearance at an NBC event...had made an impression....And then there was Dave: recalcitrant, irritable, uncooperative, Dave.

NBC refused to match CBS's offer point by point, but it did offer to make Letterman host of the "Tonight Show" when Leno's current contract expired (even sooner if Leno quit in disgust), at roughly the same salary he would get at CBS. NBC refused to give him ownership of the show. The CBS offer was better, and Letterman was free to accept it if he wanted to.

THANKS, JOHNNY

Letterman wasn't sure he wanted to go to CBS—he'd spent a lifetime working toward hosting the "Tonight Show," and he wasn't sure he wanted to give it up just because NBC was offering to make him filthy rich a little more slowly than CBS was.

Letterman couldn't make up his mind...so he called Johnny Carson and asked him what he would do in the same situation. "I'd probably walk," Carson told him. So Letterman did.

STARTING OVER

"The Late Show with David Letterman" premiered on CBS on August 30, 1993; to no one's surprise, Letterman thumped Leno's ratings on opening night.

NBC hoped that Letterman's ratings would peak and then drop off after a few weeks; even if Leno stayed in second place, he wouldn't be too far behind Letterman. They were wrong—Letterman whipped Leno in the ratings night after night, month after month, for nearly two years. Leno didn't beat Letterman in the ratings even once in more than 90 consecutive weeks.

REVERSAL OF FORTUNE

But in 1995 things began to change, thanks to two factors:

1. The collapse of CBS's programming schedule. When Letterman joined CBS in 1993, the network was #1 in prime-time ratings; it was broadcasting the NFL, the World Series, and the Olympics, and it had the strongest station lineup in the country.

By July 1995, all of that had changed. CBS was mired in third place and had lost the broadcast rights to the NFL and the World Series. Its ratings were so bad that some affiliate stations even jumped ship and signed with Fox. The Tiffany Network hit rock bottom in September 1995 and became the first of the Big Three networks to slip into fourth place in the ratings behind Fox.

2. A revamping of the "Tonight Show" format. In May 1994, Leno took his show to New York, and realized that by imitating the format created to support Carson's strengths, he'd been undermining his own. "I'm a night-club comic," he explains. "Prior to [our New York trip], we were doing the show exactly as it was for Johnny. People meant well, but I ended up doing a 'Tonight Show' by committee, instead of the one I wanted to do." As Ed Bark of the *Dallas Morning News* wrote:

> On Sept. 27 of that year, *Tonight* unveiled a new, more intimate set that allowed Mr. Leno to do his monologue virtually in the midst of a gaggle of audience members seated in a small, floor-level section. Comedy bits were stretched out and sourpuss bandleader Branford Marsalis gave way to the considerably more congenial Kevin Eubanks.... "Tonight" slowly made headway against the "Late Show."

On July 10, 1995, Hugh Grant went on the "Tonight Show" with his first post–Divine Brown public appearance. As ratings soared, Leno leaned over and asked, "What the hell were you thinking?" That week, "Tonight" had its first ratings win against the "Late Show."

By the beginning of 1997, the "Late Show" had slipped to third place behind both "The Tonight Show" and "Nightline"; as late as the summer of 1999 it was still there. "Tonight" had regained its place as King of the Night, but it was no longer the monolith that it had been under Allen, Paar, and Carson. Late-night television is now more competitive than it has ever been, and it is likely to remain so for years to come.

*   *   *

Random fact: What did Mexican War hero General Winfield Scott remember most about the time he ate dinner at the White House? A pickpocket stole his wallet, which contained $800.

DYING HARD: THE STORY OF "THE TICKING MAN"

The 1990 sale of The Ticking Man *movie script was a Hollywood milestone that jacked the price of original scripts into the stratosphere. Of course, many of them wound up as box-office bombs...and at least one—*The Ticking Man*—never got made at all. Here's a quintessential Hollywood story, written by John Lippman and first published in 1995 in the* Wall Street Journal.

ONLY IN HOLLYWOOD

It was the kind of only-in-Hollywood scenario that makes headlines. Two unemployed 29-year-olds, one a former scallop fisherman and the other a struggling writer, had just sold a movie script for $1.2 million, then a record for an original screenplay. The year was 1990, and the huge sum they managed to snare helped set off a frenzied bidding war that ratcheted up prices all over town.

Fast-forward five years. Their famous script, *The Ticking Man*, sits on a shelf. After plowing through two studios, four rewrites and more than $1 million in extra costs, it isn't any closer to being made than it was the day it was conceived.

The tortured saga of *The Ticking Man* illustrates the Alice-in-Wonderland nature of business in Hollywood. Here, studios routinely pay huge sums for a script, then spend even more to tear it up and start all over again. Considering that film budgets often top $50 million, a few million more on rewriting a script is loose change—and it offers the added benefit of buying the ego satisfaction of producers, stars and others who all want to make their mark on the project during the rewriting process. Where else would it take $2.5 million and no less than 32 different writers to turn out a script for Universal Pictures' 1994 kiddie flick *The Flintstones?*

Yet *The Ticking Man* also serves as a reminder that, for all the huge sums tossed about, Hollywood remains a place where writers reside in the nether regions of the food chain. Watching what happened to his script, says *Ticking Man* co-writer Manny Coto, was "like seeing a baby mauled."

ACCIDENT OF TIMING

That *The Ticking Man* played a starring role in inflating Hollywood script prices was largely an accident of timing. A writer's strike in 1988 left studios with few films in the pipeline by 1990. The problem was made worse by a proliferation of new studios, all fighting for the next hit. Studio executives began to panic.

Traditionally, the executives had farmed out ideas to writers who would sketch out a synopsis, frame a few scenes—and only then think about starting on a script. The process, all told, could take years. But after the strike, producers began taking notice of "spec" scripts—scripts that were already written in full, on "speculation."

That is where the two unemployed young screenwriters, Mr. Coto and Brian Helgeland, came in. Mr. Helgeland, the former fisherman, had come to Hollywood from Massachusetts five years earlier "on a lark," he says. He wrote a couple of B-movie scripts, such as *976-EVIL*, the fourth sequel of *Nightmare on Elm Street*. While on the set of that film, his agent introduced him to Mr. Coto. The two quickly hit it off, and collaborated on a horror script that they couldn't sell.

With no prospects in sight, one night on the telephone they made a vow: They wouldn't hang up until one of them came up with a movie idea they could sell for $1 million. A mere 30 minutes later, they had perfected their pitch. And after eight frantic weeks holed up in Mr. Coto's cramped one-bedroom apartment, taking meals at Barney's Beanery, a venerable greasy spoon around the corner, they had their screenplay. The premise of *The Ticking Man* was simple: a nuclear bomb becomes "sentient," and starts thinking and feeling like a human being.

BIDDING WAR

The young writers enlisted the aid of their agents...who decided to auction the script off rather than simply shop it around, hoping to create a buzz. To whip up enthusiasm a bit more, a week before the auction, Mr. Coto bought two dozen alarm clocks from a local five-and-dime store, spray painted them black, and pasted on an ominous picture of a silhouette casting a shadow on a horizon. Triad sent one to every bidder, inscribed with the words: "The Ticking Man is coming." Then Triad insisted that studios

---

Both poison oak and poison ivy are members of the cashew family.

couldn't see the script until the day of the auction the following Tuesday—and that they would have to send their own messengers to get it.

Such mundane marketing tricks probably wouldn't raise eyebrows today, but at the time the approach was unheard of, and word began to spread. On Tuesday, the first bid came in just after noon, for $250,000. By nightfall, Largo Entertainment Inc. chief Lawrence Gordon had bid up the price more than five times that, purchasing the screenplay for a production company owned by [his] brother.

Everything about Largo spelled big plans. Largo's Mr. Gordon, formerly president of the Twentieth Century-Fox Entertainment Group, was known as one of Hollywood's pre-eminent producers of "hardware" movies—big-budget action features like *Die Hard*, loaded with car crashes and explosions. At Largo, he had $100 million in backing from consumer electronics giant JVC/Victor Co. of Japan.

THE PLOT THICKENS

Mr. Gordon promised a $60 million budget and *Die Hard* star Bruce Willis in the leading role. Mr. Willis was to play Los Angeles police demolition expert Lloyd Hockett, who invents the ultimate "stealth weapon": a robot with a 20-megaton nuclear warhead implanted in its chest. But a malevolent government scientist named Dr. Jerrold sets out to "launch" the Ticking Man by giving it the power to think for itself. When the robot escapes from his Nevada compound and heads toward Moscow, the government summons Dr. Hockett to capture his creation.

Accompanied by the comely journalist Meg Sharpe, Dr. Hockett follows the Ticking Man as he leaves a trail of dead soldiers, crashed Cobra helicopters, and car collisions through airports in Las Vegas, Denver, Paris, and Berlin before ending up in New York. At the last moment, the Ticking Man confronts Dr. Hockett in a climactic showdown on the Brooklyn Bridge seconds before the robot is set to blow up the city.

PUTTING UP A PORCH

Soon after the heady auction, Mr. Gordon summoned Mr. Coto and Mr Helgeland to his office, adorned with a stuffed piranha on

Even bloodhounds cannot smell the difference between two identical twins.

his desk, and got straight to the point. Their script was about to undergo heavy rewrites. "I bought the house," one of the young writers recalls him saying. "Now I want to put on a porch."

Then, Mr. Gordon posed a question. "I want you guys to think: Does it really have to be a nuclear bomb?" The writers gasped, flabbergasted at his casual suggestion that they unceremoniously throw out the central premise of their story. It "really chilled me to the bone," Mr. Coto says. Mr. Gordon denies making the first comment and doesn't recall whether he made the second.

But that was just for starters. To accommodate Mr. Willis, Mr. Gordon quickly went about reassembling the *Die Hard* team, including producer Joel Silver.

The screenwriters were sent off to meet with Mr. Silver, a protégé of Mr. Gordon's with credits such as *Predator* and *Lethal Weapon*. He got right to the point, too: They were out of the picture, immediately. With heavy time pressure and a blockbuster budget, the producers didn't want to see if novice writers were up to the rewriting task. He was turning the script over to *Die Hard* writer Steven de Souza, who had also scored big for Messrs. Gordon and Silver with the screenplay for the Eddie Murphy–Nick Nolte action comedy *48 Hours*.

ANOTHER SLAP IN THE FACE

For the young writers, it was yet another slap in the face. For Mr. de Souza, who was tapped largely for his expertise in crafting Willis-style repartee, it was business as usual. "I was brought in because the script had a lot of problems. Larry said, 'We want a different approach,'" he recalls. For a fee of about $1 million, the screenwriter hopped on a plane for Rome, where Mr. Willis was filming *Hudson Hawk*.

In Rome, Mr. de Souza met with Gordon, Silver and Willis…and started sketching out his ideas. Rather than open the movie with the robot rampaging on the loose, Mr. Willis's hero would discover a secret government plot to build the nuclear robot and then set out to stop it. And the Ticking Man would be "half human" rather than the original screenplay's pure android.

"Everybody approved it," recalls Mr. de Souza, who immediately started banging out a 20-page "treatment," a detailed plot summary, on a laptop computer at his hotel. "But almost literally before I could get back to the U.S. and write one word of the screenplay, Bruce decided not to do the movie." Mr. de Souza was dispatched to work on other Largo projects.

QUITE A COINCIDENCE

What spooked the actor? It turned out that *The Ticking Man* bore a startling resemblance to an imminent low-budget film called *Eve of Destruction*. That film, from Orion Pictures Corp., was about a nuclear-armed robot named Eve that can think and act for itself. The robot goes haywire and an antiterrorist expert, played by Gregory Hines, is called upon to immobilize Eve. In the movie's climax, Mr. Hines faces off the robot in the subway tunnels under Manhattan seconds before it is set to explode.

The coincidences didn't end with the plot. It turns out that *Eve of Destruction* co-writers Yale Udoff and the late Duncan Gibbins had pitched the idea to Largo even before *The Ticking Man* was written. Largo executives turned down the idea, and the writers sold the script elsewhere for $100,000 (though Mr. Udoff said they later were paid an additional $300,000). When he heard about *The Ticking Man*, he says, "I kidded Larry he could have had our script for a fraction of the cost."

Eve of Destruction opened on January 18, 1991—the night U.S. jets started bombing Baghdad. Most Americans stayed home glued to their TV sets that week, and Orion pulled the movie from theaters shortly thereafter. With a slender $11 million budget, *Eve of Destruction* grossed just $4.4 million at the box office and promptly disappeared.

MR. SILVER'S ROLE

Behind the scenes, there appeared to be another reason Mr. Willis suddenly got cold feet about *The Ticking Man*. Producer Mr. Silver, who had started as Mr. Gordon's driver and assistant, was chafing to set out on his own. He had designs on Mr. Willis for his own next big movie, *The Last Boy Scout*. And so, say people close to the project, he "badmouthed" *The Ticking Man* to Mr. Willis. Both Mr. Willis and Mr. Silver declined to comment.

OOH, OOH, I'VE GOT IT!

Back at Largo, a young executive named Dan Mazur hatched an

What do cows and cats have in common? Both get hairballs.

idea for overhauling *The Ticking Man* yet again: Tell the whole story from the robot's point of view. So Largo signed up a new screenwriter, Sam Hamm, who had written the original screenplays for *Batman* and *Batman Returns*.

In late 1991 and 1992, for a $200,000 fee, Mr. Hamm banged out three new *Ticking Man* treatments. He started by getting rid of Lloyd Hockett and virtually every other principal in the *Ticking Man* cast.

Instead, in the Hamm version, the Ticking Man is a secret weapon kept dormant for years until it discovers that it is an android programmed with the memories of its creator, a brilliant inventor named Malcolm Pace who mysteriously died eight years earlier. On a test run it "goes AWOL" and sets out to find its "family." As the android learns its true destiny—a weapon of mass destruction—it wrestles uneasily with its dark existential plight and vows "to avenge the death" of Dr. Pace. In the new climactic scene, the Ticking Man threatens to blow up itself at a secret Nevada nuclear-robot factory, unaware that it will blast to pieces Dr. Pace's innocent family hidden nearby.

OH, NEVER MIND

By the time Mr. Hamm handed in his third draft, though, Largo was running into trouble. It had produced about 10 films over four and a half years and had a string of disappointments, including *The Super* and *Judgment Night*. It had moderate hits in *Unlawful Entry* and *Point Break* but had to shelve plans for a third *Die Hard* for lack of financing. (Fox, co-producer of the *Die Hard* films, ultimately produced *Die Hard With a Vengeance* with Cinergi Pictures Entertainment Inc.)

Eventually, JVC decided not to pump any more money into Largo. In January 1994, Mr. Gordon left Largo and became a producer at MCA Inc.'s Universal Pictures. He took a handful of projects with him—including *The Ticking Man*. Coto and Helgeland by this time didn't hold out much hope that they would recognize the finished product.

"I was outraged because we wrote this terrific script," Mr. Coto says. "But I shut it off after awhile. Ultimately, if you sell your script, you've got to take what comes with it."

These days, many in Hollywood think the script has been "in

turnaround" for so long that its Cold War premise is outdated and the project is finally dead. But Mr. Gordon says he still plans to make the movie—when he finds the right script. *The Ticking Man* recently showed up in Creative Artists Agency's "open assignment" book of projects searching for writers, with this revised synopsis: "A nuclear bomb expert working for the LAPD has to capture 'The Ticking Man,' a man who has just discovered that he is not human, but is a robot with a nuclear bomb inside of him."

BACK TO THE DRAWING BOARD

As for the writers of *The Ticking Man*—well, even if the movie is never made, it still could help them to live happily ever after.... Each netted about $250,000 from the sale, enough for Mr. Coto to move out of his Hollywood apartment and buy a home in the upscale Los Feliz neighborhood. He went on to produce TV shows and direct movies.

Mr. Helgeland, meanwhile, saw his "quote"—the floor price for writing a script—leap 250%, and he moved from his home near the Los Angeles airport to Malibu. He now earns well over $500,000 a year as a specialist who rewrites action-adventure films, some of them initially penned by rookie writers such as he was just a few years ago. He and Mr. Coto also helped spark a round of can-you-top-this script deals, culminating last July in a record $4 million for *The Long Kiss Goodnight*, by Shane Black, who after *The Ticking Man* sale had received $1.75 million for *The Last Boy Scout*.

"A success like *The Ticking Man* is always good for two or three jobs," explains Mr. Helgeland, who recently finished a rewriting assignment for a Sylvester Stallone action thriller called *Assassins* [made in 1995]. "I've written a bunch of stuff," he adds with evident pride. And which of his projects have we seen on the big screen? "It's all in development, as they say," he concedes. "Nothing has been made."

Ed. Note: *Helgeland wrote* Conspiracy Theory, *which was made, and starred Mel Gibson and Julia Roberts. Then, he co-wrote* L.A. Confidential, *for which Kim Basinger won an Oscar.*

One tsp. of liquid nicotine or ½ oz. of pure caffine, are considered lethal doses for a 150 lb. man.

THE DARK SIDE OF PETER PAN

"All children except one, grow up. They soon know that they will grow up…this is the beginning of the end." The first paragraph of James Barrie's classic story, Peter Pan, introduced its central theme. It sounds innocent, but a look at Barrie's life gives it a more sinister twist.

I WON'T GROW UP

"All of James Barrie's life led up to the creation of *Peter Pan*," wrote one of his biographers.

A pivotal point came in 1866 when Barrie, the youngest in a Scottish family of 10 children, was six: his brother David, the pride of the family, died in a skating accident. Barrie's mother was devastated. To comfort her, little James began imitating David's mannerisms and mimicking his speech. This bizarre charade went on for years…and only got weirder: when James reached 13, the age at which David had died, he literally stopped growing. He never stood taller than 5', and didn't shave until he was 24. He always had a thin, high-pitched voice.

SUCCESS AND FAILURE

From childhood, Barrie's main interest had been creating stories and plays. After graduating from college, he moved to London to pursue a career as a writer, and soon his work was being published.

In the 1880s, his novels about a "wandering little girl"—his mother—captured the public's imagination and put him on the road to fame and wealth. He soon became one of England's most famous writers.

Despite his professional success, the gawky Barrie was painfully shy with women, and the thought of marriage terrified him. After a nightmare, he wrote in his journal: "Greatest horror, dream I am married, wake up screaming." But that didn't stop him from putting lovely actresses on a pedestal. Barrie became enamored of leading lady Mary Ansell, who appeared in his early plays. Motherlike, she nursed him through a life-threatening bout of pneumonia. And when he recovered, they decided to marry.

Murders have claimed more American lives during the 20th century than wars have.

It was a disaster. Barrie wasn't capable of an intimate relationship and was probably impotent as well—stuck, physically and emotionally in a state of perpetual boyhood. Eventually, Mary fell in love with a young writer named Gilbert Cannan and demanded a divorce. Barrie refused, because his marriage had provided him with the appearance of being normal. But when Mary threatened to tell the world that he was impotent and had never consummated their marriage, Barrie gave in.

THE LOST BOYS

In 1899, while still unhappily married, Barrie befriended young George, John, and Peter Davies and their mother, Sylvia, in London's Kensington Park. The boy's father, Arthur Davies, was too busy tending to his struggling career as a lawyer to spend much time with his family. So childless Barrie was only too happy to play with the Davies boys. He became a frequent caller at their home, and even rented a cottage nearby when they went on vacations in Surrey.

Barrie idolized the children's beautiful mother. But it was with the children that he could truly be himself. He met with them daily in the park or at their home. They played Indians together, or pretended to be pirates, forcing each other to "walk the plank." Barrie made up stories for the boys, featuring talking birds and fairies, and acted them out.

PETER IS BORN

In 1901 Barrie ordered a printing of only two copies of a photo-essay book of his adventures with the Davies boys. He entitled it *The Boy Castaways of Black Lake Island* and gave one copy to the boy's father (who promptly left it on a train). The next year, Barrie published these adventures in a novel called *The Little White Bird*. In a story-within-a-story, the narrator tells "David" (George Davies) about Peter Pan, a seven-day-old boy who flies away from his parents to live with fairies. All children start out as birds, the story goes, but soon forget how to fly.

Peter eventually flies home, and tearfully sees through the nursery window that his mother is holding a new baby and has forgotten him. Now Peter Pan can never go home and will never grow up.

Camels are born without their humps.

The Little White Bird was popular, and readers begged Barrie to give them more of that new character, Peter Pan.

Barrie knew exactly how to bring Peter Pan back. He had often taken the Davies boys to pantomimes—dazzling Christmastime musical dramas put on for children. The plays always featured a young hero and heroine (both played by actresses), a Good Fairy, a Demon King, fight scenes, characters flying (on invisible wires) and a "transformation scene," in which the ordinary world became a fairyland. During the performances, Barrie carefully observed the boys' reactions. They seemed to love every moment.

So why not, Barrie thought, put Peter Pan in a similar children's play for the London stage?

THE DARLINGS

Barrie always acknowledged that the Davies boys' free-spirited youth was his inspiration for Peter Pan. "I made Peter by rubbing the five of you together, as savages with two sticks produce a flame," he wrote on the dedication page of the printed version of the play. More than that, however, the Davies family—loving mother, impatient father, and adorable sons—served as Barrie's model for the Darlings in the play. He even used their names:

- Mr. Darling was named after the eldest boy, George Davies.
- Jack Davies became John Darling.
- Michael and Nicholas became Michael Nicholas Darling.
- Peter Davies's name went to Peter Pan.

As for the author, he appears as Captain James Hook, whose right hand is gone. Barrie suffered paralysis of his right hand from tendonitis. Hook is relentlessly pursued by a crocodile who has swallowed a ticking clock, which biographers say was "a metaphor of Barrie stalked by cruel time." Porthos, his St. Bernard, became nurse-dog Nana, who exasperated the stuffy father (in real life, he was exasperated not with the dog, but with Barrie).

Barrie added a sister, Wendy, modeled after Margaret Henley, the deceased daughter of Barrie's friend, W. E. Henley. The six-year-old girl had called Barrie her "fwendy" (friend) and from that child-word, Barrie invented the name Wendy. It rapidly became one of England's most popular girls names.

WILL PETER PAN FLY?

Peter Pan posed a radical departure for adult theater. Barrie had an agreement with producer Charles Frohman to deliver a play manuscript. He offered Frohman another play gratis if he would only produce his "dream child," *Peter Pan.* "I'm sure it will not be a commercial success," Barrie said of *Peter.*

But Frohman, a wealthy American who liked risky ventures, said he would produce both plays. After reading the manuscript of *Peter Pan,* Frohman was so excited, he would stop friends on the street and force them to listen to passages from it. With an American staging now secured, it was easier for Barrie to find backing for a London opening.

The play was first performed at the Duke of York's Theatre on December 27, 1904, with an actress, Nina Boucicault, as Peter Pan. Having an actress play the boy—a tradition that continues to this day—began as a practical matter. The role was too demanding for a child; only an adult could handle all of the lines. And only an adult female could pass for a boy.

Peter Pan was an immediate hit, quelling Barrie's misgivings that an audience of adults wouldn't go for a play he'd originally written for children. One review compared Barrie's genius with that of George Bernard Shaw. Later, Barrie would cash in on the play's popularity by writing the novels *Peter Pan in Kensington Gardens* (1906) and *Peter and Wendy* (1911).

THE FATE OF THE LOST BOYS

But this story has no happy ending. Arthur Davies died of cancer, which left Barrie and Sylvia free to marry. Barrie went so far as to give her an engagement ring, but then she, too, died of cancer. Suddenly Barrie was the legal guardian of five boys, ages 7 to 17.

He devoted his life to them, imagining them as his own, but the boys felt he was overbearing in his possessiveness. Some biographers claim that the Davies brothers grew uncomfortable with their lives because they were always badgered about their relationship with the famous James Barrie. (On the other hand, he had little affection to bestow on his real family. Barrie was also named guardian of his brother's grandchildren when their parents died…but although he paid for their education, he refused to see them.)

Don't try this at home: Anteaters can flick their tongues 160 times a minute.

George, the eldest Davies child and Barrie's favorite, died in World War I in 1915. Michael drowned in a pool at Oxford while being taught to swim by a close friend; there were rumors of a suicide pact. John married and distanced himself from Barrie. Peter Davies committed suicide as an adult in an attempt to escape, some say, from forever being called "Peter Pan."

Barrie ended up famous and rich, but a sad and lonely man. He was described as looking prematurely old and withered. Just before he died in 1937, he willed all proceeds from the copyright of *Peter Pan* to London's Great Ormond Street Hospital for Sick Children. Millions of dollars were realized from this bequest. Under British law, copyrights may extend no longer than 50 years before becoming public property. In this special case, Parliament made an exception and allowed the hospital to continue offering the world's best pediatric care because of the boy who never grew up.

*   *   *   *

The Clapping Gamble

The play's most original and magical moment comes when the fairy Tinkerbell, in an attempt to save Peter's life, drinks poison that Captain Hook had intended for the boy. Boldy, Peter addresses the audience and calls on them to save the fairie's life. "Clap if you believe in fairies," he begs. Nina Boucicault, the first Peter, asked James Barrie, "Suppose they don't clap? What do I do then?" Barrie had no answer. The director told orchestra members to start the clapping if the audience sat on their hands. But the ploy was not necessary: the audience suspended disbelief with a vengeance and Nina-Peter wept openly with Tink's return to life.

*   *   *   *

A "lost boy" was a Victorian
euphemism for one who died young.

Call waiting: Nearly 6% of all marriage proposals are made over the telephone.

THE OTHER SIDE OF PETER PAN

*Now that you know something about James Barrie and the origins of
Peter Pan, how does it change the way you perceive the story?
Here are some quotes from the original book.*

ALL CHILDREN, EXCEPT ONE, grow up. They soon
know that they will grow up, and the way Wendy knew was
this. One day when she was two years old she was playing
in a garden, and she plucked another flower and ran with it to her
mother. I suppose she must have looked rather delightful, for Mrs.
Darling put her hand to her heart and cried, "Oh, why can't you
remain like this for ever!" This was all that passed between them
on the subject, but henceforth Wendy knew that she must grow
up. You always know after you are two. Two is the beginning of
the end.

*　　*　　*　　*

MRS. DARLING FIRST HEARD of Peter when she was tidying
up her children's minds. It is the nightly custom of every good
mother after her children are asleep to rummage in their minds and
put things straight for next morning, repacking into their proper
places the many articles that have wandered during the day.

If you could keep awake (but of course you can't) you would see
your own mother doing this, and you would find it very interesting
to watch her. It is quite like tidying up drawers. You would see her
on her knees, I expect, lingering humorously over some of your
contents, wondering where on earth you had picked this thing up,
making discoveries sweet and not so sweet, pressing this to her
cheek as if it were as nice as a kitten, and hurriedly stowing that
out of sight.

When you wake in the morning, the naughtiness and evil
passions with which you went to bed have been folded up small
and placed at the bottom of your mind; and on the top, beautifully
aired, are spread out your prettier thoughts, ready for you to
put on.

*　　*　　*　　*

Humans and Koshima Island monkeys are the only creatures that intentionally salt their food.

SUDDENLY HOOK FOUND HIMSELF face to face with Peter. The others drew back and formed a ring around them.

For a long duck the two enemies looked at one another; Hook shuddering slightly, and Peter with the strange smile upon his face.

"So, Pan," said Hook at last, "this is your doing."

"Ay, James Hook," came the stern answer, "it is all my doing."

"Proud and insolent youth," said Hook, "prepare to meet thy doom."

"Dark and sinister man," Peter answered, "have at thee."

Without more words they fell to and for a space there was no advantage to either blade. Peter was a superb swordsman, and parried with dazzling rapidity….Hook, scarcely his inferior, forced him back, hoping suddenly to end all with a favorite thrust…but to his astonishment he found his thrust turned aside again and again.

…"Pan, who art thou?" he cried huskily.

"I'm youth, I'm joy," Peter answered…"I'm a little bird that has broken out of the egg."

This, of course, was nonsense; but it was proof to the unhappy Hook that Peter did not know in the least who or what he was, which is the very pinnacle of good form.

"To't again!" he cried despairingly.

He fought now like a human flail, and every sweep of that terrible sword would have severed in two any man or boy who obstructed it; but Peter fluttered around him as if the very wind it made blew him out of the danger zone.

*   *   *   *

"PETER," WENDY SAID, "are you expecting me to fly away with you?

"Of course; that is why I have come."…

"I can't come," she said apologetically, "I have forgotten how to fly."

"I'll soon teach you again."

"O Peter, don't waste the fairy dust on me." …

Then she turned up the light, and Peter saw. He gave a cry of pain; …"What is it?" he cried again.

She had to tell him. "I am old, Peter….I grew up a long time ago…I couldn't help it."

Hippopotamus bites, experts say, are almost universally fatal. Reason: They're very large bites.

ANSWERS—Jeff's Brainteasers (page 168)

1. One train entered the tunnel at 7 a.m., the other entered at 7 p.m.

2. Start both hourglasses. When the 4-minute glass runs out, turn it over (4 minutes have elapsed). When the 7-minute glass runs out, turn it over (7 minutes have elapsed). When the 4-minute glass runs out this time (8 minutes have now elapsed), the 7-minute glass has been running for 1 minute. Turn it over once again. When it stops, 9 minutes have elapsed.

3. Nine o'clock. Since there are 12 hours between the two times, and half of that time is six, then the halfway mark would have to be 7 o'clock. If it were 7 o'clock, two hours ago, the time would now be 9 o'clock.

4. The other end of the rope isn't tied to anything.

5. Just push the cork into the bottle and shake the coin out.

6. An ear of corn.

7. Throw the ball straight up.

8. They're female boxers.

9. The dates are 1990 B.C. and 1995 B.C.

10. His parachute didn't open.

11. An Infiniti.

12. The tape recording ends with him killing himself. If he'd committed suicide, the tape wouldn't be rewound to the beginning of his statement.

13. She's playing baseball.

14. Captain Russo is bald.

15. He's playing Monopoly. The man with the "car" token has landed on a property that has a "hotel." Since he cannot afford the rent, he declares "bankruptcy.

*   *   *.

Random Fact: Henry Kissinger's favorite breakfast: "a serving of egg whites, dyed yellow to make them look like yolks."

In virtually every language on Earth, the word for "mother" begins with the letter "m".

ANSWERS—The Riddler (from page 321.)

1. An echo.
2. Holes.
3. Mount Everest.
4. Envelope.
5. A ton.
6. A priest.
7. Only one...the last one.
8. Zero...Noah took animals on the ark, not Moses.
9. Only once. After the first calculation, you will be subtracting 5 from 20, then 5 from 15, and so on.
10. A secret.
11. You can't take a picture with a wooden leg....You need a camera!
12. Darkness.
13. Footsteps.
14. A coffin.
15. An umbrella.
16. Suicide.
17. The year 1961. It reads the same upside down. Won't happen again until the year 6009.
18. The letter "V."
19. "Are you asleep?"
20. A promise.

ANSWERS—The World's Simplest Quiz (from page 307.)

1. 116 years, from 1337 to 1453.
2. November (on the 7th). The old Russian calendar was 13 days behind ours.
3. Ecuador.
4. El Salvador. It's a medicinal herb grown by the Balsam Islands.
5. The Manx shearwater. Puffins are genus *Fratercula* or *Lunda*.
6. The sheep.
7. A hard-wearing cotton fabric called moleskin.
8. They're a fruit grown in New Zealand.
9. Sixteen. The one known as Louis XVII died in prison during the Revolution, and thus never reached the throne.
10. A breed of large dogs. The Latin name was *Canariae insulae*—"Island of the Dogs."
11. Albert. When he came to the throne, he respected the wish of Queen Victoria that no future king should be called Albert.
12. The distinctively colored parts are crimson.
13. It takes place in the spring, from April 29 to May 1.
14. It is usually made of squirrel's hair.
15. Thirty years, of course—1618 to 1648.

The abbreviation for pound, "lb.," comes from the astrological sign Libra.

If you like reading our books...

VISIT THE BRI'S WEB SITE!

www.unclejohn.com
or
www.bathroomreader.com

★   ★   ★

- Introducing "The Salon"—chat with BRI staff & members
  - Visit "The Throne Room"—a great place to read!
    - Receive our *regular* newsletters via email
      - Order additional BRI books
        - Become a BRI member
      - Suggest ideas for future editions
    - Submit your favorite articles and facts

Go With the Flow!

THE LAST PAGE

FELLOW BATHROOM READERS:
The fight for good bathroom reading should never be taken loosely—we must sit firmly for what we believe in, even while the rest of the world is taking pot shots at us.

We invite you to take the plunge: Sit Down and Be Counted! by joining the Bathroom Readers' Institute. Send a self-addressed, stamped envelope to: BRI, P Box 1117, Ashland, Oregon 97520—or contact us through our Web site at: *www.bathroomreader.com*. You'll receive your attractive free membership card and a copy of the BRI newsletter (sent out monthly via email), and earn a permanent spot on the BRI honor roll!

 crð   crð   crð

UNCLE JOHN'S NEXT BATHROOM READER IS IN THE WORKS!

Don't fret—there's more good reading on the way. In fact, there are a few ways *you* can contribute to the next volume:

1. Is there a subject you'd like to see us research? Write to us or contact us through our Web site (*www.bathroomreader.com*) and let us know. We aim to please.

2. Got a neat idea for a couple of pages in the new *Reader*? If you're the first to suggest it, and we use it, we'll send you a free book.

3. Have you seen or read an article you'd recommend as quintessential bathroom reading? Or is there a passage in a book or Web site that you want to share with us and other BRI members? Tell us how to find it. If you're the first to suggest it and we publish it in the next volume, there's a free book in it for you.

Well, we're out of space, and when you've gotta go, you've gotta go. Hope to hear from you soon. Meanwhile, remember:

Go with the flow